Exploration
in animals and humans

The Comparative Psychology of Animals and Humans

Series Editor: Professor W. Sluckin, University of Leicester

The comparative perspective — viewing animals and human beings side by side — is best suited to a range of topics within psychology. The nature/nurture issue has traditionally been considered in this way, and more narrowly circumscribed areas of study, such as conditioning, have for a long time been investigated in animals as well as in humans. In more recent times, developments in the related fields of ethology and sociobiology have focused attention on the comparative approach to selected psychological topics.

The aim of this series is to produce books dealing in a comparative manner with a variety of topics. The multiple authorship of each book ensures a thorough and in-depth coverage of the topic, while at the same time great care is taken that the chapters cohere according to an overall structure provided by the book's editor. Each volume is under the separate editorship of a specialist in the given field. All the books review and evaluate research in the respective fields, and give an up-to-date summary of the present state of knowledge.

Exploration
in animals and humans

Edited by

John Archer
School of Psychology
Preston Polytechnic

and

Lynda I. A. Birke
Animal Behaviour Research Group
Department of Biology
The Open University

 Van Nostrand Reinhold (UK) Co. Ltd.

Published by Van Nostrand Reinhold (UK) Co. Ltd.
Molly Millars Lane, Wokingham, Berkshire, England

Library of Congress Cataloging in Publication Data

Main entry under title:

Exploration in animals and humans.

  Includes bibliographies and index.
  1. Curiosity. 2. Psychology, Comparative.
I. Archer, John. II. Birke, Lynda. [DNLM: 1.
Exploratory behavior. BF 323.C8 E96]
BF323.C8E94 1983   156'.3   82–8524
ISBN 0–442–30527–3   AACR2

Printed in Great Britain at the
University Press, Cambridge

Contents

v

Introduction

'Exploration' is a widely used concept in animal behaviour research, and yet it is difficult to define. In a broad sense, it refers to all those activities concerned with gathering information about the environment. These include short-term responses, usually regarded as attentional, such as the orienting reflex, which typically occurs under conditions of stimulus change and novelty. The sense organs become oriented to a source of stimulus change, and this is accompanied by physiological changes concerned with energy mobilisation. 'Exploration' more commonly refers to investigatory behaviour, a more varied collection of responses occurring over a longer period of time that are not accompanied by readily identifiable physiological changes. Both types of exploration provide ways in which an animal can increase its stimulus input. They have sometimes been distinguished as passive and active forms of exploration, referred to as inspective and inquisitive behaviour by Berlyne (1960).

If the term 'exploration' is used to refer to *all* activities concerned with gaining information about the environment, some form of exploration would appear to be involved in practically every type of animal behaviour. One influential way of studying the motivation of animal behaviour has been to divide up various activities into separate systems, such as feeding, drinking, aggression and fear. The activities associated with each individual system are then studied separately. But in practice, all these activities are interconnected: for example a hungry or frightened animal may less readily engage in sexual activities than a satiated animal. The interconnections have been studied in terms of how motivational systems interact. Such an approach is feasible where we are dealing with relatively discrete types of behaviour, such as feeding, drinking or fighting. But in the case of exploration, this is difficult as it is interconnected with *all* other aspects of behaviour. In practice, a distinction is made between extrinsic exploration, which is directed towards a biologically significant event, such as feeding (Berlyne, 1960), and intrinsic exploration, which refers to responses that cannot be linked to such an event, and hence are seen as serving to familiarize the animal with stimuli in its environment as 'an end in itself' (Berlyne 1960). The former has been viewed in terms of a separate motivational system, associated with curiosity and boredom, whereas extrinsic motivation is generally considered in relation to its particular biological endpoint. In the ethological tradition, the 'appetitive' phase of a specific motivated behaviour would correspond to extrinsic motivation, and this is viewed separately from intrinsic forms of exploration (Barnett, 1963).

These distinctions can nevertheless become blurred in practice: when an animal finds its way around its home range, presumably relying on knowledge of the spatial locality, or when it 'patrols' the boundary of a territory, it may be difficult to see these activities as wholly intrinsic or extrinsic. It is likewise difficult to place movements within a home range or territory, such as 'patrolling', into one of these two categories. Patrolling can be viewed as re-exploration, enabling the animal to detect changes in the environment (see Chapter 6).

In ethological research, appetitive behaviour has been associated with the concept of 'search image' derived from the work of Tinbergen (1960) and Gibb (1962), describing changes in the predation of specific prey related to its density. The term refers to a cognitive change whereby the animal is 'set' to respond selectively to particular patterns of stimuli. More recently, psychologists studying intrinsic exploration have also referred to hypothetical cognitive processes in seeking to explain exploration in terms of 'cognitive maps'. This concept, which originated with Tolman in the 1930s, has been used increasingly in recent studies (see Chapters 3 and 4), and has now been linked with physiological investigations (see Chapter 5).

So far, we have referred exclusively to animal exploration, since this reflects the majority of research on the subject. The composition of the book reflects this bias, and we begin with several chapters on the nature of exploration in animals, each one covering the subject from a different angle. In Chapter 1, we discuss some of the overall issues involved in research on animal exploration, notably problems of definition, theoretical approach and function. In particular we discuss the limitations of the comparative psychological approach, which has been the dominant one in research on exploration since the 1920–30s. It has involved laboratory experiments using rats or mice in artificially constructed environments, such as novel arenas or mazes, and theories formulated in terms of incentive or drive. In Chapter 2, Russell provides a detailed review of these psychological studies. He points out that psychological investigations of exploration flourished in the 1950s and 1960s both in the sense of the number of animal studies carried out and in the comprehensive theoretical accounts that were put forward then. Since this time, the subject has received little major impetus, at least from this research tradition. The remaining nine chapters represent attempts either to take a fresh look at classical psychological studies of exploration or to widen the field of enquiry and application by considering approaches from outside the comparative psychological tradition. Chapter 2 points out the deficiencies of many classical psychological studies, both methodologically and theoretically. Methodologically, they involve artificial test environments that take insufficient account of the function of exploration under natural conditions. Theoretically, they have often floundered in a number of complex explanations couched in terms of hypothetical motivational constructs such as boredom, curiosity and arousal. These were often ill defined as concepts and therefore offered little scope for precise prediction.

These two issues, highlighted in Chapter 2, are amplified throughout the book. The first, concerning lack of ecological validity, leads us to enquire whether a more ethological approach based on appreciation of the animal's natural habitat can offer a wider perspective on animal exploration. Some researchers from the ethological tradition, who were originally a group of zoologists interested in the control of rodent pests, have studied the responses of animals to novel stimuli presented in a familiar area. Other ethologists have been more concerned with exploration within an animal's familiar area, including partrolling, which we referred to earlier. Both aspects are discussed in Chapter 6. Chapter 7 considers how the captive environment affects the behaviour of captive wild animals and in particular how lack of stimulation and opportunities for exploration ('boredom') can lead to various forms of abnormal behaviour. In Chapter 8, Wood-Gush, Stolba and Miller approach the similar problem involved in housing farm animals. They ask how much exploratory behaviour is required for the wellbeing of farm animals and whether additional opportunities for exploration would eliminate some of the abnormal behaviour.

The second main issue highlighted in Russell's chapter, concerning theoretical approaches to exploration, is considered in Chapters 3, 4 and 5. These three authors discuss theories of exploration in rather different terms from the comparative psychologists' drive and incentive approaches. Toates first describes traditional behaviourist and S–R theories, then discusses the limitations of this approach, and finally considers the contributions from modern cognitive approaches to learning theory. The cognitive approach to exploration is developed further by Inglis (Chapter 4), particularly in relation to the work of Tolman in the 1930s. Inglis advances a theory of exploratory behaviour based on Tolman's work and a variety of more modern approaches, including human cognitive psychology.

Russell criticized the theoretical constructs of the 1950s for not being tied to neurophysiological events and mechanisms. The hypothetical construct favoured by Toates, and also incorporated into Inglis' discussion, is the cognitive map (referred to earlier); this has the added advantage of having being studied in relation to physiological mechanisms, and this research is discussed in Chapter 5, by Morris who also considers recent work on the motor sub-systems involved in exploratory behaviour.

Research on exploration in the 1950s and 1960s was, as we have seen, fairly narrowly based on laboratory animal studies, and any extension to human studies was largely the result of the conceptual scheme developed by Berlyne (1960) in his book *Conflict, Arousal and Curiosity*. His analysis of collative variables, such as novelty and complexity, stimulated research in several areas of human psychology. One is the study of exploration and play in children, and this is the subject of Chapter 10 by Hughes who is mainly concerned with the interrelations between object play and exploration. In Chapter 9, Einon provides more general coverage of the subject of exploration and play, including social as well as object play, in both young animals and children. The final chapter, by Sluckin, Hargreaves and Colman, covers the extension by Berlyne of his work on collative variables to the subject of human aesthetics. This is often referred to as the new experimental aesthetics (Berlyne, 1971, 1974). The authors describe research in children and adults which seeks to relate aesthetic preference to novelty and familiarity: they describe their own research on letters, words and names, and survey other studies on musical preferences.

John Archer
Lynda Birke

References

BARNETT, S. A. (1963) *A Study in Behaviour*. London: Methuen.

BERLYNE, D. E. (1960) *Conflict, Arousal and Curiosity*. New York: McGraw-Hill.

BERLYNE, D. E. (1971) *Aesthetics and Psychobiology*. New York: Appleton-Century Crofts.

BERLYNE, D. E. (1974) *Studies in the New Experimental Aesthetics*. Wiley: New York.

GIBB, J. A. (1962) L. Tinbergen's hypothesis of the role of specific search images. *Ibis*, **104**, 106–111.

TINBERGEN, L. (1960) The natural control of insects in pinewoods.
  I: Factor influencing the intensity of predation by songbirds. *Archives Neerlandaises de Zoologie*, **13**, 265–343.

CHAPTER 1

Some Issues And Problems in the Study of Animal Exploration

Lynda I. A. Birke and John Archer

Animals, as any pet owner knows, get bored. Over the last few decades, it has become increasingly fashionable for those responsible for the husbandry of captive animals to show concern not only for the animal's diet, but also that it should have adequate stimulation in its living space. The 'bored' animal may develop stereotyped behaviour, may start ingesting harmful substances, or may even start eating its fellows. All of these vices can be prevented by providing it with objects with which to play or to explore.

In everyday language, we talk of animals being bored, or, conversely, being curious, implying that they need or seek a certain level of stimulation. Although, scientifically, we may prefer to avoid such mentalistic terms, we can study the behavioural outcome of 'curiosity' or 'boredom': that is, we can study the ways in which the animal explores stimuli or its environment. In this chapter, we deal with some of the ways that such investigatory responses have been studied, outlining some of the difficulties that have beset research in this area. As will be apparent, when we outline the literature on animal exploration, we are really only talking about mammals — indeed, very few mammalian orders at that. Most of the research we discuss has used the animal much beloved by laboratory psychologists, the rat. We have not addressed the question of whether concepts of exploration might be applicable to groups other than the 'higher' vertebrates, simply because of the lack of comparative data.

Our concern in this chapter is with different approaches to the study of animal exploration, and with the main issues and problems that have arisen. For example, it has been difficult to define precisely what is meant by the term 'exploration'. In the first section, we examine the features of exploratory behaviour, to highlight some of these difficulties of definition. Another important problem is how to classify exploration in relation to other motivational systems, or, indeed, whether it is meaningful to refer to exploration as a motivational system in the way that we refer to, say, feeding or drinking. The second part of the chapter outlines the development of views on exploration as a motivational system, in order to illustrate the problems, although we do not cover these issues at any length as they are discussed more

1

fully in the following chapters of this book. Finally, we consider the question of the function of exploration: what does the animal gain in terms of survival value by exploring? In discussing this topic, we move away from psychological studies of exploration in laboratory rodents to consider more ethological and ecologically oriented research, e.g., on strategies of foraging, in the belief that this area of research will prove fruitful for future developments in the study of animal exploration.

1.1 Definition and Measurement of Exploration

What do animals do when they explore? When an animal enters a new environment, it appears to move about in an unpredictable way, seeming to investigate various features of the environment. Exploration is usually defined in terms of consequences, i.e. it is assumed to provide the animal with information about its environment, and therefore includes all those types of behaviour that seem to increase the information obtained by the animal. In the laboratory rat this will include running around and sniffing, rearing up on its hind legs, making contact with stimuli by means of vibrissae or paws and turning its head and body towards particular stimuli. Other species pick up stimulus objects and manipulate them or even put them into the mouth.

It is clear from these brief examples that many different behavioural responses are generally thought of as 'exploratory'. Simply stating that the animal explored tells us little about what it actually did, since 'exploration' is a category based on consequences rather than specific motor acts. Psychologists have employed a variety of approaches in studying exploration. In all of these, complex behaviour is reduced to relatively simple, measurable, responses: e.g. exploration may be measured by the extent of movement in a novel arena or maze, or by the choice of particular arms of a maze, during relatively short test sessions. Such studies provide information about the types of choices or responses animals might make under these controlled conditions, but they do not necessarily enable predictions to be made about behaviour in more complex environments over longer periods of time, where choices include location of food, water and other essential resources. The lack of ecological validity in psychological studies is a theme taken up in Chapter 2. We return later in this chapter to consider the paucity of more ecological evidence.

Some of the problems of defining exploration have been dealt with in the Introduction, where we referred to two broad distinctions, between passive and active forms of exploration (attentional changes and active investigation, respectively) and between intrinsic and extrinsic exploration (whether motivated by curiosity or by some other drive). These distinctions were made by Berlyne (1960), who also drew a number of other distinctions between different forms of exploration. One of these, discussed in Chapter 2, is between inspective exploration, responding *to* environmental change, and inquisitive exploration, responding *for* — or in order to initiate — a change. Another is between specific exploration, obtaining information about a specific object or event, and diversive exploration, responses directed at increasing the information obtained from *any* environmental source. This latter distinction is particularly important in research on exploration and play in children, e.g. that carried out by Hutt (1970) and described in Chapter 10.

In the remainder of this section, we discuss the different types of responses that have been regarded as 'exploratory' in laboratory studies. We begin by considering movements made by an animal in its familiar area, often referred to as 'patrolling', before going on to discuss various responses shown in novel environments or to specific novel stimuli. These are the responses that have been measured in psychological studies of exploration that form the bulk of the research on animal exploration.

1.2   Patrolling

'Patrolling' is the term used to describe systematic movements through a familiar territory. Although a subject neglected by the classical psychological studies of exploration in the 1950s and 1960s, it has been extensively studied in laboratory rodents by Barnett and coworkers in the 1970s (e.g. Barnett & Cowan, 1976; Barnett & McEwan, 1973; Cowan, 1977). This work is described more fully in Chapter 6. It has involved studying rodents living in a cross-maze, and it was found that all four arms were regularly visited even when one of them was completely empty. Arms containing food or water were visited more frequently, but the animals never completely habituated to the empty arm. Furthermore, the visits were systematic, in that animals did not return immediately to the arm they had just visited.

Cowan (1977) observed that patrolling by laboratory rats tended to occur soon after a meal had been eaten, suggesting that patrolling is a rather low-priority activity, compared to other activities such as locating and eating food. The extent to which patrolling is important for animals in the wild has not been adequately studied. It may not even be possible in practice to separate 'exploratory' behaviour from foraging for specific resources (see Introduction and later in this chapter). The extent to which this is the case may depend on the animal's feeding habits. Patrolling may be more typical of animals that tend to eat in 'meals' than of those which have to search for food over extended periods of time. The latter are likely to obtain information about their environments while searching for food or other resources, in the same way that a rat would while patrolling.

1.3   Responses to Novelty

Apart from these few studies of patrolling, all other laboratory investigations of exploration have used 'novel' situations. Hennessy & Levine (1979) distinguished between 'absolute' novelty, in which the animal is placed into an entirely unfamiliar apparatus, such as a maze, and 'relative' novelty, in which one or two stimuli are novel within more familiar surroundings. An animal's responses to these two kinds of novelty are likely to differ. In the former, initial responses may include very general changes in behaviour ('diversive' exploration), such as increased locomotion, whereas the latter is more likely to lead to direct investigation of the changed stimuli ('specific' exploration). We now consider these two in turn.

1.3.1   Responses to Novel Environments

Locomotor changes. Locomotion in a novel environment is commonly assumed to represent exploratory behaviour, and since it can be easily measured, it has frequently been used to quantify animal exploration. However, as Berlyne (1960) and others have observed, there are problems in accepting uncritically the premise that locomotion necessarily indicates exploration. An animal may move around a novel environment for other reasons, for example attempting to escape. Even leaving aside the problem that locomotion may serve other purposes, can we assume that the amount of locomotion will accurately measure 'exploration' in the sense of information acquisition? It is questionable whether the rat that moves about more is exploring more. A fast-moving rat may be relatively inattentive to environmental cues, whereas one that remains stationary may be attentively watching and sniffing the air. The problems encountered in using locomotion as a measure of exploration are discussed in some detail by Russell in Chapter 2, and therefore our discussion here is limited to a few preliminary remarks.

Prescott (1970) reviewed the often contradictory data on activity measures and suggested that increases in activity usually, but not always, consisted of increases in behaviour 'related to sampling of environmental stimuli'. How this feature of locomotion is related to other, more static forms of exploratory behaviour remains problematic, however.

Levels of locomotor activity may be influenced by various factors, both internal and external: for this reason, early drive theorists incorporated general activity as the behavioural outcome of general drive (Bolles, 1975), which could be influenced by factors such as hormonal state, or food deprivation. Hormonal state is known to influence activity levels: for example, oestrous rats have been reported to be more active than dioestrous in several different situations (e.g. Finger, 1969; Martin & Bättig, 1980) although this may be specific to certain methods of testing (Mullenix, 1981). Similarly, food or water deprivation affects activity levels in some rodent species (Campbell *et al.*, 1966). As a result of these types of influence, it is not always clear whether simple changes in activity level can be attributed to differences in 'exploration', although the more obvious influences can be controlled in experimental investigations.

Several studies suggest that locomotor activity might be separable from other investigatory responses, either through the use of statistical procedures or by physiological manipulations. Simmel & Eleftheriou (1977) analysed the exploratory behaviour of mice in a novel two-chamber arena. A factor analysis of the behavioural measures used indicated two factors, one involving behaviour related to novel stimuli, and the other relating to locomotor activity. Similarly, Leyland *et al.* (1976) reported a dissociation between activity and investigation of novel stimuli in a modified Berlyne box (an apparatus in which rats are presented with a range of patterned stimulus cards). In this apparatus, novel stimulation increased exploration but not locomotion, whereas administration of *d*-amphetamine had the reverse effect.

Activity and exploratory investigation have been separated by physiological manipulations, including injection of dopaminergic agonists (Isaacson *et al.*, 1978), lesions of septal nuclei (Kohler & Srebro, 1980) and hippocampectomy (see Chapter 5; and O'Keefe & Nadel, 1978). The latter authors note that earlier studies of the effects of hippocampectomy in rats had led to the suggestion that lesioned animals explored more. However, further studies showed that hippocampal rats were also less responsive to novel stimuli than control animals: O'Keefe and Nadel suggest, therefore, that the effect of the lesion is not to make the animals explore more, but rather to make them hyperactive.

In pointing out these limitations to the use of locomotion as a measure of exploration, we still recognize that the active animal is likely to acquire information about its environment. Confronting an animal with a novel environment, especially one containing novel objects, may well result in increased locomotion, as well as extended examination of some of the stimuli present. Nevertheless, the assumption that the level of activity provides an accurate measure of exploratory tendency should be avoided.

Reactivity levels and responsiveness to stimuli. Even if increases in locomotion are usually accompanied by increased environmental sampling as Prescott (1970) suggested, locomotor measures may omit other forms of exploration. Bindra & Spinner (1958) made this point and suggested time-sampling a wider range of behavioural acts, some of which (for example, rearing) may be defined as exploration, whereas others, such as grooming, would not. Russell considers these other exploratory responses in Chapter 2. Here, we restrict our discussion to the use of one of these to measure 'excitability' level.

Rearing is a common exploratory response of many rodents and it has been used as a measure of 'excitability level' by Lat (1963) and others, since the frequency of rearing has been found to correlate positively with other activities, such as grooming, defensive and sexual reactions. One difficulty with this formulation is that there is a danger of viewing excitability level as another term for general drive, since it is not always possible to specify the stimuli to which the animal is responding. This approach does, however, point to the need to study exploratory behaviour not only in terms of environmental changes, but also in relation to internal factors which may influence central nervous system arousal. This in turn will affect the individual's responsiveness to stimuli. As Andrew (1974) pointed out, intraindividual changes in an animal's responsiveness to stimuli have been little studied, although they have been inferred on the basis of postulated changes in CNS arousal. There is some evidence that individual responsiveness can vary; it can vary, for example, as a function of food deprivation, or in relation to hormonal state (Birke, 1979). It can also vary according to what the animal is doing at the time the stimulus is encountered (Fentress, 1968; Forrester & Broom, 1980). Thus, the response of bank voles to an overhead stimulus differed according to whether they were walking or grooming at the time (Fentress, *op. cit.*).

Adult responsiveness to stimuli may also be influenced by early experience. Joseph & Gallagher (1980), for example, note that rats reared in a restricted environment are 'overreactive' to stimuli, when compared to controls reared in enriched environments; that is, they do not readily habituate to novel stimuli, and are less able to learn responses requiring the inhibition of behaviour.

We have so far been considering two general measures of exploratory behaviour, locomotion and responsiveness to stimuli. Most of the studies employing such measures have used novel or conspicuous stimuli presented in a novel apparatus. When interpreting studies of this kind, we should bear in mind that animals may respond differently to specific stimuli in totally novel situations from the way in which they would respond in more familiar circumstances. There are few studies comparing the differential responses of animals to stimuli in unfamiliar and familiar surroundings, one exception being that of Cowan (1976) who found that commensal *Rattus rattus* showed avoidance of novel objects which were introduced into a familiar home cage, but did not avoid objects that were present at the time the rats were first introduced.

1.3.2   *Responses to Novel Stimuli*

One difficulty with many of the studies of responses to novelty is, as we have noted, that a novel stimulus is presented in equally novel surroundings, and it is not always possible to determine to what the animal is responding. Presenting a novel stimulus in relatively familiar surroundings is a common alternative to placing an animal into a completely novel environment. Here we are concerned with 'relative novelty' in the terminology of Hennessey and Levine. The distinction between 'novelty' and 'familiarity' is addressed in the next section: here, we consider the responses an animal typically shows to stimuli the experimenter might define as novel or conspicuous.

An animal may exhibit a variety of responses to a novel or conspicuous stimulus. It may show orienting responses, it might attack, it might scent-mark, it might run away or freeze, it might sniff at, or pick the object up. Much depends on the type of stimulus, the species of animal, and whether the animal has had prior experience with that type of object. Of the various responses commonly shown towards stimulus objects, two might be considered as forming part of exploratory behaviour: orienting, and direct investigation.

Orienting responses. These represent the initial attentional changes in response to a novel stimulus, referred to by Berlyne (1960) as passive exploration. Pavlov (1927) referred to the orienting response as an 'investigatory reflex', consisting of turning the head towards the source of stimulation, and bringing the sense organs to bear upon it. Berlyne (1960) similarly stressed that by bringing the sense organs to bear upon the stimulus, the animal is finding out something about it, and can be said to be exploring it.

Sokolov (1960) and Vinogradova (1970) described the orienting response as requiring perception of the stimulus, scanning through the memory store, comparing the new with relevant stored information, and opening channels of registration if a stimulus does not fit a counterpart in memory. Once the information has been stored, the response habituates. This formulation describes orientation in terms of 'finding out about the stimulus', thus classifying orientation as an exploratory response.

There are, however, some problems with Sokolov's approach to orienting behaviour, and these are relevant to its relationship to exploration. First, as Groves & Thompson (1970) pointed out, Sokolov's model assumes that, as information about the stimulus is stored, the response habituates. Increased responses (dishabituation) due to the presentation of a second stimulus different from the first cannot readily be explained by such a model. Secondly the model makes little allowance for differing rates of habituation to stimuli of different types. Seligman (1970) has argued that animals, as a result of evolutionary selection, are more able to learn responses which have some adaptive value for them, a phenomenon which he calls 'preparedness'. For example, mice will rapidly habituate to irrelevant click stimuli (Scourse & Hinde, 1973), whereas it is virtually impossible to habituate the mouse pup-retrieval response (Petrinovich, 1973). Further examples of biological preparedness are provided by the ability of passerine birds to learn species-specific song (Nottebohm, 1970).

Seligman's point is clearly important for the study of exploration. Although it may be convenient to study specific responses of animals to somewhat contrived stimuli within the laboratory, this is not the whole story. The exploring animal not only orients to, and investigates, 'novel' stimuli, but also those that are of special relevance to it; for example, it may investigate objects that tend to be associated with the odour trails of that species.

Furthermore, although certain stimuli may be particularly significant for the species, such significance may fluctuate within the individual's life. During the breeding season, animals would be expected to react to stimuli within their environment in particular ways (e.g., picking up nest material, laying scent trails), whereas they may react to the same stimuli at other times with indifference. Changing patterns of exploration and responsiveness to stimuli over long periods of time have not yet been adequately studied, or dealt with theoretically.

The third problem with the traditional view of orientation is that it is not always clear what is meant by the term. 'Orientation' might be used to describe the alignment of attention to a source of input. This is the sense in which, for example, Ingle et al. (1979) refer to visual orientation and tracking by the gerbil. Alternatively, as Posner (1980) points out, much of the work on orienting, including that of Sokolov (1960) encompasses both the initial alignment, and the subsequent analysis of the stimulus that leads to recognition. Posner, discussing human orienting, notes that:

The orienting reflex does not distinguish between the processes that occur prior to detection and those which occur subsequently. The relatively slow nature of autonomic changes often precludes such a division. Although our method of measuring orienting is via changes in the efficiency of detecting, the two mental operations must be quite distinct.

The distinction may seem trivial. However, it is relevant to an understanding of exploration, as it reminds us that 'orienting' may take many forms. The targetting and recognition phases of the orienting reflex may be mediated by different brain structures. Andrew (1975) points out that there are midbrain mechanisms that appear to be implicated in targetting in a range of vertebrates, whereas structures such as the hippocampus are implicated in processes of retrieval of central representations of stimuli. The initial alignment to a stimulus may be followed by investigation, or it may be followed by other responses, including turning away and ignoring the stimulus. If the animal has targetted onto a stimulus of some significance (which, as Siddle (1979) observed, can only be defined *post hoc*), investigatory responses will be more likely. This may include direct investigation, such as sniffing at the object, or the animal may remain where it is and scan the object visually from a distance. Van der Poel (1979) describes the phenomenon of 'stretched attention' by rats in an approach – avoidance conflict: following initial orientation, the animal scans the stimulus visually, and sniffs towards it, with the body stretched out. It is this scanning and investigating at a distance that comprises the 'exploratory' part of the orienting response in Berlyne's classification.

Posner (1980), also suggested that orienting in humans is not only a function of events external to the organism:

> It is . . . important to make a distinction between external and central control over orienting. If orienting to memory and to external stimulus events is to have a common base, it is clear that we must be able to orient attention in the absence of an external stimulus. Similarly, movements of the eyes can either be driven by stimulus input or result from a search plan internal to the organism.

This is an important point, and one familiar to ethologists. Traditionally, psychological research on exploratory behaviour has involved manipulations of the stimulus configurations to which an animal is exposed. These are often rather contrived stimuli, such as two-dimensional patterns of stripes or squares. Ethologists have, in general, paid scant attention to exploration. Nonetheless, a concept commonly used in ethology which is pertinent to Posner's distinction is that of the 'search image', where it is assumed that the stimuli to which the animal responds correspond to a hypothetical model in its head. Tinbergen (1960) used the concept of a searching image to explain the way in which predators appear to search for only one type of prey at a time, and it is now a concept used extensively in other areas of study, for example, analyses of optimal foraging strategies (e.g., Krebs, 1978).

If we are to understand the significance of orienting as a part of exploratory behaviour, a synthesis of the two approaches, psychological and ethological, is required. The first, although positing an 'exploratory drive' (see Section 1.5

8

and Chapter 2, 3 and 4), assumes that what determines a rat's decision to orient to A rather than to B is largely a matter of the characteristics of A and B. This may be so for laboratory rats provided with ad libitum food and water. In the wild, however, it is unlikely to be the case, and what we observe as exploratory behaviour probably involves decisions based upon many criteria. Thus, orientation may occur because of stimulus characteristics *per se*, such as novelty, or because the animal has some kind of 'searching image' for stimuli of that type.

Direct investigation. Perhaps the least ambiguous measure of exploration is that of direct investigation of objects, 'specific', as opposed to 'diversive' exploration in Berlyne's (1960) classification. Here, responses to specific items, rather than to general features, are examined. Usually this involves measuring responses such as sniffing at, gazing at, or manipulating objects. It thus excludes initial orientation, but is concerned with subsequent investigation of the object. Berlyne (1950) used the duration of sniffing at objects as a measure of exploration in rats. Subsequently, similar measures — such as duration of sniffing or latency to approach an object — have been used in several types of investigation: for example, comparisons of exploration in several species of rodent (Glickman & Hartz, 1964); the effects of early handling on rat investigatory behaviour (Wells & Lawlor, 1975); comparisons of isolate and socially reared rats' investigatory and play behaviour (Einon & Morgan, 1976).

Although measures of direct investigation are the least ambiguous, it is not necessarily clear what we are measuring. For the laboratory rodent, an appropriate investigatory response is to sniff the object. However, many experimental reports do not make it clear whether there was any attempt to control for effects resulting from odours of previously tested animals: we do not know, therefore, whether the animal was responding to some characteristic of the stimulus itself, or was responding to odour traces left by another animal. Archer (1974) noted that testing rats in an open-field from which odour traces had not been removed resulted in more sniffing while walking than in rats tested in a clean open-field. Similarly, Russell & Chalkly-Maber (1979) found that rats tend to spend more time in, and investigate more, the half of an open-field that had previously contained a conspecific.

1.3.3 The Problem of Novelty

Berlyne (1960) discussed the difficulties of using such terms as 'novelty' and 'complexity' as descriptions of stimuli or stimulus configurations. The fundamental problem with the concept of novelty is that novel stimuli 'cannot be distinguished (from other stimuli) by physicochemical properties' (Berlyne, p. 20): novelty, in other words, has to be defined with respect to the animal's own past experiences. We can present the animal with stimuli that we judge to be somewhat novel on the basis of our expectations of the type of stimuli that the animal is likely to have encountered. This may be an easy task under laboratory conditions, but it is less straightforward when wild or feral animals are studied.

On this basis, however, attempts have been made to distinguish different types of novelty. We have referred, for example, to the distinction between absolute and relative novelty (Berlyne, 1960; Hennessy & Levine, 1979). A similar distinction has been drawn between the terms novelty and discrepancy (Weisler & McCall, 1976), the latter implying that 'the new stimuli bear some magnitude of physical or conceptual similarity to events remembered by the organism', whereas a novel stimulus is one not previously encountered. Berlyne (1960) notes, however, that these distinctions are arbitrary, and that it is extremely unlikely that the mature organism ever meets *entirely* new stimuli:

> Any new experience, even if it does not seem to be a combination of familiar experiences, must have some definite degree of resemblance to experiences that have occurred before. It will inevitably be possible to insert it into an ordering of familiar stimuli or to assign it to values along dimensions that are used to classify them.
>
> (Berlyne, 1960, p. 19)

The concept of 'discrepancy' implies reference to a stored representation, and does not take into account developmental changes in responses to novel situations. The distinction between novelty and discrepancy is thus of limited use for descriptions of developmental changes in exploratory behaviour.

The heart of the problem is that novelty must be defined with respect to what the animal actually does. But here we fall into the trap of circularity, with exploration and novelty both being defined in terms of each other. Furthermore, exploratory responses are clearly not the only ones an animal may show to novel stimuli. The behavioural outcome will depend, for instance, on the nature of the stimulus, the animal's physiological or behavioural state at the time the stimulus is encountered, or the context in which the novel stimulus occurs. Further, different types of stimulus may be expected to elicit very different responses from different species. There are far too few comparative studies available; these are badly needed if we are to evaluate the adaptiveness of different types of responses to novelty for different species.

Finally, as we have indicated, the context in which the 'novel' stimulus is presented may be of great importance. A novel stimulus in a novel environment may on one occasion provoke avoidance, whereas on another it may reinstate investigation of familiar stimuli (Sheldon, 1969). The environmental context will, for most species, normally include conspecifics, whose presence can alter the individual's response to novelty. For example, Simmel (1962) noted that exploratory behaviour in rats (measured by locomotion) was subject to social facilitation. Similarly, passerine birds are more likely to approach and eat novel foods if they have observed others doing so (Turner, 1964).

The problems associated with defining the concept of novelty have led Barnett & Cowan (1976) to propose that 'unfamiliarity' be used instead, as it emphasizes the relationship between present and past experience, a point made earlier by Hebb (1949). It is doubtful, however, whether much is gained by such semantic changes: the problems of tautology, and the wide range of behavioural outcomes, remain.

If novelty is difficult to define, so are the other stimulus features often said to lead to exploration, such as 'complexity' or 'incongruity'. What is clear is that since novelty (and related terms) can lead to so many behavioural outcomes it cannot be used to *define* exploration.

That said, a problem remains. It is clear to anyone who has kept domestic animals that animals are 'curious' and liable to become bored. This had led some writers to argue that animals seek out 'novelty' or, more accurately, stimulus change (e.g. Fowler, 1965). If given a choice, animals tend to prefer places that are novel to those that are more familiar, at least in laboratory conditions (e.g. Hughes, 1968; Montgomery, 1953). Many species will also learn operant tasks for a variety of stimulus changes, even including changes in illumination (e.g. rodents — Kish, 1955; pigs — Baldwin & Mesee, 1977, but see Halliday, 1968, for possible interpretations of this).

The extent to which an animal seeks out stimulus change depends to some extent on the species (Glickman & Hartz, 1964; Glickman & Sroges, 1966); the fact, however, remains, that for most of the commonly studied mammals and birds, moderate levels of stimulus change are reinforcing, and 'boredom' is rather aversive. Such boredom, as any visitor to the zoo or intensive farm is frequently reminded, can lead to the development of intensely stereotyped behaviour (see Chapters 7 and 8).

1.4 What Type of Motivation is Exploration?

It would seem reasonable to suppose that 'curiosity' represents a form of motivation. Exploratory behaviour has, however, long presented difficulties for theories of motivation. It did not fit easily into Hull's theory of general drive, as it lacked obvious antecedent conditions (Bolles, 1975). For a time, exploration was thought of as a form of general activity, a view that began to change during the 1950s. Once it was realized that the opportunity to explore stimuli is itself reinforcing, exploration was considered by many to be an autonomous drive (e.g. Berlyne, 1950; Fowler, 1965; Hebb, 1949; Montgomery, 1953). Both Berlyne (1950) and Montgomery (1953), for example, referred to a 'curiosity drive', elicited by the presence of novel stimuli, and which led to investigation of those stimuli. Montgomery argued that, by analogy with other postulated drives, the curiosity drive decreased with continued exposure to the eliciting stimuli, and increased during non-exposure. Similarly, Berlyne (1960) considered exploration to be a drive, on the basis of such criteria as its ability to reinforce operant responses (e.g. Butler, 1954; Nissen, 1930).

These attempts to locate exploration within the domain of classical drive theory met many difficulties. First, much of the data simply failed to fit classical drive interpretations. Deprivation of an opportunity to explore, for example, does not always result in increased exploration, as would be theoretically predicted. Secondly, the types of behaviour subsumed under the title 'exploratory' are very heterogeneous, and this variety produces difficulties for a unitary explanation. As Halliday (1968) observed, one group of data may be best explained by one theory and another by a different theory. Glanzer (1953) put forward a 'stimulus satiation' theory (that is, the hypothesis that, with each moment that an animal continues to receive a stimulus, the tendency to make any response to that stimulus diminishes) which, as Halliday (*op. cit.*) suggests, deals adequately with some results, particularly those relating habituation to novelty, spontaneous alternation, and so on. Other findings are better explained by assuming that the opportunity to explore acts as a positive reinforcer. Finally, a unitary drive theory would predict that changes in different forms of 'exploratory' behaviour should covary. Unfortunately, the correlations between such measures have generally been low (Barnett & Cowan, 1976).

An alternative to the classical Hullian view is to suggest that exploration is motivated by fear. A relationship between exploration and fear was suggested by Hebb (1955) in his discussion of the 'conceptual nervous system'. He implied that moderate levels of fear might be rewarding and that animals tend to seek stimulation from mildly fear-provoking objects. Several authors have proposed a single 'fear' continuum along similar lines, avoidance occurring at high fear levels, and exploration (e.g. approach and investigation of a stimulus) at low to moderate levels (e.g. Halliday, 1968; Lester, 1967; also see Chapter 2). An alternative to this hypothesis is the notion of a balance between two competing tendencies — to approach (curiosity) and to avoid (fear) — a view originally proposed by Montgomery (1955). Both viewpoints are exhaustively reviewed by Russell (1973) and in Chapter 2, so we will do no more than refer to them briefly here. Russell concludes that the evidence for both theories is equivocal since attempts to define operationally concepts such as fear and exploration are elusive.

Are such theoretical disputes about the relation between exploration and fear useful? It is, of course, true that certain stimuli — which we might classify as inherently fearful to the animal, such as electric shock — are more likely to elicit responses incompatible with direct approach and investigation. Freezing or running away, for instance, are clearly not compatible with approach. It is worth stressing that in these cases we are referring to responses rather than hypothetical intervening variables. As Bolles & Fanselow (1980) observed: 'Custom has it that while fear may have motivational effects, it is basically a set of responses and it is properly defined in terms of those responses'. These responses do not normally include approach, and in fact are incompatible with approach at a motor level.

Several authors have criticized the use of fear as an intervening variable which motivates exploration in some way. Murphy (1978) considers that the use of such explanatory constructs is premature, since we know rather little as yet about the detailed relationships between specific stimuli and exploratory responses. McCullough (unpublished, see McCullough, 1979) remarks that: 'It is immaterial whether exploration occurs as a result of, or in spite of, fear; in either case the animal provides itself with information about, among other things, the safety or dangers of the explored situation'. Although the theories of fear and exploration have certainly promoted research, it is questionable whether such research has contributed much, if anything, to our understanding

12

of exploration. Certainly such theories now appear to have outlived their usefulness, and other approaches to the motivation of exploration are necessary.

Before leaving the subject of fear, we should note that fear and exploration can be regarded as broadly having something in common, in being elicited primarily by disparity. This aspect has been incorporated into discrepancy theories that have been applied to such diverse subjects as the orienting reflex (see above), imprinting and fear (Salzen, 1970), the development of fear (Kagan, 1974), and aggression and fear (Archer, 1976). Archer's (1976) model of fear and aggression, for example, incorporated disparity actuation, such that large disparity between the stimulus and internal representations (neuronal models) activates fear responses and moderate disparity activates aggressive responses. Russell discusses discrepancy theories further in Chapter 2.

Discrepancy theories do have an advantage over drive theories, in that they emphasize to a greater extent stimuli and events external to the organism, rather than relying solely on hypothetical internal states which goad the animal into action. Another approach to the nature of exploratory motivation has been in terms of incentive motivation. The idea of incentives originated with Hull, and was further elaborated by Spence (1956). For these authors, however, incentives were a learned, secondary factor acquired by stimuli which have been associated with drive reduction: incentives were thought of, then, as subsidiary to the internal drive state.

The concept has changed over the 30 years since Hull's original formulation (Bolles, 1975). A current view is to see incentive motivation as providing selective facilitation of particular responses (e.g. Bindra, 1969, 1979; Bolles, 1975; Toates & Birke, 1982). According to this view, incentive stimuli both arouse motivation and also give it direction. Bindra, for example, views the motivational state, once aroused, as sensitizing the animal to respond in particular ways to stimuli around it. For instance, in the presence of stimuli predictive of food, motivation (which we may choose to call hunger) is aroused, and this sensitizes the animal to food stimuli, facilitating appropriate responses, such as biting or chewing the food. According to this view, organismic state (e.g., fluid or energy state) affects motivation in that it influences the excitability of specific motivational circuits, which in turn determine the effectiveness of particular stimuli to elicit appropriate behaviour.

Incentive motivation provides a useful framework for considering exploratory behaviour (see Chapter 3). We consider exploration as a motivational system aroused in response to particular kinds of stimuli, and we can also relate it to other motivational systems. The freely moving, choosing animal encounters a whole range of stimuli in its environment, some of which may be incentives for feeding, others for exploration, or for copulation, or other activities. Its decisions to move between these various stimuli and choose, say, to investigate one rather than eat another will be influenced by internal state, as well as the relative incentive values of the different stimuli.

1.5 Functional Aspects: What is to be Gained by Exploring?

In functional or 'survival value' terms, whether or not an animal explores depends upon the costs and benefits to the animal which accrue as a result of exploring. The most significant costs are energy expenditure, and the risk of predation. Danger from predators is likely to reduce the amount of exploration in novel environments shown by any given species. Glickman & Morrison (1969) showed that mice that were particularly 'exploratory' in an open field were those most likely to be preyed upon, whereas those that stayed close to the edge and moved little were more likely to survive. Such costs have to be balanced against the benefits gained by animals that explore — or the costs incurred by not doing so. Presumably if a predator is nearby, an animal that is familiar with its surroundings will be better equipped to avoid predation than one that is not.

The benefits of exploration are less straightforward than the costs. Exploratory behaviour presumably provides the animal with information about the environment or about objects within it. Many studies of laboratory rodents show that investigation of novel stimuli or environments is a high priority activity; even if subjected to considerable food or water deprivation, a rat will still explore a novel environment before deciding to eat. In terms of survival value, this makes sense because in the wild, such exploration would reduce uncertainty about the environment. Only a foolish rat would eat food pellets before making sure that it was safe to do so, or that other places did not offer a more attractive menu.

Most laboratory studies use animals kept in standard cages, with a constant supply of food and water, which is most unlike the natural environment. An animal's movements around its natural habitat may be better described as a search for specific resources than as 'exploration' in the abstract. But whatever the distinction between exploration, and search (to which we return below), both provide the animal with information. We may decide that the movements of a starling across the lawn indicate that it is searching for food, but the animal must also be alert to other stimuli around it. Some of these may require immediate action whereas others may be ignored for the time being. In either case, the animal is provided with potential information about the environment, and building up external representations of its world (a point further elaborated in Chapter 4).

Purely random movements through a habitat are most unlikely, since this is a highly inefficient means of exploiting the environment. MacArthur & Pianka (1966) originally proposed the idea that an animal foraging for resources will act in ways that are rather efficient, and serve to maximize resource utilization. This has since given rise to a considerable literature on evaluating different models of 'optimal foraging' strategies (see review by Krebs, 1978).

The assumption that animals are at all times acting to maximize resource utilization is, however, one that has been disputed. Pulliam (1974), for example, suggested that models of 'optimal' behaviour, based upon principles of maximization, are probably only applicable when the resource is critical.

14

Similarly, Christensen-Szalanski *et al.* (1980) noted that food deprived rats do not always act in the most efficient manner when obtaining food. Krebs (1978) pointed out that a further assumption of optimal foraging models is that they are equilibrium condition models, i.e. it is assumed that the animal knows its environment, and how to forage optimally within it. This ignores the question of what the animal does if it encounters a new environment, a problem that has not been adequately studied from the perspective of foraging strategies.

An animal that encounters a new environment knows little about it, including the location of important resources. It might in this case be beneficial for the animal to explore the area in a general way for a while, possibly sampling different patches of resources, before searching more specifically within a patch. Apart from providing itself with information about potential hazards within the new area, the animal also gains information about the relative quality of different patches of resources, which can be used as the basis for establishing the appropriate strategy for searching the new area. Exploration of a new environment can, then, be thought of as part of a long-term strategy of optimal resource utilisation.

'Exploration' and 'search' (previously referred to as intrinsic and extrinsic exploration) may be synonymous in many species, particularly those whose energy demands are great. But in animals such as the laboratory rat, that tend to eat in defined meals, they may be different. A meal may be followed by other, lower-priority activities, such as grooming, sleeping or patrolling. Given the high costs of exploratory activities (see above), what are the benefits of patrolling? One obvious one is that the animal may thereby locate new resource sites, which can be exploited some time in the future. There is some empirical evidence to suggest that animals do learn the general location of different resource sites, so that they can act upon this knowledge later (Krebs, *op.cit.*, p. 58). Thus, although the present risks are great, the potential gain is that the animal in the future can locate a resource immediately without having to engage in lengthy searches, which would incur severe costs themselves. The benefit may not be apparent for some time: information about the environment may be remembered months later, for example, say, when building a nest. The animal that has familiarized itself with all its environment will therefore have an advantage over one that has recently migrated into that area; it will generally obtain a better nest site and be better able to exploit available food supplies and places of hiding. For this reason, Partridge (1978) questioned the use of the concept of an 'optimal' habitat, since animals occupying supposedly sub-optimal habitats may have become so well adapted to them that that habitat becomes 'optimal' for that animal. Animals can clearly remember fine details of their environment, even over long periods: for example, those that cache food supplies often remember where the food is located many months afterwards. Balda (1980) observed that nutcrackers (*Nucifraga caryocatactes*) first carry out a general survey of an area, before searching around for a specific cache site. Presumably, this survey enabled them to learn local topography, as they proved to be highly efficient at locating caches several months later.

Perhaps the most significant benefit resulting from a thorough knowledge of

15

the surroundings is for an animal to be able to adapt its strategies appropriately. Few habitats are rigid: an animal will therefore require to learn the appropriate rules for use in responding to environmental changes. For example, the habitat may yield different foods at different times of year, and each type of food may require particular strategies to enable the animal to exploit them optimally.

What is gained from exploration is, quite simply, information about the environment, enabling the animal to build up an internal model or 'map' of its world. Tolman (1932) proposed the term 'cognitive mapping' to describe this process, and his work has received renewed interest in recent years. Inglis, in Chapter 4, uses Tolman's idea of cognitive mapping as a basis for a cognitive theory of exploration that emphasizes the central importance of exploration in an animal's life. Exploration is seen as *the* process whereby an animal gains knowledge about, and hence is able to function in its environment. Several recent reviews have covered other aspects of cognitive mapping. For example, Menzel (1978) reviewed evidence that chimpanzees use cognitive maps to locate hidden objects within their living space. O'Keefe & Nadel (1978) argued that the hippocampus is essential for the formation of such maps. The brain structures involved in cognitive mapping and other aspects of exploration are considered in Chapter 5.

1.6 Conclusions

We began this chapter by outlining some of the features of exploratory behaviour. Although we made some generalizations about what constitutes exploration, it was clear that the many different approaches used to study it has resulted in many semantic and conceptual difficulties. These have hampered research on animal exploration considerably. The first half of this chapter draws largely upon research carried out some years ago, and largely carried out within a traditional psychological framework tending to use animals under strictly controlled laboratory conditions. There is a dearth of knowledge about how animals explore their natural habitats — or, indeed, if they ever do 'explore' in the rather abstract sense that the term is used in psychological research. The psychological emphasis in research on animal exploration has had several consequences. First, there has been a tendency to overemphasize responses to novelty, often studied under rather limited conditions, so that responses to more familiar environments, such as patrolling, have until recently been ignored, although they may be of greater importance in the natural habitat. Secondly, studies of the laboratory rat have been overemphasized. Until there are more comparative data, it is hard to estimate the extent to which this has impoverished our concepts of exploration. We can be almost certain that it has impoverished them to some degree: the rat's strategies of exploration may differ from those of many other mammals, and of other vertebrates. Indeed, those of the inbred laboratory rat may differ substantially from those of its wild and feral counterparts. Thirdly, exploration has not featured prominently in discussions

16

of motivational systems, largely due to its failure to fit neatly into classical drive theory.

On the other hand, ethologists have had little to say about exploration. There are some useful ideas arising from current research on foraging strategies that may be relevant to exploratory behaviour. However, a major focus of this research has been on principles of maximization of resource acquisition, which has been criticised by several authors (see above). Under conditions in which resources are not limiting, animals do not necessarily operate as maximally efficient automata, and they may even prefer to explore rather than to forage.

We have, at various points in this review, indicated directions in which future research could usefully go. These include far more comparative studies, investigations of the ways in which animals make decisions between different stimuli while exploring an area, how these decision-making processes differ between individuals or species, and further investigations of the relationship (if any) between strategies of exploration and strategies of search for specific items. The way forward, it seems to us — and to our contributors in the following chapters — is no longer to pursue the bored laboratory rat down an endless maze, but to widen our field of enquiry to encompass the questions we have mentioned in this chapter, and which are amplified in more detail in the remainder of the book.

Acknowledgements

This chapter has benefitted from discussion with members of the Open University Animal Behaviour Research Group; particularly Frederick Toates, who made helpful comments on an earlier draft.

References

ANDREW, R. J. (1974) Arousal and the causation of behaviour. *Behaviour* 51, 135-165

ANDREW, R. J. (1975) Midbrain mechanisms of calling and their relationship to emotional states. In *Neural and Endocrine Aspects of Behaviour in Birds* (Eds. P. WRIGHT, P. G. CARYL and D. M. VOWLES). Amsterdam: Elsevier.

ARCHER, J. (1974) Sex differences in the emotional behavior of three strains of laboratory rat. *Animal Learning and Behavior* 2, 43-48.

ARCHER, J. (1976) The organization of aggression and fear in vertebrates. In *Perspectives in Ethology, Vol. 2* (Eds. P. P. G. BATESON and P. KLOPFER). New York: Plenum Press.

BALDA, R. P. (1980) Recovery of cached seeds by a captive *Nucifraga caryocatactes*. *Zeitschrift für Tierpsychologie* 52, 331-346.

BALDWIN, B. A. and MEESE, G. B. (1977) Sensory reinforcement and illumination preferences in the domestic pig. *Animal Behaviour* 25, 497-507.

BARNETT, S. A. and COWAN, P. E. (1976) Activity, exploration, curiosity and fear: an ethological study. *Interdisciplinary Science Reviews* 1, 43-62

BARNETT, S. A. and McEWAN, I. M. (1973) Movements of virgin, pregnant and lactating mice in a residential maze. *Physiology and Behavior* 10, 741-746.

17

BERLYNE, D. E. (1950) Novelty and curiosity as determinants of exploratory behaviour. *British Journal of Psychology* **41**, 68–86.

BERLYNE, D. E. (1960) *Conflict, Arousal and Curiosity*. London: McGraw-Hill.

BINDRA, D. (1969) The interrelated mechanisms of reinforcement and motivation, and the nature of their influence on response. In *Nebraska Symposium on Motivation* (Eds. W. J. ARNOLD and D. LeVINE). Lincoln: University of Nebraska Press.

BINDRA, D. (1979) Motivation, the brain and psychological theory. Paper presented to American Psychological Association, New York.

BINDRA, D. and SPINNER, N. (1958) Responses to different degrees of novelty: the incidence of various activities. *Journal of the Experimental Analysis of Behavior* 1, 341–350.

BIRKE, L. I. A. (1979) Object investigation by the oestrous rat and guinea-pig: the oestrous cycle and the effects of oestrogen and progesterone. *Animal Behaviour* **27**, 350–358.

BOLLES, R. C. (1975) *The Theory of Motivation, 2nd Edn*. New York: Harper & Row.

BOLLES, R. C. and FANSELOW, M. S. (1980) A perceptual-defensive-recuperative model of fear and pain. *Behavioral and Brain Sciences* **3**, 291–323.

BUTLER, R. A. (1954) Incentive conditions which influence visual exploration. *Journal of Experimental Psychology* **48**, 19–23.

CAMPBELL, B. A., SMITH, N. F., MISANIN, J. R. and JAYNES, J. (1966) Species differences during hunger and thirst. *Journal of Comparative and Physiological Psychology* **61**, 123–127.

CHRISTENSEN-SZALANSKI, J. J. J., GOLDBERG, A. D., ANDERSON, M. E. and MITCHELL, T. R. (1980) Deprivation, delay of reinforcement and the selection of behavioural strategies. *Animal Behaviour* **28**, 341–346.

COWAN, P. E. (1976) The new object reaction of *Rattus rattus* L.: the relative importance of various cues. *Behavioral Biology* **16**, 31–44.

COWAN, P. E. (1977) Systematic patrolling and orderly behaviour of rats during recovery from deprivation. *Animal Behaviour* **25**, 171–184.

EINON, D. and MORGAN, M. (1976) Habituation of object contact in socially reared and isolated rats. *Animal Behaviour* **24**, 415–420.

FENTRESS, J. C. (1968) Interrupted ongoing behaviour in two species of vole (*Microtus agrestis* and *Clethrionomys britannicus*). I: Response as a function of preceding activity and the context of an apparently 'irrelevant' motor pattern. *Animal Behaviour* **16**, 135–153.

FINGER, F. W. (1969) Estrus and general activity in the rat. *Journal of Comparative and Physiological Psychology* **68**, 461–466.

FORRESTER, R. F. and BROOM, D. M. (1980) Ongoing behaviour and startle responses of chicks. *Behaviour* **73**, 51–63.

FOWLER, H. (1965) *Curiosity and Exploratory Behavior*. New York: Macmillan.

GLANZER, M. (1953) The role of stimulus satiation in spontaneous alternation. *Journal of Experimental Psychology* **45**, 387–393.

GLICKMAN, S. E. and HARTZ, K. E. (1964) Exploratory behavior in several species of rodent. *Journal of Comparative and Physiological Psychology* **58**, 101–104.

GLICKMAN, S. E. and MORRISON, B. J. (1969) Some behavioral and neural correlates of predation susceptibility in mice. *Communications in Behavioral Biology* **4**, 261–267.

GLICKMAN, S. E. and SROGES, R. W. (1966) Curiosity in zoo animals. *Behaviour* **26**, 151–188.

GROVES, P. M. and THOMPSON, R. F. (1970) Habituation: a dual-process theory. *Psychological Review* **77**, 419–450.

HALLIDAY, M. S. (1968) Exploratory behaviour. In *Analysis of Behavioural Change* (Ed. L. WEISKRANTZ). New York: Harper & Row.

HEBB, D. O. (1949) *The Organization of Behavior*. New York: Wiley.

HEBB, D. O. (1955) Drives and the CNS (conceptual nervous system). *Psychological Review* **62**, 243–254.

HENNESSY, J. W. and LEVINE, S. (1979) Stress, arousal, and the pituitary-adrenal system: a psychoendocrine hypothesis. *Progress in Psychobiology and Physiological Psychology, Vol.8* (Eds. J. M. SPRAGUE and A. N. EPSTEIN). London: Academic Press.

HUGHES, R. N. (1968) Behaviour of male and female rats with free choice of two environments differing in novelty. *Animal Behaviour* **16**, 92–96.

HUTT, C. (1970) Specific and diversive exploration. In *Advances in Child Development and Behaviour, Vol. 5* (Eds. H. REESE and L. LIPSITT). New York: Academic Press.

INGLE, D., CHEAL, M. and DIZIO, P. (1979) Cine analysis of visual orientation and pursuit by the Mongolian gerbil. *Journal of Comparative and Physiological Psychology* **93**, 919–928.

ISAACSON, R. L., YONGUE, B. and McCLEARN, D. (1978) Dopamine agonists: their effect on locomotion and exploration. *Behavioral Biology* **23**, 163–179.

JOSEPH, R. and GALLAGHER, R. E. (1980) Gender and early environmental influences on activity, overresponsiveness, and exploration. *Developmental Psychobiology* **13**, 527–544.

KAGAN, J. (1974) Discrepancy, temperament, and infant distress. In *The Origins of Behavior, Vol.2: The Origins of Fear* (Eds. M. LEWIS and L. A. ROSENBLUM). New York: Wiley.

KISH, G. B. (1955) Learning when the onset of illumination is used as the reinforcing stimulus. *Journal of Comparative and Physiological Psychology* **48**, 261–264.

KOHLER, C. and SREBRO, B (1980) Effects of lateral and medial septal lesions on exploratory behaviour on the albino rat. *Brain Research* **182**, 423–440.

KREBS, J. R. (1978) Optimal foraging: decision rules for predators. In *Behavioural Ecology: An Evolutionary Approach* (Eds. J. R. KREBS and N. B. DAVIES). Oxford: Blackwell.

LAT, J. (1963) The spontaneous exploratory reactions as a tool for psychopharmacological studies. In *Pharmacology of Conditioning Learning and Retention* (Ed. M. I. MIKHELSON). Proc. 2nd Internat. Pharmacol. Meeting, Prague.

LESTER, D. (1967) Sex differences in exploration: toward a theory of exploration. *Psychological Record* **17**, 55–62.

LEYLAND, M. ROBBINS, T. and IVERSEN, S. D. (1976) Locomotor activity and exploration: the use of traditional manipulators to dissociate these two behaviours in the rat. *Animal Learning and Behavior* **4**, 261–265.

MACARTHUR, R. H. and PIANKA, E. R. (1966) On the optimal use of a patchy environment. *American Naturalist* **100**, 603–609.

McCULLOUGH, M. L. (1979) The primacy of the experiment: some reservations. *Bulletin of the British Psychological Society* **32**, 409–412.

MARTIN, J. R. and BÄTTIG, K. (1980) Exploratory behaviour of rats at oestrus. *Animal Behaviour* **28**, 900–905.

MENZEL, E. W. (1978) Cognitive mapping in chimpanzees. In *Cognitive Processes in Animal Behavior* (Eds. S. H. HULSE, H. FOWLER and W. K. HONIG). Hillsdale: Lawrence Erlbaum Assoc.

MONTGOMERY, K. C. (1953) Exploratory behavior as a function of 'similarity' of stimulus situations. *Journal of Comparative and Physiological Psychology* **46**, 129–133.

MONTGOMERY, K. C. (1955) The relation between fear induced by novel stimulation and exploratory behavior. *Journal of Comparative and Physiological Psychology* **48**, 254–260.

19

MULLENIX, P. (1981) Structure analysis of spontaneous behavior during the estrous cycle of the rat. *Physiology and Behavior* **27**, 723–726.

MURPHY, L. B. (1978) The practical problems of recognizing and measuring fear and exploration behaviour in the domestic fowl. *Animal Behaviour* **26**, 422–431.

NISSEN, H. W. (1930) A study of the exploratory behavior in the white rat by means of an obstruction method. *Journal of Genetic Psychology* **37**, 351–376.

NOTTEBOHM, F. (1970) Ontogeny of bird song. *Science* **167**, 950–956.

O'KEEFE, J. and NADEL, L. (1978) *The Hippocampus as a Cognitive Map*. Oxford: Clarendon.

PARTRIDGE, L. (1978) Habitat selection. In *Behavioural Ecology: An Evolutionary Approach* (Eds. J. R. KREBS and N. B. DAVIES). London: Blackwell.

PAVLOV, I. P. (1927) *Conditioned Reflexes*. Oxford: Clarendon Press.

PETRINOVICH, L. (1973) A species-meaningful analysis of habituation. In *Habituation I: Behavioral Studies* (Eds. H. V. S. PEEKE and M. J. HERZ). London: Academic Press.

POSNER, M. I. (1980) Orienting of attention. *Quarterly Journal of Experimental Psychology* **32**, 3–25.

PRESCOTT, R. G. W. (1970) Some behavioural effects of variables which influence the 'general level of activity' of rats. *Animal Behaviour* **18**, 791–796.

PULLIAM, H. R. (1974) On the theory of 'optimal' diets. *American Naturalist* **108**, 59–75.

RUSSELL, P. A. (1973) Relationships between exploratory behaviour and fear: a review. *British Journal of Psychology* **64**, 417–433.

RUSSELL, P. A. and CHALKLY-MABER, C. J. W. (1979) Effects of conspecific odor on rats' locomotor activity in the open-field. *Animal Behaviour* **21**, 109–112.

SALZEN, E. A. (1970) Imprinting and environmental learning. In *Development and Evolution of Behavior* (Eds. L. R. ARONSON, E. TOBACH, D. S. LEHRMAN and J. S. ROSENBLATT). San Francisco: Freeman.

SCOURSE, N. J. S. and HINDE, R. A. (1973) Habituation to auditory stimuli in mice. *Behaviour* **47**, 1–13.

SELIGMAN, M. E. P. (1970) On the generality of the laws of learning. *Psychological Review* **77**, 406.

SHELDON, M. H. (1969) Preference for familiar versus novel stimuli as a function of the familiarity of the environment. *Journal of Comparative and Physiological Psychology* **67**, 516–521.

SIDDLE, D. A. T. (1979) The orienting response and stimulus significance: some comments. *Biological Psychology* **8**, 303–309.

SIMMEL, E. C. (1962) Social facilitation of exploratory behavior in rats. *Journal of Comparative and Physiological Psychology* **55**, 831–833.

SIMMEL, E. C. and ELEFTHERIOU, B. E. (1977) Multivariate and behavior genetic analysis of avoidance of complex visual stimuli and activity in recombinant inbred strains of mice. *Behavior Genetics* **7**, 239–250.

SOKOLOV, E. K. (1960) Neuronal models and the orienting reflex. In *The Central Nervous System and Behavior* (Ed. M. A. B. BRAZIER). New York: Josiah Macy Jr. Foundation.

SPENCE, K. W. (1956) *Behavior Theory and Conditioning*. New Haven: Yale University Press.

TINBERGEN, L. (1960) The natural control of insects in pine woods. I. Factors influencing the intensity of predation by song birds. *Archives Neerlandaises de Zoologie* **13**, 265–343.

TOATES, F. M. and BIRKE, L. I. A. (1982) Motivation — a new perspective on some old ideas. In *Perspectives in Ethology, Vol. 5* (Eds. P. BATESON and P. H. KLOPFER). New York: Plenum.

TOLMAN, E. C. (1932) *Purposive Behavior in Animals and Man*. New York: Century.

TURNER, E. R. A. (1964) Social feeding in birds. *Behaviour* 24, 1–46.

VAN DER POEL, A. M. (1979) A note on 'stretched attention', a behavioural element indicative of an approach-avoidance conflict in rats. *Animal Behaviour* 27, 446–450.

VINOGRADOVA, O. S. (1970) Registration of information and the limbic system. In *Short-term Changes in Neural Activity and Behaviour* (Eds. G. HORN and R. A. HINDE). Cambridge: Cambridge University Press.

WEISLER, A. and McCALL, R. B. (1976) Exploration and play: resumé and direction. *American Psychologist* 31, 492–508.

WELLS, P. A. and LAWLOR, M. M. (1975) Effects of early handling on investigatory behaviour in the rat. Paper presented at Association for the study of Animal Behaviour conference, Aberdeen, July.

CHAPTER 2

Psychological Studies of Exploration in Animals: a Reappraisal

P. A. Russell

2.1 The Psychological Approach

Although psychological studies of the exploratory behaviour of animals can be traced at least as far back as the 19th century (Small, 1899) it was not until the early 1950s that exploration began to receive systematic attention from psychologists (see reviews by Barnett, 1958; Berlyne, 1960; Fowler, 1965; Welker, 1961). It is significant that the upsurge in interest in exploration in the 1950s was due largely to a realization of its important and rather problematic implications for the psychological *theories* of animal behaviour then prevalent, theories that centred on drive motivation and drive reduction reinforcement concepts (Fowler, 1965; Harlow, 1953). Then, as now, the psychological approach to exploration tended to regard the animal as a laboratory 'preparation' exhibiting a theoretically interesting behavioural phenomenon. This contrasts with ethologically oriented approaches that emphasize the role of exploration in the wider context of its significance for animals in natural habitats (Barnett, 1958; Barnett & Cowan, 1976; see also Chapter 6). Besides its theoretical emphasis, the psychological approach is characterized by concentration on a relatively small number of species (most commonly the laboratory rat, but with some study of other rodents, birds and primates), on a similarly small number of types of environments, and on a relatively narrow range of behavioural measures.

Since the mid-1960s, there has been a perceptible decline in interest in psychologically oriented studies of animal exploration and also a decline in the importance of animal studies within the context of exploration research. One of the few major reviews of the exploration literature to appear in the 1970s (Weisler & McCall, 1976), for example, chose to deal with only a limited selection of the work on exploration in non-human primates and to ignore entirely the large literature on rodents. To some extent this trend reflects a general move away from theory-oriented studies of animal behaviour, but it also reflects the fact that some of the theoretical problems that provided the original foci for animal exploration research have been effectively resolved by subsequent theoretical developments. The original problem centred on the motivation of exploration and was closely tied up with the then-prevalent theory that all motivation stemmed from primary homeostatic drives. Since animals often engage in exploration in the apparent absence of any of these drives it was not clear what motivates it. Also, exploration generally serves to maintain or even increase the intensity or amount of stimulation (or stimulus change), and this made exploration difficult to fit into the drive reduction theory that the goal of behaviour is the reduction of intense stimulation. Thirty years on, it is easy to see that some of the 'problems' posed by exploration stemmed from what now appears as a simplistic and restrictive drive and drive reduction theory of motivation. Recognition of this has undoubtedly contributed to the decline in importance of animal exploration studies. It is important to realize, however, that the abandonment of attempts to base a comprehensive theory of motivation solely on primary drives has not in fact been accompanied by any detailed solutions to the motivational problems set by exploration and that an adequate theoretical framework for exploration is still lacking. One of the aims of this chapter is to highlight the strengths and weaknesses of existing theoretical approaches and in particular to evaluate psychological concepts from a more broadly based ethological perspective that emphasizes the adaptive nature of exploration. This perspective may also help to shed light on some persistent methodological problems and issues in the psychological work on animal exploration.

2.2 The Adaptive Significance of Exploration

Exploratory behaviour clearly plays an important part in the day to day lives of many animals and its implications for survival are not hard to see. Most animals show some degree of attachment to a particular location or area of habitat, the home range (Jewell, 1966), wherein the activities of feeding, sleeping, reproducing and so on occur. Implicit in the concept of home range is the assumption that the individual is relatively familiar with, that is possesses information about, a particular area. The adaptive significance of attachment to a familiar area is largely self-evident: survival chances must be enhanced by the possession of information about the availability and location of food, water and other essential resources, sleeping and hiding places, the presence of conspecifics and predators and so on. In this context, the importance of exploration is that it is not only central to the establishment of a familiar home range, but also to the maintenance of familiarity. Having once explored an environment, an animal will usually have to engage in some further exploration at intervals simply to maintain familiarity with it: most environments are subject to a degree of change over time, as a result of both seasonal and climatic factors and the behaviour of other animals. In many cases, maintenance of a familiar environment will necessitate regular inspections, which may take the form of systematic environmental patrolling in which different areas are visited in turn, as observed in rodents and other small mammals (Barnett & Cowan, 1976;

Cowan, 1977; Jewell, 1966; see also Chapter 6). Regular visits to the various parts of the home range are necessary to determine whether or not changes have occurred, and if they have to ensure that they are properly investigated. It is also possible that patrolling serves to 'refresh the animal's memory' of its home range.

It is possible to analyse exploration in terms of costs and benefits (Chapter 1). To highlight one example of benefit, knowledge of the environment gained through exploration is fundamental to predator avoidance in wild rats. According to Barnett (1975, p.49):

> The principle means of avoiding predators are the use of pathways under cover, and flight to a burrow or other place of concealment. These actions depend on previous experience of the topography of their living space. Given such experience, they can run from any one point to any other, by the shortest route and in the least possible time.

In considering adaptive aspects, it is helpful to bear in mind the distinction between exploration and orienting behaviour. The term exploration is sometimes used to embrace both, that is to describe any response that serves to bring receptors to bear on environmental stimuli through attention, receptor orienting, approach and contact behaviour. Attention and distal receptor orienting responses, discussed by Birke & Archer (Chapter 1), tend to occur to virtually any environmental change and may be deemed exploratory in that they play a part in obtaining information about the change. A distinction (albeit somewhat arbitrary) can be drawn between these initial responses and responses that occur subsequently, the nature of which depends upon the characteristics of the change. For example, a change that elicits orienting may be followed by approach and contact behaviour, which in turn results in distal receptors being brought closer to the source of change (e.g. walking up to and inspecting visually) and may permit proximal receptors to be used (e.g. touching, tasting). Most of the psychological literature on animal exploration is actually concerned with approach and contact behaviour, and this chapter follows the convention of referring to this as exploration, leaving the term orienting for the preceding receptor adjustments. This recognizes that exploration is only one of many possible classes of behaviour patterns which can follow orienting, depending on the characteristics of the change, for example protective responses, aggression and courtship. Protective or fear responses (Archer, 1979; Gray, 1971b; Russell, 1979) such as withdrawal, escape, flight, avoidance, hiding and freezing are particularly relevant here, inasmuch as they are generally incompatible with or antagonistic to exploration. Their general goal is the reduction or avoidance of contact with changes that are potentially harmful. The adaptive significance of fleeing or hiding from a predator is obvious, but there are many other reasons why environmental changes may elicit protective behaviour rather than exploration: a new object within the home range could harbour dangers, an unknown area beyond the home range boundary may be deficient in resources, and so on.

2.3 Adaptive Considerations and the Psychological Approach

In reviewing the psychological literature on exploration it is helpful to bear in mind that psychologists have been concerned largely with proximate causes, particularly the immediate situational determinants, eliciting stimuli and motivational mechanisms of exploration. Although they can hardly have been unaware of the adaptive significance of exploration, this has not been central to the development of psychological methods and theories. Although several major reviews recognise the information-supplying role of exploration (Berlyne, 1960; Halliday, 1968; Hutt, 1970; Weisler & McCall, 1976) this aspect has had little heuristic impact. For example the experimental and theoretical work of Berlyne, the most prolific and influential psychologist writing on exploration, was guided not by consideration of the information-supplying role of exploration but by the idea that exploration serves to effect changes in psychophysiological arousal (Section 2.5.3).

Of course it is perfectly possible to see arousal theory, and theories centering upon other concepts such as curiosity and boredom (Section 2.5.2), as an attempt to specify the proximate mechanism of exploration and there is no problem, in principle, about reconciling proximate mechanisms with adaptive considerations. Exploration may be seen as having evolved to provide organisms with information and be based upon an arousal mechanism (or some other mechanism) that has evolved to meet the requirements of information-gathering. Nor is there any reason why psychologists should not focus on proximate causes rather than consequences and functions. There is, however, some evidence that some methodological and theoretical weaknesses in the psychological approach can be traced to insufficient consideration of the adaptive aspects of exploration, particularly its contribution to survival in natural habitats.

2.3.1 Categories of Exploration

Distinctions have been drawn in the psychological literature between a number of categories or types of exploratory responses, most of these being made explicit by Berlyne (1960). Since they have been made without much regard for adaptive considerations it is instructive to re-examine them in this light.

One such distinction is between extrinsic and intrinsic exploration. Extrinsic responses are directed at obtaining information about a conventional reinforcer or other biologically significant event: observing responses giving information about the availability of food (Wyckoff, 1952) are a good example. Extrinsic exploration has not been a central issue within the area of psychological research on exploration, probably because it appears to pose few problems for primary drive theories of motivation. Psychologists have concentrated instead on intrinsic exploration, which is defined as exploration directed at stimuli of little apparent biological consequence. This is typically studied in animals that are not under any obvious primary drive state and are in environments devoid of conventional reinforcers, of which the exploration of a maze or arena (Section 2.4.1) is a typical example. From an adaptive and ecological viewpoint, it is doubtful whether the distinction between exploratory responses that produce information about a conventional reinforcer and those that do not, has much validity. Exploration of a natural habitat will supply an animal with information about various environmental features, some of which fall into the category of 'reinforcers' (food and water, for example) and some of which do not (e.g. the availability of cover and sleeping sites). It is also obvious that some of the information so gathered is of great consequence 'biologically', that is it has important implications for survival, but does not relate directly to conventional reinforcers, for example information about the environment's topography. It is even doubtful whether, in the natural habitat, there is any such thing as a change that has no 'biological significance'. Any change is *potentially* important for survival and may be expected to elicit at least transitory orienting, which may or may not be followed by exploration (or some other behaviour) depending on its nature.

Berlyne (1960) also drew attention to the potential importance of the distinction between responding *to* an environmental change, termed inspective exploration, and responding *for* a change, inquisitive exploration. Inspective exploration involves increased contact, through approach and proximal interaction, with changes in the organism's immediate stimulus field that are acting on its receptors. Inquisitive exploration, in contrast, serves to bring about contact with changes that are not already present in the immediate stimulus field and involves seeking out or producing changes. An example of inquisitive exploration is the learning of a response that is instrumental in altering the environment in some way, even when this is not associated with access to a conventional reinforcer (Section 2.4.3). The adaptive significance of inspective exploration — that is, responding to a change in the environment — is clear (Section 2.2). Inquisitive exploration, on the other hand, requires comment in the light of the theory that animals generally behave so as to maintain themselves in a familiar environment since it involves self-induced environmental changes.

The first and most obvious point is that the process of maintaining a familiar environment, such as by regularly patrolling the home range, will result in 'novelty-seeking'. When an animal moves from an area of its range in which it has spent some time, and with which it is relatively familiar, to another area it has not recently visited, and with which it is therefore less familiar, it is *de facto* seeking out change. Responding for environmental change may also be predictable on adaptive grounds if, as is widely assumed (Berlyne, 1966; Hebb, 1955; Leuba, 1955), organisms are 'set' to function at maximum efficiency in environments that present a certain level of stimulation or stimulus change. This seems likely because most natural environments will present an approximately constant and predictable level of change, to which natural selection will have 'tuned' the species. Departures from the optimum level might then be expected to lead to behaviour, including change-seeking, directed at restoring this level. The notion of an optimum degree of environmental change is not incompatible with the further idea that it can be adaptive for an organism to seek out change because this provides the opportunity for learning about the environment in a way which enables it to develop its mastery of, and competence in dealing with, its environment. Quite apart from ensuring that an animal is familiar with its home area, exploration may actually facilitate the development of new, innovative behaviour patterns that permit exploitation of the environment in new ways. This function of exploration has been particularly stressed with regard to the behaviour of primates (Baldwin & Baldwin, 1977) and applies especially clearly in the case of tool-using behaviour. Tool-use by primates and other animals is clearly adaptive in permitting increased efficiency in exploitation of the environment (Beck, 1980; Lawick-Goodall, 1970), and it seems certain that selection for tool-using ability, and particularly for the ability to develop new tool-use patterns, has resulted in pressure on a variety of traits including sensorimotor skills and, importantly in the present context, on the motivation to seek out and investigate new objects for their potential as tools.

Berlyne (1960) also distinguished between specific exploration, defined as behaviour directed at obtaining information about a *particular* changed object or event (i.e. information specific to that thing), and diversive exploration, behaviour directed at obtaining stimulus change and information from *any* environmental source. Berlyne gives the case of a person setting out to find the solution to a particular intellectual problem as an example of specific exploration and someone seeking relief from boredom through exposure to any stimulus change as an example of diversive exploration. The importance of this distinction is that specific and diversive exploration are regarded as motivationally distinct. Berlyne linked specific exploration to 'curiosity', increased arousal generated by lack of information about a specific stimulus change, and diversive exploration to 'boredom', increased arousal stemming form a lack of stimulus change of any sort. Both specific and diversive exploration can be seen as adaptive, the significance of exploring a change (specific) and seeking out changes (diversive) having already been commented on. Although studies of exploration in humans have paid particular attention to this distinction (Hutt, 1970; Hughes, Chapter 10) it has not been much drawn in animal studies.

2.4 Methods of Studying Exploration

Psychological studies of animal exploration have usually been based on exposing the animal to an environmental change that it has not experienced before or not experienced for some time, conventionally referred to as a novel stimulus or novel environment. A convenient, if rather arbitrary, division can be made into studies in which the subject is (a) confined to a novel environment, (b) exposed to discrete, localized environmental changes or (c) able to respond in order to produce a novel stimulus or open up access to a novel area. In addition, a few studies have focused upon the dimension of stimulus complexity. It is instructive to examine these methods and the interpretations that have been placed upon the data obtained from them in the light of adaptive considerations and the circumstances in which animals encounter novelty in the wild.

2.4.1 Confinement to a Novel Area

Many studies involve putting an animal briefly into a novel environment such as a maze, open field or other test chamber (see Barnett & Cowan, 1976; Halliday, 1968, for reviews). These test environments are usually relatively barren and homogeneous, often lacking in food, water, objects, cover and other animals. Because they confine the subject with no opportunity for escape they are sometimes referred to as tests of 'forced exploration'. The adoption of test environments of this sort has clearly been dictated by convenience and ease of recording behaviour rather than by any consideration of the nature of environmental changes occurring in the wild. The use of mazes in the study of animal exploration was simply a carry-over from their existing use in learning studies, although no doubt the *prima facie* similarity between mazes and the natural runways and burrows of the rats and other small rodents that are the typical subjects of such studies reflects the propensity of these animals to explore such environments.

Locomotor exploration. The assumption behind novel environment studies is that in order to explore the environment the animal must move about, and that the amount of movement is therefore an index of exploration. Typically, ambulation (walking and running) is measured by counting the number of environmental sections (e.g. floor squares or maze arms) traversed, a measure of 'locomotor exploration'.

Various problems relating to locomotor exploration measures have been identified (Berlyne, 1960; Fowler, 1965; Halliday, 1968). One is the possibility that locomotion may reflect behaviour that is actually unrelated to exploration, such as 'spontaneous activity' or 'exercising'. In rats, however, exercise in an activity wheel before placement in a novel environment does not affect exploration (Montgomery, 1953b), although, as Berlyne (1960) notes, it is just possible that environmental ambulation may provide a different kind of exercise to running in a wheel. More conclusive is the fact that rats' locomotion in a novel environment is unaffected by their having been exposed a short time before to a different novel environment that provided opportunity for locomotion (Halliday, 1966b). Also, locomotion is correlated with the degree of novelty of an environment: repeated testing in the same environment is usually accompanied by an initial decline in locomotion (Halliday, 1966b, and studies reviewed by Russell, 1973a) and this effect is attenuated if the environment is changed slightly between tests (Montgomery, 1953a). Such findings show that novel environment locomotion is not wholly a function of nonexploratory factors, although the possibility that these factors make some contribution to locomotion scores in particular cases is difficult to rule out. One finding that has been considered relevant in this connection is that positive within-subject

28

correlations between locomotor exploration and wheel activity have been reported for both rats (Montgomery, 1953b) and mice (Manosevitz, 1970). The correct interpretation of this, however, appears to be that running in a novel wheel, but not a familiar one, is influenced by factors that also influence locomotor exploration in a novel environment. This is because in both studies significant correlations were obtained only for wheel activity occurring during an initial period immediately following introduction to the wheel, and not for later wheel activity.

It is generally assumed that, although the separation of exploratory and non-exploratory locomotion may be difficult in practice, it is nonetheless possible in principle, but this is actually arguable. If an animal moves around extensively within a novel environment because it is 'exercising' or 'spontaneously active' it is conceivably obtaining more information about its environment than one moving about less, rather as a jogger may be expected to get to know more about the neighbourhood than his or her sedentary fellows, even though the collection of such information is not the primary aim of jogging. The problem centres around the fact that although exploration is defined as behaviour directed at obtaining information about the environment, a locomotion measure provides no indication of the amount of information actually gathered. Something of the same problem is seen in the often-raised query over whether or not an animal that locomotes extensively is exploring more than one moving about less but spending time in intensive investigation of one or a few areas through sniffing, pecking, or rearing and so on. Presumably they learn different things about the environment although it is difficult quantitatively to compare their behaviour.

A related issue concerns the potential distinction between exploration and escape behaviour. It is often suggested that locomotion in a novel environment may reflect the animal's attempt to escape from it (Johnston, 1964; Welker, 1957, 1959). The adaptive significance of escaping from a novel environment, particularly if it is relatively strongly lit and affords no cover, and locating an area that is familiar and/or covered and dark is especially obvious in the case of rodents and other species susceptible to predation. It has often been assumed that exploration and escape are functionally and motivationally quite distinct, so that locomotion can reflect either one or the other or, possibly, a combination of the two (Johnston, 1964; Russell & Williams, 1973; Whimbey & Denenberg, 1967). A more plausible assumption, however, is that exploration itself can have different goals and that at least one of the goals of exploratory behaviour in a novel environment is the location of a familiar, and so safe, area or a place of cover, to which retreat can be made. In this case, exploration of a new environment may itself be 'escape-directed'.

One test of the goal of locomotion in a novel environment is to provide access to an adjoining familiar or enclosed 'retreat' area and see whether animals do tend to enter and remain in the retreat. There is good evidence that rats at least do tend to leave the novel environment and locomote less in it under these 'free exploration' conditions (Blanchard et al., 1974; Hayes, 1960; Valle, 1972; Welker, 1957, 1959). In particular, the fact that they are more inclined to leave a novel environment if the retreat is familiar rather than novel (Blanchard et al.,

29

1974), argues that locomotion in a novel environment is at least in part escape-directed. Further evidence on the escape-directed nature of behaviour in a novel environment comes from observations on wild rats, which, besides rapid and vigorous ambulation, may also jump in an apparent attempt to escape, with jumping being more common on the first exposure and at the start of each exposure (Huck & Price, 1975; Price & Huck, 1976).

On the basis of these findings, it is possible to offer a tentative and essentially *post hoc* hypothesis concerning the novel environment behaviour of rats (for which the most data are available). In terms of adaptive 'strategy', there would seem to be more to be gained from immediate locomotor exploration of a new environment than from not exploring. Exploration provides information that may be crucial to survival and offers the chance of locating a familiar place or landmark or of finding cover, which may be expected to be high-priority behaviour, particularly for a species strongly susceptible to predation. Not exploring, in contrast, would lay the rat open to the hazards of an unknown environment, even though a familiar area or a hiding place may be at hand. In social species, such as the rat, exploration may also have the goal of establishing contact with conspecifics, particularly where, as is often the case, the animal has been removed from a group for testing (see Gallup & Suarez, 1980, for data on chickens). In a natural habitat a rat finding itself out of its familiar area stands a good chance of relocating that area or of finding cover through exploration, but the subject of a psychological experiment on forced exploration is denied this opportunity. It is reasonable to expect, therefore, that in the latter case the initial bout of exploration will cease once it has established that familiarity and · cover cannot be contacted: an initial intra- and inter-test decline in locomotion in such studies is well documented (review by Russell, 1973a; Russell & Williams, 1973). Once attempts at relocation have failed, the best strategy is probably to stay relatively still (freezing), since this minimizes the chance of being spotted by a predator or encountering some other danger and also minimizes contact with novel stimuli. Prolonged or repeated exposure to a novel environment, however, often results in a subsequent recovery of locomotion (Russell & Williams, 1973; Welker, 1957; Williams & Russell, 1972), which possibly reflects the fact that the animal must venture forth eventually to explore its environment again if it is to deal effectively with it. Presumably, exploration will eventually stabilise, perhaps with a cyclical pattern of patrolling (Section 2.2).

This analysis suggests a reinterpretation of data that have been regarded as inconsistent with the hypothesis that novel environment locomotion is escape-directed. Hayes (1960) argues that the escape hypothesis predicts that a high level of ambulation in a forced test, indicating strong motivation to escape, should be correlated with low ambulation in a free exploration test. Hayes' finding was that when rats were given a forced test followed by a free one, within-subject correlations were actually positive. This finding is not crucial for the escape hypothesis, however, since it is questionable whether high ambulation in the forced test is necessarily indicative of strong escape tendencies: if animals discover relatively quickly that no escape is possible, ambulation will soon be replaced by freezing. Rats most motivated to freeze on the forced test will be low ambulators and these same animals will be those most motivated to escape, so having the lowest ambulation scores, when given the free test.

It is worth emphasizing that this interpretation of rats' novel environment locomotion may well need extension to account for the effects of additional variables. For example, there are a few reports of locomotion increasing, rather than decreasing, over a series of novel environment exposures (Levine & Broadhurst, 1963; Levine et al., 1967; Williams & Russell, 1972). It is possible that novel environment behaviour depends upon the animals' previous experience and also on the nature of the environment: escape attempts may be brief or nonexistent if an animal has previously experienced inescapable situations or if the environment is small, readily searched and 'obviously' inescapable.

It is also reasonable to expect species differences in response to placement in a novel environment: the nature and extent of escape-directed behaviour may depend upon such factors as a species' susceptibility to predation and the likelihood of it encountering a novel open area in its natural habitat. Domestic chicks appear to freeze rather than move about when first placed in a novel environment (Candland & Nagy, 1969; Salzen, 1962). Glickman & Hartz (1964) reported that whereas rats and guinea pigs tended to leave an open field in a free exploration test, thus showing a significant reduction in locomotor exploration, mice, chincillas, hamsters, gerbils and African spiny mice did not.

Related to the question of escape behaviour is the possible occurrence of behaviour that is a reaction to experiences immediately before placement in the test apparatus. In particular, it has been suggested that handling by the experimenter may evoke behaviour that normally operates when an animal has been caught by a predator (Gallup & Suarez, 1980). Physical restraint of many small animals may result in an initial burst of struggling and attempts to escape which, if unsuccessful, is likely to be followed by a period of tonic immobility (Archer, 1979; Gallup, 1974, 1977; Salzen, 1979), which presumably serves to lessen the chances of injury. Depending on the details and duration of pre-test handling, then, it is conceivable that placement in a novel environment may be followed immediately by either escape behaviour, such as running away from the experimenter, or by immobility, both of which have obvious implications for the measurement of locomotor exploration. It may be significant that domestic chicks, which respond to placement in a novel environment with freezing (above), are particulary likely to show restraint-induced tonic immobility.

The kind of analysis proposed here suggests further that the conventional psychological interpretation of novel environment locomotion as being an index of exploration that may be 'contaminated' to a greater or lesser extent by such factors as activity levels and escape behaviour would be better replaced by the assumption that movement about an environment can have a variety of goals and that these goals may be different in different situations or in the same situation at different times. In particular, movement may sometimes reflect behaviour that has escape from novelty and the search for familiar sources as its goal and at other times behaviour that involves approach to novelty and information-seeking.

Finally, in this section, it is worth noting that a novel environment test, particularly of the commonly used forced kind, has little to commend it on ecological grounds; that is, it does not correspond very closely to the sort of environmental changes animals normally encounter in the wild. Since animals rarely, if ever, naturally encounter a novel confining environment, it is by no means certain that they will have evolved behaviour patterns appropriate to it or that their behaviour will 'make sense' adaptively. For most species, being plunged suddenly into a totally new environment is a fate normally only encountered in the rare event of loss of touch with the home area as a result of some accident such as falling from a branch or cliff or being chased or carried off by a predator. Even then the animal is not usually denied the chance of relocating a familiar area by insurmountable boundary obstacles. Test situations which give animals a choice of novel and familiar stimuli obviously have more to commend them on ecological grounds.

Other exploratory responses. Animals confined to a novel environment show a variety of nonlocomotor responses that are *prima facie* exploratory. In rodents, rearing and sniffing (but not visual inspection) are relatively easily recorded. Rearing and locomotion are usually accompanied by sniffing, and in general these three behaviour patterns are positively intercorrelated (Gray, 1965; Russell, 1973b; Satinder, 1968).

A few studies have increased the heterogeneity of confining novel environments by providing foci for exploratory responses. These may be objects (Einon & Morgan, 1976; Foshee *et al.*, 1965; Russell & Williams, 1973) or odour sources (Jones & Nowell, 1974; Russell & Chalky-Maber, 1979). Alternatively, they may be holes or recesses into which the animal can poke or dip its head, as in the case of the holeboard, essentially an open field with a series of holes in the floor (File & Wardill, 1975; Makanjuola *et al.*, 1977; Weinberg *et al.*, 1976). Measures of exploration derived from such situations have putative advantages over a locomotion measure, but since both environment and foci are novel the problem of whether behaviour is correctly interpreted as approach to novelty or as an attempt to avoid it is not entirely circumvented: this is especially true of the holeboard, where a head-dip response could be a search for familiar sources. Where object contact and locomotor exploration have both been recorded in the same environment, within-subject correlations tend to be positive, but not always large (Foshee *et al.*, 1965; Russell & Williams, 1973). Studies in which novel objects are presented in a familiar environment or in which object novelty is manipulated are reviewed in Section 2.4.2.

2.4.2 Exposure to Discrete, Localized Environmental Changes

An alternative to confining an animal to a novel environment is to present it with novel stimuli that are relatively discrete and localized. This gives the animal the opportunity to display a preference for some stimuli over others, and has the advantage that it is usually obvious whether behaviour is directed to or away from a particular stimulus. Another advantage is that it parallels more closely the conditions under which animals normally encounter novelty in the wild, that is as either discrete changes within a familiar environment, such as the occurrence of a new object or an odour trace from another animal, or unfamiliar areas at the boundaries of the home range (Section 2.2). Several procedural variations on the theme can be identified.

Discrete changes in a familiar area.   One of the least ambiguous tests of an animal's response to novelty involves introducing a change or changes into an environment with which it is familiar. A common technique is to place one or more new objects in or adjacent to the home cage or living area. Another is to introduce novel stimuli in an environment that is relatively, but not completely, familiar, as when the animal is 'prefamiliarized' with the test situation for a short time before testing. In the simplest case, there is a single novel source and the animal has the choice of contacting it or not: under these conditions the source may be approached and investigated or it may be avoided. For example, new objects, such as wooden blocks and rubber tubing introduced into the cages of zoo animals usually elicit sniffing, nosing, manipulating and so on, although there are marked species differences in contact time (Glickman & Sroges, 1966; Russell & Pearce, 1971). Glickman and Sroges found that primates, in particular, often spend considerable time manipulating new objects (see also primate studies reviewed by Berlyne, 1960, pp. 148–149). Often, object contact is preceded by an initial period of avoidance (or neophobia: Barnett & Cowan, 1976; see also Chapter 6).

In contrast to locomotor measures, novel stimulus contact is a relatively unequivocal index of exploration. Not only does contact behaviour decline with continued or repeated exposure, but it can be shown that a discrete environmental change results in increased time spent in the area of the change relative to the animal's previous behaviour or that of animals not experiencing the change. Corman & Shafer (1968) found that when the centre area of a relatively familiar open field was changed from black to white, rats suddenly increased the amount of time they spent in the centre area. Berlyne (1955) obtained an increase in the number of approaches rats made to an alcove when it contained a novel object and found that rats with the object made more approaches than no-object controls. A variation on the same theme involves presenting two or more localized sources differing in novelty. Berlyne (1950) exposed rats to three identical objects — cubes or cylinders — for five minutes and subsequently tested them with one of the objects changed (cube to cylinder or *vice versa*): they spent more time contacting the novel object than the familiar ones.

Where novel stimuli are discrete and localized, exploration can be measured in terms of both the number and duration of contacts, and this may make it possible to assess the influence of differences in nonexploratory activity (see Section 2.4.1) on contact behaviour. For example, Russell (1977) found that in a situation in which rats could make a head-poke response in order to explore

33

alcoves that were either novel or familiar, females initially spent more time head poking than males. This reflected a longer mean head-poke time in females, not a difference in the number of head pokes, which argues that the sex difference was not due to females coming into contact with the alcoves more often as a consequence of a higher level of locomotor activity (which is possible in view of sex differences reported in a highly familiar environment: Russell, 1973b). Leyland *et al.* (1976) have also reported 'dissociation' of activity and exploration using the technique of presenting complex novel stimuli in one section of a relatively familiar test box. Relative to controls, rats given *d*-amphetamine spent less time inspecting the stimuli but ambulated more.

Access to a new area adjacent to a familiar one. Similar considerations to those discussed in the previous section apply to studies in which an animal is given the opportunity to explore a novel area adjacent to a familiar one. Usually this involves removing a barrier between the animal's cage or living area or some other area with which it is relatively familiar and an adjoining section of environment, a technique used particularly with rats and which usually results in movement into the new area (Barnett & Cowan, 1976; Barnett & Spencer, 1951; Hughes, 1965a, 1968; Russell, 1975). As with novel objects, a novel area may be avoided at first and explored only after a delay (Blanchard *et al.*, 1974; Montgomery, 1955). This neophobia is reflected in the use of the time taken to enter a novel environment as an index of fear, emotionality or timidity (Billingslea, 1942; Williams & Wells, 1970).

Studies of this kind may be seen in the context of a feral animal that encounters novel areas at the boundaries of its home range, areas into which it is relatively disinclined to go. The fact that captive animals do eventually enter and explore a new area and may subsequently add it to their living space suggests, however, that the captive animal studies relate more to the extension of a home range artificially compressed by captivity.

Alternation between different environmental areas. It is well established that an animal's movements about an environment are seldom random and often highly predictable. In particular the animal is likely, when moving from one area to another, to tend to enter the area visited least recently, a tendency studied in psychological experiments on the phenomenon of spontaneous alternation, first described by Tolman (1925). Literature reviews are provided by Barnett (1975), Berlyne (1960) and Dember & Fowler (1958). Spontaneous alternation is often studied in a T-maze: the subject, usually a rat, is first placed in the start arm and allowed to enter one of the two choice arms. On being replaced in the start arm it is more likely to then enter the other, unvisited choice arm.

Numerous experiments have demonstrated that alternation involves the alternation of stimuli rather than responses (response alternation involves turning to the left if the first response was to the right and *vice versa*). For example, when the maze is in the form of a cross and the animal is started from a different arm on each of the two trials (say north and south) alternating the response would lead to the animal re-entering the arm it visited on the first trial, whereas in fact it tends to enter the novel arm and so repeats the turning response (Glanzer, 1953b; Montgomery, 1952a). Also, if an animal is simply confined to one choice arm for a time, without having chosen it, and then allowed to choose between the familiar arm and a novel one it is more likely to select the novel arm (Glanzer, 1953b; Sutherland, 1957). If the animal is first confined to the start arm but permitted to see the choice arms through glass partitions and then allowed to choose between them, with the partitions removed and one of the choice arms changed in some way (for example from black to white or *vice versa*), it is more likely to enter the arm that has been changed (Dember, 1956; Hughes, 1965b; Kivy *et al.*, 1956). These and other studies demonstrate that the animal is alternating its approach to different environmental areas and is most likely to enter the area least recently visited or an area which has changed in some way. Essentially the same behaviour is demonstrated by animals freely exploring a maze, where it appears as a relatively orderly sequence of maze arm entries (Lester, 1967a, 1969; Montgomery, 1952b). Rats, at least, appear to use information from several sources in alternating approach to stimuli, including environmental cues (such as extramaze stimuli), cues to spatial orientation derived from a 'spatial map' of the environment (which permits the animal to move in different directions on successive occasions) and avoidance of odour trails (Douglas, 1966; Douglas *et al.*, 1974; Sherrick *et al.*, 1979).

Psychological experiments have studied alternation behaviour during short periods of confinement to a relatively novel test environment, but in ethological studies animals confined for longer periods to a relatively familiar living area containing food and water also show an orderly sequence of visits to different parts of the environment. This has been described as regular, systematic patrolling (Barnett & Cowan, 1976; Cowan, 1977, and Chapter 6).

It is easy to see how the process of becoming familiar with, and subsequently maintaining familiarity with, an environment is facilitated by approaching the most novel area while alternation behaviour can be seen as paralleling the preference for novel sources and areas discussed earlier in this section. A further, neglected, and not necessarily incompatible, possibility is that entry to the novel arm in maze alternation experiments could actually represent an attempt to avoid novelty and contact familiar sources or cover. Rats will leave an open novel environment for a familiar or covered one if given the opportunity (Section 2.4.1). In the case of maze behaviour, an animal that has explored one arm and failed to locate familiarity or cover would be expected subsequently to enter the novel arm in search of these.

Finally in connection with alternation behaviour, it should be noted that maze alternation may not occur in all species under all conditions, although there are few systematic data on vertebrate species other than the rat (see Cogan, *et al.*, 1979; Hayes & Warren, 1963; Sinclair & Bender, 1978).

2.4.3 Response for Environmental Change

Psychological studies have also examined situations in which an animal can bring about an environmental change by responding in a particular way. These differ from those discussed in the previous section, in that the novel stimulus or change does not impinge on the animal until after it has responded, so that the response is *for*, rather than *to*, change and the behaviour is essentially inquisitive (Section 2.3.1).

Considerable attention has been focused on Skinner box set-ups in which an environmental change such as a brief period of illumination, light offset, sound or mild electric shock is contingent upon a lever press or similar operant (reviews by Berlyne, 1960; Fowler, 1971; Kish, 1966). Another variant makes a short opportunity to view the environment outside the test box contingent on responding (Butler, 1957; Stahl *et al.*, 1973). Other studies have adopted discrete trial situations in which the response is running in an alley leading to a goal box containing complex or novel stimuli (Chapman & Levy, 1957; Schneider & Gross, 1964) or turning correctly in a T-maze (or other discrimination situation) for such stimuli (Montgomery, 1954; Montgomery & Segall, 1955).

Studies of this kind have shown that response-contingent novelty will act in much the same way as a conventional reinforcer like food or water, that is it strengthens the response so that its frequency or speed are increased, an effect that has been described as sensory reinforcement (Kish, 1966). An important defining characteristic of a reinforcer is that it produces learning, a relatively permanent change in behaviour rather than a temporary, facilitatory change and, in some cases at least, sensory reinforcers do meet this criterion. For example, in the response-contingent light studies the increased response rate may be maintained for a time after the light contingency is terminated, with responding showing the same extinction effect obtained on termination of a conventional reinforcer (Barnes & Baron, 1961; Kling *et al.*, 1956).

It appears reasonable, then, to interpret sensory reinforcement effects as demonstrating that animals will learn to make responses that are instrumental in producing an environmental change. Although this fact has been seen as having some problematic implications for psychological theories of exploration (Section 2.5.2) it is predictable enough on adaptive grounds. It should be remembered that the distinction between responding for a change and to a change is not hard and fast, and that just as it is adaptive for an animal to investigate a change that is already within its sensory field so it is adaptive for it to bring itself into contact with a change: in both cases it is familiarizing itself with its environment. To take one example, an animal that runs down an alley in order to enter a goal box in which it has previously encountered changes is monitoring its environment and paying particular attention to a significant part of it, in much the same way as it might do by patrolling a natural environment and visiting areas where changes have been found to occur in the past. Such behaviour implies the operation of mechanisms through which animals 'anticipate' the possibility of changes in a particular area. These mechanisms are presumably akin to those involved in the anticipation of food or other conventional reinforcers, and acquisition and extinction phenomena are correspondingly similar. Similar considerations apply to lever-pressing experiments: in producing the change the animal is learning the properties of its environment. Light onset in a dark box is a particularly effective sensory reinforcer, probably because as well as constituting an environmental change, it permits the animal to explore the box visually, the so-called scanning or viewing hypothesis (Halliday, 1968).

2.4.4 Studies of Stimulus Complexity

An animal's response to an environmental change will depend not just upon novelty but also upon the exact nature of the change. Complexity is one factor that has been studied reasonably systematically. The concept of stimulus complexity is somewhat problematic, but broadly relates to the number of distinguishable elements and the dissimilarity of those elements (Berlyne, 1960; Walker, 1970).

There is good evidence that complex stimuli elicit more exploration and make more powerful sensory reinforcers than simple ones; they are also preferred in choice situations (see reviews by Berlyne, 1960; Kish, 1966; Walker, 1970). For example, when placed in a new environment rats spend more time in the vicinity of areas that contain objects or are otherwise heterogeneous (Berlyne, 1955; Williams & Kuchta, 1957). Chimpanzees' manipulation of object arrays is a function of the heterogeneity of the array (Welker, 1956). Taylor (1974), using the technique of familiarizing rats to one T-maze arm of moderate complexity and then allowing them to choose between this arm and one of different complexity, found a preference for the novel arm which was stronger if this arm was of higher complexity than the familiar one than if it was of lower complexity. Such findings are expected on the grounds that complex stimuli contain more information to be assimilated.

It has also been predicted that maximal exploration will be elicited by stimuli of moderate, rather than high, complexity because highly complex stimuli tend to be ignored or actively avoided (Berlyne, 1960; Dember & Earl, 1957; Walker, 1964) and there is some limited evidence for this (Sales, 1968; Walker, 1970). In an adaptive context it may be that, rather as postulated in the case of stimulus change level (Section 2.3.1), organisms are tuned to deal with stimuli lying within the particular complexity range normally encountered in the natural habitat. Where experimental situations confront them with stimuli of higher complexity, withdrawal and avoidance may result. On the other hand, it may be argued that psychological experiments invariably make use of complex stimuli that are, from the animal's point of view, relatively meaningless, such as arbitrary visual patterns or collections of objects. Although this may enable clear statements about the effects of complexity *per se*, independent of stimulus content, the complexity variable may have little relevance for understanding behaviour in natural habitats, where content is often the crucial determinant of the animal's reaction (e.g., whether an approaching object is a conspecific, a predator, or a wind-blown leaf).

2.5 Theories of Exploration

For reasons outlined in Section 2.1, psychological theories of exploration have been concerned primarily with motivational issues. This section presents a brief overview of the various approaches, with the aim of pointing up their similarities and differences and considering them in the context of exploration as adaptive behaviour.

2.5.1 Environmental Modelling and Discrepancy Theories

It is convenient to begin with theories that pay particular attention to the processes through which organisms detect environmental changes since, although these have been developed in an ethological framework rather than a psychological one, they provide a useful backdrop against which to evaluate more conventionally 'psychological' theories.

It seems clear that responding to environmental changes must involve some sort of comparator process, with current stimulus input being compared with previous inputs (past experience). This idea has been developed formally in terms of modelling theories (Sokolov, 1960), of which Salzen's (1962, 1970) application to orienting, fear, attachment and exploration is particularly relevant here. Salzen proposes that a familiar environment is embodied in a set of internal representations or neuronal models that have been built up through experience, and that a discrepancy between a model and current input arising from an environmental change serves to activate a behavioural system that has the elimination of discrepancy as its goal. Salzen suggests that relatively small discrepancies produce low levels of activation and result in approach and investigation of the source of the change (Berlyne's inspective exploration), which then serve to establish a new model and eliminate the discrepancy. More drastic discrepancies, producing intense activation, are more likely to lead to withdrawal from the discrepant source and/or attempts to locate familiar, nondiscrepant stimuli.

Some extension of this sort of theory is necessary to encompass inquisitive exploration and environmental patrolling, since, although this behaviour is consistent with the idea that organisms behave so as to maintain a familiar environment, in the short term it involves moving away from familiar stimuli towards novel ones producing more discrepancy. This is especially obvious in the case of a patrolling animal moving from a highly familiar part of its range into a part not visited recently. Behaviour of this kind may sometimes be explainable in terms of discrepancy generated by changes that are detected by distal receptors, as, for example, when an animal sees a change at a distance and moves towards it, in which case the behaviour is inspective rather than

38

inquisitive. Truly inquisitive exploration (Section 2.4.3), however, requires some other explanation. One possibility is that discrepancy is generated as a result of change in models (rather than input), through decay, interference or other forgetting processes: patrolling behaviour, in particular, could serve to 'repair' models. Inquisitive behaviour may also be accounted for by the assumption of a mechanism that anticipates environmental changes and discrepancies (Section 2.4.3).

Salzen's theory assumes that the goal of exploration is the elimination of discrepancy. An alternative assumption is that the goal is the achievement of a mild degree of discrepancy rather than a match between models and input. In the latter case, a close and/or persistent match would activate withdrawal from current sources and search for, and approach to, more discrepant ones — that is, inquisitive exploration. Both formulations are plausible, emphasizing that although modelling theory provides a framework broadly consistent with the facts of exploration, it is not strongly predictive or readily amenable to experimental test. There is no direct way of assessing the degree of discrepancy produced by a stimulus (although it may be possible to rank stimuli in terms of discrepancy). Nor is there any means of specifying in advance whether a particular change will produce a small discrepancy and give rise to exploration, or a large one, giving withdrawal.

Another problem with modelling theory is that Archer (1976) has proposed an essentially identical hypothesis to account for aggression and fear, with the difference that a small discrepancy is held to produce aggression and a large one fear, with both serving to eliminate the discrepancy. For a discrepancy theory to be predictive there must be some way of scaling stimuli for discrepancy and of specifying the discrepancy ranges over which particular types of behaviour ('exploration', 'fear', 'aggression') occur. The theory would also have to take into account the nature of the stimulus as well as the amount of discrepancy it produces. Conceivably a conspecific, a predator, a prey animal and an inanimate object can all produce a similar degree of discrepancy but will not necessarily elicit the same behaviour. It is of course possible that the concept of discrepancy modelling can be applied to several behavioural systems that are completely or partially functionally and motivationally independent.

Environmental modelling theories are clearly compatible with several other theoretical concepts that have been proposed in connection with exploration. Of these, curiosity, boredom and arousal concepts are discussed in later sections. There is also a tie-up between environmental modelling and the concept of a cognitive map, discussed by Toates (Chapter 3), Inglis (Chapter 4) and Morris (Chapter 5). The term 'cognitive map' implies a brain representation of a set of spatial and/or temporal relationships in the environment and the concept serves much the same heuristic function as that of a neuronal model. The neuronal model concept is perhaps preferable in that the cognitive map concept is difficult to divorce from an intuitive appeal based on our human experience of imagery, which may or may not be appropriate to an understanding of the processes involved in environmental modelling in other species.

Further, because discrepancy is equated with the lack of correspondence between environmental input and existing brain representations of the environment it also links up with other theoretical concepts including conflict, uncertainty and lack of information, all of which were identified by Berlyne (1960, 1966) as determinants of exploration. Discrepancy relates directly to conflict, regarded by Berlyne as the simultaneous evocation of incompatible neural reactions: in modelling theory terms, these reactions are the input and the model. Discrepancy also implies uncertainty and lack of information, which can be rectified by exploration, resulting in the formation of new models or cognitive maps and the resolution of conflict.

Finally, Salzen (1970) notes that the modelling hypothesis is in principle independent of any specification of actual brain mechanisms, although the clarification of these must be regarded as a desirable goal. One move in this direction is represented by an attempt to identify the hippocampus as the core brain structure involved in environmental mapping (O'Keefe & Nadel, 1978: see also Kimble, 1979). This work is discussed in more detail by Morris (Chapter 5).

2.5.2 Drive Theories: Curiosity and Boredom

The modelling theory notion that discrepancy leads to the activation of behavioural systems is readily translated into the language of classical drive theory. The history of the 'exploratory drive' and the concepts of curiosity and boredom are dealt with elsewhere in this volume (Chapters 1, 3 and 4).

Activation stemming from a discrepancy can be equated with curiosity, a drive deemed to be aroused by a novel stimulus and reduced by inspective exploration of that stimulus (Berlyne, 1950). This formulation is notoriously unhelpful, in that as the drive is both being inferred from and used to explain, exploration, it is essentially circular and nonpredictive (Brown, 1953; Fowler, 1965). Curiosity differs from, say, fear as a drive, since fear has proved more useful conceptually in that in principle it can be measured independently of withdrawal and any other protective behaviour that is said to accompany it, for example, in terms of autonomic and endocrine indices (Archer, 1973; Mayes, 1979 — but see also Section 2.5.4). The physiological correlates of curiosity are considerably more obscure. Although the equation of curiosity with arousal level promised at one time to overcome this problem, the promise has not really been fulfilled (Section 2.5.3).

Another difficulty with the curiosity formulation is that because contact with a novel stimulus is held both first to elicit and then subsequently to reduce curiosity, drive eliciting and drive reducing properties are being ascribed to precisely the same event, that is contact with the stimulus (Fowler, 1965). This also contrasts with fear, where the drive is elicited by contact with a stimulus and reduced by withdrawal or other protective behaviour which *reduces* contact with that stimulus. However, this is really only a problem from the point of view of the conventions of classical drive theory and there is nothing problematic about postulating, for example, that curiosity is generated by lack of information about a stimulus, or by a discrepancy between the stimulus and a model, and is reduced by exploratory behaviour that supplies information and reduces discrepancy.

The problem of independent specification applies equally to boredom, the other major psychological drive concept invoked to account for exploration. A boredom drive theory, such as that proposed by Myers & Miller (1954), identifies the motivation for exploration as a drive state generated by exposure to monotonous, unchanging stimulation, a state which is reduced by stimulus change. According to Eisenberger (1972), Myers and Miller's original formulation regarded boredom as a drive state produced by unvarying stimulation that is specific to that stimulation, the implication being that changes in other dimensions or modalities will not alleviate boredom. Other boredom formulations (Berlyne, 1960; Fowler, 1965) assume that the drive is reduced by *any* change. The concept of boredom can be linked to the discrepancy modelling theory proposal that activation stems from a close or persistent match between input and model (Section 2.5.1). It also has something in common with the concept of stimulus satiation (Glanzer, 1953a,b), according to which exposure to a stimulus generates satiation that reduces the tendency to respond to that stimulus and, by implication, increases the tendency to respond to other, novel stimuli.

Applied to inspective exploration, boredom drive theory assumes that changes in environmental stimuli are approached and explored because they reduce boredom generated by exposure to unvarying environmental conditions. The real point of the boredom conceptualization, however, is that it accounts for inquisitive exploration and novelty-seeking, explaining them as attempts to reduce boredom by self-produced exposure to change. This is important in that according to some theorists (e.g. Fowler, 1965), inquisitive exploration is difficult to account for in terms of a curiosity drive formulation: because curiosity is not aroused until the animal comes into contact with novelty, curiosity cannot motivate behaviour aimed at seeking out novel stimuli which are not actually impinging on the animal (although there is no problem if it is assumed that animals can anticipate sources of change and that inquisitive behaviour is motivated by 'anticipatory curiosity', an idea expressed more formally in terms of incentive motivation theory by Fowler, 1965, 1967).

Some theorists, including Berlyne (1960, 1966) and Fowler (1965, 1967), make use of both curiosity and boredom drive concepts although, as outlined above, just one or other of these concepts can be made to encompass both inspective and inquisitive exploration. Perhaps the most reasonable conclusion is that the two concepts are to a large extent compatible with one another, particularly when it is realized that approaching and exploring an environmental change necessarily involves moving away from familiar stimuli, that is withdrawal from and avoidance of the familiar. Exposure to an unchanging environment, then, may motivate behaviour directed away from familiar sources ('boredom') and towards new sources ('curiosity'). Viewed in this way, there is an inverse relationship between the curiosity and boredom generated by a particular stimulus. The higher the level of curiosity the more likely the animal is to explore the stimulus and the more likely it is to withdraw from other sources. Conversely, the higher the level of boredom the more likely it is to move away from the stimulus towards some other stimulus.

In assessing formulations such as this, though, it must be remembered that restating behavioural tendencies in terms of curiosity and boredom drives actually adds very little, particularly in view of the lack of independent specification of these drives.

Stimulus change, deprivation and boredom. The adaptive significance of orienting away from familiar stimuli has been commented on in Section 2.3.1 (see also Chapter 4). The concepts of boredom and stimulus satiation provide the clearest theoretical statement about such behaviour, that is that the tendency to move away from a stimulus and towards other stimuli is an increasing function of the length of exposure to the first stimulus. Experimental tests of this prediction have usually been framed in terms of deprivation of novelty or stimulus change and involve confining an animal to a specific unchanging environment before it is permitted to engage in inquisitive or inspective exploration. It should be noted that natural environments rarely, if ever, impose this particular constraint on animals, since they are normally free to move from one area to another within the home range and can readily leave a source with which they have been in contact for some time and orient towards and approach a relatively more novel source, as happens in environmental patrolling. Stimulus change deprivation experiments, involving a period of confinement to a relatively small, inescapable environment presumably result in the animal being exposed to stimuli beyond the point at which it would normally have moved away from them. In this connection, it is interesting that one definition of boredom in the context of human performance is motivation stemming from a person being forced to remain at a task beyond the point at which he or she would have voluntarily given up (Barmack, 1939).

The most compelling evidence of boredom motivation comes from studies in which an animal is first confined to an unchanging environment and subsequently permitted to make a response that is instrumental in producing change. Butler (1957) found that the frequency with which macaque monkeys pressed a plate in order to open a window and see out of the box in which they were confined increased as a function of the period of prior confinement to the box, approaching a maximum after four hours of confinement. Similarly, with light reinforcement (Section 2.4.3), response frequency has been found to be an increasing function of the period of prior confinement to the darkened box in rats (Premack *et al.*, 1957) and monkeys (Fox, 1962), and in mice responding is greater if the animals are preconfined in a dark box compared with a continuously or intermittently lit one (Kish & Baron, 1962). Using a runway, Fowler (1965, p. 48) found that when the rats were permitted to run from a start box to a goal box of opposite brightness (i.e., black to white or *vice versa*), running speed was a function of the period of prior exposure to the start box. Similar 'deprivation' effects have been demonstrated in the context of T-maze alternation behaviour, with rats' tendency to choose the novel arm on the test

42

trial increasing as a function of the length of time for which they have been pre-exposed to the other, familiar arm (Fowler, 1965, p. 45; Glanzer, 1953b). Some negative findings should be noted, however: Premack & Collier (1962) found that prior light deprivation did not increase rats' light-reinforced lever pressing and Haude & Ray (1967) found that the frequency and duration of viewing novel visual stimuli by rhesus monkeys was unaffected by the length of time for which they were preconfined to the test chamber.

One interpretation of prior confinement effects is that animals experiencing a short period of confinement respond less, or less rapidly, because they are still exploring the novel test environment, compared to animals confined for a longer period that will have become familiar with the environment. This interpretation is compatible with the boredom formulation rather than an alternative to it since, as noted in Section 2.5.2, the concept of boredom implies that an animal will tend to direct its attention away from the immediate features of the novel environment and begin seeking out less immediately available ones only after it has become familiar with the immediate features.

Another group of studies has used the technique of confining animals to one environment with reduced stimulus change and then removing them and testing them in a second environment. The results here are more conflicting and difficult to interpret. Woods (1962) found that rats confined to small solid-walled cages or to normal mesh-fronted cages for 24 h before test in a novel environment showed more sniffing and locomotion than rats confined for the same period to large, open cages containing objects. Charlesworth & Thompson (1957), however, found no difference between rats kept in normal cages and those confined in solid-walled boxes for three, six or nine days before testing and Premack & Collier (1962) noted that maintaining rats in a similar fashion *reduced* light contingent bar pressing.

It must be concluded that although some of the findings on stimulus change deprivation are consistent with the predictions of boredom theory, others are not. One reason for the conflicting findings may be that animals kept in unchanging conditions for some time may adapt to these conditions so that subsequent exposure to stimulus change results in a degree of change that is large enough to elicit withdrawal and avoidance (see also Chapter 4). Adaptation in this sense could be equated with the formation of a set of models consistent with low environmental change. Depending on the period of deprivation and on the levels of pretest and test stimulus change, then, deprivation could have a facilitatory, an inhibitory or a nil effect on approach and exploration of an environmental change. The possibility of adaptation to environmental change levels raises questions about the long-term effects of maintenance and rearing conditions upon response to novelty in captive subjects (see Inglis & Freeman, 1976; Kish, 1966).

2.5.3 Optimal Stimulation and Arousal Theories

Theories centering around the concept of optimal stimulation are reviewed by

Inglis (Chapter 4). Their theme is that organisms behave so as to maintain an optimum level of stimulation. Stimulation level is often referred to as arousal. Environmental change (novelty) is held to be an important determinant of arousal and the implications of this type of theory for exploration have been examined extensively (Berlyne, 1960; Fowler, 1965).

It is important to distinguish two variants of arousal theory. One, exemplified by Fiske & Maddi (1961), equates an unchanging environment with low arousal and regards exploration (both inspective and inquisitive) as behaviour directed at increasing arousal towards an optimum level, so that low arousal is the conceptual equivalent of boredom. Environmental change may, however, increase arousal above optimum, and there are two ways it can be reduced, through inspective exploration or through withdrawal and avoidance. In the longer term, exploration reduces arousal by rendering the change familiar but may mean 'tolerating' a temporary further increase in arousal before this happens. Withdrawal is likely to be more immediately effective. High arousal is thus broadly equatable with curiosity and with fear. In modelling theory terms, high arousal is the equivalent of a large discrepancy between input and model.

Berlyne (1960, 1963, 1967) has proposed an arousal theory that is similar to the above formulation but differs in postulating that arousal is a U-shaped function of stimulation, with not only high but also *low* levels of stimulus change being highly arousing. This formulation necessitates specifying arousal as a state defined independently of level of stimulation. Berlyne's original statements followed the ideas of Hebb (1955) and others (see Chapter 4) concerning arousal as a psychophysiological dimension with reticular system and cortical correlates, although he subsequently seems to have come to regard it as a hypothetical concept not necessarily anchored in this way (Berlyne, 1967). Berlyne's original formulation also postulated that behaviour is generally directed at *reducing* arousal, with the assumption that the optimum level is *low*, in contrast to most other formulations, which assume that a moderate or intermediate level is optimal. There are echoes here of the two variants of discrepancy theory noted in Section 2.5.1: optimal discrepancy being either nil (or very low) or intermediate. Berlyne's arguments concerning the motivational effects of high arousal stemming from a high stimulation level are much the same as Fiske and Maddi's. But for Berlyne, high arousal stemming from a low level of stimulation (boredom) can motivate inquisitive exploration, the seeking out of stimulus changes to reduce arousal. In later formulations, Berlyne (1967, 1969) appears to have modified this basic theory and, in particular, moved away from the assumption that the goal of behaviour is always arousal reduction, allowing that small or moderate increases in arousal are sometimes sought.

There is little point in elaborating theories of arousal here since it has not generally been possible to formulate them with sufficient rigour to enable detailed predictions to be made (see, e.g., Eisenberger, 1972; Fowler, 1965) and consequently the arousal concept has had little impact on animal studies. The problem is much the same as that encountered with both discrepancy modelling and drive theories, and Fowler's (1965) comment that arousal theories tend to 'explain everything' but 'predict nothing' remains apposite. The basic problem is that it is difficult to specify what the optimum level of arousal is in particular cases or to determine whether an organism is above or below its optimum. This is true of theories that equate arousal directly with level of stimulation, but is even more of a problem for a theory that maintains that both high and low stimulation levels are highly arousing. The difficulty of specifying arousal levels is further increased by the fact that arousal is held to be determined not just by the novelty of a stimulus but also by such factors as its intensity and meaning and by concurrent internal stimuli such as those associated with primary drive states.

Where the physiological correlates of arousal are specified, a theory is potentially testable since it should be possible to measure arousal independently of behaviour. In practice, however, the problems involved in defining and measuring physiological arousal (Lacey, 1967; Lacey & Lacey, 1970) have proved a stumbling block, and attempts to relate such measures as cortical EEG to exploration in animals have so far met with little success (Joseph *et al.*, 1981).

2.5.4 Fear and Exploration

That environmental changes sometimes elicit withdrawal and other protective responses rather than exploration has already been commented on (Section 2.2, and 2.4.2). Theoretically, two sorts of explanations have been proposed to account for the fact that an environmental change can elicit either exploration or withdrawal, one based on a biphasic system and the other on a monophasic one.

Biphasic theories postulate two separate but interacting motivational systems (Montgomery, 1955; Schneirla, 1959; Valle, 1972). According to Montgomery, for example, the behaviour elicited by an environmental change is the net outcome of the competition between the tendency to explore, motivated by curiosity, and the tendency to withdraw, motivated by fear. On this view, small environmental changes are likely to generate little or no fear.

Monophasic theories, in contrast, postulate a single motivational process operating with a threshold, below which exploration is more likely and above which withdrawal is more likely. Arousal theory (Section 2.5.3), for example, attributes exploration to small to moderate increases in arousal and withdrawal to large increases. A similar idea is Salzen's (1970) suggestion that small discrepancies from neuronal models lead to approach and large discrepancies to withdrawal. According to such theories, whether the underlying motivation is above or below threshold depends upon various factors, including the magnitude and precise nature of the environmental change.

Another monophasic theory is that exploration is actually motivated by the fear generated by environmental changes (Halliday, 1966a; Lester, 1967b; Mowrer, 1960). This theory agrees that high levels of fear elicit withdrawal, but adds the assumption that lower levels of fear elicit approach and investigation. Accepting the fear motivation theory at face value, much of the evidence presented in its support is equivocal, and there is other evidence that runs counter to the theory (Russell, 1973a). What has been less often remarked is that the theory suffers from several conceptual difficulties. Since these point up some more general problems associated with the psychological approach to theory, it is worth examining them in detail. Most notable is whether it is possible to distinguish a drive state of 'fear' from a drive state of 'curiosity', and whether or how these states differ from those described by apparently more general conceptions like arousal and activation. In the absence of suitable distinguishing criteria, it is difficult to formulate and test between alternatives. The fear theory is actually potentially testable, because fear has been linked to various autonomic and endocrine correlates (Section 2.5.2) that provide for independent measurement, but this approach has been little used (Russell, 1973a). There is also some dispute over whether the relationships between the various physiological measures and between these and behavioural measures can be adequately summarized in terms of a unitary fear drive concept (Archer, 1973, 1979; Gray, 1971a,b, 1979). A further problem is that even if it should prove possible to demonstrate a positive correlation between indices of fear and measures of exploration, this need not indicate a causal relationship, particularly as variables that are affecting fear are usually those that can equally well be said to affect curiosity or arousal. For example, Halliday's (1966a, 1967) argument that the fear theory is supported by the fact that rats show more locomotion in an elevated maze than in an enclosed one (an elevated maze being putatively more fear-evoking) is not conclusive, because it can be argued that the two mazes differ in novelty or some other stimulus factor that, according to rival theories, affects relevant motivational states such as curiosity (Sheldon, 1968).

One sort of evidence that has been regarded as critical for the fear theory is that animals sometimes approach, and have a preference for, distinctive stimuli (such as a section of environment painted with stripes) which have previously been associated with mild electric shock (Halliday, 1966a; Wong & Bowles, 1976). The assumption here is that it is mild fear of these stimuli that motivates exploration (more intense shocks, of course, result in avoidance of stimuli associated with them). Several alternative interpretations are possible, however. Mild, non-painful shock may simply function in the same way as any other environmental change, so that the animals are investigating an area of the environment (striped) that has previously been associated with an 'interesting' stimulus, that is they are showing 'anticipatory curiosity' (Section 2.4.3 and 2.5.2). This is not incompatible with the possibility that the area is relatively novel or incongruous because it was once, but is no longer, associated with such a stimulus. There is also some evidence that mild pretest shock can have a general facilitatory effect on exploration of a relatively complex area of the test environment independently of these specific effects (Williams, 1972) and that shock can facilitate other types of behaviour, including eating and sexual behaviour (Archer, 1979). It must also be noted that even if shock effects are interpreted in terms of fear facilitating exploration, this need not mean that mild fear is a necessary or sufficient condition for the occurrence of exploration in general.

46

2.6 Conclusions

Two major points emerge from this review of psychological approaches to exploration. One is that laboratory studies of exploration have failed to take sufficient account of the adaptive significance of exploration and of the actual circumstances under which animals typically encounter environmental changes in the natural habitat. It has been argued that studies making use of test situations that present changes against a familiar background, so providing a choice of novel and familiar stimuli, are the most valid ecologically and also the least open to conflicting interpretations. By contrast, novel confining environments such as mazes and the open field provide unnecessarily ambiguous data.

The other point is that psychological theories of exploration have not yet advanced much beyond the stage of offering hypothetical motivational constructs, such as curiosity, boredom, activation, arousal and fear, that are not tied very precisely to independently measurable events and that, therefore, offer very limited scope for prediction and testing. Those concepts do, however, at least provide a starting point for the investigation of proximate mechanisms. Future studies of these mechanisms should be conducted with appropriate attention to adaptive and ecological considerations. Two examples will serve to illustrate the importance of this point.

One concerns the question of whether, in drive theory terms, exploration is best explained in terms of curiosity or boredom. Focusing on behaviour in the natural habitat leads to the conclusion that there is a place for both concepts. An animal will move away from a familiar source either when distal receptors pick up a change elsewhere which must be investigated (curiosity) or when it embarks on environmental patrolling and checking for changes (boredom).

Consideration of natural behaviour serves also to draw attention to the fact that approaching an environmental change necessarily entails withdrawal from familiar sources and that withdrawal from a change correspondingly involves approach to familiar sources. Psychologists have traditionally used the term 'exploration' for the search for, and approach to, environmental changes, but in fact it is reasonable to suppose that the *search for, and approach to, familiar stimuli* will involve essentially identical behaviour patterns, for example locomotion, visual search and sniffing. This, combined with the fact that many psychological studies of animal exploration have used novel confining environments and that there is good evidence that animals often attempt to withdraw from such environments (Section 2.4.1), has led to some largely unremarked confusion about exploration. Where an animal's movements in a novel environment actually reflect attempts to withdraw from novelty and the search for and attempts to approach familiar sources these movements are, according to psychological usage of the term 'exploratory', exploratory in terms of their *form* but they are not exploratory in terms of their *goal*. This leads to further confusion when theoretical questions are posed about the motivation of exploration. Following conventional terminology, it would be reasonable to describe such movements as being fear-motivated and it might even be possible to correlate the strength of these movements with some other independent index of fear but, paradoxically, this could not constitute evidence for a fear motivation theory of exploration (Section 2.5.4), because the behaviour involved is not, according to the theory, exploratory. Clearly, such conceptual confusions need to be identified as a preliminary to any attempt at formulating a theory of exploration.

References

ARCHER, J. (1973) Tests for emotionality in rats and mice: a review. *Animal Behaviour* **21**, 205–235.

ARCHER, J. (1976) The organisation of aggression and fear in vertebrates. In *Perspectives in Ethology, Vol. 2* (Eds. P. P. G. BATESON and P. KLOPFER). London: Plenum Press.

ARCHER, J. (1979) Behavioural aspects of fear. In *Fear in Animals and Man* (Ed. W. SLUCKIN). London: Van Nostrand Reinhold.

BALDWIN, J. D. and BALDWIN, J. I. (1977) The role of learning phenomena in the ontogeny of exploration and play. In *Primate Biosocial Development* (Eds. S. CHEVALIER-SKOLNIKOFF and F. E. POIRIER). London: Garland Publishing.

BARMACK, J. E. (1939) A definition of boredom: a reply to Mr. Berman. *American Journal of Psychology* **52**, 467–471.

BARNES, G. W. and BARON, A. (1961) The effects of sensory reinforcement on extinction behavior. *Journal of Comparative and Physiological Psychology* **54**, 461–465.

BARNETT, S. A. (1958) Exploratory behaviour. *British Journal of Psychology* **49**, 289–310.

BARNETT, S. A. (1975) *The Rat: a Study in Behavior*. Chicago: University of Chicago Press.

BARNETT, S. A. and COWAN, P. E. (1976) Activity, exploration, curiosity and fear: an ethological study. *Interdisciplinary Science Reviews* **1**, 43–62.

BARNETT, S. A. and SPENCER, M. M. (1951) Feeding, social behaviour and inter-specific competition in wild rats. *Behaviour* **3**, 229–242.

BECK, B. B. (1980) *Animal Tool Behaviour*. New York: Garland Press.

BERLYNE, D. E. (1950) Novelty and curiosity as determinants of exploratory behaviour. *British Journal of Psychology* **41**, 68–80.

BERLYNE, D. E. (1955) The arousal and satiation of perceptual curiosity in the rat. *Journal of Comparative and Physiological Psychology* **48**, 238–246.

BERLYNE, D. E. (1960) *Conflict, Arousal, and Curiosity*. New York: McGraw-Hill.

BERLYNE, D. E. (1963) Motivational problems raised by exploratory and epistemic behavior. In *Psychology: a Study of a Science, Vol. 5* (Ed. S. KOCH). New York: McGraw-Hill.

BERLYNE, D. E. (1966) Curiosity and exploration. *Science* **153**, 25–33.

BERLYNE, D. E. (1967) Arousal and reinforcement. In *Nebraska Symposium on Motivation, Vol. 15* (Ed. D. LEVINE). Lincoln: University of Nebraska Press.

BERLYNE, D. E. (1969) The reward-value of indifferent stimulation. In *Reinforcement and Behavior* (Ed. J. T. TAPP). New York: Academic Press.

BILLINGSLEA, F. Y. (1942) Intercorrelational analysis of certain behavior salients in the rat. *Journal of Comparative Psychology* **34**, 203–211.

BLANCHARD, R. J., KELLEY, M. J. and BLANCHARD, D. C. (1974) Defensive reactions and exploratory behavior in rats. *Journal of Comparative and Physiological Psychology* **87**, 1129–1133.

BROWN, J. S. (1953) Problems presented by the concept of acquired drives. In *Current Theory and Research in Motivation*. Lincoln: University of Nebraska Press.

BUTLER, R. A. (1957) The effect of deprivation of visual incentives on visual exploration motivation in monkeys. *Journal of Comparative and Physiological Psychology* **50**, 177–179.

CANDLAND, D. K. and NAGY, Z. M. (1969) The open field: some comparative data. *Annals of the New York Academy of Science* **159**, 831–851.

CHAPMAN, R. M. and LEVY, N. (1957) Hunger drive and reinforcing effect of novel stimuli. *Journal of Comparative and Physiological Psychology* **50**, 233–238.

CHARLESWORTH, W. R. and THOMPSON, W. R. (1957) Effect of lack of visual stimulus variation on exploratory behaviour in the adult white rat. *Psychological Reports* **3**, 509–512.

COGAN, D., JONES, J. F. and IRONS, T. (1979) Spontaneous alternation in chicks using social reward. *Developmental Psychobiology* **12**, 285–290.

CORMAN, D. C. and SHAFER, J. N. (1968) Open field activity and exploratory behavior. *Psychonomic Science* **13**, 55–56.

COWAN, P. E. (1977) Systematic patrolling and orderly behaviour of rats during recovery from deprivation. *Animal Behaviour* **25**, 171–184.

DEMBER, W. N. (1956) Response by the rat to environmental change. *Journal of Comparative and Physiological Psychology* **49**, 93–95.

DEMBER, W. N. and EARL, R. W. (1957) Analysis of exploratory, manipulatory, and curiosity behaviors. *Psychological Review* **64**, 91–96.

DEMBER, W. N. and FOWLER, H. (1958) Spontaneous alternation behavior. *Psychological Bulletin* **55**, 412–428.

DOUGLAS, R. J. (1966) Cues of spontaneous alternation. *Journal of Comparative and Physiological Psychology* **62**, 171–183.

DOUGLAS, R. J., MITCHELL, D. and DEL VALLE, R. (1974) Angle between choice alleys as a critical factor in spontaneous alternation. *Animal Learning and Behavior* **2**, 218–220.

EINON, D. and MORGAN, M. (1976) Habituation of object contact in socially-reared and isolated rats (*Rattus norvegicus*). *Animal Behaviour* **24**, 415–420.

EISENBERGER, R. (1972) Explanation of rewards that do not reduce tissue needs. *Psychological Bulletin* **77**, 319–339.

FILE, S. E. and WARDILL, A. G. (1975) Validity of head-dipping as a measure of exploration in a modified holeboard. *Psychopharmacologia* **44**, 53–59.

FISKE, D. W. and MADDI, S. R. (1961) A conceptual framework. In *Functions of Varied Experience* (Ed. D. W. FISKE and S. R. MADDI). Homewood, Ill.: Dorsey.

FOSHEE, D. P., VIERCK, I.J., MEIER, J. N. and FEDERSPIEL, L. (1965) Simultaneous measures of general activity and exploratory behavior. *Perceptual and Motor Skills* **20**, 445–451.

FOWLER, H. (1965) *Curiosity and Exploratory Behavior*. New York: Macmillan.

FOWLER, H. (1967) Satiation and curiosity: constructs for a drive and incentive-motivational theory of exploration. In *The Psychology of Learning and Motivation, Vol. 1* (Eds. K. W. SPENCE and J. T. SPENCE). New York: Academic Press.

FOWLER, H. (1971) Implications of sensory reinforcement. In *The Nature of Reinforcement* (Ed. R. GLASER). New York: Academic Press.

FOX, S. S. (1962) Self-maintained sensory input and sensory deprivation in monkeys: a behavioral and neuropharmacological study. *Journal of Comparative and Physiological Psychology* **55**, 438–444.

GALLUP, G. G. (1974) Animal hypnosis: factual status of a fictional concept. *Psychological Bulletin* **81**, 836–853.

GALLUP, G. G. (1977) Tonic immobility: the role of fear and predation. *Psychological Record* **1**, 41–61.

GALLUP, G. G. and SUAREZ, S. D. (1980) An ethological analysis of open-field behaviour in chickens. *Animal Behaviour* **28**, 368–378.

GLANZER, M. (1953a) Stimulus satiation: an explanation of spontaneous alternation and related phenomena. *Psychological Review* **60**, 257–268.

GLANZER, M. (1953b) The role of stimulus satiation in spontaneous alternation. *Journal of Experimental Psychology* **45**, 387–393.

GLICKMAN, S. E. and HARTZ, K. E. (1964) Exploratory behavior in several species of rodents. *Journal of Comparative and Physiological Psychology* **58**, 101–104.

GLICKMAN, S. E. and SROGES, R. W. (1966) Curiosity in zoo animals. *Behaviour* **26**, 151–188.

GRAY, J. A. (1965) A time sample study of the components of general activity in selected strains of rats. *Canadian Journal of Psychology* **19**, 74–82.

GRAY, J. A. (1971a) Sex differences in emotional behaviour in mammals including Man: endocrine bases. *Acta Psychologica* **35**, 29–46.

GRAY, J. A. (1971b) *The Psychology of Fear and Stress*. London: Weidenfeld & Nicolson.

GRAY, J. A. (1979) Emotionality in male and female rodents: a reply to Archer. *British Journal of Psychology* **70**, 425–440.

HALLIDAY, M. S. (1966a) Exploration and fear in the rat. *Symposium of the Zoological Society of London* **18**, 45–54.

HALLIDAY, M. S. (1966b) The effect of previous exploratory activity on the exploration of a simple maze. *Nature* **209**, 432–433.

HALLIDAY, M. S. (1967) Exploratory behaviour in elevated and enclosed mazes. *Quarterly Journal of Experimental Psychology* **19**, 254–263.

HALLIDAY, M. S. (1968) Exploratory behaviour. In *Analysis of Behavioural Change* (Ed. L. WEISKRANTZ). New York: Harper and Row.

HARLOW, H. F. (1953) Mice, monkeys, men, and motives. *Psychological Review* **60**, 23–32.

HAUDE, R. H. and RAY, O. S. (1967) Visual exploration in monkeys as a function of visual incentive duration and sensory deprivation. *Journal of Comparative and Physiological Psychology* **64**, 332–336.

HAYES, K. J. (1960) Exploration and fear. *Psychological Reports* **6**, 91–93.

HAYES. W. N. and WARREN, J. M. (1963) Failure to find spontaneous alternation in chicks. *Journal of Comparative and Physiological Psychology* **56**, 575–577.

HEBB, D. O. (1955) Drives and the CNS (Conceptual Nervous System). *Psychological Review* **62**, 243–254.

HUCK, U. W. and PRICE, E. O. (1975) Differential effects of environmental enrichment on the open-field behavior of wild and domestic Norway rats. *Journal of comparative and Physiological Psychology* **89**, 892–898.

HUGHES, R. N. (1965a) Food deprivation and locomotor exploration in the white rat. *Animal Behaviour* **13**, 30–32.

HUGHES, R. N. (1965b) Spontaneous alternation and response to stimulus change in the ferret. *Journal of Comparative and Physiological Psychology* **60**, 149–150.

HUGHES, R. N. (1968) Behaviour of male and female rats with free choice of two environments differing in novelty. *Animal Behaviour* **16**, 92–96.

HUTT, C. (1970) Specific and diversive exploration. *Advances in Child Development and Behavior* **5**, 119–180.

INGLIS, I. R. and FREEMAN, N. H. (1976) Reversible effects of ambient housing stimulation upon stimulation-seeking in rats. *Quarterly Journal of Experimental Psychology* **28**, 409–417.

JEWELL, P. A. (1966) The concept of home range in mammals. *Symposium of the Zoological Society of London* **18**, 85–109.

JOHNSTON, W. A. (1964) Trends in escape and exploration. *Journal of Comparative and Physiological Psychology* **58**, 431–435.

JONES, R. B. and NOWELL, N. W. (1974) A comparison of the aversive and female attractant properties of urine from dominant and subordinate male mice. *Animal Learning and Behavior* **2**, 141–144.

JOSEPH, R., FORREST, N. M., FIDUCIA, D., COMO, P. and SIEGEL, J. (1981) Electrophysiological and behavioral correlates of arousal. *Physiological Psychology* **9**, 90–95.

KIMBLE, D. P. (1979) Hieroglyphics of the hippocampus. *Contemporary Psychology* **24**, 689–691.

KISH, G. B. (1966) Studies of sensory reinforcement. In *Operant Behavior* (Ed. W. K. HONIG). New York: Appleton-Century-Crofts.

KISH, G. B. and BARON, A. (1962) Satiation of sensory reinforcement. *Journal of Comparative and Physiological Psychology* **55**, 1007–1010.

KIVY, P. N., EARL, R. W. and WALKER, E. L. (1956) Stimulus context and satiation. *Journal of Comparative and Physiological Psychology* **49**, 90–92.

KLING, J. W., HOROWITZ, L. and DELHAGEN, J. E. (1956) Light as a positive reinforcer for rat responding. *Psychological Reports* **2**, 337–340.

LACEY, J. I. (1967) Somatic response patterning and stress: some revisions of activation theory. In *Psychological Stress* (Eds. M. H. APPLEY and R. TRUMBULL). New York: Appleton-Century-Crofts.

LACEY, J. I. and LACEY, B. S. (1970) Some autonomic-central nervous system relationships. In *Physiological Correlates of Emotion* (Ed. P. BLACK). New York: Academic Press.

LAWICK-GOODALL, J. VAN (1970) Tool-using in primates and other vertebrates. *Advances in the Study of Behavior* **3**, 195–249.

LESTER, D. (1967a) Effects of fear upon exploratory behavior. *Psychonomic Science* **1**, 117–118.

LESTER, D. (1967b) Sex differences in exploration: toward a theory of exploration. *Psychological Record* **17**, 55–62.

LESTER, D. (1969) Orderliness and activity in the exploratory behavior of rats. *Psychonomic Science* **14**, 125–127.

LEUBA, C. (1955) Toward some integration of learning theories: the concept of optimal stimulation. *Psychological Reports* **1**, 27–33.

LEVINE, S. and BROADHURST, P. L. (1963) Genetic and ontogenetic determinants of adult behavior in the rat. *Journal of Comparative and Physiological Psychology* **56**, 423–428.

LEVINE, S., HALTMEYER, G. C., KARAS, G. G. and DENENBERG, V. H. (1967) Physiological and behavioral effects of infantile stimulation. *Physiology and Behavior* **2**, 55–59.

LEYLAND, M., ROBBINS, T. and IVERSON, S. D. (1976) Locomotor activity and exploration: the use of traditional manipulators to dissociate these two behaviors in the rat. *Animal Learning and Behavior* **4**, 261–265.

MANOSEVITZ, M. (1970) Early environmental enrichment and mouse behavior. *Journal of Comparative and Physiological Psychology* **71**, 459–466.

MAKANJUOLA, R. O. A., HILL, G., MABEN, I., DOW, R. C. and ASHCROFT, G. W. (1977) An automated method for studying exploratory and stereotyped behaviour in rats. *Psychopharmacology* **52**, 271–277.

MAYES, A. (1979) The physiology of fear and anxiety. In *Fear in Animals and Man* (Ed. W. SLUCKIN). London: Van Nostrand Reinhold.

MONTGOMERY, K. C. (1952a) A test of two explanations of spontaneous alternation. *Journal of Comparative and Physiological Psychology* **45**, 287–293.

MONTGOMERY, K. C. (1952b) Exploratory behavior and its relation to spontaneous alternation in a series of maze exposures. *Journal of Comparative and Physiological Psychology* **45**, 50–57.

MONTGOMERY, K. C. (1953a) Exploratory behavior as a function of 'similarity' of stimulus situations. *Journal of Comparative and Physiological Psychology* **46** , 129–133.

MONTGOMERY, K. C. (1953b) The effect of activity deprivation upon exploratory behavior. *Journal of Comparative and Physiological Psychology* **46**, 438–441.

MONTGOMERY, K. C. (1954) The role of the exploratory drive in learning. *Journal of Comparative and Physiological Psychology* **47**, 60–64.

MONTGOMERY, K. C. (1955) The relation between fear induced by novel stimulation and exploratory behavior. *Journal of Comparative and Physiological Psychology* **48**, 254–260.

MONTGOMERY, K. C. and SEGALL, M. (1955) Discrimination learning based upon the exploratory drive. *Journal of Comparative and Physiological Psychology* **48**, 225–228.

MOWRER, O. H. (1960) *Learning Theory and Behavior*. New York: Wiley.

MYERS, A. K. and MILLER, N. E. (1954) Failure to find a learned drive based on hunger: evidence for learning motivated by 'exploration'. *Journal of Comparative and Physiological Psychology* **47**, 428–436.

O'KEEFE, J. and NADEL, L. (1978) *The Hippocampus as a Cognitive Map*. Oxford: Clarendon Press.

PREMACK, D. and COLLIER, G. (1962) Analysis of nonreinforcement variables affecting response probability. *Psychological Monographs* **76**, Whole No. 524.

PREMACK, D., COLLIER, G. and ROBERTS, C. L. (1957) Frequency of light-contingent bar pressing as a function of the amount of deprivation of light. *American Psychologist* **12**, 411 (Abstract).

PRICE, E. O. and HUCK, U. W. (1976) Open-field behavior of wild and domestic Norway rats. *Animal Learning and Behavior* **4**, 125–130.

RUSSELL, E. M. and PEARCE, G. A. (1971) Exploration of novel objects by marsupials. *Behaviour* **40**, 312–322.

RUSSELL, P. A. (1973a) Relationships between exploratory behaviour and fear: a review. *British Journal of Psychology* **64**, 417–433.

RUSSELL, P. A. (1973b) Sex differences in rats' stationary-cage activity measured by observation and automatic recording. *Animal Learning and Behavior* **1**, 278–282.

RUSSELL, P. A. (1975) Sex differences in rats' response to novelty measured by activity and preference. *Quarterly Journal of Experimental Psychology* **27**, 585–589.

RUSSELL, P. A. (1977) Sex differences in rats' stationary exploration as a function of stimulus and environmental novelty. *Animal Learning and Behavior* **5**, 297–302.

RUSSELL, P. A. (1979) Fear-evoking stimuli. In *Fear in Animals and Man* (Ed. W. SLUCKIN). London: Van Nostrand Reinhold.

RUSSELL, P. A. and CHALKY-MABER, C. J. W. (1979) Effects of conspecific odor on rats' position and behavior in an open field. *Animal Learning and Behavior* **7**, 387–391.

RUSSELL, P. A. and WILLIAMS, D. I. (1973) Effects of repeated testing on rat's locomotor activity in the open-field. *Animal Behaviour* **21**, 109–112.

SALES, S. M. (1968) Stimulus complexity as a determinant of approach behaviour and inspection time in the hooded rat. *Canadian Journal of Psychology* **22**, 11–17.

SALZEN, E. A. (1962) Imprinting and fear. *Symposium of the Zoological Society of London* **8**, 199–218.

SALZEN, E. A. (1970) Imprinting and environmental learning. In *Development and Evolution of Behavior* (Eds. L. R. ARONSON, E. TOBACH, D. S. LEHRMAN and J. S. ROSENBLATT). San Francisco: Freeman.

SALZEN, E. A. (1979) The ontogeny of fear in animals. In *Fear in Animals and Man* (Ed. W. SLUCKIN). London: Van Nostrand Reinhold.

SATINDER, K. P. (1968) A note on the correlation between open field and escape-avoidance behvior in the rat. *Journal of Psychology* **69**, 3–6.

SCHNEIDER, G. E. and GROSS, C. G. (1964) Curiosity in the hamster. *Journal of Comparative and Physiological Psychology* **59**, 150–152.

SCHNEIRLA, T. C. (1959) An evolutionary and developmental theory of biphasic processes underlying approach and withdrawal. In *Nebraska Symposium on Motivation* (Ed. M. R. JONES). Lincoln: University of Nebraska Press.

SHELDON, M. H. (1968) Exploratory behaviour: the inadequacy of activity measures. *Psychonomic Science* **11**, 38.

SHERRICK, M. F., BRUNNER, R. L., ROTH, T. G. and DEMBER, W. N. (1979) Rats' sensitivity to their direction of movement and spontaneous alternation behaviour. *Quarterly Journal of Psychology* **31**, 83–93.

SINCLAIR, J. D. and BENDER, D. O. (1978) Compensatory behaviors: suggestion for a common basis from deficits in hamsters. *Life Sciences* **22**, 1407–1412.

SMALL, W. S. (1899) Notes on the psychic development of the young white rat. *American Journal of Psychology* **11**, 80–100.

SOKOLOV, E. M. (1960) Neuronal models and the orienting reflex. In *The Central Nervous System and Behavior* (Ed. M. A. B. BRAZIER). New York: Josiah Macy Jr. Foundation.

STAHL, J. M., O'BRIEN, R. A. and HANFORD, P. (1973) Visual exploratory behavior in the pigeon. *Bulletin of the Psychonomic Society* **1**, 35–36.

SUTHERLAND, N. S. (1957) Spontaneous alternation and stimulus avoidance. *Journal of Comparative and Physiological Psychology* **50**, 358–362.

TAYLOR, G. T. (1974) Stimulus change and complexity in exploratory behavior. *Animal Learning and Behavior* **2**, 115–118.

TOLMAN, E. C. (1925) Purpose and cognition: the determiners of animal learning. *Psychological Review* **32**, 285–297.

VALLE, F. P. (1972) Free and forced exploration in rats as a function of between- vs. within-S design. *Psychonomic Science* **29**, 11–13.

WALKER, E. L. (1964) Psychological complexity as a basis of a theory of motivation and choice. In *Nebraska Symposium on Motivation* (Ed. D. LEVINE). Lincoln: University of Nebraska Press.

WALKER, E. L. (1970) Complexity and preference in animals and men. *Annals of the New York Academy of Sciences* **169**, 619–652.

WEINBERG, J., KRAHN, E. A. and LEVINE, S. (1976) Differential effects of handling on exploration in male and female rats. *Developmental Psychobiology* **11**, 251–259.

WEISLER, A. and McCALL, R. B. (1976) Exploration and play: resume and redirection. *American Psychologist* **31**, 492–508.

WELKER, W. I. (1956) Variability of play and exploration behavior in chimpanzees. *Journal of Comparative and Physiological Psychology* **49**, 181–185.

WELKER, W. I. (1957) 'Free' versus 'forced' exploration of a novel situation by rats. *Psychological Reports* **3**, 95–108.

WELKER, W. I. (1959) Escape, exploratory and food-seeking responses of rats in a novel situation. *Journal of Comparative and Physiological Psychology* **52**, 106–111.

WELKER, W. I. (1961) An analysis of exploratory and play behavior in animals. In *Functions of Varied Experience* (Eds. D. W. FISKE and S. R. MADDI). Homewood. I11.: Dorsey.

WHIMBEY, A. E. and DENENBERG, V. H. (1967) Two independent behavioral dimensions in open field performance. *Journal of Comparative and Physiological Psychology* **63**, 500–504.

WILLIAMS, C. D. and KUCHTA, J. C. (1957) Exploratory behavior in two mazes with dissimilar alternatives. *Journal of Comparative and Physiological Psychology* **50**, 509–513.

WILLIAMS, D. I. (1972) Effects of electric shock on exploratory behaviour in the rat. *Quarterly Journal of Experimental Psychology* **24**, 544–546.

WILLIAMS, D. I. and RUSSELL, P. A. (1972) Open-field behaviour in rats: effects of handling, sex and repeated testing. *British Journal of Psychology* **63**, 593–596.

WILLIAMS, D. I. and WELLS, P. A. (1970) Differences in home-cage emergence in the rat in relation to infantile handling. *Psychonomic Science* **18**, 168–169.

WONG, R. and BOWLES, L. J. (1976) Exploration of complex stimuli as facilitated by emotional reactivity and shock. *American Journal of Psychology* **89**, 527–534.

WOODS, P. J. (1962) Behavior in a novel situation as influenced by the immediately preceding environment. *Journal of the Experimental Analysis of Behavior* **5**, 185–190.

WYCKOFF, L. B. (1952) The role of observing responses in discrimination learning. Part 1. *Psychological Review* **59**, 431–442.

CHAPTER 3

Exploration as a Motivational and Learning System: A Cognitive Incentive View

Frederick M. Toates

3.1 Introduction

In this review, I shall consider a modern interpretation of exploratory behaviour, in terms of incentive and cognitive theories, and place emphasis upon 'spatial' or 'cognitive maps'. I do not intend to provide a comprehensive historical review of exploration. However, it is relevant to look at some previous models, in order to understand possible alternative ways of viewing exploratory behaviour and to contrast the older models with the ideas developed here. Theories of exploration arise in the context of more general theories of motivation and learning that are favoured at any point in time. Hence, to some extent, this chapter is also a review of some contemporary cognitive approaches to animal behaviour.

My own orientation, which is advanced here, is towards what I like to term *cognitive-behaviourism*. To some people, this expression would be an impossible compound of polar-opposites, but I do not accept that view (see Spiker, 1977, for a similar argument). I see cognitive-behaviourism as the logical development of both behaviourism and cybernetics. By 'cognitive', I mean simply that animals are able to code external events and the relationship between these events in their nervous systems (see also Chapter 4). They do this independently of whether they ever exploit this information in overt behaviour (Dickinson, 1980). By the use of the term 'behaviourism', I am making, first, a dedication to the rigours of empirical observation. Secondly, my own emphasis is upon a faith in mechanistic and cybernetic models couched in definable, and preferably quantifiable, terms. In such terms, in order to qualify as a viable explanation of the processes underlying behaviour, one should be able to build a machine that exhibits the properties of the proposed system. The line advanced here is, I believe, a logical development of the theoretical positions adopted by Hull (1952) and Tolman (1932).

This review looks at the general question of the acquisition of information by animals, of which exploratory behaviour, active investigation, is a part. An attempt is made to fit exploratory behaviour into the broader context of what

55

kind of information animals acquire and how they utilize this information. We are not yet in a position to present a model of the motivational basis of exploratory behaviour that is in any way comparable to those of, say, drinking or feeding (Toates, 1980). However, we are able to formalize some aspects of the motivational system and hopefully more formal and integrated models will thereby arise in the future.

3.2 Background

3.2.1 *Traditional Behaviourist Models and S - R Theories*

Exploration has usually fitted rather uncomfortably into general theories of motivation. For instance, the model of behaviour favoured in the first half of this century was that animals are 'pushed' into action by inner states of drive, such as those arising from energy depletion or seminal-vesicle fluid pressure (e.g. Hull, 1952). In such terms, the behaviour that results from the drive (e.g. energy gain, ejaculation) causes a reduction in drive level. It is not at all clear how one would fit exploration to such a model. Some authors have proposed a boredom drive (see Chapter 4), arising from lack of sensory stimulation: exploration would then correct the boredom. There are several problems with such a model. Beyond the parsimony of fitting exploration to a more general model, it has little or no explanatory value. One only supposes that the animal is bored because it subsequently explores; boredom is an unhelpful mentalistic construct. In addition what little evidence there is that deprivation of exploratory opportunity does energize subsequent exploration is ambiguous (see, e.g. Bolles, 1975).

3.2.2 *Two-Factor Theories of Motivation*

There is a certain attraction in devising general models that apply to any motivation system, and various attempts have been made to do that. However, other researchers have preferred to divide motivational states into two broad classes, according to whether they are primarily externally or internally driven (Grossman, 1967), a view that still arises occasionally (e.g. Roper, 1981). For example, hunger would be said to be primarily internally driven, whereas, exploration and sex would be said to be more strongly aroused by external factors. Hunger would be caused by low internal energy states, whereas the latter would be aroused by, respectively, novel stimuli and a conspecific (though hormonal factors would modulate sexual arousability). Admittedly, the dichotomy is useful in pointing to physiologically vital functions such as hydration, energy state and body-temperature, in which measurable internal states play a powerful role in the causation of behaviour. Unless these states are confined within a certain range, death will result. Nothing analogous occurs (as far as we know!) for deprivation of sex or exploratory opportunity. However, a dichotomy in terms of states that *can* reach lethal regions and states that appear not to be able to do so refers to function (McFarland & Nunez, 1978) and not to causal mechanisms. To translate uncritically from such a dichotomy back to the causal level can lead one to overlook the fact that external factors are vital in the arousal of feeding and drinking (Toates, 1981). Conversely, internal factors are vital in sex and exploration, and this is saying much more than simply that an animal needs a nervous system in order to copulate or explore. Certainly, some animals show sexual satiety and, normally, internal processes must recover before the animal can be rearoused. In the case of exploration, the supposed external cue, novelty, is not simply a fixed property of particular objects but can only be defined in terms of (1) the animal's history of exposure to various objects in various locations *and* (2) the particular object in question. Thus, the dichotomy is weak. All motivational states appear to involve internal and external factors. To attribute weightings to their importance only creates new problems. For example, how much is sex internally and how much is it externally aroused? To some extent the problems with such a dichotomy are solved if we adopt a version of incentive-motivation theory.

3.2.3   Incentive-Motivation Theories

Incentive theories emphasize the role of environmental stimuli in arousing motivational states (see also Estes, 1969); hunger is aroused by food and sexual arousal is caused by a partner. Perhaps the best known theorist in this tradition is Bindra (1969, 1978, 1979) who speaks of internal states (e.g. energy state) as 'gating' the power of external stimuli (e.g. food cues) to arouse motivational states (e.g. hunger). To use hunger as an example, if energy is deficient food will be sought, whereas in energy surfeit the same food may be avoided. In the case of hunger and thirst, an incentive-based model makes predictions that conform better to the experimental evidence than explanations in terms of simply defending fixed internal set-points (see Toates, 1981; Toates & Birke, 1982). In such terms, sexual motivation is seen as sharing important characteristics with hunger and thirst. Each is aroused by external stimuli. In both cases, internal states (energy, water or 'sexual arousability') set limits on, or accentuate, the power of external stimuli to arouse the particular type of behaviour.

Applying this logic to exploration, objects in the environment might be described as having 'potential incentive value'. Whether they do, in fact, elicit investigation depends upon factors internal to the animal. Later, the argument will be developed that this internal factor is associated with, amongst other factors, disparity between incoming information and internal models of the environment.

Let me hasten to add that, in attempting to produce a general model of motivation, I am not trying to tailor the evidence on exploration to fit a model that is really applicable only to ingestive behaviour. However, I believe it to be useful to consider *features* that these motivational systems may share, and this may lead to a more universally applicable theory.

3.2.4 What Animals Learn

Exploratory behaviour is generally described as that which has the acquisition of information as its consequence. In this review, I shall emphasize the kind of information that animals acquire and exploit. Traditional behaviourist theories made some rather specific statements in this area. Consider the question of spatial locations, and see the maze shown in Fig .3.1. The hungry rat runs from the south end and when it turns to the east it obtains food. According to a stimulus – response view, the link between stimuli at the choice point and the bodily response of turning right become strengthened by finding food. By contrast, failure to find food by turning left weakens that stimulus – response connection. A more cognitive interpretation would be that, assuming suitable landmarks are available outside the maze, then the rat learns something about the *place* of food. For example, it extrapolates from other cues associated with the direction of east. Suppose the rat is released from the north. According to S – R theory, it should turn west but according to a more cognitive view, if extra-maze cues are available, it should turn east. The answer is that, according to the circumstances, rats tend to follow one or the other strategy, but for our purposes the interesting point is that they certainly can work on the basis of place,

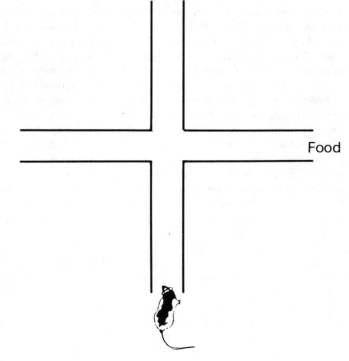

Food

Fig. 3.1   Maze.

58

independent of the actual responses involved in moving through that environment (cf. the swimming task referred to in Chapter 5). According to the S – R view, knowledge of the environment *is* nothing more than the linkage between stimulus and response; knowledge has no independent existence. We now know that although knowledge can be held in this form, it need not necessarily be. A similar argument applies to lever pressing in the Skinner box. Rats do not appear to learn simply to make a fixed muscular response of depressing the lever; a variety of actual mechanical acts may serve this end. It seems that rats learn a general rule of the kind 'lowering the lever causes food to appear', which they exploit by a variety of means (cf. Bindra, 1978; Bolles, 1972).

3.3   Evidence for a Cognitive Model

By a cognitive model, I do not mean a return to mentalism. I simply mean that, in their brains, animals form representations of objects and events in both their external and internal environments. They also code the relationships between such events. Simply by being *exposed* to stimuli, animals can form internal representations of them. These representations may, or may not, relate directly to overt behavioural reactions associated with these stimuli (Dickinson, 1980). Exploration, such as roaming in a maze or observing stimuli, is behaviour that involves the assimilation of information concerning the form of objects, their spatial lay-out and the causal relationship between events. Over the years, the cognitive position has gained strength from several sources. I shall now review some of these and show their relevance to exploratory behaviour, ultimately with reference to motivation.

3.3.1   Cognitive Maps

The classical studies of Tinbergen & Kryut (1938), showed that, on leaving the burrow, the digger wasp makes an observation of the surrounding area. It forms a memory, a cognitive map, of the landmarks and their spatial relationship. I would refer to the behaviour of flying around and observing as 'exploratory behaviour', since it is a process of information assimilation. Only later, on returning, does the wasp exploit this information in its movements.

Tolman (1932) showed that rats form 'spatial' or 'cognitive maps' of their environment. Significant features of the environment and the spatial relationship between these features are coded within the animal's nervous system. On the basis of this information, the animal can synthesize new routes and make predictions concerning routes it has experienced. Fig. 3.2 illustrates this. Rats are able to use routes 1, 2 or 3 in order to get from the start box to the goal box, and were observed to make each of these choices. Then, on a particular trial, route 1 is found to be blocked, as shown by the dotted line. On retracing its footsteps, the rat tends more often to take route 2 than route 3, i.e. it extrapolates that route 3 is also blocked by the barrier. In cognitive language, as

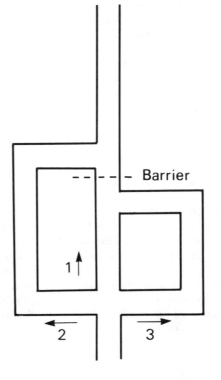

Fig. 3.2   Maze.

a result of the rat's observation, an internal representation of the route is labelled 'blocked'.

Menzel (1978) described the form of exploration in chimpanzees. When placed in a complex and novel environment, they tend, first, to establish a *base*. They then move out to explore other features of the environment, but make frequent returns to the base. These experimental observations are entirely compatible with the view that exploration is concerned with establishing cognitive maps in which important landmarks are labelled. Presumably the base would form the first point of reference in such a map.

In an experiment by Menzel, chimpanzees were able to observe (i.e. explore, in a broad sense of the word) an experimenter hiding food in various locations. They were then released and were seen to remove food from the various sites by following a very efficient route between the sites. One would conclude that locations within the animal's cognitive map were first labelled 'food' and then the label modified after the animal had removed food from that location. Similarly, in rats, exploration of a complex maze is systematic (see Olton, 1979); the rat seems to follow an optimum strategy for covering the territory in a relatively short space of time and not revisiting arms. In a sense, the rat ticks off arms as it visits them. Such results, when viewed in the context of the cognitive-map theory, suggest a systematic confirmation of the map involving goal specification of one region of the maze after the other. Such exploration may be cursory if no disparity arises, or more lengthy if disparity does appear.

Deutsch's Model. The argument that animals form cognitive maps of their environments is an interesting one, but the issue raises many problems. Possession of a map does not necessarily tell one how to act in relation to the map (Gallistel, 1980). Have we left the rat buried in thought? Does a homunculus, a map-reader, have to appear within the nervous system? A pioneering attempt at meeting such problems was made by Deutsch (1960) in a once very influential, but now somewhat neglected book entitled *Structural Basis of Behaviour.* Deutsch argued that particular objects in the rat's environment were represented by *links* in its nervous system. The details need not concern us, but the essential principle is highly relevant. One link might represent the site of food (y), whereas another might represent a landmark (x) that leads to food. Now suppose that the animal is relatively energy depleted. This energy depletion sensitizes the link associated with the site of food (y). Suppose stimuli from point y in the environment impinge upon the animal. These activate link y, which was already sensitized by energy depletion. Suppose then, by these influences, that link y becomes the most strongly activated link. Thereby, according to Deutsch, it forms the goal of the animal's behaviour. The animal then moves towards this goal.

By virtue of the fact that landmark x leads to the food site y, links x and y form an association within the animal's nervous system. Excitation of link y by food deprivation causes, in turn, excitation of link x. So now consider the case where stimuli from x impinge upon the animal, stimuli from y being out of range. Having the strongest activated link, target x will form the immediate goal of the animal's behaviour. On gaining contact with x, y will come into view and hence form the new goal. In other words, getting to food involves ascending through a series of landmarks each bringing it nearer to the goal. This is essentially an incentive model; the animal moves towards the stimulus whose link is most strongly activated.

The model should be thought of as being a viable account of how the nervous system and behaviour *could be* organized. The details may well be oversimplified, but the model is a shining example of the usefulness of a systems approach in suggesting processes underlying behaviour. In several ways, Deutsch's model is relevant to exploration. In his terms, exploration of an environment establishes internal representations of significant landmarks (links) and associations between them. We would now describe this as a *cognitive map.* The links represent sites of food, water, escape routes, etc., and cues leading to them. There is no need for the animal to be deprived of food and to ingest it for a site to be labelled as food, though this may well help. Similarly, even if the rat is passively transported through the maze, it can still learn about the configuration of the maze (see Deutsch, 1960). Deutsch's model gives a formal and scientifically precise meaning to the term 'goal-directed behaviour': the most strongly activated link forms the goal. It shows how a mechanism could yield such behaviour. If the animal is food deprived, then stimuli associated with food may provide the goal. From this it would seem a logical step to argue that various sites and objects with no particular significance as far as food, water, etc., are concerned can equally form the goals of activity, i.e. when the animal roams or patrols. In these terms, such 'neutral' objects would seem to be able to gain control of behaviour at somewhat regular intervals as reflected in the frequency of patrolling (cf. Barnett & Cowan, 1976: see Chapter 6).

O'Keefe and Nadel's Model.   O'Keefe & Nadel (1978) proposed what has become a highly influential and controversial theory of cognitive mapping that has many similarities to that of Deutsch. They closely associate the hippocampus with the function of cognitive mapping. Theirs is an extensive argument involving detailed neuroanatomy, and it goes beyond the brief of this chapter, although it is described more fully in Chapter 5. However, the model is of vital relevance to motivation theory in general, and to exploration in particular. We shall therefore need to discuss it· at some length here.

O'Keefe and Nadel suggest that the cognitive mapping system contains a map for each environment with which the organism has gained experience. They claim that:

> The animal brings to a new situation a *tabula rasa* of potential place representations. One of these is chosen to represent a specific location in the environment; this automatically determines the way in which the remainder of the locations in the environment will be represented.

More precisely, it may prove not to be the case that a *tabula rasa* is the correct expression. Similar situations may have been experienced in the past, and this might give some prior structure to the new representation.

According to the interpretation of O'Keefe and Nadel, exploration is behaviour that, first, builds, and then revises, cognitive maps. O'Keefe and Nadel propose that *misplace detectors* serve to detect disparity between incoming sensory information and the internal representations that the animal already possesses for that environment. For example, suppose an animal has extensively explored an environment. Then a large new object is placed there. On subsequently encountering this environment, the new object will not have a representation in the cognitive map in question. Therefore misplace detectors will be activated and exploration of the environment aroused until the internal representation is updated (this runs parallel to earlier views on exploration, such as those of Halliday, 1967). Even a familiar object will be explored if it is placed in an unfamiliar location. Thus, the labelling of objects is specific to the location that they normally occupy, i.e. in terms of the cognitive map.

O'Keefe and Nadel go on to discuss how the cognitive map enables desired sites to be reached, dangerous locations to be circumvented, etc. They propose an explanation that is similar to that of Deutsch. As an example, they consider an animal that has explored an environment while satiated for food, and has formed a cognitive map of the environment including a label for the food site.

62

Later, it finds itself energy depleted and in the territory concerned. How might a cognitive map guide it to food? They state:

> Let us assume that, in addition to a generalised subliminal excitation of all place representations connected together into one map which ensures whenever any two or more parts of a map are activated, hunger specifically excites those place representations where food has been experienced. These two will sum, bringing the representation of the place containing food in that environment close to activation.

The system then executes appropriate motor behaviour to take the animal from where it is presently to the food site.

O'Keefe & Nadel give a primary role to mismatch as the causal factor underlying exploration, but acknowledge that familiar stimuli are also explored. They describe this as the animal '. . . making a cursory check to ensure that nothing has changed.' I would prefer to see such exploration as lying on a continuum with mismatch-induced exploration. In this way, one can avoid mentalistic terms. Successive parts of the cognitive map form the goal of the animal's behaviour.

In the case of the rat, it would roam around making a cursory inspection of its established territory. According to this interpretation, if no mismatch occurs, exploration is rapid, otherwise a more lengthy investigation is involved. However, as much as I would agree with O'Keefe and Nadel's analysis, I would prefer to see mismatch as either one causal factor amongst several or as a factor that is itself influenced by various other factors. For instance, given an appropriate hormonal condition, odours may be particularly strongly explored. It is somewhat unconvincing just to argue that disparity is particularly high. At this point one starts to ask where exploration ceases and sexual behaviour takes over (see also Toates & Birke, 1982, for a discussion of similar problems associated with disparity as the determinant of aggression). The answer may be to see sexual arousal as accentuating exploration of certain cues.

3.3.2 Learning Theory

Cognitive maps represent information about the environment in a form that is independent of particular responses attached to the animal's commerce with that environment. Contemporary learning theory suggests that this general principle of information storage has a rather wide application as far as the nervous system is concerned.

As I have mentioned earlier, animals learn about events in their environment irrespective of whether or not, at the time of learning, a response is associated with the event (Dickinson, 1980). Take the traditional Pavlovian situation, for example. Food (the UCS) causes the response of salivation (the UCR). A bell is paired a few times with the food, and then the bell acting on its own (the CS), is able to cause salivation (the CR). A traditional behaviourist account of this phenomenon would be that the *response* of salivation simply becomes linked with the bell: 'Knowledge' *is* the S – R connection. However, there are now several examples showing that animals can learn that a stimulus (1) is associated in time with another stimulus (2) even though, at the time of learning, the stimuli were not associated with any particular response. Later, when a response is appropriate, such learning is revealed in overt behaviour. For example, suppose that, first a bell (E_1) is paired a number of times with a light (E_2). Then the light, but not the bell, is paired with shock (E_3). Subsequently, presentation of the bell alone causes a conditioned fear reaction. However the light alone is also able to cause some fear reaction, despite the fact that it has never been paired with shock (see Dickinson, 1980, for a review). A cognitive interpretation of this phenomenon is that the animal forms internal representations of E_1 and E_2 and their positive correlation of occurence, i.e. E_1 predicts E_2, represented as $(E_1 \rightarrow E_2)$. In some way, presentation of E_1 calls up an internal representation of E_2, so that, by virtue of presenting E_1 alone the animal acts, to some extent, *as if E_2* has happened. In other words it anticipates E_2's occurence. By extension of this argument, E_1 evokes an expectation of E_2, which, even in E_2's absence, evokes an expectation of E_3.

For several reasons, contemporary learning theory is particularly relevant to exploratory behaviour. Exploration, in the broad sense of the word, serves not only to establish internal representations of external objects but also external events and their causal relationships. By observing stimuli and by more active investigation, (e.g. manipulation of objects) such information can be assimilated. Animals tend to manipulate their environment. For instance, rats will perform operant responses for a change in illumination (Glow, 1970). In this experiment, depression of the lever in the Skinner box leads to a change in illumination $(E_1 \rightarrow E_2)$. Such knowledge may later be exploited to some end. Although, in this context, learning theory is relevant to understanding what the animal is assimilating, at present it is not clear as to how we translate this into an interpretation of the appropriate motivational mechanism.

An important phenomenon in contemporary learning theory is known as *surprise* (Kamin, 1969). Again, I believe that one need not abandon behaviourist principles in order to accommodate this. The following example will show what is meant by the term. Suppose that, over a series of trials, a stimulus E_1 (e.g. a tone) comes on 5 s before a shock (E_2), and the rat learns to take evasive action on presentation of the tone. Then a compound stimulus consisting of the tone (E_1) plus another stimulus, E_1^1 (e.g. a light), is presented over a number of trials and, as in the first phase of learning, is followed 5 s later by shock (for some animals E_1 is a tone and E_1^1 a light, for others, the reverse design is employed). The animal takes evasive action in response to the compound stimulus. Then the ability of E_1^1 *alone* to evoke evasive action is tested. Typically, it shows rather little power. The argument is that, under such conditions, E_2 is totally expected; E_1 adequately predicted it and so E_1^1 carries no additional information. To use the favoured expression, the shock is not surprising. When a surprising event occurs, it is as if the animal searches, in its memory, for a cue that precedes the event and that could be used in the future in order to predict the event.

64

Kamin (1969) writes:

> . . . it is necessary that the US provoke the animal into a 'backward scanning' of its memory store of recent stimulus input; only as a result of such a scan can an association between CS and US be formed, and the scan is prompted only by an unpredicted US, the occurrence of which is surprising.

There would seem to be a rather close parallel between two such kinds of 'searching', as follows. The animal's nervous system can form a predictive association between E_1 (e.g. a tone) and E_2 (e.g. shock) where little or no overt exploratory behaviour is shown, though the animal may orient towards the source of the sound. Alternatively, if a significant event occurs, animals may more actively explore their environment following the event. This would serve the function of finding a possible predictive cue for the event. For instance, the Halliday – Lester theory (see Russell, 1973, and Chapter 2 for a review) that fear increases exploration is based largely on the observation that rats tend to explore an area of a maze in which they have experienced a shock. A model based upon a search initiated by a significant event would seem a more parsimonious explanation than that fear motivates exploration. The rat's exploration is prompted by the significant event: shock. Placing a slightly different emphasis, Russell (1973) refers to possible disparity between a now-safe location and a previously dangerous location. He writes:

> . . . since the least equivocal evidence of apparent facilitatory effects of fear on exploration comes from studies demonstrating a preference for stimuli previously associated with shock, it may be possible to explain these results by assuming that the shocked rats in these studies have a greater need for information about these stimuli and so explore them more. In effect, a stimulus previously *but no longer* associated with stressful stimulation will have *greater incongruity* than it will for an animal which experiences the same stimulus without having previously had it paired with shock. Greater exploration in the former case may occur not because the animal is more motivated by its fear of the stimulus (in fact it explores *despite* a certain amount of fear) but because the stimulus is more incongruous.

Normally in classical conditioning the CS must appear *before* the UCS in order for conditioning to occur. For example, the tone should ideally appear about 1 s or so before the food in order to get good salivary conditioning. However, in the special case of a sudden aversive stimulus as the UCS, the CS may appear slightly after the UCS and still conditioning occurs (Keith-Lucas & Guttman, 1975), particularly conditioning to a predator-like object. This might seem to have adaptive significance; cues associated with a predator might only become apparent after the predator has struck. Again, we have an example of the animal establishing predictive relationships. In a particular experiment, carried out by Hudson and reviewed by Lewis (1979), post-response learning was shown. No avoidance learning to electric shock was obtained if apparatus cues were removed immediately following the shock. If, however, the animal was, to use Tolman's expression, able to 'look back and see what happened' then avoidance was learned. This seems again to be an example of a search for predictive cues being initiated by a significant event.

65

3.3.3 Memory

In experimental psychology, the study of memory has produced various models. Full discussion of these goes beyond our brief, but some aspects of this area are directly relevant to understanding exploration.

In a comprehensive theory of memory, Lewis (1979) argues against the usefulness of the short-term memory/long-term memory distinction and instead proposes a new dichotomy; active and inactive memories. A memory may be active under either of two circumstances: (1) when it is for sensory information that has just arrived; or (2) when a relatively long-established memory is actually being used in solving a problem. Active memory is a small subset of the total memory store of the animal. At any point in time, inactive memory is the vast store of memories that the animal retains but are not actually in use. Suppose that an animal has established a memory that a particular tone predicts electric shock and that the animal can avoid the shock by jumping from site A to B. In Lewis's terms, presentation of the tone would revive the memory of the shock (it would become active) and the rat would act on the basis of the shock's imminent occurrence (see also Estes, 1969, for a similar argument). Note the essential similarity with contemporary learning theory, i.e. tone → shock.

Lewis argues that following, say, an unexpected presentation of electric shock, 'the animal is trying to "make sense" out of what happened, to relate the event to the remainder of its experience'. I would express 'making sense' in the following terms. Significant events initiate a retrospective search in memory for predictive cues. They also promote exploration of the environment in order to establish predictive cues. In Lewis's terms, the animal is searching for cues that, on their future presentation, will reinstate the memory of the shock. Traditionally, in such experiments, a tone is used as the predictive cue. If no such cue ever occurs then the location in general may be labelled as dangerous. Thus, Lewis (1979) notes that an animal placed into a standard experimental environment and given a shock to the feet will attempt to:

> . . . distinguish the part of the environment that gives pain or annoyance from the other parts, to place events in context. This is, of course, further learning, but it occurs *after* the learning that the footshock (or something painful) occurred. It involves coding the target memory into a context that yields an increase in retrievability.

A cognitive view of memory that fits neatly to that of Lewis is represented by the experiment of Albert & Mah (1972) and the theoretical conclusions that these authors draw. This particular experiment looks at exploratory behaviour. In their home cages, rats had a history of obtaining water from a metal spout. Then, when not water-deprived, rats were placed in a novel environment having a nook containing an empty water spout. They spent time exploring this environment. Later, the spout was removed, and rats were returned to the environment, some being water-deprived and others not water-deprived. Time spent exploring the empty nook was significantly greater in those that were water-deprived than in those that were not. This motivation-specific exploration applied specifically to the water-spout (as a control condition, another metal object of similar size was used). Presumably, over the period of the rat's earlier experience with such spouts, it would have formed an internal representation of a spout. When placed in the test environment, the rat would have formed a cognitive map of the environment, and, with the assistance of the earlier inner representation of the spout, would have labelled the nook as a location in the map appropriate for re-hydration (though, see Tolman, 1949, for a review of the limits to which exposure to food and water is able to label the appropriate sites in a cognitive representation). Later, when the animal is put back thirsty, then presumably the state of hydration would have accentuated that aspect of the map relevant to water (the spout and nook) and this would have formed the animal's goal. Thus, even in the spout's absence it can form a goal. These authors conclude that:

> . . . in the thirsty animal the central neural circuitry representing the spout is activated at the time the animal is put into the apparatus on the test day. Presumably the rat responds behaviourally to this internally generated neural stimulus in a manner that is similar (but not identical) to its response to neural activity originating at a peripheral sense organ.

3.4   An Overview and Synthesis

Several interesting and challenging theoretical and philosophical questions are raised by the contemporary discussion of motivation and learning theory. To anchor the present section in slightly secure ground, I must state the premise that the behaviour of an animal is determined only by events *at present* occurring in its nervous system. It is necessary to make that point merely to remind the reader of the commonsense view that events in the future cannot influence what happens in the present. However, this basic assumption is not incompatible with claiming that inner *representations* of what is likely to occur in the future can influence what happens in the present. More precisely, it means that, on the basis of past experience, events not actually present, that is future (i.e. with regard to time) and distant (i.e. with regard to geographical location) events are represented (coded) within the nervous system. We have discussed examples in both the spatial and temporal domains. A distant goal, a site reached in the future, may be said to pull an animal towards it. Translated into the terms of a more precise causal mechanism, this means that parts of an inner neural model of the environment are accentuated so that they form the goal of behaviour. Consider now anticipation of future, rather than distant, events. Suppose a rat anticipates an electric shock by jumping in response to a warning tone. In causal terms, this would be translated to mean that the warning stimulus evokes a neural representation of the shock towards which the animal reacts *as if* shock were occurring. Exploration serves to build models of the world and its causal texture such that the animal is able to anticipate remote events.

Consider now the active exploration of objects, and let us try to place this in a more general context of motivation. To a considerable extent, theorizing in

67

motivation has moved away from the view that the organism is simply driven or energized by internal states. A more satisfactory model is in terms of the arousal of motivational states by biologically appropriate stimuli, acting synergistically with internal states. These stimuli arouse, say, feeding or sex. An incentive model may provide a better framework for considering exploration. Exploration appears to be aroused by synergistic properties of external stimuli *and* internal states. In such terms exploration is apparently not so very different from other motivational systems.

An incentive model does not require us necessarily to divide all examples of behaviour into exclusive categories such as sex-driven or exploration driven. Suppose a rat approaches the site of a particular sex-odour. Is this an expression of sexual behaviour or exploration? It does not need to be categorized as either one or the other. The mechanisms of exploration and sexual arousal may well act in combination to accentuate the value of the cue as a target for approach. In some cases, of course, exploration of an environment is incompatible with, say, eating from a particular food bowl in that environment.

I have so far considered the animal's interaction with objects, such as food, water, a mate or a novel object, when stimuli associated with these objects actually impinge upon the organism's sense organs. Let us now reconsider the situation where the organism is influenced by inner *representations* of objects and events that are not actually present. A great deal of what we study under the heading of motivation is actually the behaviour of getting from one site to a distant site. Escape may consist of little or nothing other than this, and, depending upon the species, food, water, warmth and a sleeping site may be relatively fixed in space. For example, energy depletion may sensitize parts of an inner model of the environment so that the animal is 'pulled' towards food sites. Alternatively, the animal may be pulled towards sites in its environment that are not directly associated with primary biological reinforcers. When in contact with these locations the animal simply explores them (e.g. patrolling). Sites appear to increase in their strength of candidature for gaining control of such exploratory visits as the length of time since the last visit increases.

A rat shows greater alternation in a T-maze if the arms lead to different goal boxes than if they lead to the same goal box (Sutherland, 1957). I would view this in terms of the accentuation of part of a cognitive map as a result of the animal not having so recently visited this part. Upon examining a location, it is as if the nervous system puts a tick against it. For a while, this site takes a lower priority as a candidate for a visit. Rats show a preference for exploring the arm of a maze that has been changed in lightness from when the rat last encountered the arm (see Chapter 4). This is to be seen in terms of disparity between incoming sensory information and stored representations of the environment. Labelling of sites within a cognitive map is an aspect of the foraging strategy of some species. For instance, when in its established territory, the Amakihi, an Hawaiian honeycreeper, rarely revisits a depleted site until a certain minimum time period has elapsed (Kamil, 1978). The time that elapses allows replenishment of nectar. It is hard to escape the interpretation that the bird forms a cognitive map of its environment involving representations of particular food sites. The 'label' attached to these sites is revised by the animals commerce in the environment (see also Olton *et al.*, 1979, for a similar demonstration in rats).

Whereas aspects of exploration, such as those just described, can only be understood in terms of a cognitive map, conversely, the construction of a cognitive map is to be understood in terms of the outcome of exploratory behaviour. In the formation of cognitive maps, landmarks are coded, along with any particular relevance to food, water, aversive stimuli, etc. Exploration serves the vital function of first establishing and then confirming this inner representation. Once an inner representation of an environment is formed, and then a primary biological reinforcer is introduced to the environment it is quickly assimilated into the matrix of established representations.

Having constructed a cognitive map, various sites within the map successively form the goal towards which movement is directed. A site is *specified* as the goal; it forms the set-point of a negative feedback system and the animal moves towards the site as specified by the set-point (see Powers, 1978, for a similar argument). One can imagine a decisionmaker being presented with various *candidate* goals; that having the highest strength would take command. Food deprivation would enhance the strength of candidature of food-related goals. A warning tone that in the past had been the cue for the occurrence of shock would accentuate sites of safety. This model would conform to the view of memory that sees a memory of the shock as being reinstated by the tone: the animal acts as if being shocked. Exploration enables such expectations to be constructed and refined. Migration would involve the specification of a distant goal that would be extrapolated on the basis of cues such as stars and the sun. I have shown how the models described by Deutsch, O'Keefe & Nadel, and others may provide (1) a mechanism for generating exploration and (2) a way of translating cognitive maps into actions, such as food seeking. It may prove possible to extend these models to cover behaviour such as migration.

To use the language of Oatley (1978), the animal needs to hold, in its head, models of the world and the causality of events in the world. Exploration is behaviour that specifically contributes to such information assimilation. Although there is a neurophysiological machinery of object inspection that comes into the service of such exploration, the animal may also assimilate information in less obvious ways — for instance in the course of being under the control of another motivational system. Models may be of particular objects (e.g. inner representation of a water spout), of the relationship between objects (e.g. the spatial map) or of the temporal relationship between events (e.g. tone predicts light). It was shown that contemporary learning theory favours the kind of explanation in which animals form relationships of the kind E_1 predicts E_2.

The idea that animals possess inner representations of external events would be heresy to traditional behaviourists, and it is with some guilt that I adopt this particular language system. It is somehow more satisfying scientifically to follow the Hullian method of avoiding cognitive terms and proposing simple statements couched in mathematical terms. For instance, to say that satiation of a thirst drive works retroactively to strengthen S – R connections seems more parsimonious than to say that rats form inner representations of water spouts. However, the evidence seems to force one into taking a more cognitive view. In some cases, it is possible to build machine analogies that show cognitive processess (e.g., the Deutsch model) and, in this way, I believe it to be possible to integrate cognitive and behaviourist approaches. On a cognitive view, it is not too difficult to propose theories as to how behaviour, such as bar-pressing, arises in hungry animals (Bindra, 1978; Bolles, 1972; Wasserman, 1981). Also the idea that animals learn $E_1 \rightarrow E_2$ relationships in situations unconnected with primary biological incentives is now convincing. In future we need to turn our thoughts to the problem of how the motivational command for exploratory responses such as bar pressing for a change in illumination arises.

References

ALBERT, D. J. and MAH, C. J. (1972) An examination of conditioned reinforcement using a one-trial learning procedure. *Learning and Motivation* 3, 369–388.

BARNETT, S. A. and COWAN, P. E. (1976) Activity, exploration, curiosity and fear: An ethological study. *Interdisciplinary Science Reviews* 1, 43–62.

BINDRA, D. (1969) The inter-related mechanisms of reinforcement and motivation, and the nature of their influence on response. In *Nebraska Symposium on Motivation* (Eds. W. J. ARNOLD and D. LEVINE), pp. 1–33, Lincoln: University of Nebraska Press.

BINDRA, D. (1978) How adaptive behaviour is produced: a perceptual – motivational alternative to response-reinforcement. *The Behavioral and Brain Sciences* 1, 41–92.

BINDRA, D. (1979) Motivation, the brain and psychological theory. Paper presented to the Centennial Symposium, American Psychological Association, New York.

BOLLES, R. C. (1972) Reinforcement, expectancy and learning. *Psychological Review* 79, 394–409.

BOLLES, R. C. (1975) *Theory of Motivation*. New York: Harper and Row.

DEUTSCH, J. A. (1960) *Structural Basis of Behavior*. Chicago: University of Chicago Press.

DICKINSON, A. (1980) *Contemporary Animal Learning Theory*. Cambridge: Cambridge University Press.

ESTES, W. K. (1969) New perspectives on some old issues in association theory. In *Fundamental Issues in Association Learning* (Eds. N. J. MACKINTOSH and W. K. HONIG), pp. 162–189. Halifax: Dalhousie University Press.

GALLISTEL, C. R. (1980) *The Organization of Action — A New Synthesis*. Hillsdale: Lawrence Erlbaum.

GLOW, P. H. (1970) Some acquisition and performance characteristics of response contingent sensory reinforcement. *Australian Journal of Psychology* 22, 145–154.

GROSSMAN, S. P. (1967) *A Textbook of Physiological Psychology*. New York: Wiley.

HALLIDAY, M. S. (1967) Exploratory behaviour. In *Analysis of Behavioural Change* (Ed. L. WEISKRANTZ), pp. 107–126, New York: Harper & Row.

HULL, C. L. (1952) *A Behavior System*. New Haven: Yale University Press.

KAMIL, A. C. (1978) Systematic foraging by a nectar-feeding bird, the Amakihi (*Loxops virens*). *Journal of Comparative and Physiological Psychology* 92, 388–396.

KAMIN, L. J. (1969) Selective association and conditioning. In *Fundamental Issues in Associative Learning* (Eds. N. J. MACKINTOSH and W. K. HONIG), pp. 42–64, Halifax: Dalhousie University Press.

KEITH-LUCAS, T. and GUTTMAN, N. (1975) Robust-single-trial delayed backward conditioning. *Journal of Comparative and Physiological Psychology* **88**, 468–476.

LEWIS, D. J. (1979) Psychobiology of active and inactive memory. *Psychological Bulletin* **86**, 1054–1083.

McFARLAND, D. J. and NUNEZ, A. T. (1978) Systems analysis and sexual behaviour. In *Biological Determinants of Sexual Behaviour* (Ed. J. B. H. HUTCHISON), pp. 615–652. Chichester: Wiley.

MENZEL, E. (1978) Cognitive mapping in chimpanzees. In *Cognitive Processes in Animal Behavior* (Eds. S. H. HULSE, H. FOWLER and W. K. HONIG), pp. 375–422. Hillsdale: Lawrence Erlbaum.

OATLEY, K. (1978) *Perceptions and Representations*. London: Methuen.

O'KEEFE, J. and NADEL, L. (1978) *The Hippocampus as Cognitive Map*. Oxford: Clarendon Press.

OLTON, D. S. (1979) Mazes, maps and memory. *American Psychologist* **34**, 583–596.

OLTON, D. S., BECKER, J. T. and HANDELMANN, G. E. (1979) Hippocampus, space and memory, *The Behavioral and Brain Sciences* **2**, 313–365.

POWERS, W. T. (1978) Quantitative analysis of purposive systems: Some spadework at the foundations of scientific psychology. *Psychological Review* **85**, 417–435.

ROPER, T. J. (1981) Book review of F. M. Toates 'Animal Behaviour — A Systems Approach'. *Quarterly Journal of Experimental Psychology* **33B**, 137–140.

RUSSELL, P. A. (1973) Relationships between exploratory behaviour and fear: A review. *British Journal of Psychology* **64**, 417–433.

SPIKER, C. C. (1977) Behaviorism, cognitive psychology, and the active organism. In *Life-span developmental psychology* (Eds. N. DATAN and H. W. REESE), pp. 93–104. New York: Academic Press.

SUTHERLAND, N. S. (1957) Spontaneous alternation and stimulus avoidance. *Journal of Comparative and Physiological Psychology* **50**, 358–362.

TINBERGEN, N. and KRUYT, W. (1938) Uber die Orientierung des Bienenwolfes. *Zeitshrift für vergleichende Physiologie* **25**, 292–334.

TOATES, F. M. (1980) *Animal Behaviour — A Systems Approach*. Chichester: Wiley.

TOATES, F. M. (1981). The control of ingestive behaviour by internal and external stimuli — A theoretical review. *Appetite* **2**, 35–50.

TOATES, F. M. and BIRKE, L. I. A. (1982). Motivation — A new perspective on some old ideas. In *Perspectives in Ethology, Vol. 5* (Eds. P. BATESON and P. H. KLOPFER). New York: Plenum.

TOLMAN, E. C. (1932). *Purposive Behavior in Animals and Man*. New York: Century.

TOLMAN, E. C. (1949). There is more than one theory of learning. *Psychological Review* **56**, 144–155.

WASSERMAN, E. A. (1981). Response evocation in autoshaping: Contributions of cognitive and comparative - evolutionary analyses to an understanding of directed action. In *Autoshaping and Conditioning Theory* (Eds. C. M. LOCURTO, H. S. TERRACE and J. GIBBON), pp. 21–54. London: Academic Press.

CHAPTER 4

Towards a Cognitive Theory of Exploratory Behaviour

I. R. Inglis

The aim of this chapter is to suggest a framework for a cognitive theory of what Berlyne (1960) termed 'intrinsic exploratory behaviour'; that is, behaviour which is seemingly an end in itself and contains no clear consummatory acts that might link it to specific needs (see Introduction and Chapter 2). A cognitive approach is one that emphasizes that animals are primarily information-processing systems that use previously encoded knowledge to impose upon their environments certain *a priori* interpretive assumptions. As the major function of intrinsic exploration would intuitively appear to be the gathering of information concerning an animal's surroundings, it is strange that cognitive explanations of this activity have been relatively rare. Instead, most workers have attempted to account for such behaviour within the explanatory moulds used for activities clearly connected with reduction of one of the classic need states (e.g. hunger, thirst). In such theories, stimulation-seeking behaviour is subordinate to activities related to need reduction. In this chapter I argue the opposite position, namely that gathering information is the dominant behavioural activity for any animal living in a stochastic environment, and that behaviour directly related to need reduction should be explained as a sub-set within a theory designed primarily to account for stimulation-seeking behaviour. This position may seem eccentric in view of the emphasis frequently placed upon 'optimal' behaviour sequences in relation to need reduction (e.g. McFarland & Houston, 1981). It is however not new, for it was advocated many years ago (e.g. the 'behaviour-primacy theory' — Woodworth, 1958) and then I believe unjustly disregarded. It is also a stance perhaps not too surprising to anyone who has tried to lure a child from a game at a mealtime.

The chapter is organized into two major sections. The first aims to give an idea of the sorts of data that have to be explained while demonstrating how the various explanations that have been founded on need reduction lines have proved inadequate: it does not provide an exhaustive survey of the literature, for there have been several good reviews concerned with exploratory behaviour (e.g. Berlyne, 1960, 1963, 1966; Butler, 1965; Eisenberger, 1972; Fowler, 1965; O'Connell, 1965; Russell, 1973). The second section presents an outline for a cognitive theory of exploratory behaviour. Many of the concepts used are not new; indeed several were proposed around the middle of the century but have been rather neglected under the reductionist climate that until recently has dominated theories of motivation. These old ideas are restated and related to recent findings on attention and memory in the hope that this may stimulate further theories in a similar cognitive vein.

4.1 The Nature of the Problem

Sporadic research on stimulation-seeking behaviour began in the 1920s (e.g. Dashiell, 1925; Nissen, 1930) when it was reported that rats would cross an electrified grid in order to explore novel surroundings. At this time motivation was explained by postulating a drive associated with a basic biological need. Exploration was thought to be a secondary or acquired drive serving one or other of the 'basic' drives, e.g. searching for food. However, the results from latent learning experiments (see Thistlethwaite, 1951) made it apparent that animals could explore and learn about their environment even when their primary needs had been sated. Further Harlow and his co-workers (e.g. Harlow, 1950; Harlow et al., 1956) discovered that hand-reared monkeys that had never had to search for food or water, would nevertheless manipulate puzzles for long periods in the absence of a primary need state. As White (1959, p.299) argued:

> In order to sustain the idea that secondary reinforcement accounts for this fact, we should have to suppose that primary rewards have often been associated with the exploration of novelties. This image may seem to fit mature animals who search the environment for food, but it certainly cannot apply to young animals before they are weaned.

The very young mammal whose attention strays from the nipple to some novel object will only find itself frustrated.

A secondary drive status for exploration was therefore dropped and instead it was proposed that this behaviour had its own drive. Certainly there were many data suggesting deprivation and satiation effects within exploration similar to those found within the classic need states. Lengthening the interval between exposures of novel stimuli has been found in many species to increase the probability of locomotor exploration (e.g. Berlyne, 1955; Fowler, 1965, 1967; Myers & Miller, 1954; Terry, 1979) of visual exploration (e.g. Butler, 1957; Rabedeau & Miles, 1959), of light-contingent bar pressing (e.g. Forgays & Levin, 1958; Fox, 1962; Premack & Collier, 1962), and of manipulation (e.g. Forgays & Levin, 1958; Premack & Bahwell, 1959.) There is a similar mass of data showing a decline in exploration within the session following such an interval; for locomotor exploration (e.g. Berlyne, 1955; Bronstein, 1972; Glanzer, 1961; Inglis, 1975a; Montgomery, 1951, 1955; Montgomery & Monkman, 1955; Montgomery & Zimbardo, 1957; Studelska & Kemble, 1979; Terry, 1979; Welker, 1957; Williams & Kuchka, 1957; Woods, 1962), for visual exploration (e.g. Butler & Harlow, 1954; Inglis, 1975b; Rabedeau & Miles, 1959), for light-contingent bar pressing (Forgays & Levin, 1958; Fox, 1962; Inglis, 1975b; Kling *et al.*, 1956; McCall, 1965, 1966; Premack & Collier, 1962, Wendt *et al.*, 1963) and for manipulation (e.g. Harlow, 1950; Kling *et al.*, 1956; McCall, 1965; Premack & Bahwell, 1959; Walker, 1956). Satiation of a non need-reducing drive was also supported by the data on spontaneous alternation. When rats were given a choice of alternative paths, they alternated consecutive selections with a greater frequency than expected by chance (see Dember & Fowler, 1958). This behaviour could not be totally explained without postulating the avoidance of further contact with the last chosen stimulus (e.g. Dember, 1956; Dember & Fowler, 1958; Eisenberger *et al.*, 1970; Fowler, 1958; Woods & Jennings, 1959). Although some workers failed to find increased exploration with longer inter-stimulus intervals (Charlesworth & Thompson, 1957; Forgays & Levin, 1958; Haude & Ray, 1967) or a decrease in within-session responding (Montgomery, 1955), the high percentage of studies revealing satiation and/or deprivation effects is impressive, and the exceptions have never been organized into a coherent alternative.

Two basic modifications of drive theory were proposed to explain these effects. The first argued that novel objects motivate exploration, and the second postulated that it was the lack of novelty that energized such behaviour. Berlyne (1950) and Harlow (1950, 1953) proposed an 'exteroceptively aroused drive' (i.e. curiosity) that was created when a novel object was encountered and was diminished by prolonged contact with that object. The novel stimulus therefore both activated and directed the drive, and exploratory behaviour was rewarded by the resultant drive reduction. However it soon became apparent that animals could learn an instrumental response with the opportunity to explore or to experience a simple stimulus change as the sole reward (e.g. Andronico & Forgays, 1962; Girdner, 1953; Hefferline, 1950; Kish, 1955; Kling *et al.*, 1956; Lavery & Foley, 1965; Long & Tapp, 1967; Montgomery, 1945; Montgomery & Segall, 1955; Robinson, 1959, 1961). As Brown (1953) pointed out, if the novel stimulus elicits the drive then learning should not take place for the drive is not produced until after the behavioural response is made that the drive is supposed to be motivating. Further, if it is argued that an initial accidental act is responsible for triggering the stimulus change then this act should be aversive, for it was accompanied by an increase in exploratory drive rather than its reduction or termination (Fowler, 1965). In addition a simple curiosity drive approach could not predict the observed avoidance of 'very' novel or incongruous stimuli (e.g. Barnett, 1958; Menzel, 1962; Montgomery, 1955; Welker, 1956).

Myers & Miller (1954, p. 434) proposed that exploration was energized by a boredom drive 'produced by homogeneous or· monotonous stimulation, enforced inaction, etc.', that could be 'reduced by sensory variety, freedom of action, etc., and that such drive reduction is the reinforcement involved in learning for "exploratory", manipulatory and exercise rewards'. A similar position was argued by Glanzer (1953). He dispensed with the idea of any energizing drive, but retained Hull's concept of reactive inhibition (Hull, 1943) by suggesting that exposure to a stimulus creates a quantity of 'stimulus satiation' to that stimulus which lowers the animal's preference for it. O'Connell (1965) argued that such theories do not allow for unique predictions concerning the direction of response. However as Fowler (1967) noted, this is incorrect, in that the least novel object is the one most resembling the boring situation and thereby the least favourable. Support for the boredom approach came not only from the many studies that demonstrated increased exploration with lengthened inter-session interval; the early experiments involving short-term human sensory deprivation (e.g. Thompson *et al.*, 1954) similarly provided data which suggested that such conditions created high levels of motivation for a change in sensory input.

Soon, however, it became apparent that there are problems with explanations of exploratory behaviour that do not contain some curiosity component — that in other words, do not allow the novel stimulus to exert some more specific influence upon the animal's preference. We still have the problem of the data that suggest that extreme novelty is aversive. Further, although Glanzer's theory was proposed specifically to explain findings on spontaneous alternation (e.g. Kivy *et al.*, 1956; Walker, 1956; Zeaman & House, 1951), the experiment of Dember (1956) suggested that such behaviour might better be explained using some curiosity-based concept. Dember placed rats in a T-maze whose arms were blocked by clear perspex on trial 1 but not on trial 2. On trial 1, one arm of the maze was black and the other was white, and on trial 2 both arms were the same colour, either black or white. The subjects preferred the changed arm even though it was a stimulus they had previously seen and was identical to that in the other arm. Fowler (1958) and Woods & Jennings (1959) successfully replicated this work, which clearly supports some 'current-change-attraction' theory.

A greater problem for boredom theories concerns the data from experiments using long periods of sensory impoverishment. Boredom explanations predict that the longer the period of sensory restriction the greater should be the subsequent level of stimulation-seeking. For example, Glanzer (1953, p. 259) states that:

> . . . the same amount of stimulus satiation develops in each successive moment. The total amount developed is, therefore, an increasing linear function of time.

However, there is a mass of data showing that this is not the case. Anecdotal accounts of people adrift on the Atlantic, lost on Polar expeditions, etc., suggest that under such conditions lethargy becomes very great, reasoning almost entirely vanishes and an increasing proportion of the day is spent sleeping, until finally a 'pseudo-coma' develops (e.g. Bombard, 1953; Brainard, 1929; Tiira, 1955). Obviously such conditions might result solely from physical exhaustion, but there are experimental human deprivation studies where this factor can be ruled out. For example, Gendreau *et at.* (1968) isolated maximum-security prison inmates under perceptual deprivation for 7 days. After this period experimental subjects and controls could select levels of light; the former group showed a lowered preference for high levels of visual input. Smith & Myers

(1966, p. 1160) reported similar 'withdrawal' symptoms in groups of volunteers deprived for only 48 h:

> ... some subjects in long term isolation seemingly make peace with their environment and develop a quiet serenity. Others develop the desire to be left alone for the duration of confinement, not wanting to receive constant reminders of the outside.

Such studies provide no support for a strong stimulus-seeking drive after relatively lengthy periods of sensory restriction.

Many animal experiments also provide results at variance with boredom theory. For example, Butler (1957) found that the rate of responding to visual stimulation by monkeys increased until 4 h of visual pattern deprivation had been reached, but from then on (up to a maximum of 8 h) the rate altered little, and in some cases dropped. Numerous studies have investigated the effects of rearing rats in environments of varying complexity upon subsequent levels of 'emotionality' and exploration. The results for exploration are contradictory. Some workers (e.g. Ehrlich, 1961; Woods *et al.*, 1960; Zimbardo & Montgomery, 1957) found that animals reared in 'restricted' environments explored more, as predicted by boredom theories. Others (e.g. Ehrlich, 1959; Montgomery & Zimbardo, 1957) failed to find such a difference. The confusions in this area that have resulted from rather anthropomorphic theorizing have been clearly indicated by Daly (1973). Further, the imposition of the differential sensory environment at a sensitive stage of maturation could easily have produced profound irreversible physiological repercussions especially within the sensory processing areas of the brain (Edward *et al.*, 1968, for example, found an increase in photic evoked potential latencies in rats that had been reared in a restricted environment). It is therefore wise not to place too heavy an emphasis on these data. Experiments in which adult rats have been subjected to such regimes are easier to interpret.

Inglis (1975a) randomly assigned adult rats, reared under identical conditions, to sensory enriched or restricted environments. When after 5 weeks the animals were placed in a novel maze, the enriched animals showed more types of behaviour indicative of exploration. Not only did they start with a higher level of exploratory activity, but they also exhibited a faster decline in such behaviour throughout the trial, suggesting that they could assimilate the novel surroundings more quickly than the restricted animals. A similar difference in habituation rate between enriched and deprived groups has also been found by Studelska & Kemble (1979). Inglis (1975b) kept adult rats in restricted environments and tested their tendencies to explore after varying numbers of days using both a novel maze attached to a familiar environment and a stimulus-contingent bar-press paradigm. In both experiments, there was a decreasing trend in stimulation-seeking behaviour with increases in the time spent under sensory restriction. An identical result was obtained using a head input operant by Inglis & Freeman (1976). Many light-contingent bar-press experiments have also revealed that rats prefer to expose themselves to light levels approximating their housing conditions rather than to novel light levels (e.g. Lockard, 1963). Similar preferences have been found in other sensory modalities, such as gravity (McCoy & Jankovitch, 1972), temperature (Deaux & Engstrom, 1973), taste (Young & Falk, 1956) and tactile sensations (Soskin, 1963).

Contrary to the prediction of boredom theories, there is therefore strong evidence that under prolonged sensory restriction, stimulation-seeking declines and is replaced by a preference for little or no change in environmental stimulation. The animals adapt in some way to their environment, in the sense that the amount of stimulus change they prefer appears to be directly related to the overall level of environmental complexity. Curiosity and boredom can be called contrast effects, the animal exhibiting either is apparently seeking a contrast, a change in its present environment. Underlying these processes, however, there seems to be an adaptation factor with a longer time constant that, under conditions of sensory restriction, slowly decreases the preferred degree of contrast. The relationship between these contrast and adaptation effects is crucial to any theory of exploratory behaviour and will be discussed in detail later in this chapter.

Since explanations of exploration using either curiosity or boredom concepts alone were not successful, it is not surprising that the remaining attempts to use drive theory involved both incentive and deprivation components. Fowler (1965, 1967) built his theory on the incentive component of drive as proposed by Spence (1956). Curiosity became the learned anticipation of novel situations, which then served to reduce a boredom drive. Many problems arise from this adoption of concepts originally proposed to explain classic need states. For example, Spence's original theory required a clear goal object and subsequent, relatively fixed, consummatory acts. In exploratory behaviour there are no clear consummatory acts. In other words the extreme variability of stimulation-seeking behaviour must cast doubt upon any postulated formation of anticipatory goal responses which, as originally conceived, require a rigid behaviour sequence for their creation. Another problem is that Fowler (1965, p. 58):

> . . . treats curiosity as a learned anticipatory reaction to the changes in stimulation contingent upon some instrumental act. Accordingly curiosity is not present when the animal encounters a novel, or unfamiliar surround, but only on subsequent occasions or trials and only as a result of the animal learning to anticipate the unfamiliar stimuli.

However, animals clearly do explore on the first experimental trial; indeed, exploratory measures are usually smaller on subsequent trials. Fowler attempts to circumvent this fact by proposing that as a result of past experience with 'similar' changing stimuli, anticipatory investigatory reactions become conditioned generally. Such a proposal is now very far from the original Spence formulation, and it is hard to see how it could explain why, for example, primates well before weaning show strong stimulation-seeking behaviour even though they have had little or no chance to acquire such 'generalized response tendencies' by exposure to 'similar' novel stimuli in the past.

Berlyne (e.g. 1960, 1963, 1967, 1969) and Fiske & Maddi (1961) proposed theories of exploratory behaviour based upon the concept of general drive (Hebb, 1949, 1955; Leuba, 1955). The growth of the arousal, activation or general drive concept has been rapid in spite of, or perhaps because of, the lack of any consistent definition of arousal (see Andrew, 1974). Berlyne, and Fiske & Maddi, argued that all incoming sensory stimulation contributes to a general arousal level and that, for a given task, there is an optimal level of arousal that the animal strives to maintain. The theories differ about the form of the relationship between the level of sensory input and arousal, but both nevertheless conclude that there will be an optimal level of sensory input that the animal will prefer to maintain. Therefore, if the level of environmental stimulation is below the optimum level, the animal will seek extra stimulation, whereas if an environment offers sensory input above the optimum level, then the animal will strive to withdraw from that environment. Unfortunately there is no generally accepted mechanism whereby the present state of arousal of an animal can be measured, let alone its discrepancy from an ill-defined optimum level. This means that practically any experimental result can be explained: Berlyne (1969), for example, offered two alternative models to describe the relationship between the reward value of stimulus variation and the arousal level. Although he offered predictions for each model for each of three ranges of arousal (subnormal, normal and supra-normal) nevertheless as Eisenberger (1972, p. 327) argued:

> Since he fails to provide an independent method for empirically identifying these ranges and since the assumed relationship between organismic activation and reward value is non monotonic, an adequate test of the models requires an ambitious experiment.

I do not propose to discuss these arousal theories further (see Chapter 2), except to point out that if arousal is conceived as a uni-dimensional, causal force (i.e. a general drive) resulting from multi-modality pooling of stimulation, then any act that changes the arousal level in the preferred direction should be reinforced. For example, Eisenberger (1972) notes that within the formulation of Fiske & Maddi, any large increases in arousal resulting from 'hunger, thirst, shock or noise should decrease the animal's performance for variation of other stimulation' (*loc. cit.* p. 324). Some studies have indeed found that rats receiving a pre-test shock or burst of high-intensity noise show a lower preference for novel stimuli than animals that have not been subjected to such aversive stimulation (e.g. Aitken & Sheldon, 1970; Haywood & Wachs, 1967; Sheldon, 1968; Thompson & Higgins, 1958). The results from other experiments, however, suggest that shock may actually facilitate exploration (e.g., Hudson, 1950; Williams, 1972; Wong & Bowles, 1976). There are also many data showing that hunger or thirst either increase preference for novelty or else have no effect upon it (e.g. Bolles & Delorge, 1962; Hughes, 1965; Richards & Leslie, 1962; Zimbardo & Miller, 1958). There is, therefore, little evidence to support the predicted pooling of classic need states and sensory input. Indeed, if the argument is turned around, a hungry or thirsty animal in a state of high arousal should be able to reduce its arousal level simply by moving into an area of lower environmental complexity; such behaviour would therefore be reinforced and yet the specific need would not have been reduced!

To conclude this brief review, I will mention two theories that, although formulated within an arousal framework, clearly have little to do with the original arousal concept. Schultz (1965) based his ideas upon the concept of 'sensoriostasis' which 'can be defined as a drive state of cortical arousal which impels the organism (in a waking state) to strive to maintain an optimal level of sensory variation' (loc. cit. p. 30). Here then the need states have been divorced from the factors underlying stimulation-seeking behaviour. The corollaries and predictions that Schultz derives from his basic concept do not in many respects differ from those of Fiske & Maddi (1961). His second prediction in particular clearly runs contrary to the evidence, already discussed, for the operation of some adaptation process in that it states that 'the sensoriostatic drive is induced by conditions of reduced sensory input and becomes increasingly intense as a function of time' (loc. cit., p. 30).

Delius (1970) moved even further from the original concept of arousal. He equated arousal solely with the overall rate of information processing as indicated by the number of logical decisions per unit time. As Andrew (1974, p. 138) points out:

> . . . two difficulties are at once encountered by such an approach. The first is the near impossibility of consistently avoiding earlier meanings of the term (i.e., arousal). The second is that no obvious method exists for measuring the rate of information processing or other related variables.

Also, there are situations in which, although an animal appears to be in a state of high arousal, it also seems not to be processing vast quantities of information; for example, humans after short periods under sensory restriction. Nevertheless, Delius' theory is important, for it highlights the possible role of information rather than simple sensory variation in controlling stimulation-seeking activity. This point had previously been made by several workers in the field of human sensory deprivation. For example, Jones (1969, p. 205) concluded a review of this literature by stating that:

> . . . deprivation of stimulus information is associated with a drive variable whilst deprivation of stimulus complexity and fluctuation does not result in evidence of a drive . . . The drive for stimulus information is not specific to the sensory system deprived of information but is a central process to which the information transmission of other modalities contributes.

I hope this section has indicated both the sorts of data that have to be explained by any theory of intrinsic exploratory behaviour and the problems encountered when an explanation is attempted on need-reduction lines. As we have seen, the motivation behind such behaviour was originally given the status of an acquired drive, then of a drive in its own right, then of a contributor to a general drive, and finally of formulations having little or nothing in common with classic need reduction. The acceptance of cognitive concepts concerned with the ability of an animal to process information seems to me to be inevitable. Therefore it may be more fruitful, first, to start with the premise that behaviour

79

associated with information gathering has a predominant role in the life of any animal living in a variable environment, secondly, to attempt to construct upon this foundation a cognitive theory of intrinsic exploration and only then, thirdly, to see if behaviour associated with need-reduction may not be parsimoniously incorporated. This procedure has been adopted in the remainder of this chapter.

4.2   The Framework of a Theory

The concepts used in this section are intervening variables describing behaviour at the 'molar' (Tolman, 1932) level of analysis. This is perhaps unusual in the present rather reductionist climate of comparative psychology and animal behaviour, as exemplified by the quest for physiological bases of behaviour and the ever-spreading mist of sociobiology. However I agree with Tolman (1932) who argued that behaviour has distinctive properties of its own, irrespective of the muscular, glandular and neural processes underlying it at the 'molecular' descriptive level. It is dangerous to presume that a detailed analysis at one descriptive level can account for all aspects at a higher level; for example, the concepts of the pressure and temperature of a gas cannot be deduced from the fine structure of the gas atom or molecule. This is not to say that concepts should be proposed that obviously fly in the face of basic physiology or genetics, but rather that an immediate justification for a concept at these levels is not necessary and could be counter productive.

The position to be argued here is based upon the following proposals:

1. Every animal has an inherent tendency to assimilate sensory input to form a representation of its environment.
2. This representation is used to modify subsequent behaviour by forming 'expectancies' that prime the animal to expect certain sensory inputs in a given context.
3. The attentional processes of the animal are biased towards gathering information concerning the stimulus input that diverges most from its expectancy as reflected in the output of a comparator mechanism.
4. The intensity of an animal's need state modifies the nature of expectancies relating to stimuli associated with the consummatory response of that particular need, so that the comparator mechanism responds to fulfilment of them as it would to a stimulus mismatch.
5. The strength of any response to a stimulus input increases with the degree of comparator activity that the input evokes.
6. The efficiency of the processes that assimilate novel sensory input into the cognitive representation vary with the capacity to attend to the discrepant input and with the complexity of the environmental representation of the environment at that time.
7. Whether an animal explores the source of a given sensory input or tries to avoid or change that source, is dependent upon the level of

comparator output at that time in relation to the efficiency of the assimilation processes, such that a gross imbalance in either direction is aversive.

Berlyne (1960) coined the term 'collative variables' (i.e. variables brought together for comparison) for the environmental parameters that seemingly affect exploration; under this heading he included such characteristics as novelty, surprisingness, ambiguity, incongruity and complexity. Clearly these are in the main properties of an organism – environment interaction rather than of the environment itself; apart from complexity, they clearly imply an expectancy by the subject. All collative variables appear to induce a degree of uncertainty in the organism. As the novel – familiar dichotomy is crucial for any explanation of exploration, it is clear that the animal must possess a comparator, a mechanism for comparing past and present input. The first two proposals provide the basis for such a mechanism. The fundamental assumption underlying them is that an animal's perception of sensory input is always influenced by its previous experience. In the late 19th century, Helmholtz proposed that raw sensory data, 'perzeption', were modified by previous experience through a learned, imaginal factor, 'vorstelling', before they became a true perception or 'anschaung' (Boring, 1950). In this he was following rationalist philosophers such as Kant (1781) although similar concepts can be traced back at least to the fifth century, to the Buddhist 'Consciousness-only school' of Hsuan-tsang. This school believed that there was a 'storehouse' consciousness that stored the 'seeds' or effects of previous deeds and was constantly being 'perfumed' or modified by incoming cognitions of external stimuli while at the same time endowing these cognitions with certain 'energies' so that they became true 'manifestations' (Chan, 1963). More recently the same basic assumptions have underlain several Gestalt theories of learning and it is from the Sign-Gestalt theory of Tolman (e.g. 1932, 1959) that the terms used in the first two proposals have been taken. Their meanings in the present context will now be discussed.

4.2.1 Competence and Behaviour-Primacy Theories of Motivation

Proposal 1 is that every animal has an inherent tendency to assimilate sensory input to form a representation of its environment. The phrase 'inherent tendency' clearly implies that there is no necessity to look to reinforcement for the growth of the animal's environmental representation in the same way that you do not look for reinforcement underlying, say, the eye-blink reflex. The function of the latter is to protect the eye while the former functions as an evergrowing data base that enables animals living in stochastic environments to make predictions concerning the whereabouts of food, mates, predators, etc. It therefore seems rather obvious that the gathering of information associated with the development of the cognitive model must be the predominant, continuing preoccupation of the animal for without the predictions derived from the model the environmental contexts appropriate to the reduction of specific needs are far less likely to be found. The widespread emphasis placed upon need reduction in determining behaviour is surprising although it is worth noting that there were several early exceptions to this trend.

White (1959) coined the term 'competence' referring (*loc. cit.*, p. 297):

> . . . to an organism's capacity to interact effectively with its environment. In organisms capable of but little learning, this capacity might be considered an innate attribute, but in the mammals and especially man, with their highly plastic nervous systems, fitness to interact with the environment is slowly attained through prolonged feats of learning.

He argued that in view of the persistence of behaviour whose sole purpose appeared to be to promote such learning (i.e., exploration or play) competence should be considered a motivational variable, but one that cannot be explained on the basis of drives or instinct. These forms of behaviour were thought to create 'a feeling of efficacy' resulting from the efficient use of the environment. Early studies in child development have clearly shown that being able to influence your surroundings, i.e., to be a cause, is rewarding (e.g. Gross, 1901; Piaget, 1952). Many other theorists have proposed competence-like concepts. For example Hendrick (1942, 1943) modified Freudian theory to include an 'instinct to master' the environment, postulating that every organism has a basic need to use and perfect each function as it develops in order to control and alter its surroundings by actions that create varying degrees of positive reinforcement according to their efficiency. Perhaps the most complete theory founded on these lines is that of Woodworth (1958). He drew a distinction between the 'need-primacy' theories of the time (e.g. Freud, 1935; Hull, 1943, 1952) and his 'behaviour-primacy' theory, which proposed that all behaviour is primarily directed towards dealing efficiently with the environment. Thus, rather than argue that all so-called incidental behaviour, such as exploration and play (Woodworth, 1958, p. 125):

> . . . is secondarily motivated by the organic needs or other great motives, we insist that the incidental behaviour represents the primary drive to deal with the environment and that large-scale purposive activities are based on this primary drive. In order to motivate food seeking, the hunger drive has to break into the on-going behaviour and give it a special direction.

The behaviour-primacy theory regards the tendency to deal with the environment as a primary drive, and indeed as *the* primary drive in behaviour. The various capacities for dealing with the environment afford outlets for the general behaviour drive and give it different forms — given the necessary environmental opportunities.   (*loc. cit.*, p. 133)

Thus rather than exploration being linked to one or more of the classical need states or being shown only when these have been satiated, Woodworth proposed the position adopted here, namely that exploration and allied behaviour is given pride of place, and classical need states have to become sufficiently great to disrupt the ongoing 'incidental' behaviour. Earlier work (e.g. Whiting & Mowrer, 1943) had already shown that hungry rats in a novel maze frequently explored so much that they ignored any food rewards present. This obviously makes functional sense; it is maladaptive in unfamiliar surroundings for an animal to make straight for the food and start to eat if it misses a predator hiding in the vicinity.

4.2.2 The Representation of the Environment and the Creation of Expectancies

Proposal 2 states that the representation is used to modify subsequent behaviour by forming 'expectancies' that prime the animal to expect certain sensory inputs in a given context. If an animal is to create a cognitive model of a variable habitat in order to predict events, some 'chunking' of the sensory input must take place. Predictions cannot be made on the basis of a series of unique stimuli, thus classification is a vital first step. Ayer (1973, in his *Construction of the Physical World*) added to the qualia of colour, size and shape a set of patterns whose descriptions are taken from the physical objects with which they come to be classified. He argued (*loc. cit.*, p. 91) that the observer does not characterize:

> . . . these patterns as patterns. He notices them implicitly, in the sense that it is his registering of them that governs his identification of the physical objects which he thinks he sees. They provide the main visual clues on which everyday judgements of perception are based.

The cognitive model therefore contains symbols for instances and also symbols for classes composed of them. Every perceptual instance has the potential for the occurrence of a class of similar events and therefore could become the prototype for that class. Tversky (1977, p. 347) suggested that an object is a prototype if it 'exemplifies' the category to which it belongs that does not necessitate it being 'the most typical or frequent member of its class'. He found that common features, as opposed to distinctive features, were weighted more heavily in judging 'prototypicality' than in judging 'similarity'. Categories therefore appear to be formed on the basis of a series of overlapping common features, or 'family resemblances' (Wittgenstein, 1968), no one of which may be necessary or sufficient for the classification.

Categories need to be fluid, changing with time to represent pragmatically some optimal level of abstraction, neither too specific nor too general (e.g. Hofstadter, 1979; Tversky, 1977). Thus if the frequency of encountering a given stimulus object, not prototypical of its class, suddenly increases dramatically, it may be more efficient to re-define the class around this object or to create an additional class. The threshold for category reclassification is likely to vary with the functional importance of the stimulus object. For example, it would be crucial to split a 'predator category', even if encounter rates with predators were low, when different responses were required for different predators. Category fusion would occur if, over a period of time, it became apparent that two or more stimulus objects of different categories reliably occurred in close spatial and/or temporal contiguity.

Hofstadter (1979, p. 352–353) argues that instances frequently inherit many of their properties from the classes to which they belong:

These are built into the class symbol as expected links to other symbols (i.e. potential triggering relations) and are called *default options*. In any freshly minted instance symbol, the default options can be easily overridden, but unless this is explicitly done, they will remain in the instance symbol, inherited from its class symbol.

Instances therefore determine the prototypicality of their class. However the default options created by the class prototype may influence the perceived nature of future instances of that category, as clearly indicated by Bruner's work on 'perceptual readiness' (e.g. Bruner, 1957). There is, therefore, an implicit circularity in the categorization process. As we shall see, expectancies are thought to consist in the main of default options derived from their class symbol.

The problem of the 'chunking' or classification of sensory input (see Rosch & Lloyd, 1978) is central to certain theories of human attention and memory (e.g Anderson & Bower, 1973; Estes, 1972; LaBerge, 1973, 1976). It would appear, however, that the cognitive processes of other 'higher' animals must also employ some classification of concepts. Certainly there is evidence that animals other than human beings can form complex categories including those that lack necessary and sufficient sensory features for their classification, i.e. 'polymorphous concepts' (Ryle, 1951). For example, chimpanzees can be taught a symbolic language that includes concepts such as 'open' (Gardner & Gardner 1975) and porpoises can learn categories such as 'novel behaviour' (Pryor *et al.*, 1969). Nor is this ability confined to the higher mammals for pigeons at least, can use polymorphous concepts (e.g. Hernstein, 1979; Herrnstein & Loveland, 1964; Lubow, 1974; Morgan *et al.*, 1976; Poole & Lander, 1971).

In order to explain how instance and class symbols might be used in learning, I think it is valuable to reconsider the Sign – Gestalt theory of Tolman (e.g. 1932, 1948, 1955, 1959, 1966), since the subsequent work on the problems of categorization means that many of Tolman's concepts are now more amenable to empirical test. Tolman's theory was based upon the premise that an animal forms a cognitive map of its surroundings by learning meanings within the environment rather than a series of movements or habits as suggested by stimulus – response (S – R) theories. Despite the many advantages of this approach (see, e.g., White, 1943), particularly in the fields of reward expectancy (e.g. Cowles & Nissen, 1937; Tinklepaugh, 1928), latent learning (MacCorquodale & Meehl, 1954; Thistlethwaite, 1951) and place learning (Menzel, 1978), the reductionist approach of S – R theory became the more popular. However there have been some exceptions to this trend. For example, Bolles (1972), after reviewing the many situations in which reinforcement fails to control behaviour (e.g. polydipsia, auto-shaping), concluded that it was necessary to return to a Tolman-like theory of learning:

What is learned is that certain events, cues (S), predict other, biologically important events, consequences (S*). An animal may incidentally show new responses but what it learns is an expectancy that represents and corresponds to the S – S* contingency (*loc. cit.*, p. 402)

More recently, too, an increasing number of workers in many areas of animal learning (e.g. Pavlovian conditioning — Rescorla, 1978; blocking effects — Dickinson, 1980, Fowler 1978, Mackintosh, 1978a; serial pattern learning — Hulse, 1978) have indicated a growing awareness of the immense value of a cognitive approach like that of Tolman. Indeed, Hearst (1978), writing about visual feature selection, states that (*loc. cit.*, pp. 55–56):

> . . . it seems unfortunate that many of us who received training along strongly behaviouristic lines have had little or no exposure to the views of these writers [i.e. Tolman, Woodworth and the Gestalt psychologists]. In my opinion, several of the major issues and alternative explanations that they raised deserve careful consideration.

Whereas Mackintosh (1978b) concluded a review of the present state of knowledge on conditioning with the opinion that (*loc. cit.*, p. 57):

> . . . it is time that psychologists abandoned their outmoded view of conditioning and recognized it as a complex and useful process whereby organisms build an accurate representation of their world.

Tolman envisaged his cognitive map as an intricate network of 'means – end readinesses'. Each of these (Tolman, 1959, p. 113):

> . . . is equivalent to what in ordinary parlance we call a 'belief' (a readiness or predisposition) to the effect that an instance of this *sort* of response, will lead to that *sort* of further stimulus situation.

By emphasizing the 'sort' of stimulus situation Tolman was clearly imagining his beliefs to be composed of the default options of their respective categories. Tolman proposed that beliefs were acquired when the animal was acting under one or other of the classic drives but remained 'whether or not instances of the type of stimuli and responses in question are present at the moment' (Tolman, 1959, p.106). Initially every major drive was thought to have an associated 'exploratory tendency' (see Tolman, 1932, p. 94). Later, on the basis of the work of Berlyne (1955) and Montgomery (1952, 1954), a 'pure curiosity drive' was added, whose goal 'is the experience of distant stimuli *per se* and it is also accompanied by its own trial and error' (Tolman, 1959, p. 101). However, as we have seen, not only is a curiosity drive an inadequate concept, it is also redundant, for there is no need to invoke any reinforcement process to account for information gathering.

Within the Sign – Gestalt theory expectancies were beliefs that had been 'activated' or given 'valence', by need states. Those categories of the belief structure became expectancies that had been associated with the attainment of the consummatory act relevant to a particular need state within the context the animal found itself. I think this emphasis upon need states was misplaced and that beliefs are continually being activated by prior sensory input regardless of whether or not the animal is acting under one of the classic need states. The crucial point, as we shall see later, is whether the expectancies thus triggered control attention. They can do this if (a) they are not 'fulfilled' by subsequent sensory input or (b) the animal is indeed behaving under a deficit need state and the expectancy has been associated with it in the manner suggested by Tolman.

Tolman & Brunswik (1935), in a classic paper, argued that beliefs must be probabilistic since the causal nature of the environment would permit only stochastic predictions. Brunswik (1939) found a measure of agreement between the choices made in a simple maze by hungry rats and the probabilities that food would be found in these areas. There has since been a mass of work concerned with the 'matching laws' governing response/reinforcement relationships (e.g. Baum, 1974; Herrnstein, 1970). As beliefs are probabilistic they can have 'strength' in two distinct ways (Tolman, 1959, p. 124):

> Thus a belief may have strength because it holds that the S_2 type of stimulus will follow the S_1 type of stimulus in a high percentage of cases. Or a belief may have strength (even though the expected frequency of the S_2 consequence is very low) in the sense that it is held to very strongly.

A belief has a value based upon the expected probability of reinforcement, but also, and perhaps more importantly, it has a confidence rating, derived from the variance of the results of expectancies triggered from the belief. Tolman used the concept of confidence ratings in his explanation of the partial-reinforcement effect. A question now arises concerning the factors likely to be important in determining how an animal would choose between a belief having a high value but low confidence rating and one having the reverse. The strangely neglected work of Smedslund (1955) provides a possible answer.

Smedslund (1955) conducted experiments on multiple probability learning in which students tried to predict a lever position that was probabilistically determined by combinations of prior visual cues. Under such conditions the subjects formed what Smedslund called 'perceptual hypotheses' that appear to be functionally equivalent to expectancies. The subjects' learning curves showed almost cyclical patterns of dependence upon various combinations of the perceptual cues. Also their criteria for considering whether a perceptual hypothesis about a particular combination of cues was relatively successful and satisfactorily decreased as the experiments progressed. In trying to explain these results, Smedslund started from the same position as Tolman in supposing that

> . . . every perceptual hypothesis involves not only anticipation of future events but also an anticipation of the relative frequency of success of these anticipations. (*loc. cit.*, p. 45)

He applied classic adaptation level theory (see Helson, 1959) in proposing that the verification probabilities of all the perceptual hypotheses formed in a given context created a 'level of probability adaptation' that was some 'kind of weighted average'. He then suggested that whether a particular expectancy was held to be 'satisfactory' was dependent upon its discrepancy relative to this level of probability adaptation rather than to some absolute scale.

The minimum value of the level was thought to be determined by a number of factors. Amongst these the strength of the motivation for the success of the expectation was empirically found to be very important in that

> . . . the stronger the motivation of the person the slower is the downward displace-

ment of the level of probability adaptation and the higher is the minimum value. (*loc. cit.*, p. 49)

Finally Smedslund introduced his concept of a 'subjective confidence limit'. In extinction experiments it was noted that subjects could be well aware that the relative frequency of verification of an expectancy had decreased and yet be reluctant to discard it, feeling that the decrement may have been 'accidental'. The ease with which the expectancy was rejected was directly related to the amount of the subject's experience of it. It was argued that the subjects in effect applied some sort of significance test to the decrement. The subjective confidence limit is 'the size of the difference that is regarded as just barely "reliable" '(*loc. cit.*, p. 53) and is directly proportional to the momentary motivational strength to keep the expectancy, and inversely proportional to the amount of relevant experience. The cyclical preference for the various perceptual hypotheses could now be explained on the basis of a decrease in the subjective confidence limit with increasing experience:

> In other words we think that the declines occur when the S has had enough experience to be *certain* that the future relative frequency of verification will remain lower than his level of probability adaption. (*loc. cit.*, p. 67)

Using Smedslund's approach it can be seen that whether an animal will prefer a belief with a high value and low confidence rating, or one with a low value and high confidence rating, will vary with the level of the relevant motivation. Thus if a need state is high, the higher is set the minimum level of probability adaptation, with the result that only those beliefs with the highest confidence ratings will be preferred. In other words the animal will avoid risks in conditions where the value of any of the alternative beliefs is sufficient to reduce the need. As the need state is reduced, beliefs with higher values but lower confidence ratings may come to be preferred (Pubols, 1962). There have been numerous studies concerned with how humans perceive risk (e.g. Kaplan & Schwartz, 1975) particularly within a gambling context (e.g. Coombs *et al.*, 1978; Slovic,1967). Interestingly, one general finding has been that the perceived 'riskiness' of a coin toss increases with the denomination of the coin (e.g. Coombs & Meyers, 1969), which seems to fit Smedslund's scheme since the motivation to win will presumably increase with the amount to be won. It is also interesting to note that the major theory attempting to account for the results of studies on perceived risk in humans, the Portfolio theory (Coombs, 1975; Coombs & Avrunin, 1977), proposes that preferences for risky options are determined by two dimensions, expected value and perceived risk, and that, for each expected value, an individual has an ideal level of risk at which preference is maximal such that deviations from the ideal point to either higher or lower risk would reduce the preference. The two dimensions of expected value and perceived risk are clearly reminiscent of Tolman's two types of strength for a belief.

Studies on 'impulse conditioning' suggest that perceived risk may also be important in determining the behaviour of animals other than humans. Pigeons and rats for example tend to prefer a small reward now to a potential larger reward sometime in the usually uncertain future (e.g. Ainslie, 1974; Logan, 1965; Rachlin & Green, 1972). More direct evidence comes from the recent work of Caraco *et al.* (1980) who found that foraging birds are sensitive to the variance as well as to mean probability of reward within a given locality. If the birds' expected intake was greater than their expected energy requirements, then they avoided risk by reducing their mean reward in order to reduce the reward variation. Caraco (1980) suggested that a risk-prone forager would have to accept a higher probability of starvation. Stevens (1981), however, illustrates an example of a situation where choosing a riskier, in the sense of being a less certain, option could reduce the probability of starvation. Certainly, if an animal is to increase the reliability of its environmental representation then it should favour the gathering of information about those beliefs that have the lowest confidence ratings. The studies on blocking effects (e.g. Kamin, 1969; Wagner, 1971) show how sensitive animals are to the predictive properties of sensory input and (Mackintosh, 1978b, p. 52):

> . . . blocking is, in fact, only one instance of a general phenomenon; conditioning occurs selectively to relatively good predictors of reinforcement at the expense of relatively poor predictors.

Only when a specific need is strong enough to control behaviour would we expect strong preferences for the most certain of the expectancies relevant to reduction of that need. The following section considers how behavioural control could be determined.

4.2.3 Attention and Needs

Proposal 3 suggests that the attentional processes of an animal are biased towards gathering information concerning the source of the stimulus input that diverges most from its expectancy. It is therefore implicitly accepted that an animal may not be able simultaneously to process all discrepant sensory input. The evidence for limitations within the sensory processing system comes from work on human attention. Cherry (1953) conducted one of the earliest experiments. Subjects were presented with a different message to each ear and instructed to attend to, or 'shadow' one message and to ignore the other. Subsequently they were unable to recall the unshadowed information or even remember whether the language in which it had been presented had changed during the experiment. However they could pick up a gross change in the physical properties of the unshadowed message (e.g. a change in pitch). Later experiments (e.g. Moray, 1959; Triesman, 1960) demonstrated that the unshadowed message may receive deeper analysis, in that its meaning as well as its gross physical characteristics are sometimes recalled. That there is a processing bottleneck is commonly accepted, although theories differ however as to its position with respect to the depth of analysis of the input (cf. Broadbent, 1958; Deutsch & Deutsch, 1963; Norman 1968, 1969).

In order to explain why behavioural routines come with practice to involve

88

fewer conscious decisions, it has been suggested that there are two processing pathways (e.g. LaBerge, 1973; Neisser, 1967; Schneider & Shiffrin, 1977; Shiffrin & Schneider, 1977). One is a parallel system having a very large or unlimited capacity for processing data at an automatic, unconscious level. The other is a serial system requiring the limited capacity of a short-term, or working, memory store for analysis of data at a controlled, flexible, conscious level. It is proposed that repetition of a behavioural routine allows relatively simple rules to be developed and then stored within a long-term memory which in many respects seems equivalent to a cognitive model. Once rules have been formed then automatic routines can control information flow and direct attention thereby allowing capacity within short-term memory to be reallocated to other, less obvious, tasks.

The idea that attention can be viewed as an allocatable resource was put forward by Kahneman (1973). He drew his evidence from experiments like that of Zelniker (1971) who combined shadowing with delayed auditory feedback. As her subjects repeated the shadowed message their voices were tape recorded and played back a fraction of a second later to their 'unattending' ears. Such delayed feedback upsets speech and causes stuttering. When the shadowing task was difficult, stuttering was less than when the task was easy. This suggests that more of a limited attentional capacity was being allocated in the difficult shadowing condition than in the easy one, thereby leaving less available to process the disruptive message from the 'unattending' ear. The reallocation of capacity for a complex task was thought by Kahneman (1973) to give rise to the feeling of 'cognitive effort'. Shiffrin & Schneider (1977, p. 183) argue that only controlled processing within short-term memory usually involves effort:

> The development of automatic processing provides a means of improving performance independently of the effort put into controlled processing. In fact, the effort required is usually greatly reduced by the development of automatic processing even though performance improves.

Since reallocation of processing capacity, as well as modification of a cognitive representation, is a change of state it must involve work and thus it may ultimately be possible to measure the cost of 'cognitive effort' in terms of energy usage. The resource allocation/cost approach to information processing has been logically extended by Navon & Gopher (1979) by their use of economic theory to describe capacity allocation within the processing systems.

The very fact that a novel stimulus is novel means that rules for automatically processing the discrepant input will not be available. Processing of unexpected input requires capacity within short-term memory, and Proposal 3 suggests that allocation priority within short-term memory is given to novel input. Being in unusual surroundings could potentially be very dangerous or very useful to an animal and therefore if it is to survive it needs the ability to respond quickly and flexibly to novel events.

As it is suggested that novel input is given priority within short-term memory, this implies that the input has been recognized as discrepant before this stage. Andrew (1976) put forward an attention-based theory of animal behaviour founded on the proposal that before any processing can occur an input must activate one or more 'recognition units' (Treisman, 1960). He proposed that 'if a novel stimulus fails to activate a recognition unit then no mismatch is possible' (*loc. cit.*, p. 101) and also that 'it is possible for elaboration of a new recognition unit to occur during examination of a novel stimulus without responses associated with mismatch being evoked' (*loc. cit.*, p. 102). This seems a curious position for it is not clear how 'examination' of the novel stimulus is initiated or maintained if there is no processing of the novel input and none of the attending behaviours that would be associated with mismatch. The position adopted here is that all input is continually being compared with expectancies at the automatic processing level. This does not mean that all input is completely analysed as suggested by Deutsch & Deutsch (1963); this would be wasteful if only part of it was to be consciously processed afterwards. Rather, as Norman (1968, p. 528) argued, 'the automatic matching of a stimulus with its stored representation does not imply knowledge of everything related to that stimulus', for as we have seen expectancies are thought to consist of their class default options. Thus Wittgenstein (quoted in Kenny, 1973, p. 527), in his treatment of anticipation and intention, stated that:

> . . . looking for something presupposes that I know what I am looking for, without what I am looking for *having* to exist. I'd once have expressed this by saying that looking for something presupposed the elements of the complex, but not the actual combination I am looking for.

Grossman (1980) has indicated how a comparator mechanism could have evolved as a consequence of a more basic property, namely noise suppression, and how a relatively simple process involving lateral inhibition interactions affecting each cell over a prescribed spatial extent can accomplish pattern matching.

The above arguments predict that surprising events should be afforded deeper processing than expected events and this proposal is supported by evidence from recent experiments on the mechanisms of animal learning (for an excellent review see Dickinson, 1980). As a result of this work it has been suggested that surprising events are 'rehearsed' within short-term memory. If a stimulus event is retained in such a manner within this limited capacity store then obviously it has priority in the sense that it is denying access to other events. Also it has been argued that permanent associations within long-term memory develop to the degree that their components have been jointly active within short-term memory (e.g. Konorsky, 1967; Shiffrin & Schneider, 1977; Wagner & Terry, 1975). Therefore a surprising event, through its being rehearsed, is more likely to form such associations than an event that is either not represented in short-term memory or is not rehearsed there. The evidence that unexpected stimuli are given processing priority comes mainly from the elegant experiments of Wagner and his co-workers (for a review see Wagner, 1978). For example, Wagner *et al.* (1973), in a series of conditioning experiments with rabbits, demonstrated that receiving an unexpected post-trial shock disrupted learning. This interference was not simply the result of the physical nature of the post-trial event, i.e. the shock, for a surprising event consisting of the omission of an expected post-trial shock created just as much disruption. These results are clearly consistent with the following proposals; that there is a limited capacity to the learning mechanism, that processing continues after the end of a trial and that surprising events have the ability to override such post-trial processing. By giving the surprising post-trial event at increasing intervals after the trial Wagner *et al.* (1973) were able to show a decreasing level of interference thereby giving a clue as to the time required to form long-term associations.

If an animal is, for example, starving it obviously must be capable of responding to expected sensory input that signals a source of food. There must be a mechanism whereby such input can override the priority usually afforded to unexpected stimuli. Proposal 4 suggests that the intensity of an animal's need state modifies the nature of expectancies relating to stimuli associated with the consummatory response of that particular need, so that the comparator mechanism responds to the fulfilment of these expectancies as it would to a stimulus mismatch. In other words the need state adds to the expectancy some factor that signals the importance of that expectancy even if, particularly if, the expectancy is fulfilled. The strength of this additional factor is further thought to be directly correlated with the intensity of the need.

There is nothing new in this proposal. Norman (1968, 1970) put forward a theory of attention and memory whereby only input with the highest levels of 'pertinence' could control attention. Pertinence was thought to be based upon several factors including motivational state. Thus Norman suggested that a hungry animal, for example, will be in a drive state that will cause the pertinence of stored memories associated with food to increase whether or not they are expected in the immediate future. Inputs matching these highly pertinent memories would thus be attended to. As seems so often the case, pertinence, when derived in this manner, appears to have much in common with one of Tolman's early concepts, namely the 'valence' of a stimulus. Tolman (1932) argued that the past pairing of a stimulus with a consummatory act endowed that stimulus with a potential attractive property of 'cathexis' that varied with the number of such pairings. However the actual attractive power of the stimulus, its 'valence', was held to be a product of its 'cathexis' and the momentary level of the relevant 'need', the latter being a function of deprivation time. Thus the valence of the stimulus is directly correlated with the strength of the relevant need. It should be remembered that Tolman's belief structure was composed of a network of 'means-ends-readinesses'; stimuli could be categorized as means to others as well as possibly ends in themselves. All stimuli associated, however remotely, in the past with consummatory acts could have attained a degree of valence and therefore a series of 'means' stimuli leading up to the consummatory act served to direct the animal's behaviour; each became a sub-goal which when reached allowed access to the next valenced stimulus in the chain. The idea of a chain of sub-goals was subsequently elaborated in the behavioural theories of Deutsch (1960) and Miller *et al.* (1960).

Proposal 4 therefore summarizes how need states are thought to be able to 'break into' the prevailing stream of exploration. The valence they endow upon expectancies that have been associated with the reduction of that need, becomes functionally equivalent to comparator mismatch. Hence these expectancies even when verified can still compete for processing priority within short term memory. Whether such stimuli come to control attention will depend upon their valence excitation relative to any mismatch excitation received at the same time. As this proposal predicts changes in capacity allocation with variation in need state, it would be interesting to conduct a shadowing experiment using subjects who were experiencing varying degress of hunger or thirst and to present stimuli reliably associated with eating or drinking to the unshadowed ear. The level of deprivation should influence the degree of awareness of the unattended stimuli.

I have mentioned data that suggest that hunger rarely decreases active exploration but either increases or has no effect upon it. These findings would be predicted by the present framework. If hunger is low, then input matching the expectations associated with it may still accrue insufficient valence to attain priority within short-term memory. Exploration would therefore be expected to differ little between these deprived rats and satiated ones. If hunger is sufficient to enable such input to control attention, then we would expect an increase in behaviour associated with food finding. However the wild rat is an opportunistic feeder (e.g. Ewer, 1971, for the black rat), normally actively seeking out food and frequently finding it in novel surroundings. Exploration in this species is therefore often associated with need reduction, and thus we should not be surprised if hungry rats when placed in novel surroundings sometimes increase their locomotory exploration. Experiments clearly need to be conducted with a species whose foraging behaviour is incompatible with exploration; for example, one that lies in wait to ambush passing prey.

Proposal 5 suggests that the vigour and persistence of behaviours triggered by a stimulus input are directly related to the degree of comparator activity that is evoked by that stimulus. As we have seen, there are thought to be two sorts of comparator activity, that resulting from expectancy/input mismatch and that resulting from the fulfilment of a valenced expectancy.

The orienting response is a cluster of physiological changes evoked by reception of unexpected sensory input; experiments by Sokolov (e.g. Sokolov, 1969) suggest that the greater the stimulus discrepancy the more prolonged is the orienting response and the longer it is before the animal ignores that input. Sokolov's detailed explanation of the orienting response has many features in common with the position suggested here. In a given situation, hypotheses, equivalent to expectancies, are triggered from a long-term memory store together with associated *a priori* probabilities that each particular hypothesis will in fact be verified. After observation of the input there are derived *a posteriori* probabilities that the input does or does not correspond to one or more of the hypotheses. If the *a posteriori* probabilities are such that the input could be assigned to a number of hypotheses, then the entropy of the system is said to be high. If this entropy exceeds a given threshold then an orienting response occurs:

The orienting response terminates as soon as the probability of one of the hypotheses has become significantly greater than that of the others, and the entropy of the system decreased to a point below the threshold value. (*loc. cit.*, p. 689)

Since the amount of entropy depends upon the number of hypotheses being used, a reduction in the system of hypotheses leads to a decrease in the scope and duration of the orienting response. This corresponds to the extinction of the orienting response with repetitions of the same stimuli. (*loc. cit.*, p. 680)

The orienting response remains until the situation has been clarified and some categorization of the discrepant input has occurred. The complexity of the cognitive model in terms of the number and diversity of its categories is therefore an important factor and will be discussed further in the following section.

The second sort of comparator activity involves valenced expectancies. It seems reasonable to suppose that a strongly motivated animal will persist in attempting to reach the source of sensory input which has reliably preceded reduction of that particular need longer than will a less motivated animal strive to attain a source of input that has only occasionally signalled subsequent need reduction. This is in effect all Proposal 5 suggests with respect to the fulfilment of valenced expectancies for, as we have seen, the valence of a stimulus is proportional to the momentary need of the animal and to the number of times that the stimulus has led to reduction of the need (i.e. to the confidence rating of the stimulus).

4.2.4   Contrast, Adaptation and Affect

In this section I return to the important question concerning what determines whether an animal will approach or avoid a source of discrepant input. In particular an attempt is made to provide a framework that can account for data suggesting the operation of the contrast and adaptation phenomena already discussed.

McClelland & Clark (1953) elaborated the original concept of an adaptation level (Helson, 1947, 1959, 1964) by proposing that positive and negative affect (i.e. 'rewarding' and 'aversive' states) result from the degree of discrepancy between incoming stimulation and the adaptation level, a weighted log mean of all previous stimuli within that modality. No discrepancy was associated with 'indifferent' affect, although small discrepancies created positive affect and large discrepancies negative affect. Results of experiments using psychologically simple stimuli supported this proposal (e.g. Haber, 1958, using temperature), whereas work involving more complex stimuli did not (e.g. Verinis *et al.*, 1968, using texts concerned with blind dates). Most relevant in the present context are experiments that varied one of the collative variables. Complexity has been the one most commonly used as it is the easiest to grade and an inverted quadratic relationship between complexity and positive affect has been found (e.g. Dorfman, 1965; Sackett, 1967; Vitz, 1966b), although there have also been reports of only a monotonically increasing or decreasing relationship (Jones, 1964; Thomas, 1966).

Helson (1959, 1964) suggested that there may be adaptation levels not only for individual stimulus dimensions but also a general level to which several sensory modalities contributed. There is some evidence that a change in one stimulus dimension can alter preferences within other stimulus dimensions (e.g. Berlyne et al., 1966; Glow et al., 1971; Isaac, 1962) and that restriction within one modality can enhance thresholds in other modalities (e.g. Schutte & Zubek, 1967; Zubek et al., 1964). Dember & Earl (1957) proposed in effect a multi-modal adaptation level based upon stimulus unexpectedness. Stimulus discrepancies that fall outside a range on either side of this level were thought to produce negative affect. Stimuli whose discrepancies fell within this range were termed 'pacers'; these created positive affect and helped to 'raise' the adaptation level, i.e. to move it towards the complex pole of a simple – complex axis. The adaptation level (C') could only be 'raised':

> . . . the C' change is uni-directional: with experience C' takes on increasing values. The individual can only get more able. (loc. cit., p. 94–95)

Several experiments have investigated the predicted unidirectional shifting of the adaptation level: most have provided their subjects with stimuli varying in heterogeneity and have assumed that the more heterogeneous the stimulus, the greater was its unexpectedness. The common finding has been the predicted slow increase in preference for the more complex stimuli (e.g. Dember et al., 1957; May, 1968; Sackett, 1967; Thomas 1969; Walker & Walker, 1964). Nevertheless these experiments have been conducted for only relatively short periods and as we have seen there is good evidence that several days of pre-test sensory restriction can create a decrease in preference for unexpected stimulation suggesting that stable regression of the adaptation level can occur. Admittedly Dember & Earl (1957, p. 95) did add in a footnote that 'regression of C' results from anxiety; the individual in this paper is always non-anxious'. Yet there are many behavioural and physiological indications that encounters with novelty almost always induce some degree of stress or anxiety. Indeed Russell (1973) has reviewed theories of exploratory behaviour that argue that it is the fear elicited by novel objects that controls the type of behaviour shown towards them. Eisenberger (1972, p. 331) has listed other ambiguities and inconsistencies within the theory; for example, the:

> . . . assumption that an animal will not respond to a set of stimuli which lacks a pacer stimulus contradicts their other assumption that the preferred level of unexpectedness is less than that of the pacer range.

Thomas (1971) discusses problems, common to both the above discrepancy theories, associated with the assumptions required to make clear empirical predictions. The prime distinction between theories concerns where the factor of maximum reinforcement lies along the discrepancy continuum, and therefore the major assumption is that 'responses to stimuli satisfy the criterion of a unidimensional ordinal scale' (loc. cit., p. 252). It would seem that most psy-

94

chologically complex stimuli (e.g. poems, Kammann, 1966) are unlikely to satisfy this criterion. Thomas (1969) used Coombs' (1964) unfolding theory to check the validity of his test stimuli but such thoroughness is the exception. Yet if stimuli are not evaluated in this way, the interpretation of results suggesting complex preference functions (e.g. bimodal patterns, Kammann, 1966) is unclear. Since techniques for unfolding multi-dimensional scales have been developed (e.g. Kruskal, 1964a, 1964b; Shepard, 1962), it might be possible to expand discrepancy models into the multi-dimensional case for use with those complex stimuli that fail to fit on a uni-dimensional scale.

Glanzer (1958, pp. 311–312) based his multi-modality adaptation level upon the information content or variability of the incoming stimulation:

> The organism is viewed as an information processing system that requires certain amounts of information per unit time . . . the organism's information requirements are set by its past experience. An organism that has had a high flow of information directed at it in the past would have a high requirement or standard. An organism that has lived in an impoverished informational environment would have a low requirement or standard.

Eisenberger (1972) has illustrated the difficulties that arise from ambiguity in Glanzer's definition of variation. For example, does an animal taken from a familiar heterogeneous environment and placed in a novel homogeneous environment experience a decrease or an increase in the rate of experienced variation? Also Vitz (1966a, p. 74) has argued that the use of an information formula can account:

> . . . for the number of elements and their probabilities but because it is insensitive to the metric character of the stimulus events, it fails to reflect the size of the differences or discrepancies between them.

McReynolds (1962, p. 313) proposed a scheme very similar to that of Glanzer (1958) based upon changes in the rate of assimilation of novel sensory input:

> The process of cognitive restructuring, in order to assimilate new input, can be thought of as going on over time. As such it can be conceptualized in terms of *rate*. I have elsewhere referred to this variable as *perceptualization rate* (PR). A high PR would imply considerable elaboration in cognitive organization per unit time. This could be occasioned by a high rate of input of novel stimuli which the animal was able to assimilate. A low PR would imply little change or elaboration in cognitive structure per unit time. This could be the case when an animal is in a very familiar situation. It is postulated that an animal has an *optimum* PR, a rate which it *prefers*. This optimum would vary as a function of a number of variables, probably including species and strain, age, level of arousal, level of anxiety, and previous experience.

The animal is said to be able to move its PR towards the optimum 'by behaving in such a manner as to increase or decrease the input of novel stimuli' (*loc. cit.*, p. 313).

McReynolds never explains exactly in what respects the optimum PR is optimal or why a below-optimal PR is aversive. However he does suggest that 'anxiety is a function of unassimilated perceptual material' and therefore an above-optimum PR could induce considerable anxiety as a result of the build up of such material. Also in common with Glanzer (1958, p. 315):

> . . . it is postulated that the optimum PR for an animal is determined in part by adaptation level principles. This is to suggest that the rate of novelty input at which an animal is reared or lives for a long period of time tends to become the preferred rate for that animal.

A major problem with this theory is that no indication is given as to how the various determinants of the optimum PR are thought to interact. For example, what are the relative contributions of the 'level of arousal, level of anxiety and previous experience', even supposing that we can empirically distinguish them?

The approach adopted here follows from McReynolds' theory, in that the rate at which novel sensory input can be assimilated is thought to be of crucial importance in determining whether an animal will initially approach or avoid the source of that input. Proposal 6 suggests that the efficiency of the processes that assimilate novel sensory input into the cognitive model will vary with the capacity to attend to the discrepant input and also with the complexity of the representation of the environment at the time. There are thought to be two distinct determinants of the time taken for assimilation, the degree of stimulus discrepancy and the efficiency of the processes by which assimilation is achieved.

The degree of stimulus discrepancy must vary with the nature of the cognitive model at the time the discrepant input is perceived. The larger the number of categories and the lower the average confidence ratings of these categories, the greater would seem to be the likelihood that an encountered stimulus will approximate one or more of the existing categories and hence require less assimilation than if the model had had few categories with, on average, high confidence ratings. Therefore the nature of the cognitive model will influence the efficiency of sensory assimilation such that a 'complex' model will have a higher potential efficiency than a 'simple' model.

How rapidly a given stimulus discrepancy can be assimilated will depend upon the processing capacity available for this task. As we have seen, it has been suggested that the re-allocation of short term memory capacity requires 'cognitive effort' and that any modification of the belief structure also must involve work. The capacity for doing such work is determined by the energy available; energy reserves set the upper limits of processing capacity which can be allocated over the range of possible activities according to the expected demands of each. For an animal to be successful it must be attuned to its environment. In other words, we might expect the efficiency of a given process to be greatest when expectation that the process will be needed is high. So far we have discussed the belief structure only with respect to external stimuli but it must also contain expectancies associated with internal processes, e.g., digestion, respiration. These would tend to be reliably regular and thus only occasionally provide a discrepancy sufficient to control attention. It is proposed that a part of the belief structure, the 'comparator belief', is concerned with the level of comparator output to short-term memory; a category in effect consisting

96

of an adaptation level for comparator output. In this way it would be possible for an animal to anticipate novel input, in the sense that it might expect that at a certain time within a given sort of environment comparator output will be high. This expectancy would serve to 'reserve' capacity for processing discrepant input thereby saving the time and energy costs involved in reallocation. Certainly rhythms in the general level of stimulation-seeking have been found (e.g. Barry & Symmes, 1963; File & Day, 1972; Richter, 1967; Thor & Hoats, 1968).

Proposal 7 suggests that a gross imbalance between the level of comparator output and the efficiency of the assimilation processes is aversive. As the concept of a comparator belief has now been discussed, Proposal 7 can be restated to the effect that negative affect occurs when there is a large discrepancy between the expected levels of comparator output and the actual levels. The creation of this negative affect does not mean that the animal will necessarily avoid novel stimuli, for the quality of this aversive state is thought to be different according to the direction of the discrepancy. When the rate of novel input is high and thus comparator output is high, and the assimilation efficiency is low as a result of the expected comparator output being too low, then one sort of negative effect (i.e. fear, anxiety) is thought to accrue. Obviously, when faced with an environment so novel that the input from one aspect of it can not be assimilated before another discrepant input is perceived, it is advantageous for the animal to retreat. It is adaptive for small portions of the novel environment to be familiarized one after another thereby allowing escape to a familiar and safe locale to be more easily made if danger threatens. If the rate of novel input is low and the assimilation efficiency is high (i.e. a discrepancy between actual and expected comparator output in the reverse direction) then the other sort of negative affect (i.e. boredom) results. As the efficiency of the assimilation process is high, this is the most effective time to seek novel sensory input in an attempt to improve the predictive capabilities of the cognitive model. Boredom functions to help ensure that the central capacity that has already been allocated for detailed sensory processing is not wasted. Positive affect, i.e. a rewarding state, therefore occurs when there is little or no discrepancy between the expected and actual levels of comparator output. In effect all Proposal 7 implies is that an animal prefers the greatest degree of discrepant input to occur when it is best able to assimilate that input (see Munsinger & Kessen, 1964; Walker, 1973); or, to put it another way, the degree of stimulus mismatch that creates the least negative affect increases with increase in assimilation efficiency.

So far the affect relationship can account for the homeostatic effects of curiosity and boredom, but more needs to be said concerning the effects of long term sensory enrichment or deprivation, and in particular the connection between contrast and adaptation phenomena. Perhaps the easiest way to tackle this question is to imagine an animal taken from a sensory stimulating and varied environment and placed under sensory restriction. What should occur according to the theory proposed here?

Immediately the animal will perceive a high level of discrepant input derived from the novel surroundings. Comparator activity will be high, but as the animal has just come from an enriched evironment it is likely the assimilation efficiency will also be high. Positive affect will result and the animal will explore. Soon, however, the features, such as they are, of the restricted environment will have been assimilated and comparator activity will fall. Expectancies appropriate to the previous environment of the subject will still be triggered from time to time, and these will not be fulfilled. Hence a small amount of comparator activity will continue while the confidence ratings attached to the non-occurrence of these 'old' categories slowly rise, as do the confidence ratings attached to the new categories derived from the restricted environment. As the animal has only recently come from an enriched environment, it will take some time before the expected comparator values approximate the new level. Therefore the second major phase is associated with negative affect; boredom is derived from the still relatively high assimilation efficiency and the relatively low comparator output. Any small environmental discrepancy now has sufficient salience to control attention, and the animal will exhibit increased stimulation-seeking behaviour if given the opportunity; that is, to show evidence of a 'rebound' contrast effect.

Slowly the belief structure will degenerate, becoming composed of fewer categories associated with higher confidence ratings. This will lower the potential level of assimilation efficiency but also, more directly, the comparator belief values will have been adapting so that less capacity is being allocated for the assimilation processes. Any strong diurnal rhythm in stimulation-seeking behaviour should weaken as the restricted environment provides less contrast in levels of novel sensory input between day and night. A new 'lower' balance point between comparator output and assimilation efficiency will thus be reached. There will be little external discrepant input to control attention and therefore internal stimuli, which normally would not have sufficient salience, may gain priority. For example, the increase of hallucinatory experience under sensory deprivation (e.g. Zuckerman, 1969) has been thought to indicate attempts to regain some optimal arousal level. Here, it would be argued such sensations represent imagery that normally remains at a sub-conscious level while awake, only becoming conscious within dream states, but now being able to control attention and reach a conscious level. The few discrepancies now controlling attention will require only 'shallow processing' and hence the 'general level of consciousness' will be low. The homeostatic processes of curiosity and boredom will operate around the new balance point, but if the animal is given the opportunity to explore then such behaviour will be at a much lower intensity than that shown to identical test stimuli before the environmental change. The stimuli would now create too high a comparator output to 'balance' the lowered assimilation efficiency.

If the animal is replaced in the enriched environment, then the same processes operate but in reverse. In other words, there will be an initial period of extreme anxiety created by the imbalance between high comparator output and low assimilation efficiency. However, the latter will adapt in response to the more varied environment, and exploration will increase until a new 'higher' balance point is reached. Assimilation efficiency will increase slowly for the following reasons. First, perception of novel input sufficient to create a level of comparator output greater than expected will lead to extra capacity being allocated with associated increase in cognitive effort and therefore to a modification of the comparator belief. The latter process means that in similar circumstances in the future more capacity will be allocated for sensory processing, although obviously this cannot go on indefinitely. Second, the belief structure will be becoming more complex and, therefore, novel stimuli are likely to create smaller discrepancies. In other words, the growth in comparator output will tend to slow down since, I would suggest, there is no ceiling to the complexity of a belief structure. We can continue to know more and more about less and less as long as we remain in a complex, stochastic environment. The time lag between environmental change and reaching the new 'balance point' is that needed for the revision of the belief structure including, most importantly, the updating of the comparator belief category. The time required will thus depend upon the degree of contrast between the two environments, including their levels of variability for the confidence ratings have to be modified as well as the basic stimulus categories.

I think that a theory along these lines can account for a large portion of the data already reviewed. For example the observed differences between 'enriched' and 'deprived' animals when exposed to a novel environment follow from the proposed changes in assimilation efficiency which predict a greater latency to explore and a lower rate of decline in exploration once begun, in 'deprived' animals than in 'enriched' ones. In addition these proposals result in clear predictions concerning the relationship between contrast and adaptation effects. First, following a gross environmental change initially there should be evidence of a rebound contrast effect. In other words, if the animal is taken from a complex and varying sensory environment and placed in simple and constant surroundings, it should show an increase in stimulation-seeking activity when given the opportunity. An environmental change in the reverse direction should result in a decrease in such activity. Second, this rebound effect should be transitory as the animal slowly adapts to the new environment. Third, these effects should be reversible. Unfortunately, there have been very few relevant studies that have reported contrast and adaptation effects within a single paradigm.

The first study, by McCall (1966), found that initially the rats would respond for both increases and decreases in light intensity. The bar-press rate increased with increasing discrepancy in either direction and seemed not to be dependent upon any initial light intensity. After 3 days of testing, however, this stimulus contrast effect was replaced by a preference for low intensity illumination. McCall (1966, p. 41) argued that:

> . . . the pattern of results suggests that as 'novelty' of the light change decreased equally for both increment and decrement groups it was replaced by the natural more stable light preference of the organism, i.e. preference for the dimmest levels. Hence, decreasing the light remained reinforcing while increasing it did not.

McCall was thus suggesting that the adaptation effect stemmed from the 'nocturnal nature of the rat'.

Certainly the ecology of the subject can be very important: for example, King (1970) has found species-specific restrictions upon the range of illuminations through which an animal's preference can be measured. However the results of a second study, Lockard & Haerer (1968), suggest that ecological adaptations are not the sole processes that determine stable preference values. They found contrast effects which were only apparent when animals had been given less than 8 days prior adaptation to certain housing conditions. If rats were given longer than 8 days prior adaptation they exhibited preferences related to the adaptation conditions. The fact that maintenance related preferences could be established with as little as 8 days prior adaptation suggests that there are also more immediate processes operating than 'the nocturnal nature of the rat'.

Although these experiments are interesting, they provide no evidence for the reversibility of effects. If we are looking for true reversibility, it is not sufficient to determine whether an effect decays after cessation of a particular set of conditions. Rather, these conditions must be subsequently re-imposed to see whether the effects can be repeatedly re-set to their former levels. Good evidence for reversibility comes from the experiment of Inglis & Freeman (1976), which was specifically designed to test the predictions stated above.

Inglis & Freeman (1976) tested mature rats in an arena whose walls contained holes through which the animals could push their heads. A head input either caused a visual stimulus to be illuminated at the end of an alley behind the hole or the alley remained dark. The rats were randomly assigned to groups that differed in their maintenance histories before their test by being kept for differing lengths of time under the normal, sensory-enriched, animal-house conditions (N) or under sensory-restricted conditions (R). Thus 20R5N will be used to indicate a group was kept for 20 days under sensory restriction (R) and then for 5 days in the animal house (N) before the trial. The eight experimental groups were 0R, 5R, 10R, 20R, 20R5N, 20R10N, 20R20N, and 20R20N20R. Inglis and Freeman (1976, p. 412) write:

> If group 20R exhibits less exploration than group 0R and if the predicted full reversibility of effects occurs, the behaviour of group 20R20N should be like that of group 0R. This is tantamount to predicting a perfect cubic trend in a particular direction over the groups 0R, 20R, 20R20N and 20R20N20R.

Significant cubic trends were found in the three measures, latency to explore, rate of head input to photic stimuli and relative preference for photic stimuli. The other measure examined, mean duration of head input, revealed no significant inter-group differences. It is interesting that a dissociation between duration and rate measures has often been found in studies using both bar pressing (e.g. Glow et al., 1971; McCall, 1966) and head input (e.g. Sales, 1968) operants.

The data from the intermediate groups provided evidence of the symmetrical nature of the process underlying the cumulative effects observed after each environmental shift. The latency and rate measures revealed significant quadratic trends over data taken from all groups except 20R20N20R. However, most importantly, the preference data from these groups revealed a highly significant cubic trend. This was caused by a systematic displacement of the points of inflexion from 0R to 5R and from 20R to 20R5N. Animals moved from normal to restricted environments showed after 5 days a decrease in preference for the no-change stimulus, whereas rats moved in the reverse direction, showed an increase in this preference after 5 days in the new environment. Here then is evidence of the predicted homeostatic rebound effect directly preceding a reversible adaption effect. Inglis & Freeman (1976) speculated that, as their time units were arbitrarily chosen, testing at intervals less than 5 days might reveal similar rebound effects in the other measures. It would be valuable to conduct experiments using recycling environments with paradigms that should be able to detect the predicted changes in capacity allocation. I have already discussed two possible procedures that might be used in this way; the shadowing/delayed auditory feedback technique (Zelniker, 1971) for human subjects, and the use of a surprising post-trial event at varying intervals after a learning trial (Wagner et. al., 1973) for animals.

4.2.5 A Summary of the Entire System

Fig. 4.1 depicts how the concepts discussed in the previous three sections fit together. The symbols depicted in the cognitive model represent specific beliefs containing both category and confidence rating aspects. The system can perhaps best be summarized by considering each symbol in turn. The 'cross' is a belief that is activated by feedback from the results of prior expectancies previously associated with it, to produce an expectancy. The animal expects a stimulus input corresponding to 'cross' to occur. The comparator compares this expectancy with the 'cross' sensory input, there is no mismatch and the result is a feedback which enhances the confidence rating of the 'cross' belief within that context.

The 'open square' is a belief that has in the past been associated with the consummatory act of a need state. The animal is now acting under this need state, which endows the expectancy triggered from this belief with a level of valence dependent upon the level of the need state and the confidence rating of the expected connection between that belief and the opportunity to reduce the need state. The valenced expectancy is symbolized by the 'solid square'. The 'solid square' is matched with the 'open square' input and there is no mismatch in the configurations. However, the valence factor is equivalent to such a mismatch, and thus processing is continued within short-term memory. Capacity is allocated to this stimulus according to its priority in relation to other valenced or discrepant input being received at the same time. If the input is sufficient to control attention, then the animal will attend to that stimulus and behave in ways that have in the past been appropriate for enabling a reduction of the need state. There will also be feedback to enhance the confidence rating of the belief within the cognitive model and also possibly to modify the category component of that belief if the focal search provides subsequent input that necessitates shifts in emphasis within the default options of the belief.

The 'triangle' is a belief whose expectancy is not fulfilled by the 'circle' input.

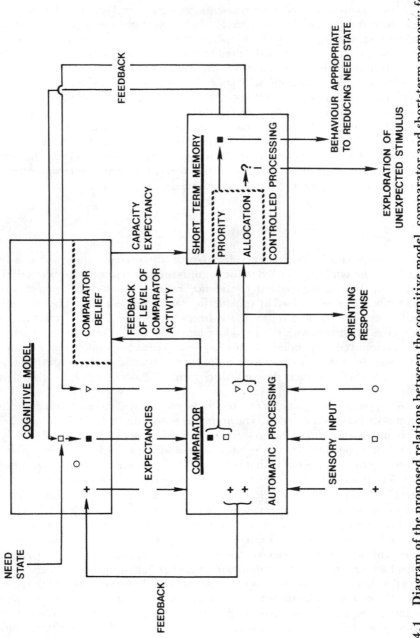

Fig. 4.1 Diagram of the proposed relations between the cognitive model, comparator and short-term memory: for explanation of the symbols see text Section 4.2.5.

This mismatch triggers the orienting response and processing is continued within short-term memory. The capacity priority given to the stimulus again depends upon the activation levels of the other discrepant, or valenced, input being received at that moment. It should be remembered that even if there is sufficient capacity for two or more inputs to be processed simultaneously, there may be behavioural incompatibility in the responses appropriate to each and thus only the behaviour corresponding to the highest priority input will be shown. If the discrepant input controls attention, then exploration of that input will occur and feedback will alter the confidence rating of the 'triangle' belief associated with the present context. This feedback will also trigger other expectancies that have in the past occasionally been verified within the present context until, finally, either (a) an existing 'circle' belief is activated and no mismatch occurs whereupon exploration ceases and the confidence rating of the 'circle' belief is enhanced, or (b) a category corresponding to the 'circle' input is created, possible through modification of existing categories, and again exploration ceases.

High-intensity stimuli reliably evoke a group of phasic arousal changes that together have been termed the 'defence reflex' (e.g. Sokolov, 1963). These changes could be incorporated into the model shown in Fig. 4.1 on an *ad hoc* basis by postulating that sensory input as well as expectancies could be weighted by some factor. If an input has an intensity above some threshold within the sensory receptor, then it would be weighted by this factor such that the comparator output for that sensory input would receive greater priority within short-term memory and the defence reflex would be triggered.

As discussed in the last section, whether the animal will immediately approach and actively explore the source of discrepant input or will withdraw and then only slowly examine the novel object, depends upon the capacity available within short term memory in relation to the output of the comparator. Fig. 4.1 shows feedback of information on the levels of comparator output to the comparator belief that uses these data to set future capacity limitations via the capacity expectancy. It may not always be possible to reserve sufficient capacity; for example, the animal may be sick or physically exhausted, and thus sufficient energy reserves may not be available for the complex processing conducted within short-term memory. If the comparator output to short-term memory requires more capacity than is present, either because the capacity expectancy was too low or because the capacity expectancy could not be fulfilled, then negative affect results. Similarly if the comparator output is too low for the allocated capacity then negative affect again occurs and stimulation seeking behaviour is shown in an attempt to increase the comparator output.

4.3 Conclusion

In the first section of this chapter it was argued that theories of intrinsic exploration founded upon need reduction principles are inadequate and it was suggested that a cognitive, information-processing, approach might be a better alternative. I then attempted in the following section to assemble concepts from several areas of study into a basic framework for such a cognitive theory. At the functional level the present system emphasizes that exploration serves to gather information concerning contingencies between perceptual events (including proprioceptive and other feedback from behavioural responses). These data are assimilated into a cognitive representation, or model, of the environment which is adaptive, in that it enables the animal to predict events with increasing accuracy. The gathering of information must be the dominant activity for any animal living in an unpredictable habitat, and a knowledge of the ecological niche of a species should enable us to assess the general level of stimulation-seeking behaviour that that species will show.

At the level of the proximal mechanism, curiosity, boredom and adaptation effects have been explained by showing how the first two could arise as a result of the discrepancy between the speed of an environmental change and the time required before adaptation processes once more attune the animal to its environment: contrast effects result from delayed adaptation. The suggested relationships between the mechanisms underlying the contrast and adaptation effects and other motivational systems, have broad implications. For example, an animal should only strive 'optimally' to reduce a specific need when the relevant deprivation state is sufficiently intense to gain attentional priority. Therefore 'optimal' behaviour should become 'less optimal' as the deprivation state is reduced for the valence of the need-related expectancies will fall, thereby enabling other environmental cues successfully to compete for attentional priority, with the result that stimulation-seeking behaviour will increasingly take over from behaviour appropriate to reduction of the need. It is possible that such a process might partly explain the satiation curve that, as McCleery (1977, p. 1011) writes:

> . . . has always presented a problem for the theorist of optimal behaviour sequences. Why, for example, does the animal not take its food or water at a constant rate until satiation has been achieved?

Although the present system contains few novel components, nevertheless the way in which these have been assembled does, as we have seen, create new, testable predictions and also suggests a fresh methodological technique, namely the use of recycling environments (Inglis & Freeman, 1976). However as the title of this chapter suggests, the present proposals should be seen only as an approximation towards a complete cognitive theory; I have side-stepped several important theoretical issues. For example, in what form is knowledge represented in the cognitive model: is it declarative or procedural in nature (Anderson, 1976; Winograd, 1975)? A declarative memory contains knowledge of relationships between perceptual events in a way that does not imply how this information should be used. A procedural memory, however, has programmes of action incorporated with the knowledge of such perceptual contingencies, thereby laying down how the information should be used. If a declarative mode is employed, then some separate action system is needed; thus Miller *et al.* (1960) distinguished between general procedural PLANS and a common declarative data bank that could supply parameters for the plans. The problem with this approach concerns what (or who?) chooses between alternative plans of action. A procedural memory obviates the need for a separate action system but, as Dickinson (1980, pp. 23–24) points out, just because certain uses are pre-programmed 'simple integration and inference is not possible with certain limited forms of procedural representation'. Tolman envisaged his network of beliefs as symbolizing 'meanings in the environment', a-what-leads-to-what relationship. A belief could be a 'means' as well as an 'end', thus implying that beliefs are often nested hierarchies of other beliefs, and that they are mainly procedural in nature. A rigid dichotomy between declarative or procedural modes is thus probably misleading; many theories have been proposed in which the basic memory unit can possess both aspects (e.g. 'scheme' — Piaget, 1952; 'schemata' — Neisser, 1976). In terms of the present system, I think that the nature of a belief may vary with its confidence rating. Thus a belief will become more rigidly procedural as its confidence rating increases; this would enable action to proceed automatically once an expectation triggered from the belief had been fulfilled (i.e. to form a habit). Processing within short-term memory would involve the dissociation of the declarative and procedural components of a belief, for only in this way could be formed new routines incorporating information from several, previously distinct, beliefs. Dissociation would become more difficult the more rigidly procedural the belief; in other words, habits are hard to break as a result of the previously high confidence ratings associated with them.

Since the 1960s there have been relatively few theories concerned with intrinsic exploration and, probably as a result, the number of experiments related to this topic has fallen sharply. In spite of the shortcomings of the present system I hope it may help to stimulate further experiments leading to better theories in a similar vein. I believe that only by accepting a strong cognitive bias in our explanations of behaviour can we hope to explain the functional significance of such attributes as imagination and self-awareness; but that is another, and even more speculative story.

Acknowledgements

I would like to thank J. Lazarus, D. H. Broom and N. H. Freeman for their constructive criticisms of earlier drafts of this chapter, and Gill Wilson for drawing the figure.

References

AINSLIE, G. W. (1974) Impulse control in pigeons. *Journal of Experimental Analysis of Behaviour* **21**, 485–489.

AITKEN, P. P. and SHELDON, M. H. (1970) Electric shock and rats preference for the familiar arm of a maze. *British Journal of Psychology* **61**, 95–97.

ANDERSON, J. R. (1976) *Language, Memory and Thought*. Hillsdale, NJ: Lawrence Erlbaum Associates.

ANDERSON, J. R. and BOWER, G. H. (1973) *Human Associative Memory*. Washington, DC: Winston.

ANDREW, R. J. (1974) Arousal and the causation of behaviour. *Behaviour* 31, 10–163.

ANDREW, R. J. (1976) Attentional processes and animal behaviour. In *Growing Points in Ethology* (Eds. P. P. G. BATESON and R. A. HINDE). Cambridge: Cambridge University Press.

ANDRONICO, M. P. and FORGAYS, D. G. (1962) Sensory stimulation and secondary reinforcement. *Journal of Psychology* 54, 209–219.

AYER, A. J. (1973) *The Central Problems of Philosophy*. London: Weidenfeld and Nicolson.

BARNES, G. W. and BARON, A. (1961) Stimulus complexity and sensory reinforcement. *Journal of Comparative and Physiological Psychology* 54, 466–469.

BARNETT, S. A. (1958) Experiments on 'neophobia' in wild and laboratory rats. *British Journal of Psychology* 49, 195–201.

BARRY, H. and SYMMES, D. (1963) Reinforcing effects of illumination change in different phases of the rat's diurnal cycle. *Journal of Comparative and Physiological Psychology* 56, 117–119.

BAUM, W. K. (1974) On two types of deviation from the matching law: bias and undermatching. *Journal of Experimental Analysis of Behavior* 22, 231–242.

BERLYNE, D. E. (1950) Novelty and curiosity as determinants of exploratory behaviour. *British Journal of Psychology* 41, 68–80.

BERLYNE, D. E. (1955) The arousal and satiation of perceptual curiosity in the rat. *Journal of Comparative and Physiological Psychology* 48, 238–246.

BERLYNE, D. E. (1960) *Conflict, Arousal and Curiosity*. New York: McGraw-Hill.

BERLYNE, D. E. (1963) Motivational problems raised by exploratory and epistemic behaviour. In *Psychology: A study of a Science* (Ed. S. KOCH) New York: McGraw-Hill.

BERLYNE, D. E. (1966) Curiosity and Behavior. *Science* 153, 25–33.

BERLYNE, D. E. (1967) Arousal and reinforcement. *Nebraska Symposium on Motivation* 15, 1–110.

BERLYNE, D. E. (1969) The reward value of indifferent stimulation. In *Reinforcement and Behavior* (Ed. J. T. TAPP). New York: Academic Press.

BERLYNE, D. E. KOENIG, I. D. V. and HIROTA, T. (1966) Novelty, arousal and the reinforcement of diversive exploration in the rat. *Journal of Comparative and Physiological Psychology* 62, 222–226.

BOLLES, R. C. (1972) Reinforcement, expectancy and learning. *Psychological Review* 79, 394–409.

BOLLES, R. C. and DELORGE, J. (1962) Effects of hunger on exploration in a familiar locale. *Psychological Reports* 10, 54.

BOMBARD, A. (1953) *Voyage of the Heretique*. New York: Simon & Schuster.

BORING, E. G. (1950) *A History of Experimental Psychology*. New York: Appleton-Century-Crofts.

BRAINARD, D. L. (1929) *The Outpost of the Lost; An Arctic Adventure*. Indianapolis: Bobbs-Merrill.

BROADBENT, D. E. (1958) *Perception and Communication*. London: Pergamon Press.

BRONSTEIN, P. M. (1972) Repeated trials with the albino rat in the open field as a function of age and deprivation. *Journal of Comparative and Physiological Psychology* 81, 84–93.

106

BRUNER, J. (1957) On perceptual readiness. *Psychological Review* **64**, 123-152.

BRUNSWIK, E. (1939) Probability as a determiner of rat behavior. *Journal of Experimental Psychology* **25**, 175-197.

BUTLER, R. A. (1957) The effect of deprivation of visual incentives on visual exploration motivation in monkeys. *Journal of Comparative and Physiological Psychology* **50**, 177-179.

BUTLER, R. A. (1965) Investigative behavior. In *Behavior or Non-human Primates* (Eds. A. M. SCHRIER, H. F. HARLOW and F. STOLLNITZ). New York: Academic Press.

BUTLER, R. A. and HARLOW, H. F. (1954) Persistence of visual exploration in monkeys. *Journal of Comparative and Physiological Psychology* **47**, 258-263.

CARACO, T. (1980) On foraging time allocation in a stochastic environment. *Ecology* **61**, 119-128.

CARACO, T., MARTINGDALE, S. and WHITHAM, T. S. (1980) An empirical demonstration of risk-sensitive foraging. *Animal Behaviour* **28**, 820-830.

CHAN, W. T. (1963) *A Source Book in Chinese Philosophy*. London: Oxford University Press.

CHARLESWORTH, W. W. and THOMPSON, W. R. (1957) Effect of lack of visual stimulus variation on exploratory behavior in the adult white rate. *Psychological Reports* **3**, 509-512.

CHERRY, E. C. (1953) Some experiments on the recognition of speech with one and with two ears. *Journal of the Acoustical Society of America* **25**, 975-979.

COOMBS, C. H. (1964) *A Theory of Data*. New York: Wiley.

COOMBS, C. H. (1975) Portfolio theory and the measurement of risk. In *Human Judgement and Decision Processes* (Ed. S. SCHWARTZ). New York: Academic Press.

COOMBS, C. H. and AVRUNIN, G. S. (1977) Single-peaked functions and the theory of preference. *Psychological Review* **84**, 216-230.

COOMBS, C. H. & MEYERS, D. E. (1969) Risk preference in coin-toss games. *Journal of Mathematical Psychology* **6**, 514-527.

COOMBS, C. H., DONNELL, M. L. and KIRK, D. B. (1978) Risk preference in lotteries. *Journal of Experimental Psychology: Human Perception & Performance* **4**, 497-512.

COWLES, J. T. and NISSEN, H. W. (1937) Reward expectancy in delayed responses of chimpanzess. *Journal of Comparative and Physiological Psychology* **24**, 345-358.

DALY, M. (1973) Early stimulation of rodents: a critical review of present interpretations. *British Journal of Psychology* **64**, 435-460.

DASHIELL, J. F. (1925) A quantitative demonstration of animal drive. *Journal of Comparative Psychology* **5**, 205-208.

DEAUX, E. and ENGSTROM, R. (1973) The temperature of ingested water: its effect on body temperature. *Physiological Psychology* **1**, 152-154.

DELIUS, J. D. (1970) Irrelevant behaviour, information processing and arousal homeostasis. *Psychologische Forschung. Zeitschrift fur Psychologie. Berlin*, **33**, 165-188.

DEMBER, W. N. (1956) Response by the rat to environmental change. *Journal of Comparative and Physiological Psychology* **49**, 93-95.

DEMBER, W. N. and EARL, R. (1957) Analysis of exploratory, manipulatory and curiosity behaviours. *Psychological Review* **64**, 91-96.

DEMBER, W. N. and FOWLER, H. F. (1958) Spontaneous alternation behavior. *Psychological Bulletin* **54**, 62-64.

DEMBER, W. N. EARL, R. W. and PARADISE, N. (1957) Response by rats to differential stimulus complexity. *Journal of Comparative and Physiological Psychology* **50**, 514-518.

DEUTSCH, J. A. (1960) *The Structural Basis of Behavior*. Chicago: University of Chicago Press.

DEUTSCH, J. A. and DEUTSCH, D. (1963) Attention: Some theoretical considerations. *Psychological Review* **70**, 80-90.

DICKINSON, A. (1980) *Contemporary Animal Learning Theory*. Cambridge: Cambridge University Press.

DORFMAN, D. D (1965) Aesthetic preference as a function of pattern information. *Psychonomic Science* **3**, 85–86.

EDWARD, H. P., BARRY, W. F. and WYSPIANSKI, J. O. (1968) Early environment effects on rat photic evoked potentials. *Revista Interamericana de Psicologia* **2**, 85–92.

EHRLICH, A. (1959) Effects of past experience on exploratory behaviour in rats. *Canadian Journal of Psychology* **13**, 248–254.

EHRLICH, A. (1961) Effects of past experience on the rats response to novelty. *Canadian Journal of Psychology* **15**, 15–19.

EISENBERGER, R. (1972) Explanations of rewards that do not reduce tissue needs. *Psychological Bulletin* **77**, 319–339.

EISENBERGER, R., MYERS, A. K. SANDERS, R. and SHANAB, M. (1970) Stimulus control of spontaneous alternation in the rat. *Journal of Comparative and Physiological Psychology* **49**, 549–552.

ESTES, W. K. (1972) An associative basis for coding and organization in memory. In *Coding Processes in Human Memory* (Eds. A. W. MELTON and E. MARTIN). New York: Wiley.

EWER, R. F. (1971) The biology and behaviour of a free living population of black rats (*Rattus rattus*). *Animal Behaviour Monographs* **4**, 127–174.

FILE, S. E. and DAY, S, (1972) Effect of time of day and food deprivation upon exploratory behaviour in the rat. *Animal Behaviour* **20**, 758–763.

FISKE, D. W. and MADDI, S. R. (1961) A conceptual framework. In: *Functions of Varied Experience* (Eds. D. W. FISKE and S. R. MADDI). Homewood, Ill.: Dorsey.

FORGAYS, D. G. and LEVIN, H. (1958) Learning as a function of sensory stimulation in food-deprived and food-satiated animals. *Journal of Comparative and Physiological Psychology* **51**, 50–54.

FOWLER, H. (1958) Response to environmental change: A postive replication. *Psychological Reports* **4**, 506.

FOWLER, H. (1965) *Curiosity and Exploratory Behaviour*. New York: Macmillan.

FOWLER, H. (1967) Satiation and curiosity: Constructs for a drive and incentive motivational theory of exploration. In *The Psychology of Learning an Motivation* (Eds. K. W. SPENCE and J. T. SPENCE). New York: Academic Press.

FOWLER, H. (1978) Cognitive associations as evident in the blocking effects of response-contingent CS.$_S$. In *Cognitive Processes in Animal Behavior* (Eds. S. H. HULSE, H. FOWLER and W. K. HONIG). Hillsdale: Lawrence Erlbaum Associates.

FOX, S. S. (1962) Self-maintained sensory input and sensory deprivation in monkeys. *Journal of Comparative and Physiological Psychology* **55**, 438–444.

FREUD, S. (1935) *A General Introduction to Psycho-analysis*. New York: Liveright Publishing Corporation.

GARDNER, B. T. and GARDNER, R. A. (1975) Evidence for sentence constituents in the early utterances of child and chimpanzee. *Journal of Experimental Psychology* **104**, 244–267.

GENDREAU, P. E., FREEDMAN, N., WILDE, G. J. S. and SCOTT, G. D. (1968) Stimulation seeking after seven days of perceptual deprivation. *Perceptual and Motor Skills* **26**, 547–550.

GIRDNER, J. B. (1953) An experimental analysis of behavioural effects of a perceptual consequence unrelated to organic drive states. *American Psychologist* **8**, 354–355.

GLANZER, M. (1953) Stimulus satiation: an explanation of spontaneous alternation and related phenomena. *Psychological Review* **60**, 257–268.

108

GLANZER, M. (1958) Curiosity, exploratory drive and stimulus satiation. *Psychological Bulletin* **55**, 302–315.

GLANZER, M. (1961) Changes and interrelations in exploratory behaviour. *Journal of Comparative and Physiological Psychology* **54**, 433–438.

GLOW, P. H., RUSSELL, A. and KIRBY, N. H. (1971) Sensory reinforcement using paired stimuli from different modalities. *Australian Journal of Psychology* **23**, 133–137.

GROSS, K. (1901) *The Play of Man* (Trans. by E. L. BALDWIN). New York: D. Appleton.

GROSSMAN, S. (1980) How does a brain build a cognitive code? *Psychological Review* **87**, 1–51.

HABER, R. N. (1958) Discrepancy from adaptation level as a source of affect. *Journal of Experimental Psychology* **56**, 370–375.

HARLOW, H. F. (1950) Learning and satiation of response in intrinsically motivated complex puzzle performance by monkeys. *Journal of Comparative and Physiological Psychology* **43**, 289–294.

HARLOW, H. F. (1953) Motivation as a factor in the acquisition of new responses. *Nebraska Symposium on Motivation* **1**, 24–48.

HARLOW, H. F., BLAZEK, N. C. and McCLEARN, G. E. (1956) Manipulatory motivation in the infant rhesus monkey. *Journal of Comparative and Physiological Psychology* **49**, 444–448.

HAUDE, R. H. and RAY, O. S. (1967) Visual exploration in monkeys as a function of visual incentive duration and sensory deprivation. *Journal of Comparative and Physiological Psychology* **64**, 332–336.

HAYWOOD, H. C. and WACHS, T. D. (1967) Effects of arousing stimulation upon novelty preference in rats. *British Journal of Psychology* **58**, 77–84.

HEARST, E. (1978) Stimulus relationships and feature selection in learning and behaviour. In *Cognitive Processes in Animal Behavior* (Eds. S. H. HULSE, H. FOWLER, and W. K. HONIG). Hillsdale: Lawrence Erlbaum Associates.

HEBB, D. O. (1949) *The Organization of Behaviour*. New York: Wiley.

HEBB, D. O. (1955) Drives and the conceptual nervous system. *Psychological Reviews* **62**, 243–254.

HEFFERLINE, R. F. (1950) An experimental study of avoidance. *Genetic Psychology Monographs* **42**, 231–334.

HELSON, H. (1974) Adaptation level as a frame of reference for prediction of psychophysical data. *American Journal of Psychology* **60**, 1–28.

HELSON, H. (1959) Adaptation level theory. In *Psychology: A Study of a Science, Vol. 1* (Ed. S. KOCH). New York: McGraw-Hill.

HELSON, H. (1964) *Adaptation-Level Theory*. New York: Harper & Row.

HENDRICK, I. (1942) Instinct and the ego during infancy. *Psychoanalytical Quarterly* **11**, 33–58.

HENDRICK, I. (1943) The discussion of the 'instinct to master'. *Psychoanalytical Quarterly* **12**, 561–565.

HERRNSTEIN, R. J. (1970) On the law of effect. *Journal of Experimental Analysis of Behavior* **13**, 243–266.

HERRNSTEIN, R. J. (1979) Acquisition, generalization and discrimination reversal of a natural concept. *Journal of Experimental Psychology: Animal Behavior Processes* **5**, 116–129.

HERRNSTEIN, R. J. and LOVELAND, D.H. (1964) Complex visual concept in the pigeon. *Science* **146**, 549–551.

HOFSTADTER, D. R. (1979) *Godel, Escher, Bach: An Eternal Golden Braid*. Harmondsworth: Penguin Books.

HUDSON, B. B. (1950) One trial learning in the domestic cat. *Genetic Psychology Monographs* **41**, 99–145.

109

HUGHES, R. N. (1965) Food deprivation and locomotor exploration in the white rat. *Animal Behaviour* **13**, 30–32.

HULL, C. L. (1943) *Principles of Behavior*. New York: Appleton-Century-Crofts.

HULL, C. L. (1952) *A Behavior System: An Introduction to Behavior Theory Concerning the Individual Organism*. New Haven: Yale University Press.

HULSE, S. H. (1978) Cognitive structure and serial pattern learning by animals. In *Cognitive Processes in Animal Behavior* (Eds. S. H. HULSE, H. FOWLER and W. K. HONIG). Hillsdale: Lawrence Erlbaum Associates.

INGLIS, I. R. (1975a) Enriched sensory experience in adulthood increases subsequent exploratory behaviour in the rat. *Animal Behaviour* **23**, 932–940.

INGLIS, I. R. (1975b) Exploratory behaviour in the hooded rat. Ph.D. Thesis, University of Bristol.

INGLIS, I. R. and FREEMAN, N. H. (1976) Reversible effects of ambient housing stimulation upon stimulation-seeking in rats. *Quarterly Journal of Experimental Psychology* **28**, 409–417.

ISAAC, W. (1962) Evidence for a sensory drive in monkeys. *Psychological Reports* **11**, 175–181.

JONES, A. (1964) Drive and incentive variables associated with the statistical properties of sequences of stimuli. *Journal of Experimental Psychology* **62**, 126–137.

JONES, A. (1969) Stimulation seeking behavior. In *Sensory Deprivation: Fifteen Years of Research* (Ed. J. P. ZUBEK). New York: Appleton-Century-Crofts.

KAHNEMAN, D. (1973) *Attention and Effort*. Englewood Cliffs NJ: Prentice-Hall.

KAMIN, L. J. (1969) Predictability, surprise, attention and conditioning. In *Punishment and Aversive Behaviour* (Eds. B. A. CAMPBELL and R. M. CHURCH) New York: Appleton-Century-Crofts.

KAMMANN, R. (1966) Verbal complexity and preferences in poetry. *Journal of Verbal Learning and Verbal Behaviour* **5**, 536–540.

KANT, E. (1781) *Critique of Pure Reason* (Translated by N. Kemp Smith). London: Macmillan, 1928.

KAPLAN, M. F. and SCHWARTZ, S. (Eds) (1975). *Human Judgement and Decision Processes*. New York: Academic Press.

KENNY, A. (1973) *Wittgenstein*. London: Allen Lane.

KING, J. A. (1970) Light reinforcement in four taxa of deermice. *Journal of Comparative and Physiological Psychology* **71**, 22–28.

KISH, G. B. (1955) Learning when the onset of illumination is used as a reinforcing stimulus. *Journal of Comparative and Physiological Psychology* **48**, 261–264.

KIVY, P. N., EARL, R. W. and WALKER, E. L. (1956). Stimulus context and ratiation. *Journal of Comparative and Physiological Psychology* **49**, 90–92.

KLING, J. W., HOROWITZ, L. and DELHAGEN, J. E. (1956) Light on a positive reinforcer for rat responding. *Psychological Reports* **2**, 337–340.

KONORSKY, J. (1967) *Integrative Activity of the Brain*. Chicago: Chicago University Press.

KRUSKAL, J. B. (1964a) Multi-dimensional scaling by optimizing goodness of fit to a nonmetric hypothesis. *Psychometrika* **29**, 1–28.

KRUSKAL, J. B. (1964b) Nonmetric multidimensional scaling. A numerical method. *Psychometrika* **29**, 29–42.

LABERGE, D. (1973) Attention and the measurement of perceptual learning. *Memory & Cognition* **1**, 268–276.

LABERGE, D. (1976) Perceptual learning and attention. In *Handbook of Learning and Cognitive Processes: Attention and memory* (Ed. W. K. ESTES) Hillsdale: Lawrence Erlbaum Associates.

LAVERY, J. J. and FOLEY, P. J. (1965) Bar pressing by rats as a function of auditory stimulation. *Psychonomic Science* **3**, 199–200.

LEUBA, C. (1955) Toward some integration of learning theories: the concept of optimal stimulation. *Psychological Reports* **1**, 27–33.

LOCKARD, R. B. (1963) Self regulated exposure to light by albino rats as a function of rearing luminance and test luminance. *Journal of Comparative and Physiological Psychology* **56**, 558–564.

LOCKARD, R. B. and HAERER, H. (1968). Time course of change in light preference resulting from prolonged exposure to adapting stimuli. *Journal of Comparative and Physiological Psychology* **65**, 529–537.

LOGAN, F. A. (1965) Decision making by rats: Delay versus amount of reward. *Journal of Comparative and Physiological Psychology* **59**, 1–12.

LONG, C. J. and TAPP, J. T. (1967). Reinforcing properties of odors for the albino rat. *Psychonomic Science* **7**, 17–18.

LUBOW, R. E. (1974) High order concept formation in the pigeon. *Journal of the Experimental Analysis of Behaviour* **21**, 475–483.

MACCORQUODALE, K. and MEEHL, P. E. (1954). Edward C. Tolman. In *Modern Learning Theory* (Ed. W. K. ESTES). New York: Appleton-Century-Croft.

MACKINTOSH, N. J. (1978a) Cognitive or associative theories of conditioning: implications of an analysis of blocking. In *Cognitive Processes in Animal Behavior* (Eds. S. H. HULSE, H. FOWLER, and W. K. HONIG). Hillscale: Lawrence Erlbaum Associates.

MACKINTOSH, N. J. (1978b) Conditioning. In *Psychology Survey No. 1.* (Ed. B. M. FOSS). London: George Allen & Unwin.

MAY, R. B. (1968) Pretest eposure, changes in pattern complexity and choice. *Journal of Comparative and Physiological Psychology* **66**, 139–143.

McCALL, R. B. (1965). Stimulus-change in light-contingent bar pressing. *Journal of Comparative and Physiological Psychology* **59**, 258–262.

McCALL, R. B. (1966) Initial-consequent-change surface in light-contingent bar pressing. *Journal of Comparative and Physiological Psychology* **62**, 35–42.

McCLEERY, R. H. (1977) On satiation curves. *Animal Behaviour* **25**, 1005–1016.

McCLELLAND, D. C. and CLARK, R. A. (1953) Antecedent conditions for affective arousal. In *The Achievement Motive* (Eds. D. C. McCLELLAND, J. W. ATKINSON, R. A. CLARK, and E. L. LOWELL). New York: Appleton-Century-Crofts.

McCOY, D. F. and JANKOVITCH, J. P. (1972). Effects of continuous exposure to high gravity preference in rats. *Journal of Comparative and Physiological Psychology* **78**, 305–310.

McFARLAND, D. and HOUSTON, A. (1981). *Quantitative Ethology*. London: Pitman Books.

McREYNOLDS, P. (1962). Exploratory Behavior: a theoretical interpretation. *Psychological Reports* **11**, 311–318.

MENZEL, E. W. (1962) The effects of stimulus size and proximity upon avoidance of complex objects in rhesus monkeys. *Journal of Comparative and Physiological Psychology* **55**, 1044–1046.

MENZEL, E. W. (1978) Cognitive mapping in chimpanzees. In *Cognitive Processes in Animal Behavior* (Eds. S. H. HULSE, H. FOWLER and W. K. HONIG). Hillsdale: Lawrence Erlbaum Associates.

MILLER, G. A., GALANTER, E. and PRIBRAM, K. H. (1960). *Plans and the Structure of Behavior*. New York: Holt, Rinehart & Winston.

MONTGOMERY, K. C. (1951) Spontaneous alternation as a function of time between trials and amount of work. *Journal of Experimental Psychology* **42**, 82–93.

MONTGOMERY, K. C. (1952) Exploratory behavior and its relation to spontaneous alternation in a series of maze exposures. *Journal of Comparative and Physiological Psychology* **45**, 287–293.

MONTGOMERY, K. C. (1954) The role of exploratory drive in learning. *Journal of Comparative and Physiological Psychology* **47**, 60–64.

MONTGOMERY, K. C. (1955) The relation between fear induced by novel stimulation and exploratory behaviour. *Journal of Comparative and Physiological Psychology* **48**, 254–260.

MONTGOMERY, K. C. and MONKMAN, J. A. (1955) Relation between fear and exploratory behaviour. *Journal of Comparative and Physiological Psychology* **48**, 132–136.

MONTGOMERY, K. C. and SEGALL, M. (1955) Discrimination learning based upon the exploratory drive. *Journal of Comparative and Physiological Psychology* **48**, 225–228.

MONTGOMERY, K. C. and ZIMBARDO, P. G. (1957) Effect of sensory and behavioural deprivation upon exploratory behaviour in the rat. *Perceptual and Motor Skills* **7**, 223–229.

MORAY, N. (1959) Attention in dichotic listening: Affective cues and the influence of instructions. *Quarterly Journal of Experimental Psychology* **11**, 56–60.

MORGAN, M. J., FITCH, M. D., HOLMAN, J. G. and LEA, S. E. G. (1976) Pigeons learn the concept of an 'A'. *Perception* **5**, 57–66.

MUNSINGER, H. and KESSEN, W. (1964) Uncertainty, structure and preference. *Psychological Monographs* **78**, whole No. 586.

MYERS, A. K. and MILLER, N. E. (1954) Failure to find a learned drive based on hunger: evidence for learning motivated by exploration. *Journal of Comparative and Physiological Psychology* **47**, 428–436.

NAVON, D. and GOPHER, D. (1979) On the economy of the human processing system. *Psychological Review* **86**, 214–255.

NEISSER, U. (1967) *Cognitive Psychology*. New York: Appleton-Century-Crofts.

NEISSER, U. (1976) *Cognitive and Reality*. San Francisco: Freeman.

NISSEN, H. W. (1930) A study of exploratory behaviour in the white rat by means of the obstruction method. *Journal of Genetic Psychology* **37**, 361–376.

NORMAN, D. A. (1968) Toward a theory of memory and attention. *Psychological Review* **75**, 522–536.

NORMAN, D. A. (1969) Memory while shadowing. *Quarterly Journal of Experimental Psychology* **21**, 85–93.

NORMAN, D. A. (1970) *Models of Human Memory*. New York: Academic Press.

O'CONNELL, R. H. (1965) Trials with tedium and titillation. *Psychological Bulletin* **63**, 170–179.

PIAGET, J. (1952) *The Origins of Intelligence in Children*. New York: International University Press.

POOLE, J. and LANDER, D. G. (1971) The pigeon's concept of pigeon. *Psychonomic Science* **25**, 157–158.

PREMACK, D. and BAHWELL, R. (1959) Operant-level lever pressing in a monkey as a function of interest interval. *Journal of the Experimental Analysis of Behaviour* **2**, 127–131.

PREMACK, D. and COLLER, G. (1962) Analysis of nonreinforcement variables affecting response probability. *Psychological Monographs* **76**, 1–178.

PRYOR, K. W., HAAG, R. and O'REILLY, J. (1969) The creative porpoise. Training for novel behaviour. *Journal of the Experimental Analysis of Behaviour* **12**, 653–661.

PUBOLS, B. H. (1962) Constant versus variable delay of reinforcement. *Journal of*

Comparative Physiological Psychology **55**, 52–56.

RABEDEAU, R. and MILES, R. C. (1959) Response decrement in visual exploratory behaviour. *Journal of Comparative and Physiological Psychology* **52**, 364–367.

RACHLIN, H. and GREEN, L. (1972) Commitment, choice and self-control. *Journal of Experimental Analysis of Behavior* **17**, 15–22.

RESCORLA, R. A. (1978) Some implications of a cognitive perspective on Pavlovian conditioning. In *Cognitive Processes in Animal Behavior* (Eds. S. H. HULSE, H. FOWLER and W. K. HONIG). Hillsdale: Lawrence Erlbaum Associates.

RICHARDS, W. J. and LESLIE, G. R. (1962) Food and water deprivation as influences on exploration. *Journal of Comparative and Physiological Psychology* **55**, 834–837.

RICHTER, C. P. (1967) Psycopathology of periodic behaviour in animals and man. In *Comparative Psychopathology of Animals and Humans* (Eds. J. ZUBIN and H. F. HUNT). New York: Grune & Stratton.

ROBINSON, J. S. (1959) Light onset and termination as reinforcers for rats under normal light conditions. *Psychological Reports* **5**, 793–796.

ROBINSON, J. S. (1961) The reinforcing effects of response-contingent light increment and decrement in hooded rats. *Journal of Comparative and Physiological Psychology* **54**, 470–473.

ROSCH, E. and LLOYD B. B (Eds.) (1978) *Cognition and Categorization.* New Jersey: Lawrence Erlbaum Associates.

RUSSELL, P. A. (1973) Relationships between exploration and fear: A review. *British Journal of Psychology* **64**, 417–433.

RYLE, G. (1951) *The Concept of Mind.* London: Hutchinson.

SACKETT, G. P. (1967) Response to novelty and complexity as a function of rats' early experiences. *Journal of Comparative and Physiological Psychology* **63**, 369–375.

SALES, S. M. (1968) Stimulus complexity as a determinant of approach behavior and inspection time in the hooded rat. *Canadian Journal of Psychology* **22**, 11–17.

SCHNEIDER, W. and SHIFFRIN, R. M. (1977) Controlled and automatic human information processing: 1. Detection, search and attention. *Psychological Review* **84**, 1–66.

SCHULTZ, D. P. (1965) *Sensory Restriction: Effects on Behavior.* New York: Academic Press.

SCHUTTE, W. and ZUBEK, J. P. (1967) Changes in olfactory and gustatory sensitivity after prolonged visual deprivation. *Canadian Journal of Psychology* **21**, 337–345.

SHELDON, M. H. (1968) The effect of electric shock on rats choice between familiar and unfamiliar maze arms: a replication. *Quarterly Journal of Experimental Psychology* **20**, 400–404.

SHEPARD, R. N. (1962) The analysis of proximities: Multidimensional scaling with an unknown distance function. *Psychometrika* **27**, 125–140.

SHIFFRIN, R. M. and SCHNEIDER, W. (1977) Controlled and automatic human information processing: II. Perceptual learning, automatic attending and a general theory. *Psychological Review* **84**, 127–190.

SLOVIC, P. (1967) The relative influence of probabilities and pay-offs upon perceived risk of a gamble. *Psychonomic Science* **9**, 223–224.

SMEDSLUND, J. (1955) *Multiple Probability Learning.* Oslo: Akademisk Forlag.

SMITH, S. and MYERS, T. I. (1966) Stimulation seeking during sensory deprivation. *Perceptual and Motor Skills* **23**, 1151–1163.

SOKOLOV, E. N. (1963) Higher nervous functions: the orienting reflex. *Annual Review of Physiology* **25**, 545–580.

SOKOLOV, E. N. (1969) The modelling properties of the nervous system. In *A Handbook of Contemporary Soviet Psychology* (Eds. M. COLE and I. MALTZMAN). New York: Bask Books.

SOSKIN, R. A. (1963) The effect of early experience upon the formation of environmental preferences in rats. *Journal of Comparative and Physiological Psychology* **56**, 303–306.

SPENCE, K. W. (1956) *Behavior Theory and Conditioning*. New Haven: Yale University Press.

STEVENS, D. W. (1981) The logic of risk-sensitive foraging preferences. *Animal Behaviour* **29**, 628–629.

STUDELSKA, D. R. and KEMBLE, E. D. (1979) Effects of briefly experienced environmental complexity on open field behaviour in rats. *Behavioral & Neural Biology* **26**, 492–496.

TERRY, W. S. (1979) Habituation and dishabituation of rats' exploration of a novel environment. *Animal Learning & Behavior* **7**, 525–536.

THISTLETHWAITE, D. L. (1951) A critical review of latent learning and related experiments. *Psychological Bulletin* **48**, 97–129.

THOMAS, H. (1966) Preference for random shapes: Ages six through nineteen years. *Child Development* **37**, 843–859.

THOMAS, H. (1969) Unidirectional changes in preference for increasing visual complexity in the cat. *Journal of Comparative and Physiological Psychology* **68**, 296–302.

THOMAS, H. (1971) Discrepancy hypotheses: methodological and theoretical considerations. *Psychological Review* **78**, 249–259.

THOMPSON, W. R. and HIGGINS, W. H. (1958) Emotion and organized behavior: Experimental data bearing on the Leper-Young controversy. *Journal of Psychology* **12**, 61–68.

THOMPSON, W. R., HERON, W. and SCOTT, T. (1954) The effect of early restriction on activity in dogs. *Journal of Comparative and Physiological Psychology* **47**, 77–82.

THOR, D. H. and HOATS, D. L. (1968) A circadian variable in self exposure to light by the rat. *Psychonomic Science* **12**, 1–2.

TIIRA, E. (1955) *Raft of Despair*. New York: Dutton.

TINKLEPAUGH, O. L. (1928) An experimental study of representative factors in monkeys. *Journal of Comparative Psychology* **8**, 197–236.

TOLMAN, E. C. (1932) *Purposive Behavior in Animals and Men*. New York: Appleton-Century-Crofts.

TOLMAN, E. C. (1948) Cognitive maps in rats and men. *Psychological Review* **55**, 189–208.

TOLMAN, E. C. (1955) Principles of performance. *Psychological Review* **62**, 315–326.

TOLMAN, E. C. (1959) Principles of purposive behavior. In *Psychology: A Study of a Science, Vol. 2* (Eds. S. KOCH) New York: McGraw-Hill.

TOLMAN, E. C. (1966) *Behavior and Psychological Man*. Berkeley: University of California Press.

TOLMAN, E. C. and BRUNSWIK, E. (1935) The organism and the causal texture of the environment. *Psychological Review* **42**, 43–77.

TREISMAN, A. M. (1960) Contextual cues in selective listening. *Quarterly Journal of Experimental Psychology* **12**, 242–248.

TVERSKY, A. (1977) Features of similarity. *Psychological Reviews* **84**, 327–352.

VERINIS, J. S., BRANDSMA, J. M. and COFER, C. N. (1968) Discrepancy from expectations in relation to affect and motivation: Tests of McClelland's hypothesis. *Journal of Personality and Social Psychology* **9**, 47–58.

VITZ, P. C. (1966a) Affect as a function of stimulus variation. *Journal of Experimental Psychology* **71**, 74–79.

VITZ, P. C. (1966b) Preference for different amounts of visual complexity. *Behavioral Science* **11**, 105–114.

WAGNER, A. R. (1971) Elementary associations. In *Essays in Neobehaviorism: A Memorial Volume to Kenneth W. Spence* (Eds. H. H. KENDLER and J. T. SPENCE). New York: Appleton-Century-Crofts.

WAGNER, A. R. (1978) Expectancies and the priming of STM. In *Cognitive Processes in Animal Behavior* (Eds. S. H. HULSE, H. FOWLER and W. K. HONIG). Hillsdale: Lawrence Erlbaum Associates.

WAGNER, A. R. and TERRY, W. S. (1975) Backward conditioning to a CS following an expected vs a surprising UCS. *Animal Learning and Behavior* **3**, 370–374.

WAGNER, A. R., RUDY, J. W. and WHITLOW, J. W. (1973) Rehearsal in animal conditioning. *Journal of Experimental Psychology Monograph* **97**, 407–426.

WALKER, E. L. (1956) The duration and course of reaction decrement and the influence of reward. *Journal of Comparative and Physiological Psychology* **49**, 167–176.

WALKER, E. L. (1973) Psychological complexity and preference: a hedgehog theory of behavior. In *Pleasure, Reward, Preference* (Eds. D. E. BERLYNE and K. B. MADSEN). New York: Academic Press.

WALKER, E. L. and WALKER, B. E. (1964) Response to stimulus complexity in the rat. *Psychological Record* **14**, 489–497.

WELKER, W. I. (1956) Some determinants of play and exploration in chimpanzees. *Journal of Comparative and Physiological Psychology* **49**, 84–89.

WELKER, W. I. (1957) Free vs. forced exploration of a novel situation by rats. *Psychological Reports* **3**, 95–108.

WENDT, R. H., LINDSLEY, D. F., ADEY, W. R. and FOX S. S. (1963) Self maintained visual stimulation in monkeys after long-term visual deprivation. *Science* **139**, 336–338.

WHITE, R. K.(1943) The case for the Tolman – Lewin interpretation of learning. *Psychological Review* **50**, 157–186.

WHITE, R. W. (1959) Motivation reconsidered: the concept of competence. *Psychological Review* **66**, 297–333.

WHITING, J. W. M. and MOWRER, O.H. (1943) Habit progression and regression — a laboratory study of some factors relevant to human socialization. *Journal of comparative Psychology* **36**, 229–253.

WILLIAMS, C. D. and KUCHKA, J. C. (1957) Exploratory behaviour in two mazes with dissimilar alternatives. *Journal of Comparative and Physiological Psychology* **50**, 509–513.

WILLIAMS, D. J. (1972) Effects of electric shock shock on exploratory behaviour in the rat. *Quarterly Journal of Experimental Psychology* **24**, 544–546.

WINOGRAD, T. (1975) Frames, representations and the declarative-procedural controversy. In *Representation and Understanding* (Eds. D. G. BOBROW and A. COLLINS). New York: Academic Press.

WITTGENSTEIN, L. (1968) *Philosophical Investigations* (3rd edn. trans. by G. E. M. ANSCOMBE). Oxford: Blackwell.

WONG, R. and BOWLES, L. J. (1976) Exploration of complex stimuli as facilitated by emotional reactivity and shock. *American Journal of Psychology* **89**, 527–534.

WOODS, P. J. (1962) Behaviour in a novel situation as influenced by the immediately preceding environment. *Journal of the Experimental Analysis of Behavior* **5**, 185–190.

WOODS, P. J. and JENNINGS, S. (1959) Response to environmental change: a further confirmation. *Psychological Reports* **5**, 560.

WOODS, P. J., RUCKELHAUS, S. I. and BOWLING, D. M. (1960) Some effects of 'free' and 'restricted' environment rearing conditions upon adult behaviour in the rat. *Psychological Reports* **6**, 191–200.

WOODWORTH, R. S. (1958) *Dynamics of Behavior*. New York: Holt, Rinehart & Winston.

YOUNG, P. T. and FALK, J. L. (1956) The acceptability of tap water and distilled water to non thirsty rats. *Journal of Comparative and Physiological Psychology* **49**, 336–338.

ZEAMAN, D. and HOUSE, B. J. (1951) The growth and decay of reactive inhibition as measured by alternation behaviour. *Journal of Experimental Psychology* **41**, 177–186.

ZELNIKER, T. (1971) Perceptual attenuation of an irrelevant auditory verbal input as measured by an involuntary verbal response in a selective attention task. *Journal of Experimental Psychology* **87**, 52–56.

ZIMBARDO, P. G. and MILLER, N. E. (1958) Facilitation of exploration by hunger in rats. *Journal of Comparative and Physiological Psychology* **51**, 43–46.

ZIMBARDO, P. G. and MONTGOMERY, K. C. (1957) Effects of 'free' environment rearing upon exploratory behaviour. *Psychological Reports* **3**, 589–594.

ZUBEK, J. P., FLYE, J. and AFTANAS, M. (1964) Cutaneous sensitivity after prolonged visual deprivation. *Science* **144**, 1591–1593.

ZUCKERMAN, M. (1969) Theoretical formulations. In *Sensory deprivation: Fifteen Years of Research* (Ed. J. P. ZUBEK). New York: Appleton-Century-Crofts.

CHAPTER 5

Neural Subsystems of Exploration in Rats

Richard G. M. Morris

5.1 Introduction

At the intersections of city streets in the United States, illuminated signs indicate when it is safe to cross. A message on the sign alternates between the commands WALK and DON'T WALK. There are similar signs in Britain, but there is a different approach here, with the signs flashing CROSS and WAIT to the pedestrian. Clearly it is acceptable in Britain to pace up and down impatiently at the kerbside while waiting for the traffic lights to change; in America, running across the road is apparently and wisely forbidden.

In formulating descriptions of exploratory behaviour, there is often indecision, even conflict, between whether a description should be couched in terms of the movements that an animal performs while exploring, or in terms of the goal or purpose of the behaviour observed. A sharp distinction between these two types of description may not always be possible, but the study of putative neural mechanisms of exploratory behaviour is predicated, in part, on a decision about what constitutes an acceptable behavioural description.

Efforts to understand the neural basis of exploratory behaviour have so far failed to reveal any discrete area of the brain, neurotransmitter or neurophysiological system that is uniquely related to it. We should not be surprised about this for what an animal does in search of and in response to novelty reflects the operation of diverse brain mechanisms including those involved in sensorimotor coordination, motivation, cognition and memory. Recently two new analyses of exploratory behaviour have been proposed. They differ both with respect to the descriptions of exploratory behaviour they are based on and with respect to the type of explanation of exploration they offer. The first approach, summarized by Teitelbaum (1981) and by Teitelbaum, *et al.* (1980), is concerned with constructing an essentially 'geometrical' description of exploratory behaviour. The second, due to the work of O'Keefe & Nadel (1978), is concerned with how an animal's movements and experience in an environment allows it to construct a 'spatial' or 'cognitive' representation.

The two approaches have a lot in common. Both use brain lesions and either neurochemical or neurophysiological techniques to investigate the underlying neural mechanisms of exploration. Both employ detailed behavioural descriptions, the former concentrating on the movement trajectories of discrete body parts, the latter on the animal's position in space and its interaction with the environment. Borrowing Teitelbaum's terminology, it is useful to think of these two approaches as being concerned with putative 'movement subsystems' and 'cognitive subsystems' of exploration, respectively. This review will be largely sympathetic to these approaches, but it is important to note that both lines of work are highly controversial. In order to restrict discussion, I shall concentrate exclusively on those aspects that refer specifically to exploration, leaving aside related work on drug-induced stereotypes (Robbins & Sahakian, 1981), the 'geometry' of social interaction (Golani, 1982; Moran et al., 1981) and the widely discussed relationship between human amnesia and the effects of hippocampal lesions in animals (Weiskrantz, 1982). This chapter is not, nor is it intended to be a comprehensive review of movement subsystems or the spatial mapping theory.

5.2   Movement Subsystems

5.2.1   Neurological Recovery of Sensorimotor Function

It is well known that lesions of the lateral hypothalamus (LH) produce aphagia (Anand & Brobeck, 1951). Teitelbaum & Stellar (1954) discovered that if maintained by means of intragastric feeding initially, some animals will recover and that the course of recovery is characterized by a series of distinct stages (Teitelbaum & Epstein, 1962) until eventually a 'recovered lateral' rat will drink water and eat dry food (though abnormalities in response to glucoprivation and hydrational challenge do remain). Although early work concentrated on the anorexic effects of LH lesions, recent studies have emphasised a wider range of abnormalities that hypothalamic lesions can cause including, in particular, sensorimotor disturbances (Marshall et al., 1971; Robinson & Whishaw, 1974).

Large LH lesions make rats profoundly akinetic and cataleptic. That is, the animals remain immobile for long periods, often in quite awkward postures. They are also somnolent (Levitt & Teitelbaum, 1975) but will occasionally intersperse brief bouts of grooming and face-washing between longer periods of apparently inattentive immobility, during which the rats fail to respond to light touch, visual or auditory cues. These sensorimotor disturbances are not a bizarre side effect of a primarily motivational disorder, but may actually contribute to at least the early stages of the feeding disturbances. Moreover, the sensorimotor behaviour also recovers and (Teitelbaum et al., 1980, p. 139):

> . . . by analyzing the disturbances of movement in recovery from akinesia and in other aberrations in locomotion, we have revealed independent behavioural subsystems that may form the substrate for exploration and orienting to goal objects.

118

Teitelbaum *et al.*'s (1980) use of the term 'subsystem' is not entirely clear. Like the term 'model system' presently being used in studies of learning, there is danger that it could mean all things to all people. However, roughly speaking, it is an empirically isolated set of movements that occur together (e.g., forward locomotion), whether in response to a stimulus, at a given stage of the recovery process or following administration of a drug. These and other variables allow a dissociation between different subcomponents of action and so identify the natural organization of sensorimotor behaviour.

Consider the exploratory behaviour of a normal rat in a novel environment. Descriptions of this behaviour commonly employ concepts such as habituation, attention or fear. The movement subsystems approach attempts to avoid their use by concentrating, rather directly, on what the rat is actually doing. A typical sequence usually includes an initial period of immobility followed by narrow and later wide scanning movements of the head. Soon the animal may turn around and then walk, staying close to the side walls of the enclosure, rearing up on its hindlegs from time to time. Only later will the rat break out into open space, investigating objects that may have been placed in various parts of the environment. Novel objects are typically investigated first, with a very stereotyped 'prostrate' approach in which the four paws remain at a distance, firmly anchored to the ground, while the animal moves its entire body forward in a longitudinal fashion until the snout and vibrissae contact the object. This hesitant manner then gives way to active vibrissae contact and, in the case of small movable objects, manipulation by the forelimbs. Eventually, the entire environment and objects in it will have been covered and the animal will find a corner and drift into slow-wave sleep. Had food been available, a hungry rat may have cut short the initial exploration, but would have interspersed eating with vigorous face-washing and bouts of further exploration. It is sometimes observed that a rat grooms in a single fixed location in the environment to which it repeatedly returns to continue grooming.

The movement subsystems approach takes this kind of description as its starting point. Thus, one important aspect of the normal rat's exploration is how components of the behaviour occur in rather prescribed ways, such as the use of strictly longitudinal movements in the initial exploration of a novel object. Golani (1982) notes how changes in the direction of progression of a quadruped (such as a rat) always involve movements of the head to the preferred orientation followed by antagonistic counterrotation of the neck as the trunk rotates to line up with the new direction of movement. A third example (Golani, 1982, p. 7) is snout contact with the ground in rats:

> During exploratory behaviour, rats keep invariant the minimal distance between their snout and the ground by coupling the movements of the lower, middle and upper torso, and neck and head (contact fixation). A change in the tilt of any of the above body segments in the vertical involves simultaneous antagonistic changes in the vertical tilt of some or all of the other serially connected segments, so that the sum total of the movements results in the snout maintaining steady light contact with the ground.

It seems that the structure of exploratory movement is far from random and

119

involves specific subcomponents to realize specific goals.

Golani *et al.* (1979) have studied the recovery of exploratory movement after LH lesions using the Eshkol – Wachmann movement notation system which allows coordinated movements to be described in terms of the relative movements of constituent parts. For this, the rat is viewed as a 'series of connected limb and body segments' and the angles between them are recorded continuously with the aid of film and videotape. Various frames of reference are used including, in particular, the longitudinal axis of the body. Golani *et al.* (1979) discovered that movement recovers after LH lesions along several purportedly independent dimensions which reappear at different times. Initially, the LH rat is immobile, barring a few automatisms (e.g. chewing). Lateral head-scanning movements recover first: the head rotates around a neck axis with the snout along the floor in successively larger arcs; later the entire anterior parts of the body rotate with the head (Fig. 5.1). Thus recovery proceeds in a cephalo-caudal direction, and this can be precisely described using the movement notation system. Specifically, the point or 'root' caudal to which no movement is observed at the early stages of recovery can be precisely located at a given body segment along the longitudinal axis. The root moves caudally as longitudinal head movements appear, forelimb movements being followed by vertical rearing and finally hindlimb locomotion. Recovery of postural support also proceeds in a cephalo-caudal fashion, though this is incomplete as 'recovered laterals' walk in a digitigrade or 'pointed toe' manner with a high arched back.

During the later stages of recovery, periods of arrest between brief moments of activity become shorter, but when movement recurs after a rest, the initiation of movement follows the same temporal sequence as that of recovery itself. Movements thus seem to 'grow' in amplitude or 'warm-up', beginning with lateral head and forelimb movements. One or both hindlimbs may remain immobile for as long as a minute or two until eventually full forward locomotion emerges. Golani *et al.* (1982) have recently noted a similar 'warm-up' phenomenon in an extensive and detailed study of the ontogeny of exploration in rats and other infant mammals. The precise details are different, but the principle is the same.

Studies of sensorimotor recovery after other brain lesions have also been conducted. Whishaw *et al.* (1981) have conducted an extensive analysis of the motor and feeding deficits associated with total decortication. One difference in the orientation behaviour of normal and decorticate rats that they observed was that although normal rats will often orient to the point in space where a probe touches their ventral body surface, decorticate rats are substantially slower and will never search for it after it has been removed. This finding suggests that certain sensorimotor deficits may be secondary to memory changes.

5.2.2 *Behavioural Traps*

In conjunction with the cephalo-caudal principle, the concept of movement sub-

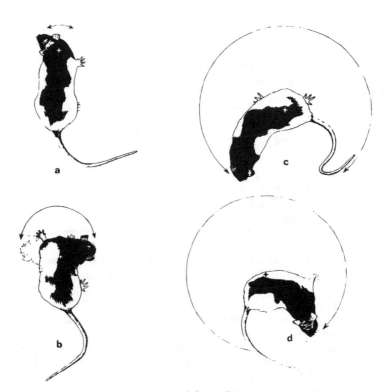

Fig. 5.1   Schematic drawings traced from films showing the top view of a rat performing increasingly larger amplitude horizontal lateral movements during 4 successive phases of reovery. The arrows indicate the amplitude of movements and the + sign indicates the root of the movement beyond which there is practically no recruitment of limb and body segments. Recruitment proceeds in a cephalocaudal order. (Reprinted from I. Golani, D. Wolgin and P. Teitelbaum (1979) *Brain Research* 164, 237–264, by permission.)

system helps to make sense of the otherwise bizarre behaviour of LH lesioned rats in 'behavioural traps'. When a normal rat explores the corner of an apparatus, it will move into the corner, rear up, sniffing at the side walls, turn and move away. However, a rat with LH lesions may engage in '. . . repeated head and forelimb movements so stereotyped as to resemble a waltz' (Golani *et al.*, 1979, p. 251). What happens is that the rat may have reached a point in recovery when lateral and forelimb movements are possible but sequential hind-limb stepping, essential for turning, is not yet recovered. The 'root' of the movements possible is still well forward along the longitudinal axis. Another case is shown in Fig. 5.2, in which a rat with LH lesions climbs into the behavioural trap of the top of a wall. This rat has recovered to the point where locomotion and climbing are still possible (6 days postoperatively but scanning

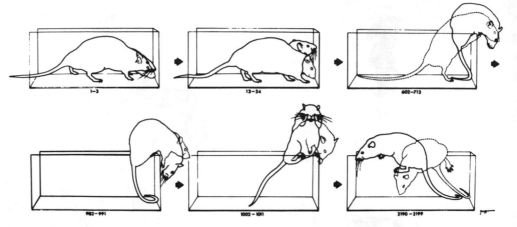

Fig. 5.2 Behavioural trap of the top of a wall. Six days postoperatively. Drawings were taken from a single 2.5 min film sequence. Numerals indicate frame numbers. Each drawing represents two adjacent positions of the rat. The frames chosen show warm-up along the vertical dimension (top row, approx 50 s), scanning along surfaces and face-washing with snout remote from a surface (bottom row). Because the rat cannot make snout contact with the ground surface, it is trapped on top of the wall. (Reprinted from I. Golani, D. Wolgin and P. Teitelbaum (1979) *Brain Research* 164, 237–264, by permission.)

movements of the snout must be in contact with surfaces. Face-washing is possible, but movements that release the snout from contact with vertical surfaces are not. The rat cannot release snout contact from the outside vertical surface while simultaneously maintaining scanning. Consequently, it remains trapped on top of the wall. The example is instructive as it illustrates that the trap need not necessarily be a confined area such as a corner — it is an essentially behavioural trap.

5.2.3   Pharmacological Dissociations between Movement Subsystems

Other work that has helped to unravel separable movement subsystems includes the study of drugs or neurotoxins which produce syndromes that resemble aspects of the LH sensorimotor deficit. Marshall *et al.* (1974) have noted similarities between the effects of damage to the nigrostriatal bundle (which courses through the lateral hypothalamic area — Ungerstedt, 1971) and LH lesions. It is likely that some of the LH lesion induced feeding and sensorimotor disturbances are due to damage to ascending dopamine fibres. Schallert *et al.* (1978) describe how intraventricular injections of 6-OHDA (which depletes brain catecholamines) produce an akinetic state resembling Parkinsonism.

Administration of an anticholinergic drug (e.g. atropine) released a dose-dependent pattern of short-step locomotion. Lateral scanning movements were absent and the atropinized, catecholamine-depleted rats became indefinitely trapped in 45° corners. The authors suggest that movement subsystems responsible for forward locomotion and lateral turning may be dependent upon different neurotransmitters and note that L-DOPA (a dopamine precursor that crosses the blood-brain barrier) will reverse akinesia by introducing circling rather than forward locomotion. The pharmacological dissociation between forward locomotion and sideways scanning is vividly illustrated in one of Whishaw's excellent films (Whishaw, 1979)

Recently, Szechtman et al. (1980) have described how apomorphine (a dopamine receptor agonist) induces a 'behavioural regression' sequence that appears (in part) to be opposite to what occurs in neurological recovery. Behaviour which appears late in recovery from LH lesions disappears first under apomorphine, but over a quite different time-scale. Marshall (1980) has also shown that dopamine is both necessary and sufficient for the recovery of normal sensorimotor function after 6-OHDA injections into the substantia nigra.

Schallert et al. (1980) have shown that large doses of atropine cause enhanced 'snout thigmotaxis' and consequent deficits in behavioural traps. However, this is not an inevitable effect of atropine: Sutherland et al. (1981b) did see snout-contact release in their atropinized rats after they had escaped from water in an open-field swimming task.

Immobility also seems to exist in different forms. De Ryck et al. (1980) have described how haloperidol-induced catalepsy is characterized by enhanced bracing reactions and resistance to postural shifts; whereas morphine-induced catalepsy involves a loss of postural support and an immobility that is actually preparatory to movement. Under morphine induced catalepsy only, the slightest stimulus will 'activate' movement (e.g. forward locomotion).

5.2.4 Critique

What, if anything, do these apparently bizarre stereotypes have to do with the rapid, coordinated expression of exploration shown by normal rats? The short answer to this question is that we just do not know. Teitelbaum et al. (1980) claim that these movement subsystems 'may form the substrate for exploration and orienting to goal objects'. They argue that the separate emergence of movement components over the long time scale of neurological recovery, the recapitulation during 'warm-up', the similarities to infant development and the consistent dissociation of components by drugs makes the assertion that normal behaviour is composed of movement subsystems as, at the very least, a viable hypothesis. However, the very different time scales of neurological recovery and normal exploration make this hypothesis very hard to test. To be sure, Szechtman et al. (1980) see a pattern of behavioural regression over a time period of a few hours that seems to be a mirror image of recovery after LH lesions that occurs over weeks. But beyond noting similarities, it is not clear what specific predictions the hypothesis makes about an animal's movements in a given situation. For example, Golani *et al.*'s (1979) claim is unclear: is it that movements that are absent cannot be made, or is it that they are not usually made? Some of Teitelbaum's own data support the latter, and weaker interpretation, such as the experiments on 'activation' by strong sensory stimuli (Marshall & Teitelbaum, 1978). In addition, it had been known since Robinson & Whishaw's (1974) study of posterior hypothalamic lesions that profoundly akinetic animals can not only swim in water but also that their ability to do so is affected by water temperature. These findings suggest that certain movement components may not be absent so much as concealed by the absence of appropriate sensory activation.

A second point is that the movement notation system is an essentially geometric description in which movement sequences are annotated, the sequential information retained but the global time domain lost. Sometimes, the occurrence of different movements at different times provides the basis for a dissociation between subsystems, as in the strict rule that caudal movement never occurs before rostral movement during recovery from LH lesions. On other occasions, such as exploration by normal rats, where movements occur in prescribed sequences but in virtually any combination, the time-domain is virtually disregarded. I shall return to the issue of the time-domain shortly.

A third issue is that much of this research on recovery is strictly empirical, in the sense that it has been conducted in the absence of any formal theory of the organization of movement subsystems. To some, this is part of its appeal. But in consequence, the interpretation of certain phenomena, such as the fact that '. . . a normal rat does not seem to be able to walk or run forward and scan or orient at the same time' has an air of special pleading about it. Teitelbaum *et al.* (1980) introduce this observation as evidence that the subsystems of head-orientation and forward locomotion are 'independent' and 'mutually antagonistic', descriptions which seem to contradict one another. If two movement subsystems are independent, then they should be able to operate separately, together or with varying degrees of temporal overlap. However, if two such systems are mutually antagonistic, a reasonable interpretation is that a common neural mechanisms may be responsible for both and that it can operate in one or other mode. Kimura (1981) makes extensive use of this latter argument in her discussion of the evolution of human communication, and draws upon observations concerning interference between speech and complex manual tasks which, she argues, share a common neural basis (Lomas & Kimura, 1976).

Fourthly, a wider issue is whether it is reasonable to describe the effects of large brain lesions of the lateral hypothalamus and cortex, the effects of neurotoxins and massive doses of drugs without reference to concepts such as anxiety, attention or learning (Iversen & Fray, 1981). Detailed discussion of this issue would require a separate review. However, my understanding is that these physiological procedures are here being used primarily as neurological tools to investigate movement rather than as techniques for localizing function in any

124

exclusive sense. To take an extreme example, the residual glucoprivation deficit in 'recovered laterals' cannot be explained in terms of a movement disorder; but then, nor can it be viewed as evidence against the movement subsystems hypothesis. Conducted cautiously, the work on movement subsystems can therefore proceed independently of other studies of, for example, forebrain catecholamine systems. However, it would still be valuable to know how the various deficits relate to one another; and I have already noted in the case of Whishaw *et al.*'s (1981) study of decorticate rats that some of the apparently sensorimotor deficits could be secondary to disturbances of memory.

The dissociations between movement subsystems that Teitelbaum (1981) has recently reviewed are clearly important and provide fascinating new insights into both recovery of function and the microorganization of exploratory behaviour. However, a major limitation of the approach that cannot be ignored concerns the changes seen in exploratory behaviour over time. As objects and places in a novel environment are successively investigated, their relative novelty declines and the probability and pattern of exploration changes. This is not to deny that certain 'invariants' of motor behaviour, to borrow Golani's (1981) terminology, may be invariant to changes in the probability of the behaviour of which they are a part. The example of cephalo-caudal warm-up in LH lesioned rats, is a case in point. But why does exploration in a novel environment wane over time? The usual generic approach, and the one pursued in all cognitive hypotheses, is to assume that the sources of spontaneity in exploratory behaviour are exclusively endogenous. Teitelbaum *et al.* (1980, p. 140), in an intriguing passage, point out that much of what triggers subcomponents of complex action sequences may actually be exogeneous:

> Behavioural traps in partial enclosures reveal that much of what seems 'spontaneous' in motivated behaviour is not so: the variety of actions that yield the illusion of spontaneity is caused by the variety of stimuli successively encountered as a result of each automatic response to the previous stimulus.'

Golani (1982) also attempts to dull the normally sharp distinction between 'goals' and 'strategies' with reference to the idea of 'attractors' that are essentially 'points of stability' (e.g. snout contact with the ground) within complex movement sequences. It may be that many components of apparently 'voluntary' action are exogenously reflexive (see also Evarts & Tanji, 1976); but there is, on strictly logical grounds, no way in which the study of movement subsystems can explain how the probability of exploratory behaviour changes as a function of prior exploration. Whether it be through the scanning manipulatory or locomotor movements that comprise exploration, information is taken in, processed and some sort of representation of the environment put together. Learning occurs.

5.3   Cognitive Subsystems

In the remainder of this chapter, one of several cognitive approaches to the study of exploration will be considered — O'Keefe & Nadel's (1978) 'spatial mapping' theory of hippocampal function. Unlike the movement subsystems approach, O'Keefe & Nadel explain exploration in terms of neural mechanisms responsible for representing the environment. On their view, exploration consists and must be described not merely in terms of the movements that an animal performs when exploring but also in terms of the goal of such movements. Both the instigator and goal of exploration is the detection of novelty, particularly in respect of the spatial layout of the environment.

The main aspects of the theory have been summarized and discussed in detail recently (O'Keefe & Nadel, 1979; with commentator's replies). Briefly, it makes three main claims. First, it proposes that animals can learn about the spatial relationships of objects and events in their environment in a form that is independent of their behaviour. The classical distinction between learning and performance is, therefore, accepted as axiomatic. Second, the theory proposes that learning about 'places' (the 'locale' system) is different from learning to approach specific visible or audible cues (the 'taxon' system). Finally, third, O'Keefe & Nadel propose that a specific anatomical system — the hippocampus (including a number of adjacent structures such as the septum, fimbria-fornix, subiculum and entorhinal cortex) is the neural substrate for place-learning. The first and third of these claims are directly relevant to the study of exploratory behaviour.

5.3.1 Novelty, Context Specificity and Mismatch

A relevant starting point to O'Keefe & Nadel's discussion of exploration is their distinction between 'novelty' and 'noticeability' (1978, p. 240). Many objects or events may attract attention and be noticed irrespective of their relative familiarity. Such stimuli will typically elicit reflex movements (e.g., head turning by a rat in response to the tactile stimulus of a von Frey hair). The term 'noticeability' refers to the extent to which a stimulus can elicit such movements, a loud sound that startles a rat having high noticeability. One implication of the work on movement subsystems is that stimuli with ostensibly low noticeability may play a very important role in the structure of behaviour (e.g. surfaces with respect to snout contact in the rat, as discussed above).

Novelty, on the other hand, typically consists of 'new configurations of familiar elements' (1978, p.241) Thus, novelty varies not only (sometimes not even) as a function of time since an object has last been seen, but as a function of exposure, of the extent to which the object has been thoroughly explored, and of mismatch. This approach differs from Gaffan's (1974) treatment of recognition memory, which emphasizes time-dependent changes in absolute and relative recency. Gaffan argues that an event is 'unfamiliar' if it has not been seen for a long time, whereas O'Keefe & Nadel's definition of novelty emphasizes that novelty is context specific. By way of example, the Keeper of Elephants at the London Zoo who happened upon an elephant while driving down Buckingham Palace Road would regard the event as 'novel' (also downright suspicious) although he sees the animal everyday. Were he also to drive down Buckingham Palace Road regularly on his way to work, it would be neither the place nor the animal that would be unfamiliar, but the conjunction of the two.

Although the example may seem trite, the role of context in exploration is central to the spatial mapping theory. O'Keefe & Nadel argue that an item or place is novel if it is not represented in the animal's spatial map, irrespective of the relative or absolute recency of the item. There are two logically separate aspects of this claim. First, that the animal's representation of the environment is spatial. Second, that novelty is context specific. The approach differs from several contemporary accounts of animal learning (Mackintosh, 1975; Moore & Stickney, 1980; Pearce & Hall, 1980) on both counts. These theories attempt to incorporate context or what are euphemistically called 'background cues' into accounts of conditioning, as if they were a single cue against which other discrete events were to be discriminated, rather than as a set of cues whose relative positions can be learned. Further, although these theories argue that 'associability', like novelty, can be changed as a function of exposure or reinforcement (unlike Rescorla & Wagner's, 1972, original model), they nevertheless assume that associability is a discrete property of objects or events. Thus, their treatment of associability is more akin to O'Keefe & Nadel's concept of noticeability — with the added assumption that noticeability can be changed. The implication is that on the first occasion that a rat is exposed to a familiar stimulus in a novel environment, that stimulus would have low associability. O'Keefe & Nadel's treatment of novelty is different. A situation is novel — on the first exposure trial — if there is any mismatch detected by the spatial mapping system. The mismatch may arise either out of gross changes in the environment, via more subtle changes, such as introducing new objects, or by moving familiar ones to new places. The role of context has been discussed more fully by Nadel & Willner (1980) and by Nadel (1981) who also note that their treatment of context has several points of similarity with Wagner's (1978) theory of priming of short-term memory.

Several experiments support the idea that familiarity is context specific. Cowan (1976; see also Chapter 6) has shown that wild rats (*Rattus rattus*) will temporarily avoid a familiar food basket put in a new position in a plus maze; and they will avoid a novel food basket in the familiar food position. Surprisingly, Cowan did not find avoidance of a new food itself, but perhaps the new food (millet) was greatly preferred to the familiar diet (rat pellets). Wilz & Bolton (1971) have shown that general activity and approaches to specific objects by laboratory rats are disinhibited when the spatial arrangement of familiar objects in a familiar environment is altered. Activity rose as high after the rearrangement as it had been during the initial exploration of the then unfamiliar environment. Willner (1980), taking a different approach, reports that latent inhibition is context specific. Latent inhibition refers to the retardation of conditioning by prior nonreinforced exposure to a stimulus. To investigate context specificity, Willner exposed two groups of rats to a saccharin solution, one group in clear plastic cages, the other in their home cage. A third group were not pre-exposed. Then the rats were given a brief period to consume a saccharin solution in their home cages and poisoned with lithium chloride. In two-bottle preference tests given several days later, Willner found that the group that had received the exposure trials in the plastic cages showed a significantly stronger aversion to saccharin than the group that had received exposure trials in the home cage. Thus latent inhibition is, at least partially, context specific. Willner went on to show that context specificity can be spatial. He did this by exposing two groups of rats to saccharin from drinking cups that could be in either of two locations. For one group, the conditioning trial took place at the same location as the exposure trials. For the other group, the exposure and conditioning locations were different. The results showed that the group conditioned in a different location showed a significantly stronger aversion in the preference tests than the group conditioned in the same location.

These experiments show that shifts in the spatial location of familiar stimuli can trigger both exploration and enhanced learning. As it is the mismatch between the current stimulus situation and the spatial representation that is critical, there need be no discriminable local cues marking the changed point in space. Corman & Shafer (1968) have explicitly demonstrated this by placing rats in a large open field with the floor surface painted black except for a small centre square painted white. Exchanging the white centre square for a black one triggered exploration.

Recently, I have shown that rats do not even require local cues to learn to navigate to specific points in space (Morris, 1981). Their ability to do this is predicted by the spatial mapping theory because it argues that the animal represents the environment in terms of places and their position relative to one another. A rat should therefore be able to go to a particular place from any direction solely using distal information indicating the rat's relative position in the familiar environment. Local cues emanating from the particular position that it wishes to approach, though usually present, are not necessary.

Rats were trained to escape from water onto a small platform hidden beneath the water surface. The platform was hidden by rendering the water opaque (using a small quantity of milk). The animals quickly learned (*circa* 6 trials) to swim towards the platform and escape from the water from any of several starting positions (Fig. 5.3). Rats for whom the platform moved around from one place to another randomly over successive trials learned to escape, but their behaviour lacked directionality. In the group for whom the platform was in a fixed location, subsequent tests indicated that moving it to a new position resulted in persistent search in the previously safe place. However, as soon as the rats found the new position, they would soon (2–4 trials) learn to avoid the old location and swim directly to the new safe place.

Recently, Sutherland *et al.* (1981a) have shown that movement of a hidden platform to a new place in a pool is accompanied by a disinhibition of rearing to levels as high as those occurring in the early trials of initial training. This presumably reflects the rat's attempts to locate its new position indicating that some, if not all, of the relevant exploratory learning occurs after the animal has escaped from the water. In support of this idea, Garrud (unpublished observations) has shown that rats escaping onto a visible platform fixed in one

Fig. 5.3 On each trial, the rat were placed into the apparatus facing the side-walls. They swam about the pool until they found the escape platform and then climbed on. Normal rats will quickly learn to take short, relatively direct paths towards the hidden platform.

place and allowed to remain on it for 60 s, showed a spatial bias to its position in a later transfer test; whereas rats removed immediately they climbed onto the platform during training did not show any bias.

Thus, place learning can occur at a separate time from the directional escape behaviour it supports. But how quickly can it occur? In a recent study (Morris, 1982), I have examined one-trial learning in this paradigm as follows. Rats were given two trials per day. On trial 1, the hidden platform could be in one of four positions — the centre point of each of the four quadrants of the pool (SW, NW, NE and SE). The rats were placed in the water at any of several starting positions and allowed to escape onto the platform where they stayed for 30 s. For trial 2, the rats were divided into two groups. Half were returned to the pool with the platform in the same location (Group Same); the other half were given a second trial in which the platform could again be in any of the four positions (Group Random). The full design of the experiment is shown in Fig. 5.4. The results (Fig. 5.5) show that on trial 2, Group Same escaped faster than Group Random. Somewhat surprisingly, the effect was not schedule-dependent. Rapid escape was shown by Group Random on that subset of trials (25%) for which the platform remained in the same location on trial 2. That is, all rats (Group Same and Group Random) showed a 'win – stay' tendency (cf. Olton, *et al.*, 1981). The rule appeared to be: 'Return to the vicinity of the previously safe place irrespective of whether this place is subsequently differentially reinforced'. The implication is that although swimming to escape from water may be reinforced by the consequent successful escape, the directionality of swimming on trial $n + 1$ is determined by knowledge about the position of the platform on the preceding trial, trial n. This finding illustrates the very close relationship between spatial learning and exploration.

In summary, O'Keefe & Nadel's proposition that animals can learn about the spatial relationships of objects in their environment is supported by several lines of evidence. In particular, mismatch between the representation of the environment stored in memory and the current state of the environment initiates exploration.

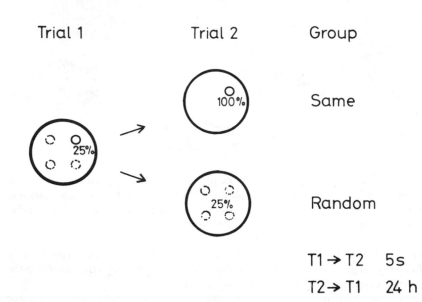

| Trial 1 | Trial 2 | Group |

T1 → T2   5s
T2 → T1   24 h

Fig. 5.4 Design for the one-trial learning experiment. Each day consisted of 2 trials. On trial 1, the hidden platform was placed in one of four positions. On trial 2, Group Same had the platform in the same location as trial 1, whereas Group Random was again given the platform in any one of the four quadrants. Complete circle = hidden platform; dotted circle = possible platform position.

5.3.2   The Role of the Hippocampus

The second relevant aspect of the spatial mapping theory is O'Keefe & Nadel's (1978) claim that the hippocampus is the critical structure. Two main lines of evidence support this proposal: first, that there are cells in the hippocampus which respond only in specific places in a familiar environment. And second, that damage to the hippocampus results in spatial deficits in exploration and learning. Both claims are factually correct, but there is widespread disagreement about their interpretation (see discussion after O'Keefe & Nadel, 1979; see also Gray, 1982; Olton *et al.*, 1979). I shall consider these two lines of evidence in detail rather than explore wider aspects of the current controversy.

Unit recording studies.   O'Keefe & Dostrovsky (1971) presented a preliminary report about the spatial characteristics of the receptive fields of cells in area CAl of the hippocampus. O'Keefe (1976) describes 'place', 'misplace' and 'displace' cells in more detail. Cell firing was recorded by means of micro-electrodes attached to a miniature microdrive mounted on the skull of the freely moving rat. The microelectrodes was lowered into the pyramidal cell layer of areas CAl and CA3 of the hippocampus, or into the granule cell layers and hilus

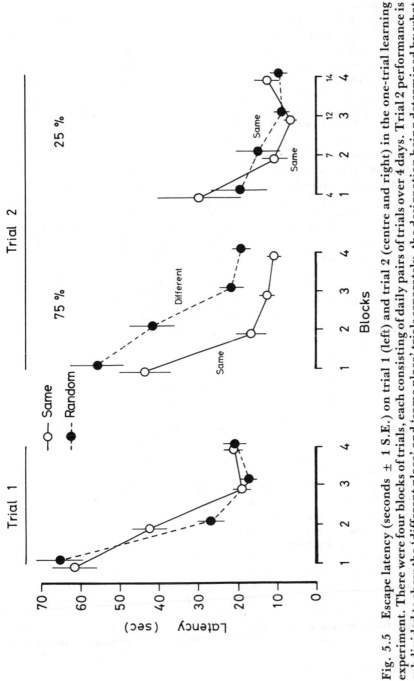

Fig. 5.5 Escape latency (seconds ± 1 S.E.) on trial 1 (left) and trial 2 (centre and right) in the one-trial learning experiment. There were four blocks of trials, each consisting of daily pairs of trials over 4 days. Trial 2 performance is subdivided to show the 'different place' and 'same place' trials separately, the designation being determined by what was scheduled for Group Random. Note that escape latency on trial 2 is equally fast in both groups on same-place trials; whereas trial 2 performance of Group Random on different place trials is no better than that shown on trial 1. The 'win – stay' effect on trial 2 in both groups is apparent from the beginning of training.

of the dentate gyrus. The available evidence collected from several laboratories (see O'Keefe, 1979, for review) suggests that place cells are pyramidal cells (though not all pyramidal cells are place cells); that interneurons in CA1 and possibly CA3 are 'displace' or 'theta' cells (Ranck, 1982) and that some granule cells of the dentate gyrus may also be 'theta' cells (Rose, 1982). The problem of anatomical identification is a complex one. Physiological criteria (e.g. collision experiments) and anatomical criteria (e.g. dye injection) are technically difficult, particularly in freely moving animals. Moreover, as emphasized by Bland *et al.* (1980), specific cells may have several modes of firing under different conditions.

Of the various types of cells reported, the place cells (or place cell firing mode) have attracted particular interest. Place cells have now been reported from several laboratories. Ranck (1982), who originally proposed a different classification of receptive field types (Ranck, 1973), now accepts the notion of a 'place' field. Olton *et al.* (1978), using a semi-automated analysis technique, have also observed place-fields (excitatory and inhibitory) in rats searching for food in a radial maze. In each of these studies, the accepted definition has been of cells that fire preferentially in specific part(s) of a familiar environment. A common procedure is to find a cell that fires with complex-spikes during slow-wave sleep and then subsequently search for a possible place field in the awake animal. Place fields (the surface area of the environment in which the cell firing is elevated) vary in size from *circa* 10 cm^2 to *circa* 100 cm^2. Some cells respond in two or more locations, and cells from which recordings have been taken in different environments often have place fields in each. Kubie & Ranck (1981) report that the background firing rate (i.e. the rate outside the place field) is discriminably different across environments. This may imply that a single cell can code both for place within context (place field) and for context itself (background rate). Alternatively, it may be an artefact of 'microfields' arranged in several places outside the primary place-field (O'Keefe, personal communication). A further possibility is that the background rate is determined by tonic influences such as odour, rather than specifically spatial features of the environment. More data on the characteristics of the background firing rate of place cells are required to settle the issue.

What the animal does in a place field can influence the rate of response (e.g. sniffing), but (a) no behaviour is sufficient for a cell to respond (e.g. outside the primary place field) and (b) no behaviour is necessary for a cell to respond (with the exception that some place cells are directionally specific). Experiments by Hill (1978) indicate that place fields may be acquired very rapidly, even instantaneously under certain circumstances — a puzzling result. Conversely, Kubie & Ranck (1981) report that place fields develop slowly during exploration of a novel radial maze over a period of 5 min. Other recent findings include work by O'Keefe & Conway (1978) who have shown that no one of several controlling cues in a cue-controlled enclosure is necessary for a place cell to respond, whereas Miller & Best (1980) have found that lesions of the fornix (a major extrinsic fibre pathway of the hippocampus) can influence place-field characteristics. The place fields are not destroyed by the lesion, but they are more sensitive to intramaze cues than in normal rats.

132

Critique What are the implications of these findings? Unfortunately, it is difficult to answer this question. Gray (1982) is clearly very suspicious about the whole enterprise. 'There is', he writes (*loc. cit.*, p. 209):

> . . . something more than a little miraculous about constructing an *ad hoc* environment like the one shown [in the figure], which no rat has ever encountered before, sticking a wire into the middle of the brain and pulling out place fields just like that.

Miracles apart, place fields have now been recorded in *ad hoc* environments in London, New York, Michigan, Virginia and, of course, California — perhaps in other places too. Clearly, they exist. More worthy of discussion are two issues: specificity and function.

Little is known about the anatomical specificity of place cells. The proportion of cells which have place fields is not known exactly (See Table 1 in O'Keefe, 1979) and, as noted above, Bland *et al.*'s (1980) findings imply that no fixed figure can be offered. Place cells may exist outside the hippocampus — a report by Mitchell & Ranck (cited by O'Keefe, 1979) indicates their presence in entorhinal cortex. No one, to my knowledge, has yet looked in detail in other areas of the brain (e.g. frontal cortex). To make matters worse, experimenters are generally somewhat constrained by the behavioural procedures they use and no systematic examination of single unit characteristics across a suitable variety of behavioural paradigms has yet been reported. It would be interesting to know, for example, if the novelty-detecting units described by Vinogradova (1975) are misplace cells or displace cells. Are they directly coding novelty in nonspatial sensory input, firing in response to the arousal input that is more strikingly evident in the rabbit brain than the rat, or are they firing in conjunction with small movements that the rabbits may be making in response to novelty? In the absence of experiments comparing different behavioural paradigms, the inescapable conclusion is that the existence of place cells is no more than circumstantial evidence that the hippocampus is specifically or uniquely involved in place learning.

Specificity aside, there remains the question of function: what are the place cells doing? One logical obstacle to accepting that they are the neurophysiological substrate of a spatial map concerns how the map would be used. Several (unpublished) investigations have begun to examine whether cell firing is influenced by the behavioural task — whether the rat is exploring, running for food or performing a working-memory task. To date such experiments (which are extremely difficult given that cells can at best be 'held' for only a few hours) have been disappointing or are incomplete. I regard this as a serious problem for two reasons. First, the system must have a mechanism indicating for the rat in place A the position of a desired goal object in place B. It follows that a cell whose place field is not where the rat is presently located must nevertheless, at least occasionally, fire — such as when the rat wishes to approach place B from A. This may in fact explain why place cells have a background firing rate, but this is unlikely. No one has systematically observed anticipatory firing of a place cell marking the vicinity of food for a hungry rat who has learned to approach it from a distance. But something along these lines must occur if the rat really is to use the spatial map to direct behaviour in the way that O'Keefe & Nadel's theory proposes. A second problem concerns the existence of place fields of a single cell in different environments. On the face of it, this phenomenon is inconsistent with the claim that the hippocampus is the site of storage of spatial maps unless (a) the maps are moved around within the structure, or (b) a specific place in a particular environment is uniquely associated with the simultaneous firing of a large number of place units. The latter proposal is only superficially attractive for, as O'Keefe (1976) notes, adjacent cells in the pyramidal cell layer usually have widely differing place fields. Although the idea that a given place is encoded by many cells is reasonable and in keeping with general principles of neural redundancy, it is puzzling that the many cells corresponding to a given place may be distributed across wide regions of the hippocampus. This is surely an extraordinary way for the nervous system to be organized. More than anything, what is required are more detailed mathematical models of how hippocampal neurons might interact. Rossler (1982) is attempting to do just that.

Lesion studies of exploration and place learning.   Hippocampal lesions cause impairments in exploratory behaviour. O'Keefe & Nadel (1978, p. 255) argue that such lesions abolish it because the animals can no longer build a maplike representation of space. However, the lack of exploration is not accompanied by inactivity; on the contrary, hippocampal lesions can cause an increase in general activity (Kimble, 1963), as can more restricted lesions such as transections of the fornix (Myhrer, 1975). To complicate matters further, the decline in general activity in an open-field over time occurs more slowly in hippocampal lesioned rats, a finding that might mislead one into supposing that damage to the hippocampus increases exploration.

However, as Archer (1973) and others (see Chapters 1 and 2) have pointed out, lesion or drug-induced changes in general activity may arise for a host of reasons, including changes in arousal, anxiety, or reactivity to novelty. A recent report by Osbourne & Seggie (1980) highlights the difficulties of interpretation. They report that rats with fornix lesions are slower to initiate movement around an open field, but are subsequently more active (on a measure of number of squares crossed) than controls. Had their measurement intervals been different, at least the latter finding may not have been obtained. Fortunately, their analysis was thorough and included a fairly detailed behavioural protocol as well as measurements of corticosterone and prolactin changes following exploration. The frequency of interactions with objects in the environment were similar in the normal, sham and experimental groups, but the fine structure of the behaviour was quite different (*loc. cit.*, p. 544):

> Normal rats exhibited longer duration interactions with objects, often involving manipulative contact, and these interactions showed predictable sequential organisation (spatially adjacent objects are highly favoured). The object interactions of rats with fornix lesions were of shorter duration and more random sequential organisation. Thus in an environment with spatially separated novel objects, as in the present experiment,

the same frequency of object interactions is accompanied by greater activity in rats with fornix lesions.

These findings suggest that exploration as distinct from general activity (whatever the latter's causes) is impaired by fornix lesions but in ways that are very difficult to describe quantitatively.

Much recent research on the effect of hippocampal lesions has concentrated on whether deficits occur in spatial memory, recognition memory or working memory. Arguments about the spatial mapping model centre on such questions as whether (a) the spatial memory deficit that is seen is secondary to a strictly spatial encoding deficit, (b) the spatial deficit is an absolute or relative one and (c) the deficit is exclusively spatial. I have discussed the broader issue of the relationship between spatial and working-memory elsewhere (Morris, 1982). Accordingly, I shall concentrate on these three questions only.

When presented with a choice between a familiar and a novel place as in spontaneous alternation, rats with hippocampal lesions show a severe and lasting impairment (Dalland, 1976). A study by Gaffan (1972) emphasized an impairment in 'recognition memory' as responsible, but his results are equally interpretable in spatial terms. Normal and fimbria-fornix lesioned rats were given two trials: the first to view a black and a white arm of a T-maze from the choice point; the second to choose between either two black or two white arms. On trial 2, normal rats chose the changed arm more frequently than the lesioned rats (who were at chance levels of responding) except after a loud and probably frightening noise when they chose the unchanged arm more frequently. Lesioned rats showed no evidence of recognizing that the brightness of one or the other arm had been changed.

The deficit observed by Gaffan (1972) could arise either because fornix lesions impair encoding of spatial cues, or because of a failure of memory (of storage, consolidation or retrieval). Several experiments suggest that both, or the first, explanation is more likely. Stevens (1973) reported that increasing the confinement time after the first trial of a spontaneous alternation experiment increased the level of alternation in hippocampal lesioned rats. O'Keefe et al. (1975) found deficits in place-learning after fimbria-fornix lesions but that some lesioned animals were eventually able to learn their task. The results of both studies are consistent with a strictly 'impaired encoding' hypothesis. Sinnamon et al. (1978, p. 152) point out that their demonstration of an impairment in a spatial delayed matching to sample task is consistent with both an encoding or a memory interpretation, though they tend to favour the former, partly on the grounds that lesioned rats were unable to perform the task at even the shortest memory interval (15 s). However, O'Keefe & Conway (1980) report results that point to a memory deficit in addition to encoding difficulties. Using a delayed spatial matching to sample task in which the cues could be removed during the delay interval, fornix lesioned rats showed memory deficits even after performing effectively at the minimum delay interval (5 s). Kesner (1981) has recently found impaired primacy but normal recency effects in hippocampal lesioned animals, using a serial order analysis of performance on Olton & Samuelson's (1976) radial-maze. The procedure was as follows. Rats were placed in an 8-arm radial maze in which (a) they could be confined in the centre and (b) could be allowed entry to individual arms in serial order. Training consisted of a forced-trial procedure in which rats visited one arm after another until all 8 arms (in a spatially random way) had been sampled. Food was available in each. The rats were then allowed to choose between the 1st and 2nd arms visited, or the 4th and 5th arms, or the 7th and 8th arms, respectively. They were selectively rewarded on the probe trials for revisiting the earlier visited of each pair of arms. Normal rats showed both a primacy (1 *versus* 2) and a recency (7 *versus* 8) effect, but chose equally often between arms 4 and 5. Hippocampal lesioned rats failed to show a primacy effect but did show a recency effect. Kesner's results imply that lesioned rats can distinguish two spatially separate arms of a radial maze but that they can only remember this information for a very short period (*circa* 5–10 s). This interpretation was supported by a follow-up study in which a short retention interval intervened between the final forced trial and the first test trial. This abolished the recency effects in both normal and hippocampal lesioned animals while leaving intact the primacy effect in the normal rats.

Kesner's results raise a puzzle as to why the performance of hippocampal and fornix-lesioned rats on the 'normal' radial maze task (in which free choice is permitted on each trial) is at chance. If lesioned rats are able to encode spatial cues and remember this information for 5–10 s, performance in lesioned rats should be well above chance because they would consistently avoid the most recently chosen arm (although they might later return to it). Olton (personal communication) has pointed out that this does not occur, and the published data (e.g. Becker *et al.*, 1980) supports his claim. If the difficulty in encoding place cues is a relative rather than an absolute one, fimbria-fornix lesioned rats should slowly, but steadily, improve on the radial maze. They do not do this. Whereas, if the encoding deficit is an absolute one, it is not clear why Kesner's (1981) lesioned rats showed a recency effect. Olton *et al.* (1982) have recently shown that fornix lesioned rats can postoperatively learn to avoid the 2 never-rewarded arms of an 8 arm maze, but never learn to avoid retracing their way to any of 3 initially rewarded arms. Learning to avoid 2 never rewarded arms was slower in the lesioned group (suggesting a partial encoding deficit for places), but the more striking dissociation was between performance on what Olton *et al.* (1979) have called the reference and working-memory components of the task.

These learning experiments may seem remote from strictly exploratory behaviour, but the putative psychological processes of recognition-memory, spatial-encoding or working-memory would almost certainly be involved in structuring normal exploration and determining the patterns of interaction with familiar and novel objects in an open field. Moreover, the question of whether hippocampal lesioned rats have any mapping or place-learning capacities intact is crucial to O'Keefe & Nadel's theory, far more so than showing that the lesion-induced deficit is not exclusively spatial. Such experiments (e.g. Olton & Feustle, 1981) show only that the theory is incomplete; whereas observations of successful spatial localisation in hippocampal lesioned animals would surely show the theory to be wrong.

136

Puzzled by the discrepancies in the literature, I have recently used the swimming pool procedure to examine both place-learning and working-memory. Morris *et al.* (1981) have reported that total hippocampectomy results in a profound and lasting impairment in the specifically place-navigation version of this task. Normal (n = 8), cortical lesioned (n = 13) and hippocampal (n = 10) rats were trained to escape onto a small platform placed at the centre of one of the four quadrants of the pool, platform position being counterbalanced within groups. The design of this experiment entailed training rats on the place-navigation task first (finding the hidden platform); then switching them to the cued navigation task (approaching a visible platform 1 cm above the water surface) having moved the platform to a new but fixed position; and finally, returning the animals to the place-navigation task to examine whether the intervening cued task could improve performance permanently (see Fig. 5.6 for summary of design).

The results are shown in Fig. 5.7. On a measure of latency to escape, hippocampal lesioned rats were severely impaired on the place task. The deficit virtually disappeared when they were switched to the cued task showing that it was not the correlated motor, motivational or reinforcement aspects of the procedure that were responsible for the initial deficit. Then, in the final part of the experiment, the place deficit reappeared, suggesting that the improvement in performance shown in the cued task requires the presence of local visible cues to be maintained.

However, showing a deficit in place learning does nothing to resolve the question of whether it is a relative or absolute one. Three lines of evidence indicate that the deficit was substantial. First, the hippocampal lesioned rats were no quicker at escaping in the place task than normal rats had been in the experimental group described earlier for whom the platform had been moved

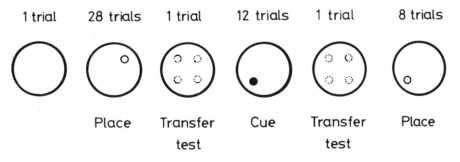

1 trial	28 trials	1 trial	12 trials	1 trial	8 trials
	Place	Transfer test	Cue	Transfer test	Place

Fig. 5.6 Design for hippocampal lesion experiment. After a single habituation trial lasting 60 s, all groups were given 28 trials on the place-navigation task followed by a transfer test in which the platform was removed from the apparatus. Complete circle = hidden platform; filled circle = visible platform; dotted circle = annulus. The diagram is drawn for a rat trained to find the hidden platform in the NE quadrant. Other rats were trained to find the platform in one of the other quadrants.

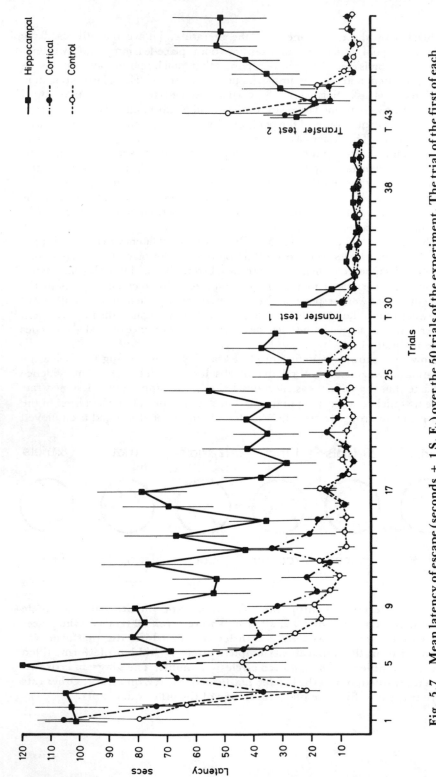

Fig. 5.7 Mean latency of escape (seconds ± 1 S. E.) over the 50 trials of the experiment. The trial of the first of each series of daily trials is shown on the horizontal axis, as are the 2 transfer tests. Note the re-emergence of the hippocampal deficit during trials 43–50.

around randomly from place to place. Hippocampal lesioned rats may therefore learn how to escape, but not where to escape. Second, as illustrated in Fig. 5.8, the hippocampal lesioned rats used longer paths to reach the platform with no apparent directionality. And finally, on transfer tests conducted after trials 28 and 41, the hippocampal lesioned group were no more likely to visit or search near the vicinity of the platform after it had been removed from the pool than they were to visit any of three other comparable locations (Fig. 5.9).

Together with other data investigating the effects of fornix lesions on the one-trial 'working-memory' version of the task (Morris, 1982), these results point to an absolute spatial deficit in lesioned rats. When required to locate a single place in the pool, under conditions in which local cues have been completely removed, hippocampal lesioned rats totally fail. Damage to the intrinsic hippocampal circuitry (Sutherland *et al.*, 1981a) also causes impairments which are as large as those shown by normal rats searching for a randomly moving platform.

Unfortunately, the finding that hippocampal lesioned rats do not generally learn about places need not imply that they cannot do so. Becker & Olton (1981) report the results of an experiment in which normal and fornix lesioned rats successfully discriminated between two objects on the basis off their appearance or position. Rats were allowed to explore an open field and climb onto the objects to find food. Later, food was hidden on top of only one of the objects and the rats had to learn to approach it, starting from any of several doorways at the periphery of the open field. The results show an impairment on the spatial task after fornix lesions (and an impairment in spatial reversal), but also (a) that the lesioned rats could eventually learn the spatial task and (b) that they eventually performed adequately on transfer tests in which the rats had to enter the open field from novel positions. A follow-up study (Becker *et al.*, 1982) shows that the fornix lesioned rats are more reliant on intra-maze cues than normals.

The discrepancy between Becker & Olton's (1981) and Morris *et al.*'s (1981) results could be trivial if Becker & Olton's animals were following odour trails,

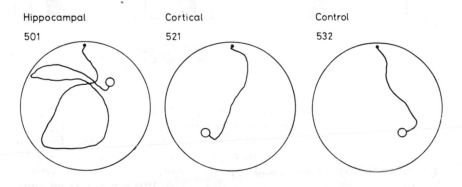

Hippocampal	Cortical	Control
501	521	532

Fig. 5.8   The actual navigated path of the median rat (median of path lengths) in each group on trial 28 just before the first transfer test.

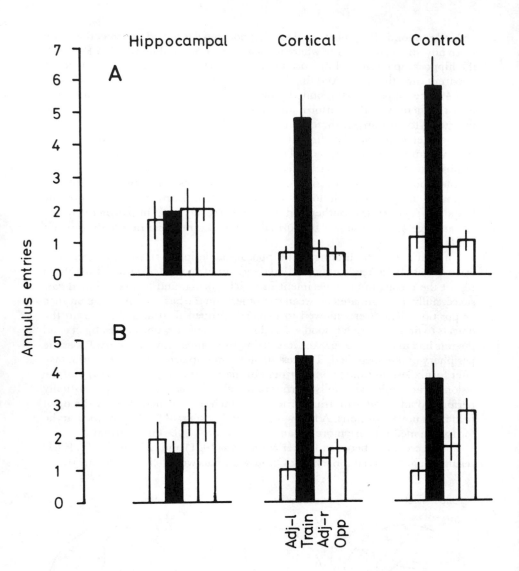

Fig. 5.9 Mean crossing of each of the annuli (± 1 S. E.) marking the former platform positions during transfer test 1 (A) and test 2 (B). The data have been grouped such that crossings of the training location for each animal (Train), the annulus in the adjacent quadrant to the left (Adj-1), adjacent to the right (Adj-r) and opposite (Opp) were grouped together. Note that the hippocampal deficit is absolute — this group was no more likely to pass through the annulus marking the training location than any other.

particularly near the fixed object. Odour trails are, of course, controlled in the swimming task. But an alternative and more interesting possibility is that some kind of spatial mapping by fornix lesioned rats is possible, provided it is based on local intra-maze cues. We should note that Miller & Best (1980) have shown that fornix lesions do not destroy place-fields — they only render them more susceptible to intra-maze cues. Becker & Olton (1981) used fornix lesions whereas Morris *et al.* (1981) used total hippocampal lesion.

Critique. I have concentrated on the absolute *versus* relative encoding deficit issue because this is particularly crucial to O'Keefe & Nadel's account of hippo-campal involvement in exploration. If hippocampal lesions do not totally abolish place-learning, then whatever else these lesions also do, O'Keefe & Nadel's (1978) theory is wrong. Some residual mapping capabilities imply the existence of allocentric spatial representation systems in the brain that lie outside the hippocampus.

Our own studies of hippocampal and fornix lesioned rats (Morris, 1982; Morris *et al.*, 1981) support the spatial mapping theory, but we are inclined to be cautious in the face of evidence (Becker & Olton, 1981; Becker *et al.*, 1982; Olton & Feustle, 1981; Olton & Papas, 1980), which not only indicates that the spatial mapping theory is incomplete but also points to residual mapping abili-ties in fornix lesioned rats. Further work is required to establish whether fornix lesions do produce a syndrome identical to that of total hippocampal ablation.

It is, moreover, important to distinguish between claiming that the mapping theory is wrong and claiming that it is incomplete. If the hippocampus and adjacent structures are the only areas of the brain involved in allocentric spatial perception and memory, intensive study of spatial tasks will be extremely fruit-ful, particularly in physiological studies such as recent work on senescence (Barnes & McNaughton, 1980). This claim holds irrespective of whether place-learning is a special category of learning.

5.4 Conclusion

This chapter has concentrated on two new approaches to exploratory behaviour. One line of work has discovered movement subsystems that may form components of exploratory behaviour; the other has discovered that a neural system — the hippocampus — is intimately involved in spatial memory, which thereby plays a role in structuring normal exploration.

However, both approaches are plagued with serious logical problems: movement components that are apparently absent during early stages of neuro-logical recovery may only be concealed in the absence of strong sensory stimula-tion; the conceptual link between 'place cells' and spatial mapping remains obscure; and some residual spatial mapping may be possible in the absence of certain extrinsic fibre systems of the hippocampus if not the hippocampus itself.

Irrespective of how these issues are resolved, these two aproaches to explora-tion present a paradox. To observe exploration requires that the experimenter leave the animal alone in a novel environment. This behavioural simplicity makes the use of open-field activity and other simple measures of exploration attractive for screening the effects of brain lesions or drugs, but it belies the true complexity of what may be happening in terms of underlying mechanisms. It has required studies of neurological recovery to learn about the sensorimotor subsystems of exploration; and study of cognitive subsystems clearly requires more complex analytical experiments on learning and memory. Thus, exploratory behaviour involves, but is unsuited for, studying some of the very neural mechanisms responsible for its coordinated expression.

Acknowledgements

This work was supported in part by the Medical Research Council and through private funds. I am grateful to Professor P. Teitelbaum and Dr. I. Golani for sending me copies of diagrams and preprints; to Ian Whishaw for introducing me to work on movement subsystems; to John O'Keefe, David Olton and Nick Rawlins, with whom I have discussed aspects of this work; and to Norma Hansell for drawing Fig. 5.3.

References

ANAND, B. K. and BROBECK, J. R. (1951) Hypothalamic control of food intake. *Yale Journal of Biology and Medicine* **24**, 123–140.

ARCHER, J. (1973) Tests for emotionality in rats and mice: a review. *Animal Behaviour* **21**, 205–235.

BARNES, C. A. and MCNAUGHTON, B. L. (1980) Spatial memory and Hippocampal synaptic plasticity in senescent and middle aged rats. In *The Psychobiology of Aging* (Ed. D. STEIN). New York: Elsevier.

BECKER, J. T. and OLTON, D. S. (1981) Cognitive mapping and hippocampal system function. *Neuropsychologia* **19**, 733–744.

BECKER, J. T., WALKER, J. A. and OLTON, D. S. (1980) Neuroanatomical bases of spatial memory. *Brain Research* **200**, 307–320.

BECKER, J. T., OLTON., D. S. ANDERSON, C. A. and BREITINGER, E. R. P. (1982) Cognitive mapping in rats: The role of hippocampal and frontal systems in retention and reversal. *Behavioural Brain Research* **3**, 1–22.

BLAND, B. H., ANDERSEN, P., GANES, T. and SVEEN, O. (1980) Automated analysis of rhythmicity of physiologically identified hippocampal formation neurons. *Experimental Brain Research* **38**, 205–219.

CORMAN, C. D. and SHAFER, J. N. (1968) Open field activity and exploration. *Psychonomic Science* **13**, 55–56.

COWAN, P. (1976) The new object reaction of Rattus rattus: The relative importance of various cues. *Behavioral Biology* **16**, 31–44.

DALLAND, T. (1976) Response perseveration of rats with dorsal hippocampal lesions. *Behavioral Biology* **17**, 473–484.

De RYCK, M., SCHALLERT T. and TEITELBAUM, P. (1980) Morphine versus Haloperidol catalepsy in the rat: A behavioural analysis of postural support mechanisms. *Brain Research* **201**, 143–172.

EVARTS, E. V. and TANJI, J. (1976) Reflex and intended responses in motor cortex pyramidal tract neurons of monkey. *Journal of Neurophysiology* **39**, 1069–1080.

GAFFAN, D. (1972) Loss of recognition memory in rats with lesions of the fornix. *Neuropsychologia* **10**, 327–341.

GAFFAN, D. (1974) Recognition impaired and association intact in the memory of monkeys after transection of the fornix. *Journal of Comparative and Physiological Psychology* **86**, 1100–1109.

GOLANI, I. (1982) The search for invariants in motor behaviour. In *Issues in Behavioural Development*, The Bielefeld Interdisciplinary Conference (Eds. K. IMMELMANN, L. PETRINOVITCH & G. M. BARLOW). In press.

GOLANI, I., WOLGIN, D. L. and TEITELBAUM, P. (1979) A proposed natural recovery from akinesia in the lateral hypothalamic rat. *Brain Research* **164**, 237–267.

GOLANI, I., BRONCHTI, G., MOUALEM, D. and TEITELBAUM, P. (1982) 'Warm-up' along dimensions of movement in the ontogeny of exploration in rats and other infant mammals. *Science*, in press.

GRAY, J. A. (1982) *The Neuropsychology of Anxiety: An enquiry into the functions of the Septo-Hippocampal System*. Oxford: Oxford University Press.

HILL, A. J. (1978) First occurrence of hippocampal spatial firing in a new environment, *Experimental Neurology* **62**, 282–297.

IVERSEN, S. D. and FRAY, P. J. (1981) Brain catecholamines in relation to affect. Unpublished manuscript.

KESNER, R. P. (1981) Memory for lists of items in rats: Role of the hippocampus. *Society for Neuroscience Abstracts* **7**, 80.12.

KIMBLE, D. P. (1963) The effects of bilateral hippocampal lesions in rats. *Journal of Comparative and Physiological Psychology* **56**, 273–283.

KIMURA, D. (1981) Neuromotor mechanisms in the evolution of human communication. In *Neurobiology of Social Communication in Primates: An Evolutionary Perspective* (Eds. H. D. STEKLIS and M. J. RALEIGH). New York: Academic Press.

KUBIE, J. L. and RANCK, J. B. Jr. (1981) Sensory behavioural correlates in individual neurons of the rat across four situations. *Society for Neuroscience Abstracts* **7**, 119.2.

LEVITT, D. R. and TEITELBAUM, P. (1975) Somnolence, akinesia and sensory activation of motivated behaviour in the lateral hypothalamic syndrome. *Proceedings of the National Academy of Sciences* **72**, 585–606.

LOMAS, J. and KIMURA, D. (1976) Interhemispheric interaction between speaking and sequential manual activity. *Neuropsychologia* **14**, 23–33.

MACKINTOSH, N. J. (1975) A theory of attention: Variations in the associability of a stimulus with reinforcement. *Psychological Review* **82**, 276–298.

MARSHALL, J. F. (1980) Basal ganglia dopaminergic control of sensorimotor functions related to motivated behaviour. In *Neural Mechanisms of Goal Directed Behavior and Learning* (Eds. R. F. THOMPSON, L. H. HICKS, and V. B. SHVYRKOV). New York: Academic Press.

MARSHALL, J. F. and TEITELBAUM, P. (1978) New considerations in the neuro-psychology of motivated behaviours. In *Handbook of Psychopharmacology, Vol 7*. (Eds. L. L. IVERSEN, S. D. IVERSEN and S. H. SNYDER). New York: Plenum Press.

MARSHALL, J. F. TURNER, B. H. and TEITELBAUM, P. (1971) Sensory neglect produced by lateral hypothalamic damage. *Science* **174**, 523–525.

MARSHALL, J. F., RICHARDSON, J. S. and TEITELBAUM, P. (1974) Nigrostriatal function and the lateral hypothalamic syndrome, *Journal of Comparative and Physiological Psychology* **87**, 808–830.

MILLER, V. M. and BEST, P. J. (1980) Spatial correlates of hippocampal unit activity are altered by lesions of the fornix and entorhinal cortex. *Brain Research* **194**, 311–318.

MOORE, J. W. and STICKNEY, K. J. (1980) Formation of attentional-associative networks in real time: Role of the Hippocampus and implications for conditioning. *Physiological Psychology* **8**, 207–217.

MORAN, G., FENTRESS, J. C. and GOLANI, I. (1981) A description of relational patterns of movement during 'ritualised fighting' in wolves. *Animal Behaviour* **29**, 1146–1165.

MORRIS, R. G. M. (1981) Spatial localisation does not require the presence of local cues. *Learning and Motivation* **12**, 239–260.

MORRIS, R. G. M. (1982) An attempt to dissociate 'Spatial mapping' and 'Working memory' theories of hippocampal function. In *Molecular, Cellular and Behavioral Neurobiology of the Hippocampus* (Ed. W. SIEFERT). New York: Academic Press.

MORRIS, R. G. M., GARRUD, P. and RAWLINS, J. N. P. (1981) Hippocampal ablation causes spatial reference memory deficit in the rat. *Society for Neuroscience Abstracts* **7**, 80.10.

MYHRER, T. (1975) Locomotor, avoidance and maze behaviour in rats with selective disruption of hippocampal output. *Journal of Comparative and Physiological Psychology* **89**, 759–777.

NADEL, L. (1981) Cognitive mapping: at the choice point again, *Cognitive Science Series* No. 12, University of California, Irvine.

NADEL, L. and WILLNER, J. (1980) Context and conditioning: a place for space. *Physiological Psychology* **8**, 218–228.

O'KEEFE, J. (1976) Place units in the hippocampus of the freely moving rat, *Experimental Neurology* **51**, 78–109.

O'KEEFE, J. (1979) A review of the hippocampal place cells. *Progress in Neurobiology* **13**, 419–439.

O'KEEFE, J. and CONWAY, D. H. (1978) Hippocampal place units in the freely moving rat: why they fire where they fire. *Experimental Brain Research* **31**, 573–590.

O'KEEFE, J. and CONWAY. D. H. (1980) On the trail of the hippocampal engram, *Physiological Psychology* **8**, 229–238.

O'KEEFE, J. and DOSTROVSKY, J. (1971) The hippocampus as a spatial map. Preliminary evidence from unit activity in the freely moving rat *Brain Research* **34**, 171–175.

O'KEEFE, J. and NADEL. L. (1978) *The Hippocampus as a Cognitive Map*, Oxford: Oxford University Press.

O'KEEFE, J. and NADEL. L. (1979) Precis of O'Keefe and Nadel's 'The hippocampus as a cognitive map'. *The Behavioral and Brain Sciences* **2**, 487–533.

O'KEEFE, J., NADEL, L., KEIGHTLY, S. and KILL, D. (1975) Fornix lesions selectively abolish place learning in the rat. *Experimental Neurology* **48**, 152–166.

OLTON, D. S. and FEUSTLE, W. A. (1981) Hippocampal function required for nonspatial working memory, *Experimental Brain Research* **41**, 380–389.

OLTON, D. S. and PAPAS, B. C. (1980) Spatial memory and hippocampal system function. *Neuropsychologia* **17**, 669–681.

OLTON, D. S. and SAMUELSON, R. J. (1976) Remembrance of places passed: spatial memory in rats. *Journal of Experimental Psychology. Animal Behaviour Processes.* **2**, 97–116.

OLTON, D. S., BRANCH, M. and BEST, P. J. (1978) Spatial correlates of hippocampal unit activity. *Experimental Neurology* **58**, 387–409.

OLTON, D. S., BECKER, J. T. and HANDELMANN, G. E. (1979) Hippocampus, space and memory. *The Behavioral and Brain Scences* **2**, 313–315.

OLTON, D. S., BREITINGER, E. R. P. and ANDERSON, E.R.P. (1982) Hippocampal function and memory processing: The amnesic syndrome following fimbria-fornix

144

lesions in rats and its relation to human amnesia. *The Journal of Neuroscience*, in press.

OLTON, D. S., HANDELMANN, G. E. & WALKER, J. A. (1981) Spatial memory and food searching strategies. In *Foraging Behavior: Ecological, Ethological and Psychological approaches* (Eds. A. KAMIL and T. D. SARGEANT). New York: Garland Press.

OSBOURNE, B. and SEGGIE, J. (1980) Behavioural, corticosterone and prolactin responses to novel environment in rats with fornix transections. *Journal of Comparative and Physiological Psychology* **94**, 536-546.

PEARCE, J. M. and HALL, G. (1980) A model for Pavlovian learning: Variation in the effectiveness of conditioned but not of unconditioned stimuli. *Psychological Review* **87**, 532-552.

RANCK, J. B. Jr. (1973) Studies on single neurones in dorsal hippocampal formation and septum in unrestrained rats. *Experimental Neurology* **41**, 461-555.

RANCK, J. B. Jr. (1982) Sensory-behavioural correlates of Hippocampal Neuronal firing: space and context. In *Molecular, Cellular and Behavioural Neurobiology of the Hippocampus* (Ed. W. SIEFERT). New York: Acadamic Press.

RESCORLA, R. A. and WAGNER, A. R. (1972) A theory of Pavlovian conditioning. Variations in the effectiveness of reinforcement and nonreinforcement. In *Classical Conditioning II* (Eds. A. H. BLACK and W. F. PROKASY). New York: Appleton-Century-Crofts.

ROBBINS, T. and SAHAKIAN, B. J. (1981) Behavioural and neurochemical determinants of drug-induced stereotypy. In *Metabolic Disorders of the Nervous System* (Ed. F. CLIFFORD ROSE). London: Pitman.

ROBINSON, T. and WHISHAW. I. Q. (1974) Effects of posterior hypothalamic lesions on voluntary behaviour and hippocampal electroencephalograms in the rat. *Journal of Comparative and Physiological Psychology* **86**, 768-786.

ROSE, G. (1982) Physiological and behavioural characteristics of dentate granule cells. In *Molecular, Cellular and Behavioral Neurobiology of the Hippocampus* (Ed. W. SIEFERT). New York: Academic Press.

ROSSLER, O. (1982) Artificial Cognitive-plus-Motivation and Hippocampus. In *Molecular, Cellular and Behavioral Neurobiology of the Hippocampus* (Ed. W. SIEFERT). New York: Academic Press.

SCHALLERT, T., WHISHAW, I. Q., RAMIREZ, V. D. and TEITELBAUM, P, (1978) Compulsive, Abnormal Walking caused by anticholinergics in akinetic 6-hydroxydopamine treated rats. *Science* **199**, 1461-1463.

SCHALLERT, T., DE RYCK, M. and TEITELBAUM, P. (1980) Atropine stereotypy as a behavioral trap: a movement subsystem and electroencephalographic analysis. *Journal of Comparative and Physiological Psychology* **94**, 1-24.

SINNAMON, H. M., FRENIERE, S. and KOOTZ, J. (1978) Rat hippocampus and memory for places of changing significance. *Journal of Comparative and Physiological Psychology* **92**, 142-155.

STEVENS, R. (1973) Effects of duration of sensory input and intertrial interval on spontaneous alternation in rats with hippocampal lesions. *Physiological Psychology* **1** 41-44.

SUTHERLAND, R. J., WHISHAW, I. Q. and KOLB, B. (1981a) A behavioural analysis of spatial localisation following electrolyic, kainate or colchicine induced damage to the hippocampal formation in the rat. *The Journal of Neuroscience*, in press.

SUTHERLAND, R. J., WHISHAW, I. Q. and REGEHR, J. C. (1981b) Cholinergic receptor blockade impairs spatial localisation using distal cues in the rat. Paper submitted for publication.

SZECHTMAN, H., ORNSTEIN, K., HOFSTEIN, R., TEITELBAUM, P. and GOLANI,

I. (1980) Apomorphine induces behavioural regression: a sequence that is the opposite of neurological recovery. In *Enzymes and Neurotransmitters in Mental Disease* (Eds. E. USDIN, T. L. SOURKES, & M. B. H. YOURDIN).

TEITELBAUM, P. (1981) Disconnection and antagonistic interaction of movement subsystems in motivated behaviour. In *Changing Concepts of the Nervous System* (Eds. A. MORRISON and P. STRICK). New York: Academic Press.

TEITELBAUM, P. and STELLAR, E. (1954) Recovery from the failure to eat produced by hypothalamic lesions. *Science* **120**, 894–895.

TEITELBAUM, P. and EPSTEIN, A. N. (1962) The lateral hypothalamic syndrome: Recovery of feeding and drinking after lateral hypothalamic damage. *Psychological Review* **69**, 74–90.

TEITELBAUM, P., SCHALLERT, T., DE RYCK, M., WHISHAW. I. Q. and GOLANI, I. (1980) Motor subsystems in motivated behaviour. In *Neural Mechanisms of Goal Directed behavior and learning* (Eds. R. F. THOMPSON, L. H. HICKS & V. B. SHVYRKOV). New York: Academic Press.

UNGERSTEDT, U. (1971) Adipsia and aphagia after 6-hydroxydopamine induced degeneration of nigrostriatal dopamine system. *Acta Physiologica Scandanavica, Supplement* **367**, 95–122.

VINOGRADOVA, O. (1975) Functional organisation of the limbic system in the process of registration of information: facts and hypotheses. In *The Hippocampus, Vol. 2* (Eds. R. L. ISAACSON and K. H. PRIBRAM). New York: Plenum Press.

WAGNER, A. R. (1978) Expectancies and the priming of STM. In *Cognitive processes in Animal Behavior* (Eds. S. H. HULSE, H. FOWLER and W. K. HONIG). Hillsdale, NJ: Lawrence Erlbaum Associates.

WEISKRANTZ, L. (1982) Comparative aspects of studies of amnesia. *Proceedings of the Royal Society, Series B*, in press.

WHISHAW, I. Q. (1979) Catecholamine depleted rats as a model of Parkinsonism, 16mm Colour Film, University of Lethbridge, Alberta.

WHISHAW, I. Q., SCHALLERT, T. and KOLB, B. (1981) An analysis of feeding and sensorimotor abilities of rats after decortication. *Journal of Comparative and Physiological Psychology* **95**, 85–103.

WILLNER, J. A. (1980) Spatial factors in latent inhibition. Paper presented at 51st meeting of Eastern Psychological Association.

WILZ, K.J. and BOLTON, R. L. (1971) Exploratory behavior in response to the spatial rearrangement of familiar stimuli. *Psychonomic Science* **64**, 117–118.

CHAPTER 6

Exploration in Small Mammals: Ethology and Ecology

P. E. Cowan

6.1 Introduction

The 'curiosity' of small mammals has long been noted. Small (1899) described the restless movements of infant rats as 'premonitions of curiosity' and Pavlov (1927) referred to the 'investigatory' or 'what-is-it' reflex in his early studies of orienting behaviour by dogs. Nonetheless, little systematic analysis was attempted; rather, much effort was concentrated on the analysis of the behaviour of rats in mazes, and on the cues they used to learn the path to food or water (Munn, 1950). However, Blodgett (1929) related maze learning and exploratory movements by demonstrating that rats use information acquired during unrewarded exposures to a maze in their later learning of that maze for conventional rewards. The importance of this relationship in the behaviour of free-living animals is discussed in Section 6.3.2.

Independently of the workers on laboratory rats (reviewed by Barnett, 1975), zoologists interested in the control of rodent pests began to analyse the exploratory behaviour and movements of wild rats and mice (Chitty & Southern, 1954). Wild rats, in particular, display a new-object avoidance reaction quite unlike the response of laboratory rats (Barnett, 1958; Shorten, 1954). Wild mice, also, behave much less predictably than do laboratory strains (Southern, 1954). Thus, the approach to, and investigation of, novel phenomena obviously has an opposite, the avoidance of strange stimuli in a familiar environment.

This dichotomy between neophilia and neophobia (Barnett & Cowan, 1976), in colloquial terms attributed to curiosity and fear, is apparent rather than real (see Section 6.4.2). However, observations and comparisons of the behaviour of wild and domestic mammals permit explanations of exploratory behaviour in terms of its effects on the survival of individuals and the selective forces impinging upon them (Hamilton, 1964).

As has been said before (e.g. Lockard, 1968), the study of behaviour has been greatly restricted by, amongst other things, a concentration on laboratory studies of laboratory-bred species, and by the questions which have been asked

147

about behaviour. To partly redress this balance, I have purposely chosen to explore some aspects of the relationships between behaviour, exploratory behaviour and ecology, and to examine ways in which these relationships affect the survival of individuals. Where laboratory studies are discussed, they provide, I hope, some insight into the fine detail of field observations of behaviour. For illustration, I have chosen mostly what is familiar to me, namely small mammals; but, in some instances, birds provide more relevant examples. In any case, the principles which govern the exploratory behaviour of small mammals are probably general throughout the animal kingdom.

6.2   The Concept of Exploration

6.2.1   The Definition of Exploratory Behaviour

Behaviour can be defined in one of two ways, either by its consequences or function (definition by the properties of the behaviour), or by the stimuli that elicit it (definition by the operations required to demonstrate the phenomenon) (Jensen, 1961).

Exploratory behaviour is often stated to be difficult to define in a rigorous way (e.g. Berlyne, 1963; Fowler, 1965). The real source of difficulty, as Berlyne (1963) said, is that probably all behaviour has some component of exploratory response or function. Most definitions have been by property: exploratory behaviour alters the animal's stimulus field (Berlyne, 1963); increases the rate of change of stimulation falling on an animal's receptors and is not impelled by homeostatic or reproductive need (Barnett, 1975); familiarizes the animal with the source of stimulation (Hinde, 1966); provides the animal with additional perceptions of its surroundings (McReynolds, 1962); gives the animal information about its surroundings (Halliday, 1968); acquaints the animal with the topography of the surroundings included in its range (Shillito, 1963). All such definitions are based on the idea that exploratory behaviour supplies information to the animal. Such definitions have, however, little practical use. Exploratory acts such as sniffing are elicited by certain specific classes of events which are open to experimental manipulation. A working definition can be based only on the identification of these classes of events.

6.2.2   The Classification of Exploratory Behaviour

Problems with the definition of exploratory behaviour also plague attempts to classify the diverse set of observations variously described as exploration. Berlyne (1960) suggested a distinction between *extrinsic* exploration, where there is an obvious goal (e.g. food searching), and *intrinsic* exploration, where there is none. Allied to these are *specific* exploration which provides stimulation from a definite source (e.g. looking for something in particular), and *diversive*

148

exploration which provides 'interest' with little reference to source or content (Berlyne, 1963; Hutt, 1970).

A more useful descriptive classification is that of *inquisitive* and *inspective* exploration (Berlyne, 1960). Inquisitive exploration brings an animal into contact with unfamiliar stimuli (e.g. searching for food or nest materials, patrolling home range, excursions outside usual ranges); inspective exploration yields further different information from partially familiar situations (e.g. response to new objects; chewing an object whose visual appearance and odour have been assessed; some types of play).

Physiological analysis has not, however, progressed far enough to enable us to identify 'motives' of animals, and unless we assume that, for example, a hungry rat explores only to find food, these general classifications have little operational value. These classifications, and others (e.g. McReynolds, 1962) were derived principally to describe behavioural observations of exploratory behaviour with little reference to the natural history or ecology of the species concerned. An ecologist would almost certainly regard the range of topics discussed here — exploration of new objects, movements within and outside home ranges, foraging and homing — as a curious hodge-podge, loosely related and with conceptual differences (J. A. Gibb, personal communication). How these topics are related can, I hope, be clarified by two general statements:

(i) Animals, when they are deprived of food, water, sensory stimulation, mates, or whatever, engage in behaviour directed at correcting their deficit; that is, they 'search' or 'explore' for specific requirements.
(ii) In the absence of such deficits, much of an animal's time, not spent on other homeostatic activities, is spent gathering information, a process usually referred to as exploratory behaviour.

6.2.3 Determinants of Exploratory Behaviour

Exploratory behaviour should not be considered as an act in itself; rather, it represents a shift in the frequencies of various acts common in an animal's behavioural repertoire (Bindra, 1961). The 'novelty' of a particular stimulus is the most commonly referred to determinant of exploratory behaviour (discussed by Barnett & Cowan, 1976). Unfamiliarity is perhaps a preferable term since it emphasizes the relationship between past and present experience. It can also be precisely operationally defined both in terms of the physical difference between familiar and unfamiliar stimuli and by the observed difference in the response of the animal — an unfamiliar object may differ from a familiar object in, say, size or in the amount of sniffing it evokes.

Berlyne (1950, 1955) clearly demonstrated that rats respond to the discrepancy between a familiar object and one differing only in one stimulus characteristic, such as colour or shape. The magnitude of the discrepancy is also an important determinant of the response. A change to a more complex stimulus (defined by its information content) evokes more response than one to a stimulus of lesser complexity (Taylor, 1974), and highest response rates for

149

sensory contingent bar pressing were by subjects experiencing the most discrepant stimuli (Barnes & Baron, 1961).

The magnitude of stimulus change and its effects may also be measured indirectly by studying animals as they familiarize themselves with an initially unfamiliar environment or object. In general, response declines with the duration of continuous exposure (Berlyne, 1950, 1955), and with repeated exposures from day to day (see also Chapter 2).

6.2.4   The Relationship between Exploration and Fear

It has often been suggested that animals approach moderately intense stimuli and withdraw from extremely intense ones (e.g. Berlyne, 1963; Halliday, 1966; Lester 1968). Two main theories have been proposed to explain the relationship between exploratory behaviour and 'fearfulness': (i) unfamiliar stimuli evoke both approach and withdrawal (curiosity and fear) and exploration reflects the balance of these two tendencies, and (ii) fear aroused by unfamiliar stimulation results in avoidance when the animal is very fearful and exploration when it is only moderately so. Russell (1973) and Barnett & Cowan (1976) have reviewed this debate.

If exploration provides an animal with information about its environment, then it may also reduce the animal's fear or avoidance of that environment. Exploration may thus reduce fear, but fear need not motivate exploration. Exploration is determined by the shifting balance between approach and avoidance; its function may simply be the acquisition of information (Cowan, 1975; O'Keefe & Nadel, 1974).

6.2.5   Novelty as a Reward and Source of Information

The opportunity to explore or manipulate unfamiliar objects acts as an effective reward for learning tasks. Laboratory rodents readily learn the path in a Y-maze leading to a Dashiell maze rather than one leading to a blind alley (Montgomery, 1954), or to press a bar in a Skinner box for nothing more than a clicking sound or a change in the level of illumination (Kish & Antonitis, 1956); and they continue to respond when tested regularly over long periods (Glow, 1970).

In some circumstances, small mammals seem actively to seek problems (Berlyne, 1963); hungry rats offered two routes to food, one direct, the other longer and with varied blind alleys, often choose the longer, more varied route (Hebb & Mahut, 1955). Prokasy (1956) used a maze with a single choice point from which the goal boxes were not visible; food was presented equally on both sides, but on one side a cue was available such that the rat could tell in advance of reaching the goal box whether it contained food. Rats developed a preference for the arm in which they received advance information. Access to information is thus a powerful determinant of behaviour.

Accession of information for its own sake underlies exploratory (latent) learning; animals allowed to explore an environment, such as a maze, without other immediate incentive learn to run in that maze for food or water more readily than animals without previous experience of the maze (reviewed by Barnett, 1975). The value of such storage of information for free-living mammals moving about stable home ranges and having to adapt to changing environmental conditions is obvious.

6.3 Patterns of Movement

6.3.1 Patrolling

Exploratory learning is shown by small mammals in the regular patrolling of their home ranges. Many small mammals have a home range over which they move at intervals, often along a system of trails (reviewed by Jewell, 1966). Patrolling of these ranges is not random, but is highly ordered both in space and time; parts of the range are visited systematically in a night and over several nights (Brown, 1969). Such patrolling is generally observed after animals have been feeding for some time; then all parts of the range may be visited, and other conspecifics approached and investigated (Crowcroft & Rowe, 1963; Mykytowycz, 1958).

Observations in the field. Patrolling has been described for commensal *Rattus norvegicus*; *Mus musculus*; *Apodemus sylvaticus*; several species of *Peromyscus*; rabbits *Oryctolagus cuniculus*; weasels and stoats, *Mustela nivalis* and *M. erminea*; pine martens *Martes martes*; and raccoons *Procyon lotor* (references in Cowan, 1975).

Fitzgerald *et al.* (1981), studying feral house mice (*Mus musculus*) in lowland native forest in New Zealand, found that although most mice had home ranges of more than 0.5 ha, many parts of them were visited each night; one male however, with a range of more than 2 ha, visited a different part of its range each night, and took three nights to cover its whole range (Fig. 6.1).

Among the animals for which patrolling has been reported, and which live in colonies or groups, the dominant male or female is usually the only animal which systematically and regularly reinvestigates the whole area occupied by the group (Brown, 1966, 1969; Crowcroft & Rowe, 1963; Ely, 1971; Mykytowycz, 1958). Wood mice (*Apodemus sylvaticus*), for example, live in groups of 2 to 4 males and 4 to 6 females; one male is dominant over all others within the group, or 'superfamily' (Brown, 1966). The subordinate males and females occupy overlapping areas within the entire home range of the group. Only the dominant male patrols the entire home range (up to 2.6 ha); different sections are systematically visited during some 2 to 3 weeks. Unfamiliar objects, such as tracking stations, are investigated and marked with urine. On one night, the dominant male visited about 80% of the stations in the area it was currently occupying, while each subordinate male visited only about 30%. When the dominant male in one area died, the dominant males from

151

surrounding areas extended their ranges to occupy the vacant areas (Brown, 1966, 1969).

The repeated investigation of familiar areas during patrolling results in the early detection of changes and also increases the chance of animals finding fresh sources of food and water. During the early part of the evening, raccoons (*Procyon lotor*) spend most time around known food sources; after they have fed, they move away and spend time in areas where food is sparse. If a new food source is found in a minor food area, raccoons return to the new source earlier on successive nights (Bider *et al.*, 1968).

During patrols, animals may also refamiliarize themselves with the areas over which they move, by leaving scent at points about their range (Johnson, 1973; Ralls, 1971), and refamiliarize themselves with their neighbouring conspecifics (Barash, 1974).

Laboratory findings. Analogous behaviour to the patrolling of free-living animals has been recorded in simple artificial environments (Barnett *et al.* 1978; Cowan, 1977b). Regular patrolling by both wild and laboratory rodents has been studied in an automated environment, the plus-maze (Fig. 6.2). A central nest box gives access to four arms, each of which may contain some incentive such as food and water, or be empty. Each entry to an arm and its duration are recorded automatically, and animals may live undisturbed in such an environment for long periods (Barnett & Cowan, 1976).

The regular and systematic patterns of movement in the plus-maze can be analysed by regarding the nest box as the choice point of a symmetrical maze. Pairs of visits may be either repeated (AA, BB, . . .) or non-repeated (AB, BC, . . .); similarly, higher-order interactions may be examined by analysing repeating or non-repeating triplets or quadruplets. Of particular interest are non-repeating triplets in which each visit is to a different arm (ABC) as opposed to one in which any two visits are to the same arm (AAB, ABA, . . .); that is, the counterpart of spontaneous alternation (Douglas, 1966).

As rats adapt to the maze, they develop a pattern of visits influenced by the incentives offered in each arm. Although an empty arm receives fewer and briefer visits than one with food or water, it is always regularly and frequently visited (Cowan, 1975). Even mice, kept in the plus-maze during pregnancy, on the day of parturition, still make about 15% of their total visits to an empty arm (Barnett & McEwan, 1973).

Rats adapted to living in the maze with food in one arm, water in another and two arms empty, have about 13 distinct bouts of activity per day; 11 of these in the dark phase of the 12 h light/dark cycle. Five to seven visits are made in a bout, and of the 15 min spent in the maze arms, 12 min (80%) are spent in the food and water arms. Usually, each arm is visited at least once. When an arm is not visited in a bout it is usually an empty arm (29% of bouts) rather than the water (17%) or food arm (4%) which is omitted; and such incomplete patrols are much more common during the day (50% of bouts) than at night (32%; $p < 0.05$) (Cowan, 1975).

Similar observations have been made on rats deprived of food and water for

152

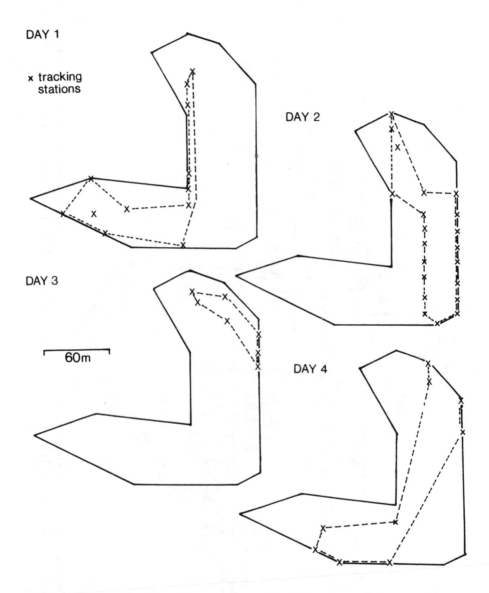

DAY 1

x tracking
stations

DAY 2

DAY 3

60m

DAY 4

Fig. 6.1 Records of tracking stations visited by one ♂ *Mus musculus* on
four successive nights, superimposed on its home range at that time. (After
B. M. Fitzgerald, B. J. Karl and H. Moller (1981) *Journal of Animal Ecology*
50, 489–518, by permission.)

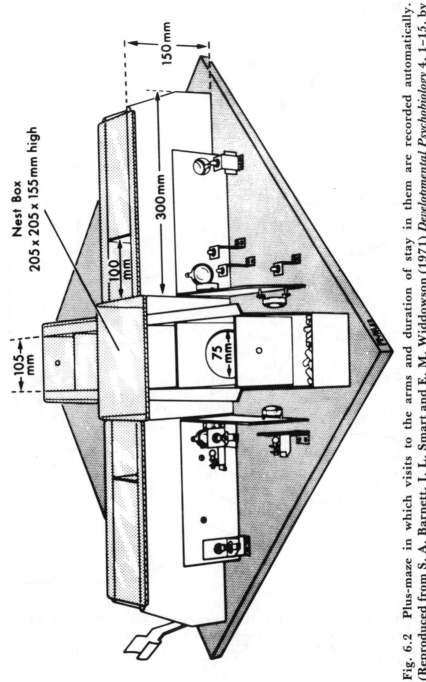

Fig. 6.2 Plus-maze in which visits to the arms and duration of stay in them are recorded automatically. (Reproduced from S. A. Barnett, J. L. Smart and E. M. Widdowson (1971) *Developmental Psychobiology* 4, 1–15, by permission.)

Nest Box
205 x 205 x 155mm high

150 mm

300 mm

100 mm

105 mm

75 mm

21 h daily (see Fig. 6.3; Cowan, 1977b). Over 8 days, rats adapted to the restricted schedule by increasing time spent feeding; but the rate of patrolling, measured by visits to and time spent in the empty arms, did not change significantly. Barnett *et al.* (1978) describe similar behaviour for wild *R. norvegicus*.

Patrolling typically occurred either at the start of the period of access to the arms, or after prolonged periods of feeding and drinking (Cowan, 1977b), regardless of whether access to the arms was restricted or not (Fig. 6.4; Cowan, 1975).

Bouts occurring at the start of periods of access, or after rest periods for rats with free access, may result from competition between exploration and feeding and drinking; bouts after a meal may result from the disinhibition of alternative activities by partial satiation (Cowan, 1977b. McFarland, 1976). Similar effects may underlie, for example, the changing patterns of raccoon behaviour discussed above.

In general, within each activity bout, rats move from one arm to another as they move around the maze, so that each part of the maze is systematically visited. The very highly significant statistical departures from random movement derive from a reduction in the frequency of repeated visits and triplets where any two visits are to the same arm, and an increase in the frequency of non-repeated visits and alternations (Cowan, 1975). Movement into an arm depended on the identity of at least the two preceding arms visited; the sequence of visits was at least a second-order process and probably at least a third-order process (Cowan, 1975).

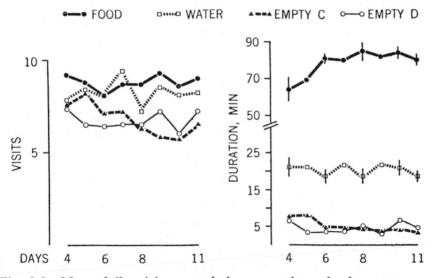

Fig. 6.3 Mean daily visits to and time spent in each plus-maze arm during 8 days when rats were restricted to 3 h/day access to the maze arms. (Reproduced from P. E. Cowan (1977) *Animal Behaviour* **25**, 171–184, by permission.)

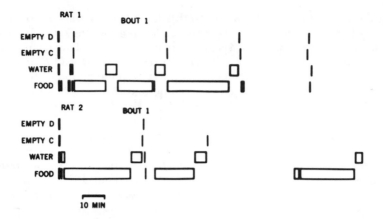

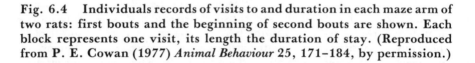

Fig. 6.4 Individuals records of visits to and duration in each maze arm of two rats: first bouts and the beginning of second bouts are shown. Each block represents one visit, its length the duration of stay. (Reproduced from P. E. Cowan (1977) *Animal Behaviour* 25, 171–184, by permission.)

The orderliness in the pattern of visits made by animals in the plus-maze is to an extent affected by the way in which incentives are presented in the arms and by the small number of alternatives. But it is not dependent on incentives; with all arms empty, whether rats are tested for short periods only or live in the maze with food and water in the nest box, the pattern of visits is similar. Rats move from one arm to a different one each time they pass through the nest box (Cowan, 1975).

Olton & Samuelson (1976) have made similar observations using a non-residential 8-arm maze; rats visited all the arms during an exposure of only a few minutes, with little repetition.

The role of social factors on patrolling has also been examined. Ely (1971) studied the behaviour of groups of male and female laboratory mice in complex cages consisting of eight nest boxes interconnected by tubular runways. Males were classed either as dominant, rival or subordinate from observations of their social behaviour. Generally, there was one dominant and one rival male; the dominant male had three times the rate of movement, and ten times the patrolling rate of the next most active male, the rival. When the dominant male was removed from a colony, the rival increased its activity and rate of patrolling.

There are thus close parallels between the field observations and laboratory studies of patrolling. To summarize, animals patrol regularly and they patrol systematically so that all parts of their range are visited; in social groups of small mammals, patrolling is largely an activity of the dominant individual. Based on these observations, patrolling should occur more frequently in strongly territorial species, or in species which hold stable ranges and are opportunistic feeders. This hypothesis remains to be tested.

Exploration and homing.   Although many small mammals maintain stable home ranges, there have been many observations of apparently exploratory movements well outside those ranges (e.g. Stickel, 1979). For example, mice (*M. musculus*) marked by Newsome (1969) in a reed-bed adjacent to wheat fields were occasionally caught in a wheat field up to 200 m away one day but back in the reed-bed the day after that; range-lengths within the reed-bed rarely exceeded 30 m.

Usually nothing other than their occurrence is known about such forays. An exception is a radiotracking study of brush-tailed possums, *Trichosurus vulpecula*; Ward (1978) located and followed 4 radiotagged possums for 3 nights/month over two years. Most excursions beyond the usual home range were associated with feeding on seasonal, highly attractive food sources or with sexual activity during the breeding season (Fig. 6.5).

But regardless of the end point of such excursions for both mice and possums, the exploratory activity involved must result in an animal being aware of a much larger area than just its usual home range. One use to which they apparently put this additional information, namely homing, has been much studied. Mice and possums are both capable of returning to their home ranges when displaced distances beyond normal range-lengths (How, 1972; Sims & Wolfe, 1976). Newsome *et al.* (1982) found that 84% of mice displaced on average twice their normal range-lengths outside their ranges returned home, and 65% displaced four times their normal range-lengths did likewise; of the mice which returned, 78% and 77% respectively had returned home after only two days.

There are many similar observations on a wide variety of mammals, and such 'exploratory migration' (defined as migration beyond the premigration limits of a familiar area during which the ability to return to that familiar area is retained, though not necessarily exploited) has recently been incorporated into a more general model of animal migration (Baker, 1978). Baker (1978) suggests a role for exploratory migration in resource exploitation in patchy habitats based on ranking of habitats visited during such exploration; animals then patrol ranked habitats primarily to reassess their suitability.

Exploration and foraging.   As Bider *et al.* (1968) showed, exploratory wanderings by raccoons after they had fed resulted in the rapid and efficient use of new sources of food located in areas not normally associated with feeding. I have found that brush-tailed possums (*T. vulpecula*) provided with additional food in the form of apples, one every 15 m distributed on the ground over a 6 ha area of forest in lines 30 m apart, ate more than 80% of the apples the first night they were put out; after only three feedings at three-nightly intervals all apples were repeatedly eaten (Cowan, unpublished findings). Possums in this habitat normally spend less than 20% of their time foraging on the ground (Ward, 1978).

Similar behaviour is shown by possums feeding at non-toxic bait stations

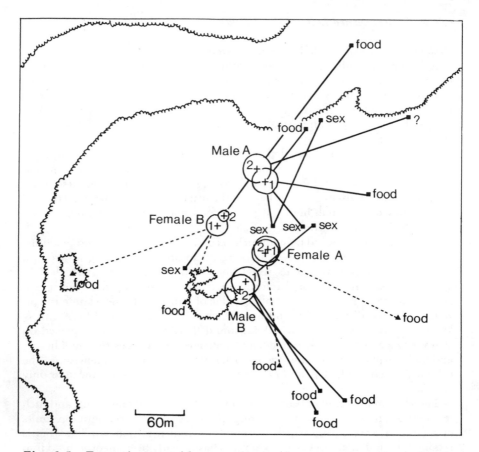

Fig. 6.5 Excursions outside normal range by two male and two female brush-tailed possums fitted with radiotransmitters. Normal range is given by mean nightly range size inscribed about the respective annual centres of activity for two years. Food was seasonally available flowers or fruit. (After G. D. Ward (1977) *Forest and Bird* No. 204, May 1977, by permission of the Royal Forest & Bird Protection Society of New Zealand.)

(Bamford, 1970; Jane, 1979). Bamford showed that the rapid increase from night-to-night in baits taken resulted initially from possums returning to feed at stations where they had found bait before, but later from possums actively searching for bait stations. When bait stations were spaced at least 40 m apart, this latter effect disappeared.

Smith & Sweatman (1974) and Krebs & Cowie (1976) have shown that foraging animals explore and sample their environment continuously and can use the information when the environment changes; less profitable food patches are sampled more than expected, and when patch quality is changed, foraging behaviour changes appropriately (Krebs, 1978).

6.4 Neophobia and Neophilia

6.4.1 Neophobia

Commensal *R. norvegicus* and *R. rattus* display two types of behaviour that protect them from control measures: (a) they avoid strange objects in a familiar place (new-object reaction, an unlearned response — Shorten, 1954) and (b) they learn to avoid foods which make them ill (poison shyness) (Barnett & Cowan, 1976; Barnett, *et al.*, 1978). Laboratory rats also display poison shyness (Rozin & Kalat, 1971), but they do not display typical new-object reaction (Section 6.4.2). Cowan (1977a) has suggested that the marked avoidance reaction of commensal rats may be due to selection in man-made environments for initial avoidance of traps or piles of poisoned bait in the rat's familiar home range. Certainly, the more usual response by small mammals to unfamiliar objects is tentative approach (reviewed by Barnett & Cowan, 1976; Wolfe, 1969).

The relative importance of various cues. Analysis of the new-object reaction of commensal rats in the plus-maze and in small cages has revealed some of the cues important in evoking the response (Cowan, 1976, 1977a).

If wild *R. norvegicus* or *R. rattus* adapted to living in the plus-maze are confronted with strange objects in the arm containing food, they often fail to enter that arm and instead starve themselves, sometimes for days. By contrast, when a previously closed arm is opened — a new area — it is quickly entered and explored (Fig. 6.6).

Objects are not avoided if they are present as part of the new environment when rats are first put in the maze (Fig. 6.7); but they are strongly avoided if they are introduced after rats have become familiar with the maze. Thus, novelty is a prime determinant of the avoidance reaction, as it is for approach (Section 6.2.3).

Further tests were conducted in the rats' familiar home-cages. The response of rats which were accustomed to feeding from two identical food baskets was measured when one basket was given a variety of treatments; relative food consumption was used as a measure of avoidance. Removing a rat's own smell from one basket or replacing its odour with that of an unfamiliar conspecific has little effect. Bull (1972) also found that altering the smell of familiar food containers with a variety of attractants or repellents had little effect on feeding activities of wild *R. norvegicus*. When only one food basket was available initially, however, moving it and later introducing a second identical basket did not evoke avoidance; nor did replacing a familiar food with an unfamiliar highly palatable one. If, however, one basket is then moved to an unfamiliar position, or if it is replaced by one of a different shape, it is usually avoided. If the alternative food source is withdrawn, some rats starve themselves for more than 4 days before eating from the differently shaped basket (Cowan, 1976).

The new-object reaction of the two commensal species is markedly different from that of domesticated laboratory rats, or of two species of wild, non-

159

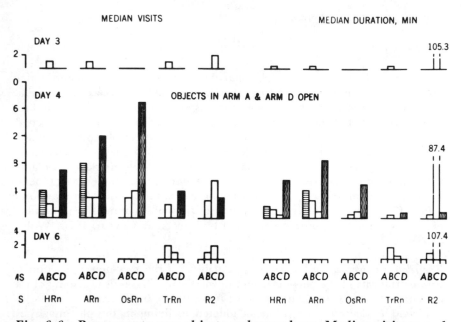

Fig. 6.6 Responses to new objects and new places. Median visits to and time spent in each maze arm in the 2 h after daily readings on day 3, and in the same period on day 4 when white-painted cubes were first put in arm A and arm D was opened, and on day 6. Rn = *Rattus norvegicus*; R2 = *Rattus rattus*; H = hooded; A = Agouti; OS = 9th generation laboratory-bred wild rats; tr = recently trapped. Six of eight *R. rattus* slept in arm C. (Reproduced from P. E. Cowan (1975) Ph.D. Thesis, Australian National University, Canberra.)

commensal rats, *R. fuscipes* and *R. villosissimus* (Cowan, 1977a: Fig. 6.8). The latter have not been subject to intense human predation and evidently do not typically avoid new objects.

Variation.   In the experiments described in Section 6.4.1, there was marked individual variation; even among wild *R. norvegicus*, where the new-object reaction is most fully developed, some animals showed little avoidance of new objects. Breeding under standard laboratory conditions for 9 to 12 generations did not reduce this variation (Cowan, 1975), although other aspects of the rat's behaviour had changed (Barnett & Stoddart, 1969). Similar variation is shown by both wild and laboratory-bred *R. rattus*.

Individuals are, however, in general persistent avoiders or non-avoiders (Cowan, 1975). *R. rattus* were tested repeatedly in the plus-maze with either the same object on each test or a different one. If a rat avoided the first object, it responded similarly on subsequent trials; non-avoiders remained so, even when confronted with different objects (Table 6.1).

160

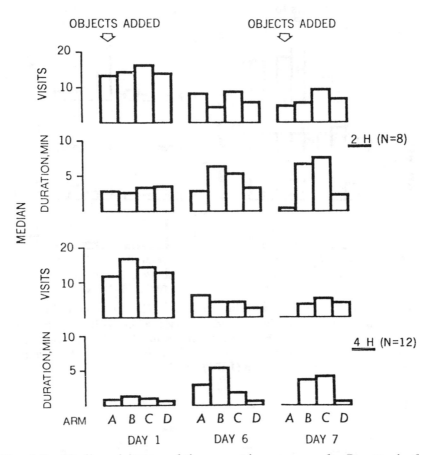

Fig. 6.7 Median visits to and time spent in maze arms by *R. rattus* in the 30 min after arms were opened each day. Rats had either 2 h (2H) or 4 h (4H) access per day to the maze arms. On day 1, unfamiliar objects were present in arm A when the rats first had access to the arms; on day 7, different unfamiliar objects were put in arm A. No objects were present on days 2–6. (Reproduced from P. E. Cowan (1975) Ph.D. Thesis, Australian National University, Canberra.)

Rats that displayed the most extreme new-object reaction on each trial were, in general, siblings, though from different litters. Crowcroft & Jeffers (1961) suggest genetical differences as a basis for variation in the response of wild house mice to traps.

Effects of age. Young *R. rattus*, not yet sexually mature, displayed typical new-object reaction, though like adults there was much individual variation (Fig. 6.9); however, they accepted a new food in a familiar basket more readily than adults (Cowan, 1975).

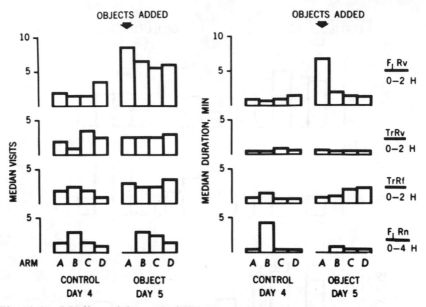

Fig. 6.8 Median visits to and time spent in each maze arm in the 2 h or 4 h after daily readings on day 4, and on day 5 when white-painted cubes were first put in arm A. F_1 = first generation laboratory-bred; Tr = trapped; Rf = *R. fuscipes*; R. v. = *R. villosissimus*; Rn = *R. norvegicus*. (Reproduced from P. E. Cowan (1975) Ph.D. Thesis, Australian National University, Canberra.)

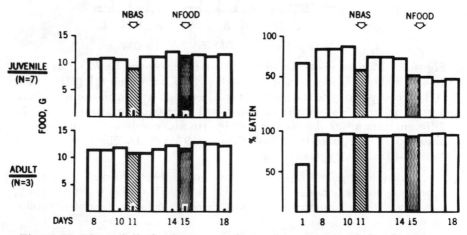

Fig. 6.9 Mean daily food consumption and percentage of total food eaten from the treated basket by juvenile (< 50 days old) and adult *R. rattus*. Initially food pellets were available in two identical baskets; on day 11 (NBAS) one basket was replaced by a new, different, container; on day 15 (NFOOD), a new food was offered in the remaining original basket. (Reproduced from P. E. Cowan (1975) Ph.D. Thesis, Australian National University, Canberra.)

Table 6.1   Percentage of Rats Avoiding Objects in the plus-maze

Group I had 3 trials with the same object: Group II had 3 trials, each with a different object.

	Number of objects avoided (% of animals)			
	All 3	None	Any 1	Any 2
GROUP I (n = 12)	42	8	17	33
GROUP II (n = 25)	60	12	12	16

Sex differences.   I have found no consistent differences in a variety of experiments between male and female commensal rats of both species in their new-object reaction; however, many females underwent irregular oestrous cycles or were anoestrous for prolonged periods during the experiments (Cowan, 1975; unpublished findings). Archer (1975), in an extensive review of sex differences in the behaviour of rodents, noted that female rats typically explored more than male rats when introduced into an unfamiliar environment. Also, female laboratory rats more rapidly patrol a complex maze at oestrus than either before or after (Martin & Battig, 1980). Oestrus in female laboratory rats is also associated with a general increase in activity and decreased feeding (Martin & Battig, 1980).

I found similar responses were shown by a few wild *R. rattus* which displayed regular oestrus (Cowan, unpublished data); a typical example is shown in Fig. 6.10. There was a consistent peak of visits to the plus-maze arms every four days. Associated with the peak of visits were a few brief visits to the one arm containing unfamiliar objects which the rat had been completely avoiding. On the subsequent 3 days the arm with the unfamiliar objects was again completely avoided. These effects persisted for more than 50 days under a variety of treatments. (Fig. 6.10).

The change in the balance between approach and avoidance associated with oestrus may have been due to a change in responsiveness to the object itself, to an increase in approach or a decrease in avoidance (or both), or to the general increase in the rate of visits. Cyclical changes in the odour detection thresholds of female (but not male) laboratory rats are associated with the oestrous cycle, with maximum sensitivity on the day of oestrus (Pietras & Moulton, 1974). High oestrogen and low progesterone levels have marked effects on the functioning of various aspects of the peripheral and central nervous system. The reticular activating system is particularly responsive. Its extensive central nervous connections (reviewed by Monier, 1968), and the marked effects of oestrogen and progesterone on EEG arousal thresholds in response to its stimulation (Kawakami & Sawyer, 1967) suggest a possible physiological basis for the changes in responsiveness associated with oestrus.

163

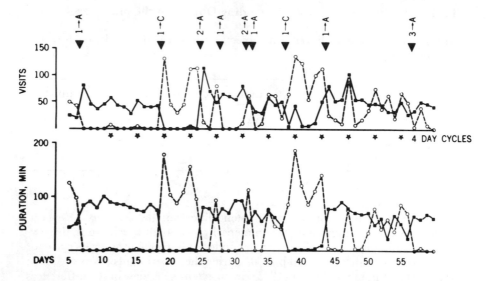

Fig. 6.10   Record of total visits and duration in plus-maze arms A and C of one *R. rattus* which showed regular 4-day activity cycles. Food was available in maze arms A and C. (1 → A: new-object 1 put in arm A and left there until next change; e.g. 1 → C.) (Reproduced from P. E. Cowan (1975) Ph.D Thesis, Australian National University, Canberra.)

6.4.2   Do Laboratory Rodents Display Neophobia?

Barnett & Cowan (1976) have suggested that the domestication of rodents in laboratories has resulted in greatly reduced new-object reaction. A series of experiments, some described in Section 6.4.1, generally support this contention (see also, Barnett, 1958; Corey, 1978; Cowan, 1976, 1977a; Cowan & Barnett, 1975). Mitchell (1976) and Mitchell *et al.* (1975) have suggested that this apparent absence of neophobia may result from the insensitivity of the measures employed. When they confronted rats with familiar and unfamiliar food containers for short periods only, the response of the laboratory strains more nearly resembled that of the wild rats; that is, long delays before feeding from the unfamiliar container and little consumption of food there.

Neophobia is, however, not an all-or-none response; as discussed in Section 6.4.1, some wild rats do not avoid unfamiliar objects or food containers. Rather, neophobia and neophilia represent opposite ends of a continuum of response. The responses of wild and laboratory rats differ quantitatively more than qualitatively; when confronted with unfamiliar objects both strains show a repeated pattern of approach-sniff-retreat (Cowan, 1975; Taylor *et al.*, 1974). The strains differ markedly, however, in the persistence of this response; in most situations laboratory rats quickly shift to actual contact with the unfamiliar object whereas wild rats may persist in avoiding it, but still repeatedly checking its presence, for days (Cowan, 1975).

164

Obviously, as Mitchell (1976) has shown, the persistence of avoidance in laboratory rats can be enhanced by appropriate environmental manipulation, particularly by maintaining unchanging conditions for long periods before the introduction of change and by arranging competition between exploration and feeding. But given sufficient experience all rats, whether laboratory or wild strains, eventually explore the changes in their environment. The level of initial response — extreme avoidance, or hesitant approach, or rapid approach and investigation — can, however, be altered by experience. Wild rats living in a constantly changing environment (a rubbish dump) exhibited little new-object reaction compared with the extreme avoidance of rats from more stable environments (Boice & Boice, 1968).

Laboratory mice in individual cages were presented with five identical unfamiliar objects one at a time for 5 min at 3 min intervals, and the time they spent in contact with, sniffing and biting, the object was measured: the set of trials was repeated three times at weekly intervals. As expected, total time spent exploring the object decreased from the first trial to the last in each series; but this effect was much more marked ($p < 0.01$) in the third set of trials than in the first. The pattern of exploration also changed with experience; not until the last of the first series of trials, and clearly in the second and third series, did the maximum amount of contact with the object occur in the first minute of a trial ($p < 0.05$; Fig. 6.11). Thus, with experience, the behaviour of the mice changed from initial hesitant approach and brief contact to rapid approach, contact and habituation (Cowan, unpublished findings).

Similarly, Sheldon (1969) exposed rats each day to one of 14 different objects; on the first trial only 30% of the rats approached the novel object while by the 14th trial, 75% did so.

Thus stimulus change may alter the balance between approach and withdrawal — displayed as neophobia or neophilia — in different directions depending on the magnitude of the change and the recent experiences of an animal with change.

6.4.3 A Model

Fig. 6.12 describes a model of my interpretation of the relationship between approach and avoidance and the expression of exploratory behaviour in domesticated and commensal rodents. This model is based on premises noted below, all of which require verification, but which derive from the results described in previous sections.

1. Exploration is determined by the shifting balance between approach and avoidance.
2. For individuals, approach is the predisposed response.
3. The maximum of both the level of approach and of avoidance are fixed in an individual (but may be altered by, for example, early experience).
4. The tendency to avoid is more labile than that to approach.

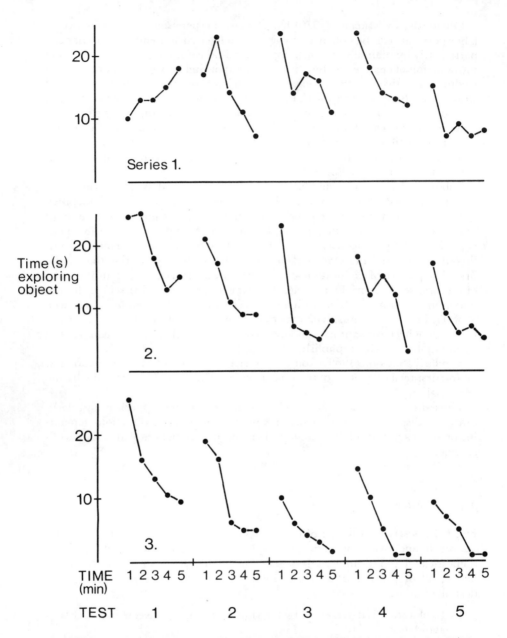

Fig. 6.11 Mean time spent sniffing and biting a white-painted cube in each minute of a series of five 5-min trials by laboratory mice (n = 10). A fresh cube was provided for each trial; the three series of trials were given one week apart. (Cowan, unpublished findings.)

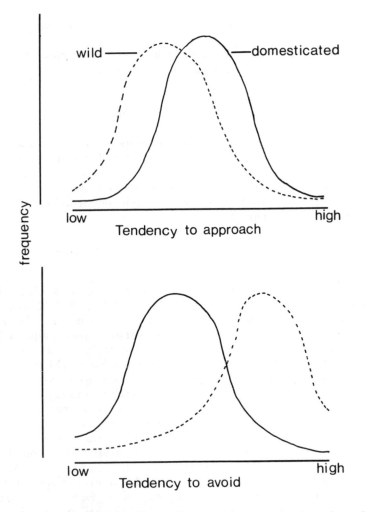

Fig. 6.12 Hypothetical curves of tendency to approach and tendency to avoid new-objects of commensal and domesticated rodents.

5. How strongly an individual responds depends on the various parameters of the situation; e.g. magnitude of stimulus change, recent experience, age, stage of oestrus, etc.
6. The tendency to approach in a particular situation is reduced by approach, but always remains positive.
7. The tendency to avoid in a particular situation has an inbuilt decay function which can be experimentally altered (by drugs, experience, etc.). Decay is accelerated by the expression of approach behaviour.
8. Selection during domestication has shifted the tendencies to approach and

avoid; avoidance has decreased to a greater extent than any change in approach.

9. Selection for commensalism has markedly increased the tendency to avoid without much, if at all, reducing that of approach.

6.5 The Survival Value of Exploratory Behaviour

Exploratory behaviour enhances the survival of individuals in two ways, by reducing factors (such as vulnerability to predation) influencing mortality and by increasing factors (such as foraging ability) which contribute directly to survival. Whether differences between individuals of the same species in their exploratory behaviour can be related to differences in their reproductive success (fitness) remains to be explored.

6.5.1 Protective Advantages

Protection from predators. Predation may act selectively on certain individuals within populations of small rodents (Brown, 1965; Dice, 1947). Commensal rodents, once they leave their nests, are subject to predation, which they avoid mainly by the use of runways under cover and flight to temporary refuges. Rats are more vulnerable if they are in unfamiliar surroundings (Shorten, 1954). *Microtus pennsylvanicus* (Ambrose, 1972) and *Peromyscus leucopus* (Metzgar, 1967) put in an unfamiliar area containing nest boxes were preyed upon by captive owls much more than mice previously given several days to explore the new environment before the owls were introduced. New animals were more vulnerable probably because they moved about more in the unfamiliar area compared to the residents, and they lacked familiar pathways and knowledge of the topography of the refuges. Glickman and Morrison (1969) found that, within groups of albino laboratory mice, those which had moved about and reared most, and made most entries to the central squares in an open field test, were also the first to be captured when the groups were given access from their home cages to an unfamiliar area to which an owl also had access.

Protection from trapping. If commensal *R. norvegicus* and *R. rattus* behaved as do laboratory rats, their rapid investigation of new objects would soon result in their being trapped. New-object avoidance, as of freshly set traps (new objects in familiar places), provides protection (Shorten, 1954).

Protection from poisoning. Commensal rats may be protected from piles of poison bait by new-object reaction when bait is first laid (Shorten, 1954). But protection against poisoned food also involves an initial hesitation to eat new foods, with low initial intake and long intervals between meals, and the ability to associate the effects of sub-lethal poisoning with a particular food, mostly as a result of the pattern of food intake (reviewed by Rozin & Kalat, 1971). These

168

responses are common to many species of small mammals (Barnett & Cowan, 1976).

6.5.2 Aids to Survival

The importance of patrolling and of exploratory excursions has already been discussed (Section 6.3), particularly in relation to foraging and homing, though the argument is readily extended to many resources, such as mates, for which an animal must search. Davies & Houston (1981) have recently elegantly modelled the relationship between foraging and patrolling for the pied wagtail, *Motacilla alba*. Pied wagtails defend winter feeding territories along a river, feeding on insects washed up on the banks. After a stretch had been depleted, time was needed for prey abundance to return to a profitable level. The wagtail's feeding rate depended on the elapsed time since a stretch was last depleted. Systematic search and exploration around the territory increased feeding rate by reducing this interval. Systematic search by the territory holder also resulted in the early eviction of intruders who exploited food available to resident territory holders; systematic resource exploitation meant that the effects of intruders on the available food were also reduced since they often fed on recently depleted areas.

The analysis of exploration and foraging was then extended to include the costs and benefits of territorial behaviour. Territories were sometimes shared with a subordinate (satellite). On days of high food abundance, owners tolerated satellites since the benefits, measured as increased feeding rate, resulting from help with territory defence outweighed the costs incurred through sharing the food supply; on days of low food abundance when an owner would have a higher feeding rate by being alone, satellites were evicted.

As Davies & Houston (1981) comment, the simple case where a territory is shared between two animals may help us to understand the conditions under which group territoriality has evolved.

6.6 Final Comment

Exploratory behaviour is all pervasive — because of its nature, the role of exploratory behaviour, its function, cannot be evaluated in isolation from other aspects of behaviour and ecology. I have tried to demonstrate these interactions and to show how they might affect the survival and fitness of individuals. Baker (1978) provides similar examples from a wide variety of both vertebrates and invertebrates.

Selection has altered exploratory behaviour in direct ways. For example, marked avoidance of new objects is shown only by commensal rats, probably in response to the selective forces associated with attempts at pest control (see Section 6.4.1), analogous to the appearance of rats resistant to anticoagulant poisons (Cowan, 1975). Recent declines in the success of field poisoning operations against rabbits both in Australia and New Zealand have also been attributed to increased neophobia resulting from selection of those animals avoiding baits as new objects (J. Bell, A. J. Oliver; personal communication). Changes in the levels of exploratory behaviour of individuals occur during population fluctuations in many small mammals (Gaines & McClenaghan, 1980; Krebs, 1970), and there are differences in exploratory behaviour between animals which disperse from populations during such cycles and those which remain (Gaines & McClenaghan, 1980).

At a more general level, some aspects of the relationships between exploratory behaviour and ecology have been explored. Baker (1978) has pointed out for terrestrial mammals how body size and weight, home range size and the extent of pre-reproductive exploratory migration seem to form an adaptive complex; selection for change in any one automatically imposes selection on each of the others.

What remains is the need for a greater integration of the findings of psychological analyses of exploratory behaviour with field studies of behaviour and ecology, so that specific testable hypotheses can be erected. The study of exploratory behaviour has many implications for other aspects of behaviour and ecology. To give but one example (discussed in Section 6.3.1), many mammals which do not hold exclusive territories but which have extensive range overlap with neighbours appear to maintain a social system by regular patrolling of those ranges according to specific timetables (Baker, 1978; Connolly, 1979).

Finally, exploratory behaviour is also implicitly bound up with the demographic processes of populations. The dispersal of individuals from their native population facilitates gene flow and the maintenance of genetic variability, and promotes the use of new or more sparsely populated areas (Gaines & McClenaghan, 1980). Dispersing individuals, in effect, venture into the unknown. Probably at no other time have the selective forces shaping exploratory responses more opportunity to affect the survival and fitness of individuals.

6.7 Summary

In the wild, many small mammals regularly patrol (re-explore) their familiar home ranges. Such patrolling is accompanied by storage of information (topographical and other learning) which can be used later; this is illustrated with particular reference to foraging and homing. Patrolling has also been analysed in an artificial environment, the plus-maze, in which animals may live for long periods while their movements are recorded automatically. Patrolling is persistent — it changes little with time and is displayed under a wide variety of experimental conditions (e.g. deprivation, pregnancy) — and systematic — animals tend to visit those parts of the environment least recently visited.

Patrolling enables animals to detect changes in their environment. New objects in a familiar place are usually approached and investigated. But the commensals, *Rattus norvegicus* and *R. rattus*, are exceptions; evidently selection resulting from human predation by trapping and poisoning has led to the

170

avoidance of such objects (neophobia). Similar avoidance is not shown by non-commensal *Rattus* or domesticated laboratory rats.

The balance between approach and avoidance determines the nature and extent of exploratory behaviour; a model is suggested for the different response of wild and domesticated rodents. The ways in which studies of exploratory behaviour impinge on both ethological and ecological analyses are described, particularly in relation to the survival value of exploratory behaviour.

References

AMBROSE, H. W. (1972) Effect of habitat familiarity and toe-clipping on rate of owl predation on *Microtus pennsylvanicus. Journal of Mammalogy* **53**, 909–912.

ARCHER, J. (1975) Rodent sex differences in emotional and related behaviour. *Behavioral Biology* **14**, 451–479.

BAKER, R. R. (1978) *The Evolutionary Ecology of Animal Migration*. Sevenoaks, Kent, Hodder & Stoughton Educational.

BAMFORD, J. (1970) Evaluating opossum poisoning operations by interference with non-toxic baits. *Proceedings of the New Zealand Ecological Society* **17**, 118–125.

BARASH, D. P. (1974) Neighbor recognition in two 'solitary' carnivores: the raccoon (*Procyon lotor*)and the red fox (*Vulpes fulva*). *Science* **185**, 794–796.

BARNES, G. W. and BARON, A. (1961) Stimulus complexity and sensory reinforcement, *Journal of Comparative and Physiological Psychology* **54**, 466–469.

BARNETT, S. A. (1958) Experiments on 'neophobia' in wild and laboratory rats. *British Journal of Psychology* **49**, 195–201.

BARNETT, S. A. (1975) *The Rat: A Study in Behavior*. Chicago: University of Chicago Press.

BARNETT, S. A. and COWAN, P. E. (1976) Activity, exploration, curiosity and fear: an ethological study. *Interdisciplinary Science Reviews* **1**, 43–62.

BARNETT, S. A., DICKSON, R. G., MARPLES, T. G. and RADHA, E. (1978) Sequences of feeding, sampling and exploration by wild and laboratory rats. *Behavioural Processes* **3**, 29–43.

BARNETT, S. A. and McEWAN, I. M. (1973) Movements of virgin, pregnant and lactating mice in a residential maze. *Physiology and Behaviour* **10**, 741–746.

BARNETT, S. A. and STODDART, R. C. (1969) Effects of breeding in captivity on conflict among wild rats. *Journal of Mammalogy* **50**, 321–325.

BERLYNE, D. E. (1950) Novelty and curiosity as determinants of exploratory behaviour. *British Journal of Psychology* **41**, 68–80.

BERLYNE, D. E. (1955) The arousal and satiation of perceptual curiosity in the rat, *Journal of Comparative and Physiological Psychology* **48**, 238–246.

BERLYNE, D. E. (1960) *Conflict, Arousal and Curiosity*. New York: McGraw-Hill.

BERLYNE, D. E. (1963) Motivational problems raised by exploratory and epistemic behavior. In *Psychology: a Study of a Science, Vol.5* (Ed. S. KOCH). New York: McGraw-Hill.

BIDER, J. R., THIBAULT, P. and SARRAZIN, R. (1968) Schemes dynamiques spatiotemporels de l'activite de *Procyon lotor* en relation avec le comportement, *Mammalia* **32**, 137–163.

BINDRA, D. (1961) Components of general activity and the analysis of behavior. *Psychological Review* **68**, 205–215.

BLODGETT, H. C. (1929) The effect of the introduction of reward upon maze performance of rats. *University of California Publications in Psychology* **4**, 113–134.

BOICE, R. and BOICE, C. (1968) Trapping Norway rats in a landfill. *Journal of the Scientific Laboratories of Dennison University* **49**, 1–4.

BROWN, L. E. (1966) Home range and movement of small mammals. *Symposium of the Zoological Society of London* **18**, 111–142.

BROWN, L. E. (1969) Field experiments on the movements of *Apodemus sylvaticus* L. using trapping and tracking techniques. *Oecologia* **2**, 198–222.

BROWN, L. N. (1965) Selection in a population of house mice containing mutant individuals. *Journal of Mammalogy* **46**, 461–465.

BULL, J. O. (1972) The influence of attractants and repellents on the feeding behaviour of *Rattus norvegicus*. In *Proceedings: Fifth Vertebrate Pest Conference* (Ed. R. E. MARSH). Fresno, California.

CHITTY, D. and SOUTHERN, H. N. (Eds.) (1954) *The Control of Rats and Mice*, 3 Vols. Oxford: Clarendon Press.

CONNOLLY, M. S. (1979) Time-tables in home range usage by gray squirrels (*Sciurus carolinensis*). *Journal of Mammalogy* **60**, 814–817.

COREY, D. T. (1978) The determinants of exploration and neophobia. *Neuroscience and Biobehavioral Reviews* **2**, 235–253.

COWAN, P. E. (1975) Activity, new object and new place reactions of several *Rattus* species. Ph.D. Thesis, Australian National University, Canberra.

COWAN, P. E. (1976) The new object reaction of *Rattus rattus* L.: the relative importance of various cues. *Behavioral Biology* **16**, 31–44.

COWAN, P. E. (1977a) Neophobia and neophilia: new object and new place reactions of three *Rattus* species. *Journal of Comparative and Physiological Psychology* **91**, 63–71.

COWAN, P. E. (1977b) Systematic patrolling and orderly behaviour of rats during recovery from deprivation. *Animal Behaviour* **25**, 171–184.

COWAN, P. E. and BARNETT, S. A. (1975) The new object and new place reactions of *Rattus rattus* L. *Zoological Journal of the Linnaean Society* **56**, 219–234.

CROWCROFT, P. and JEFFERS, J. N. R. (1961) Variability in the behaviour of wild house mice (*Mus musculus* L.) toward live traps. *Proceedings of the Zoological Society of London* **137**, 573–582.

CROWCROFT, P. and ROWE, F. P. (1963) Social organization and territorial behaviour in the wild house mouse (*Mus musculus* L.). *Proceedings of the Zoological Society of London* **140**, 517–531.

DAVIES, N. B. and HOUSTON, A. I. (1981) Owners and satellites: the economics of territory defence in the pied wagtail, *Motacilla alba*. *Journal of Animal Ecology* **50**, 157–180.

DICE, L. R. (1947) Effectiveness of selection by owls of deer-mice (*Peromyscus maniculatus*) which contrast in color with their background. *Contributions from the Laboratory of Vertebrate Biology of the University of Michigan* **34**, 1–20.

DOUGLAS, R. J. (1966) Cues for spontaneous alternation, *Journal of Comparative and Physiological Psychology* **62**, 171–183.

ELY, D. L. (1971) Physiological and behavioural differentiation of social roles in a population cage of magnetically tagged CBA mice, *Dissertation Abstracts International* **32** (6).

FITZGERALD, B. M., KARL, B. J. and MOLLER, H. (1981) Spatial organization and ecology of a sparse population of house mice (*Mus musculus*) in a New Zealand forest, *Journal of Animal Ecology* **50**, 489–518.

FOWLER, H. (1965) *Curiosity and Exploratory Behavior*. New York: Macmillan.

GAINES, M. S. & MCCLENAGHAN, L.R. (1980) Dispersal in small mammals, *Annual*

Review of Ecology and Systematics, **11**, 163–196.

GLICKMAN, S. E. & MORRISON, B. J. (1969) Some behavioral and neural correlates of predation susceptibility in mice. *Communications in Behavioral Biology* **4**, 261–267.

GLOW, P. H. (1970) Some acquisition and performance characteristics of response contingent sensory reinforcement in the rat. *Australian Journal of Psychology* **22**, 145–154.

HALLIDAY, M. S. (1966) Exploration and fear in the rat, *Symposium of the Zoological Society of London* **18**, 45–59.

HALLIDAY, M. S. (1968) Exploratory behavior. In *Analysis of Behavioral Change* (Ed. L. WEISKRANTZ). New York: Harper & Row.

HAMILTON, W. D. (1964) The genetical theory of social behaviour, I & II. *Journal of Theoretical Biology* **7**, 1–52.

HEBB, D. O. and MAHUT, H. (1955) Motivation et recherche du changement perceptif chez le rat et chez l'homme. *Journal de Psychologie Normale et Pathologique* **52**, 209–221.

HINDE, R. A. (1966) *Animal Behaviour*. London and New York: McGraw-Hill.

HOW, R. A. (1972) The ecology and management of *Trichosurus* species (Marsupialia) in NSW. Ph.D. Thesis, University of New England, Armidale, Australia.

HUTT, C. (1970) Specific and diversive exploration. In *Advances in Child Development and Behavior* (Eds. H. W. REESE & L. P. LIPSITT), New York and London: Academic Press.

JANE, G. T. (1979) Opossum density assessment using the bait interference method. *New Zealand Journal of Forestry* **24**, 61–66.

JENSEN, D. D. (1961) Operationism and the question 'Is this behavior learned or innate?' *Behaviour* **17**, 1–8.

JEWELL, P. A. (1966) The concept of home range in mammals. *Symposium of the Zoological Society of London* **18**, 85–109.

JOHNSON, R. P. (1973) Scent marking in mammals. *Animal Behaviour* **21**, 521–535.

KAWAKAMI, M. and SAWYER, C. H. (1967) Effects of sex hormones and antifertility steroids on brain thresholds in the rabbit. *Endocrinology* **80**, 857–871.

KISH, G. B. and ANTONITIS, J. J. (1956) Unconditioned operant behavior in two homozygous strains of mice. *Journal of Genetic Psychology* **88**, 121–129.

KREBS, C. J. (1970) *Microtus* population biology : behavioral changes associated with the population cycle in *M. ochrogaster* and *M. pennsylvanicus. Ecology* **51**, 34–52.

KREBS, J. R. (1978) Optimal foraging: Decision rules for predators. In *Behavioural ecology: an evolutionary approach* (Eds. J. R. KREBS and N. B. DAVIES). Oxford: Blackwell.

KREBS, J. R. and COWIE, R. J. (1976) Foraging strategies in birds. *Ardea* **64**, 98–116.

KREBS, J. R. and DAVIES, N. B. (1978) *Behavioural Ecology: an Evolutionary Approach*. Oxford: Blackwell.

LESTER, D. (1968) The relationship between fear and exploration in rats. *Psychonomic Science* **14**, 128–129.

LOCKARD, R. B. (1968) The albino rat: a defensible choice or a bad habit? *American Psychologist* **23**, 734–742.

MCFARLAND, D. J. (1976) Form and function in the temporal organization of behaviour. In *Growing Points in Ethology* (Eds. P. P. G. BATESON and R. A. HINDE). Cambridge: Cambridge University Press.

MCREYNOLDS, P. (1962) Exploratory behavior: a theoretical interpretation. *Psychological Reports* **11**, 311–318.

MARTIN, J. R. and BATTIG, K. (1980) Exploratory behaviour of rats at oestrus. *Animal Behaviour* **28**, 900–905

METZGAR, L. H. (1967) An experimental comparison of screech owl predation on resident and transient white-footed mice (*Peromyscus leucopus*). *Journal of Mammalogy* **48**, 387–391.

MITCHELL, D. (1976) Experiments on neophobia in wild and laboratory rats: a re-evaluation. *Journal of Comparative and Physiological Psychology* **90**, 190–197.

MITCHELL, D., KIRSCHBAUM, E. H. and PERRY, R. L. (1975) Effects of neophobia and habituation on the poison-induced avoidance of exteroceptive stimuli in the rat. *Journal of Experimental Psychology; Animal Behavior Processes* **1**, 47–55.

MONIER, M. (1968) Mesorhombencephalic organization of visceral performance (reticular and cerebellar integrations). In *Functions of the Nervous System, Vol. 1, General Physiology: Automonic Functions*. Amsterdam: Elsevier.

MONTGOMERY, K. C. (1954) The role of exploratory drive in learning. *Journal of Comparative and Physiological Psychology* **47**, 60–64.

MUNN, N. L. (1950) *Handbook of Psychological Research on the Rat*. Boston and New York: Houghton Mifflin.

MYKYTOWYCZ, R. (1958) Social behaviour of an experimental colony of wild rabbits, *Oryctolagus cuniculus* (L.). 1. Establishment of the colony, *CSIRO Wildlife Research* **3**, 7–25.

NEWSOME, A. E. (1969) A population study of house-mice permanently inhabiting a reed-bed in South Australia. *Journal of Animal Ecology* **38**, 361–377.

NEWSOME, A. E., IVES, P. and COWAN, P. E. (1982) Homing behaviour of house mice (in press).

O'KEEFE, J. & NADEL, L. (1974) Maps in the brain. *New Scientist* **1974**, 749–751.

OLTON, D. S. & SAMUELSON, R. J. (1976) Remembrance of places passed: spatial memory in rats. *Journal of Experimental Psychology: Animal Behavior Processes* **2**, 97–116.

PAVLOV, I. P. (1927) *Conditioned Reflexes*. London: Oxford University Press.

PIETRAS, R. J. and MOULTON, D. G. (1974) Hormonal influences on odor detection in rats: changes associated with the oestrous cycle, pseudopregnancy, ovariectomy, and administration of testosterone proprionate. *Physiology and Behavior* **12**, 475–491.

PROKASY, W. F. (1956) The acquisition of observing responses in the absence of differential external reinforcement. *Journal of Comparative and Physiological Psychology* **49**, 131–134.

RALLS, K. (1971) Mammalian scent marking. *Science* **181**, 443–449.

ROZIN, P. and KALAT, J. W. (1971) Specific hungers and poison avoidance as adaptive specializations of learning. *Pyschological Review* **78**, 459–486.

RUSSELL, P. A. (1973) Relationships between exploratory behaviour and fear: a review. *British Journal of Psychology* **64**, 417–433.

SHELDON, A. B. (1969) Preference for familiar versus novel stimuli as a function of the familiarity of the environment. *Journal of Comparative and Physiological Psychology* **67**, 516–521.

SHILLITO, E. E. (1963) Exploratory behaviour in the short-tailed vole, *Microtus agrestis*. *Behaviour* **21**, 145–154.

SHORTEN, M. (1954) The reaction of the brown rat towards changes in its environment. In *Control of Rats and Mice, Vol. 2. Rats* (Ed. D. CHITTY) Oxford: Clarendon Press.

SIMS, R. A. and WOLFE, J. L. (1976) Homing behavior of the house mouse (*Mus musculus* L.). *Journal of the Mississippi Academy of Sciences* **21**, 89–96.

SMALL, W. S. (1899) Notes on the psychic development of the young white rat. *American Journal of Psychology* **11**, 80–100.

SMITH, J. N. M. and SWEATMAN, H. P. A. (1974) Food searching behaviour of titmice in patchy environments. *Ecology* **55**, 1216–1232.

SOUTHERN, H. N. (1954) *Control of Rats and Mice, Vol. 3. Mice*. Oxford: Clarendon Press.

STICKEL, L. F. (1979) Population ecology of house mice in unstable habitats. *Journal of Animal Ecology* **48**, 871–887.

TAYLOR, G. T. (1974) Stimulus change and complexity in exploratory behavior. *Animal Learning and Behavior* **2**, 115–118.

WARD, G. D. (1978) Habitat use and home range of radio-tagged opossums *Trichosurus vulpecula* (Kerr) in New Zealand lowland forest. In *The Ecology of Arboreal Folivores* (Ed. G. G. MONTGOMERY). Washington, DC: Smithsonian Institution Press.

WOLFE, J. L. (1969) Observations on alertness and exploratory behavior in the eastern chipmunk. *American Midland Naturalist* **81**, 249–253.

CHAPTER 7

The Captive Environment: its Effect on Exploratory and Related Behavioural Responses in Wild Animals

Miranda F. Stevenson

7.1 Introduction

Human beings have been exploiting the animal world for over 10 000 years. We have kept animals such as dogs, which we have trained to work for us, and we have maintained animals in captivity to serve as food supplies: these were the ancestors of our present domestic stock. About 4000 years ago, captive wild animals were first maintained purely for prestige and amusement. The ancient Egyptian princes kept large herds of antelope, which probably served as symbols of power; the greatest collection of captive animals was that of Ptolemy II, which contained, among other exotics, the first chimpanzee to be exhibited in captivity. The Romans from about 55 BC used wild animals, not only as exhibits to amuse, but also in 'games' where the beasts were killed in spectacular shows. Later, it became fashionable for great leaders to maintain private menageries. Charlemagne had several zoos, and William the Conquerer founded the first zoo in England in the Tower of London; this royal menagerie went through various stages of expansion and contraction under different monarchs, until it was closed on the opening of Regent's Park Zoo in 1826. This was one of the first of the 'Zoological Societies' which showed a change of policy. Not only were they to exhibit animals for entertainment but also for scientific research, although at this time the research was mainly of a taxonomic and anatomic nature. However the single animals in small cages, showing the behavioural responses to their environment and the public, that we now term 'abnormal', were the amusement that attracted people to zoos. It was not until the 20th century that people began seriously to question this manner of exhibiting wildlife. The change in approach was partly due to the naturalists returning from the wild with descriptions of the natural behaviour of the species, and partly to the newly emerging science of ethology, which examined the social behaviour of animals scientifically.

The pioneering work of Hediger (1950, 1955) and Meyer-Holzapfel (published in English in 1968), drew the zoo world's attention to what it was doing to the wildlife entrusted to it. It has, however, only been in the last 20 years that scientists began to examine seriously the relationship of the caged environment and the composition of the captive group to resultant behaviour, and to compare and relate those responses to the repertoire and social groupings observed in the natural environment. Many psychologists and ethologists have also disregarded the effects that the cage environment might have on the animals whose behaviour they are studying. One exception is Humphrey (1976) who points out that the captive environment might have an effect on the cognitive development of his rhesus monkeys, and hence on the experimental results.

There is still appallingly little scientific research on the effects of different environmental stimuli and changes to the environment on the behaviour of captive wild animals (Sackett, 1968). In this chapter I shall deal only with work carried out on captive wild animals, that is those species that have, or are assumed to have, undergone a minimal amount of genotypic change due to captive breeding programmes. Chapter 8 deals with farm animals, and earlier chapters have covered research on those highly inbred strains of laboratory animals such as rats and mice that have been used for psychological experiments.

The captive environment may be lacking in novel stimuli, and therefore it provides less stimulation for exploratory behaviour. The captive animal may thus have little outlet for curiosity, and this may result in inactivity and boredom. Captivity may therefore provide too little novel stimulation, so that the animal is underaroused, inactive and 'bored', or it may have too much so that the animal is overaroused and 'stressed'. I intend to examine the possible effects of captivity on the behaviour of the animal and how environmental changes may increase or decrease the degree of arousal in different species. It is important to remember that a species' responses to the different aspects of captivity must relate to its repertoire in the wild (Morris, 1964). It is also important to consider the effect of different natural environments on the repertoire of a species, and what an individual animal's concept of its environment is. However, it is all too easy to refer to the captive environment as a 'bad' and deprived situation for an animal to be in, and perhaps people are too quick to blame the captive state for producing some of the behaviour we regard as abnormal and as artefacts of captivity. I intend to examine these concepts in detail, referring where possible to relevant field data.

7.2   What is the Environment to an Individual?

Before examining the nature of the relationship of the environment to activity levels and abnormal behaviour observed in captive wild animals, it is necessary to consider what the surrounding environment means to an individual animal. Von Uexküll (1934) suggested that the environment offered a reservoir of stimuli from which the animal constructed, and lived in, its own specific world. The individual's responses to environmental stimuli not only vary with different species but change with ontogenetic stages (Baldwin & Baldwin, 1977), as does the animal's concept of its environment.

7.2.1 The Neonate and Infant

For a neonate mammal, the first behaviour consists of reflexes that result in the orientation of the infant towards the nipple area, and the first exploratory movements are rooting and nipple seeking, which result in suckling and obtaining milk, which in turn reinforces the behaviour (Baldwin & Baldwin, 1977). In a nidicolous species, the neonate's first experiences will be of the mother, nest area and perhaps littermates. In an infant marmoset (Stevenson, 1978), the first exploratory movements are on the carrier's pelage where the infant bites and handles the hair; in the second week the infant begins to reach for, and handle objects. Eventually, in the third week, it moves off the carrier, locomoting, biting and handling objects in the environment. Thus, to the infant the surrounding environment is a constant source of new objects and is an expanding medium: the young animal is receiving constant sensory stimulation from the environment, which, in a group-reared animal, contains both objects and conspecifics.

7.2.2 The Response to the Stimulus

It is convenient at this point to consider the interpretation of the mechanisms involved in eliciting an exploratory response, discussed in Chapters 2, 3 and 4. The concept of arousal (Hebb, 1955), has been used to explain the different responses of captive animals to varying stimuli (see also Chapter 8). These ideas have been expanded by other workers (Baldwin & Baldwin, 1977; Mason, 1968), and suggest that a high level of stimulation is overarousing and produces an aversive response; a medium level is optimal for producing an exploratory response, and a low level is underarousing and may produce responses such as lethargy and 'boredom'. When a young animal explores the environment, it receives further sensory stimulation, which reinforces the continuation of exploration, (Baldwin & Baldwin, 1978). The optimal threshold for exploratory responses may vary with age or experience, and there are probably significant generic and individual differences. Birke & Archer (Chapter 1) also point out that intraindividual changes in an animal's responsiveness have been little studied. Although it is difficult to quantify arousal levels, and the concept is, in some respects, an oversimplification (see Chapter 2), it does provide a useful reference system when comparing the behavioural responses of individuals to different environments.

7.2.3 The Older Animal

As the infant grows, it experiences various stages of social interaction (e.g. play, grooming) with peers, sibs or parents, depending on the species. It commences eating solid food, foraging or hunting. From these early experiences it learns to communicate with conspecifics and avoid potential predators; its behaviour is

178

also affected by food and water availability and by climate. The captive environment, to an individual reared in a social group, is a complex interrelationship of the physical size of the cage, complexity, climate, food supply (quality, quantity and method of presentation), other group members, proximity to other groups of conspecifics and other species (Fig. 7.1). Although normally abundant in supplies of food and water, the captive environment is lacking in complexity and change. The captive environment, especially to the adult animal, is impoverished, in that it contains few novel sensory stimuli. The animal is normally familiar with the entire area and does not have to hunt or forage. Food is provided, often in a form that makes it easier and quicker to eat: time spent feeding is therefore reduced. The animal, if social, is probably living with fewer group-mates than it would in nature; there are no intruding animals, either conspecific or otherwise, nor are there many novel objects to investigate. Thus adults have 'spare time'. One must be careful, however, not to assume this of all species. For example lions in the wild spend on average, only 4 h active per day (Bertram, 1978): it is therefore somewhat ironic that this species is frequently given large enclosures in zoos.

7.3   Behaviour

The types of behaviour commonly assumed to be 'abnormal', occurring in direct response to the captive environment, have been detailed by several workers (e.g. Erwin & Deni, 1979; Hediger, 1950, 1955; Meyer-Holzapfel, 1968; Morris, 1964). Broadhurst (1963) correctly pointed out that there are no animals of whose normal behaviour we have so complete a knowledge as to be able to pinpoint exactly what is 'abnormal'. However, it is necessary to consider which forms of behaviour are induced by aspects of the captive environment: this gives us a greater understanding of the repertoire of the species and also enables us to ascertain which aspects of the environment require improvement. It is thus profitable to consider some of the abnormal behaviour. Meyer-Holzapfel (1968) defines as abnormal that which is uncommon or absent from the repertoire of free-ranging animals, some of which may be adaptive and some maladaptive to the captive environment. This approach has been taken up by several workers, although Erwin & Deni (1979) found it convenient to divide abnormal behaviour into two categories: (a) qualitative, in which the behaviour occurs in the captive, but not in the wild, environment; and (b) quantitative, in which the behaviour occurs significantly more or less frequently than it does in the natural environment. The first category includes postural movements, self mutilation, self-clasping, various sexual disorders, masturbatory behaviour, coprophagia, vomiting and eating of vomitus, and stereotypic movements. The second includes abnormal levels of activity, both social and solitary, and hyper-aggressiveness. Unfortunately at present, there are species about whose behaviour in the wild we know almost nothing, and none where we can claim to know the entire repertoire. It is probably more profitable, therefore, to compare the relative frequency and occurrences of some of these types of behaviour in various captive and natural environments.

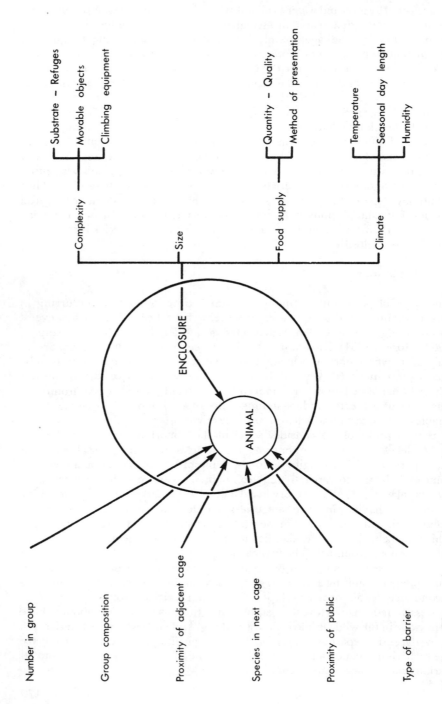

Fig. 7.1 The captive environment as it is to an individual animal.

7.3.1 Behaviour in the Natural Environment

In recent years much new information has been collected and published from field studies; most of the studies, however, have been on primates, and as the major portion of captive studies has also been on primates, many examples will be taken from that order. Some species may occur in very different environments in terms of food supply and availability, climate and degree of cover (e.g. forest and savannah). Crook (1965, 1970) was one of the first ethologists to demonstrate that the size and composition of groups, area occupied and territorial defence, could vary for a particular species depending on the richness of habitat. He illustrated these ideas with examples from birds (1965) and primates (1970). Kruuk (1972)working on the spotted hyena, found that in the Ngorongoro Crater, where food was abundant, that animals occurred in social groupings and they defended territories; in the Serengeti, where food was seasonal, animals occurred most frequently in ones and twos and did not defend fixed areas. He also noted that intergroup fights could result in injuries. Some species of antelope (e.g. springbok — Bigalke, 1972; and see review by Jarman, 1974) may occur in large herds in the wet season and split into smaller groups when the food supply becomes scarce.

Baldwin & Baldwin (1974) in a review of squirrel monkeys in different environments found that group size varied with habitat and food availability, and that the rate of development of infants could vary in different wild and captive environments. In one sparse area the young were not observed to play. Baldwin & Baldwin (1976) conducted laboratory experiments that illustrated that the frequency of social play was significantly lowered when the animals had difficulty in obtaining food (that is the food supply was made difficult to obtain). Loy (1970) found that the frequencies of social interactions changed, and that of play decreased, in Cayo Santiago rhesus when the food supply became depleted.

There are few observations on orphaned infants from the wild that allow some comparison with studies on captive rearing conditions. Goodall (1971) described abnormal behaviour shown by orphaned chimpanzee infants: extreme depression, reduction in social interaction and play and inappropriate responses to the behavioural advances of other chimpanzees. Berman (1981) noted that a rhesus monkey orphaned at 11 weeks ceased social play, became less active, exhibited a hunched posture and showed some of the behaviour associated with abnormal captive rearing. Rhine et al. (1980), working on yellow baboons, described the effects of maternal death and separation on infants: they showed hunched posture and subdued behaviour similar to that observed in captive primates artificially separated from their mothers. It is interesting that social play is the one behaviour that is always observed to occur at a lower frequency in sub-optimal conditions in the natural environment: social play, however, may occur at high frequencies in captive animals (Stevenson & Rylands, 1983).

Meyer-Holzapfel (1968) includes infanticide and hyperaggressiveness, resulting in severe injury or death in group members, as part of the abnormal captive repertoire. Recent results from long-term field studies have shown that similar behaviour, resulting in injury or death to a conspecific, can occur in certain situations in the natural environment. There are examples from several genera of males killing infants (e.g. lions — Bertram, 1975; langurs — Hrdy, 1974; gorilla — Harcourt *et al.*, 1981; and see review by Hrdy, 1979). There are examples of adult conspecific killings (chimpanzee — Goodall, 1979; torque monkeys — Dittus, 1977; vervet monkeys — Wrangham, 1981); and the infliction of serious injuries (gorilla and orang-utan — Harcourt, 1981; red deer stags — Clutton-Brock *et al.*, 1979). Some conspecific killings may be aggravated by stressful situations, e.g. lack of water in the case of Wrangham's vervets and abnormally high population densities in the case of the langurs (Curtin & Dolhinow, 1978). However, the fact remains that certain behavioural activities previously classified as being artefacts of the deprived captive environment, are observed in nature in certain circumstances.

7.3.2 Deprived Early Experience

The captive environment can become especially abnormal to infants when they are removed for handrearing and maintained in various artificial situations. Some of the behaviour observed in adult zoo and laboratory animals can be directly attributed to early rearing experiences, either removal and handrearing the infant from birth or by capturing it at a young age in the wild and subsequently rearing it in relative isolation. Here one comes up against the additional problem of mal-imprinting, (Morris, 1964). Behaviour includes incorrect mating postures, self-mutilation, self clasping, hyperaggressiveness, neophobia and certain stereotypic movements.

It is beyond the scope of this work to discuss the different types of rearing deprivation (e.g. total isolation, peer isolation, raising only with peers) or the effects of different lengths of isolation periods at various ages, and possible subsequent reversal of the effects by later socialisation. Most of the detailed research has been carried out on primates (see review by Mitchell, 1970) but similar behavioural consequences can be observed in other orders (Meyer-Holzapfel, 1968; Morris, 1964). The most extreme forms of abnormal behaviour are shown by primates that were reared in total isolation for the first year of life: they may exhibit hyperaggression or extreme fear at the sight of conspecifics, low level of play, inappropriate social responses, or sexual abnormalities, and those females that produce offspring are poor mothers. They also show stereotypic pacing, jumping and rocking, as well as self clasping and biting. Mason (1968) showed that stereotypic rocking could be eliminated by rearing on a moving, instead of a stationary, surrogate.

Workers at Cambridge, (see review by Hinde, 1972), tried to assess the effects of a short period of isolation (6 days) on normal group-reared infant rhesus monkeys. These were tested against normal infants, and it was found that even 2 years after the separation period, when exposed to novel or mildly stressful stimuli, the animals showed less locomotory behaviour and more reluctance to approach a novel object than their 'normal' peers.

A young animal must experience certain types of stimulation as it develops so that it learns to respond to novel and complex stimuli. When the novelty becomes stressful or overarousing, it can return to the mother. If deprived of this early experience it may later exhibit responses of fear and aggression towards slightly arousing social and non-social situations. Some abnormal behaviour observed in captive animals may thus be due to early experience and are not a direct response to the present environment.

7.4 Responses to Captivity

Berlyne (1960) suggested that 'specific exploration' occurred as a direct response to novelty and decreased with exposure and habituation. Birke & Archer (Chapter 1) have already discussed the problem of what comprises a 'novel' stimulus, and this argument will not be further expanded here. Many species live within restricted ranges in the wild (Davies, 1978), spending most of their time within a familiar environment; therefore most stimuli encountered would fall into the 'familiar' category of Berlyne. Although animals in the wild do change the extent of their ranges, depending on food availability and season of the year, the sudden removal of an individual to a completely new (novel) environment is an artefact normally found only in captivity, which is stressful to the animals and would therefore be expected to produce 'abnormal' responses.

As previously stated, the concept of novelty is different in young and adult animals, and immature animals habituate less rapidly than older ones to novel stimuli (Berlyne, 1960). Thus many of the behavioural responses attributed to the sterile captive environment (such as boredom, inactivity, behavioural stereotypies) should be observed more in adults than in mother or group reared young.

7.4.1 Degree of 'Wildness' and the Environment

Little work has been carried out on the possible effects of long-term captivity on the behavioural responses of a species, or subtle changes in the repertoire that may result from breeding several generations in a captive environment (See Maple, 1975; Ratner & Boice, 1975). Kummer & Kurt (1965) found certain patterns of behaviour missing from the repertoire of captive-born hamadryas baboons. Wild animals maintained in captivity have gone through some form of selection process: firstly the initial stock has been selected for those individuals that survived the transposition to captivity, and subsequent selection for those that breed successfully. Hediger (1950) suggested that the individuals that thrive are those that adapt to taming, i.e. they show a reduced flight tendency towards human beings. Thus wild animals in captivity have undergone some degree of domestication: this may result in responses to some stimuli being different from those of the wild animal. Although certain stressors, such as lack of food and presence of predators, have been removed, others, to which the species is not adapted, have been added, and these may prove overarousing and stressful.

Glickman & Sroges (1966) pointed out that the captive environment must affect an individual's responsiveness to novel stimuli, either because the animal is deprived of novel stimuli or because it has become habituated to the captive environment and as a result is less responsive to novelty. Both Glickman & Sroges (1966) and Muckenbeck Fragaszy (1979) stress the importance of species-specific and individual differences in responsiveness to novelty. Thus when observing the behaviour of the captive animal, one has to consider not only the environment, but also the previous experience of the individual in captivity and the natural tendencies of the species (Fig. 7.2.)

7.4.2   Stereotypies

Some of the commonest movements observed in captive animals are various kinds of stereotypic movements. Odberg (1978) goes to some lengths to try and decide what is meant by the term, and concludes that there are three components: (a) the movements are identical; (b) they are repeated regularly; (c) the behaviour has no obvious function. This may, however, be an exaggerated form of a purposeful behaviour (Kiley-Worthington, 1977), for example pacing at boundary of cage adjacent to a conspecific.

There are basically two forms of movement: pacing, in which the animal moves repeatedly back and forth in a straight line, circle or figure of eight; and stationary, where the animal is not locomoting but performs a repeated act, such as rocking, somersaulting, headtossing or weaving (swaying from side to side). It is possible for two of these to be combined, e.g. a monkey may headtoss in the same place on each locomotory curcuit. Stereotypies also occur in domestic animals (see Chapter 8), and it is probable that certain species show certain stereotypies more readily than others (see Meyer-Holzapfel, 1968).

Some of these types of behaviour are acquired as a result of early rearing conditions, and may remain even after environmental improvement; although members born into the group subsequently do not show the behaviour. This factor, and the lack of experimental work on the effect of environmental changes on stereotypies, make the exact cause of the behaviour difficult to deduce. Although there are certain conditions that commonly result in stereotypic movements (Kiley-Worthington, 1977); these may be both dull (underarousing) and stressful (overarousing). It is interesting to discuss some of the situations that may produce stereotypic behaviour.

7.4.3   Possible Environmental Stimuli

Draper & Bernstein (1963) concluded from their work on primates, that cage size was a critical factor and that more stereotypic movements occurred in small cages. This is a commonly held view and Morris (1964) suggested that stereo-

184

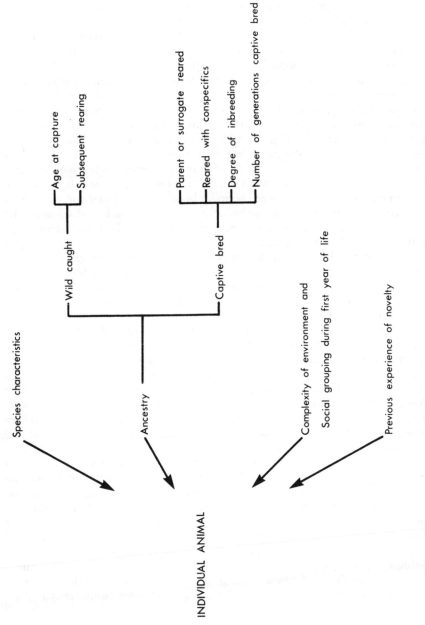

Fig. 7.2 Past experiences that may affect the behaviour of an individual in its present environment.

Species characteristics

Ancestry
- Wild caught
  - Age at capture
  - Subsequent rearing
- Captive bred
  - Parent or surrogate reared
  - Reared with conspecifics
  - Degree of inbreeding
  - Number of generations captive bred

Complexity of environment and
Social grouping during first year of life

Previous experience of novelty

INDIVIDUAL ANIMAL

typic pacing was a direct result of restricted space, developed as a modified form of territorial patrolling (see Chapter 6). However, one has to be careful in the use of the term 'patrol'; animals do not pace around the boundaries of their territories in the wild, but visit them frequently, in some species depositing scent marks. Hediger (1950) gives an example of stereotypic scent marking in a pine marten, which could be interpreted as a response to too small a cage. Odberg (1981), however, found that fewer voles showed stereotypic pacing in small rich environments than in large sparse ones. As 'cage size' plays such an important part in these discussions, it is important to point out that the term is very relative and that a big cage to one worker might be a small cage to another. Laboratory primates are usually caged in pens many times smaller than a zoo cage, and although no one has made a quantitative comparison, much more extreme stereotypies are observed in these small cages, which are also unable to hold a social group of animals. It is therefore a fact that very small cages do result in the inmate exhibiting stereotypic movements.

These movements are the result of the animal adapting its locomotory capacities to the type of confinement and will vary, not only with size and complexity of the cage, but also with the type of barrier between the animal and the public. Stereotypies are the result of a combination of several factors. I consider the main ones to be as follows: (a) early rearing deprivation; (b) a small sparse cage environment; (c) lack of complexity or features required by species, e.g. a substrate for digging animals to dig; (d) proximity to other groups of conspecifics, other species and the public; and (e) external and internal stress-producing factors. In this latter category one would include the 'thwarted intention movements' remarked on by Morris (1964) and the animal showing a 'super-normal' response to a stimulus.

The figure of eight pathway is often observed, when the animal is attracted or aroused by an animal in an adjacent enclosure. Meyer-Holzapfel (1968) explained this by suggesting that the animal begins by repeatedly moving back and forth along the perimeter fence, it then moves away, is attracted back to the fence, and ends up in a figure of eight pattern. Many movement patterns can be explained by assuming two conflicting types of motivation: an animal is attracted to the public (novel stimulus) at the cage front, but also experiences fear of the novel object (neophobia) thus returning to the rear of the cage; this movement then forms a stereotypic pacing.

The presence of a prey species in an adjacent cage can cause pacing in a predator (personal observation), but in time the predator may become habituated to this and cease pacing at that boundary. Stereotypic movements have been observed to increase when an animal expects food to be brought; this can be explained as a conflict between wishing to approach the food and being unable to do so. It is interesting to consider here whether the type and nature of the boundary fence, which affects the animal's view and concept of the public and other species, might be a relevant factor. It is possible that an animal separated from the public by a natural ditch or moat is less likely to develop stereotypic movements than one that comes right up to the public through glass or mesh.

186

Morris (1964) suggested that some stereotypic pacing could be due to responses to sub-optimal stimuli, i.e. a result of 'boredom'. This sort of pacing should be cured by the introduction of a more complex environment. Inhelder (1955) cited an example of an isolated female brown hyena that showed constant stereotypic movements that ceased when she was placed with a male. Inhelder also mentions that the frequency of stereotypic pacing decreased when the visitors were further removed from the cage front.

It is not easy to determine the cause of a stereotype as this example from Edinburgh Zoo serves to illustrate. The zoo had a single Asiatic Elephant female which was kept in an elephant house, consisting of two indoor enclosures and one outdoors. In 1976 a young female African was obtained and initially caged in one of the indoor enclosures. The idea was to introduce the African to the outdoor enclosure on her own, and introduce her subsequently to the Asiatic Elephant. However the new elephant would not venture outside and showed a strange stereotype, of always having one hind foot on the inside of the doorway and swaying with the rest of the body. Every method possible was tried for 3 years, but the animal would not move outside. After the death of the old Asiatic female the younger animal was given access to the other inside enclosure; after 8 days she ventured into the other pen and then three days later, to the outside. It was therefore not enclosure design that had caused the abnormal behaviour but the presence in the same house, of the older elephant.

Stereotypies can be caused by stressful situations (Odberg, 1978). A previously normal antelope, about to be caught up, may start to perform repeated running movements along the perimeter of the enclosure. Similarly, that which have been frightened or startled by a sudden noise or movement, may perform the same behaviour (personal observation). These movements are almost impossible to break by the introduction of new stimuli (e.g. food) and the animal can be said to be in a trance-like state. There are wide individual differences in the threshold of the overarousing stimuli that elicit the response. Some drugs (morphines, amphetamines) may also produce stereotypic behaviours (Randrup et al., 1978). The physiological effects of some of these drugs are similar to those of 'stress' hormones such as adrenaline, and it would seem important to investigate this aspect further.

Although some forms of stereotypic behaviour can be explained by stating that they are a response to 'boredom' and sensory deprivation, they can also be caused by several other variables.

7.4.4   Abnormal Behaviour that could be a Direct Response to 'Boredom'

In this section, I shall deal with behaviour that could be directly attributed to the animal receiving an abnormally low sensory input, and therefore a low level of arousal. As a result, the animal may develop various types of abnormal behaviour: these may be the consequence of either a super-normal response, or varied responses to a stimulus, or behaviour that increases the complexity of the environment (i.e. the animal is seeking out stimulus change). It is convenient to divide these responses into two types: (a) pathological, i.e., those that could actually do harm to the animal and are maladaptive; and (b) non-pathological, those that are harmless and might even be considered adaptive to captivity.

Pathological responses.   *Self-mutilation* involves biting of the limbs, tail or parts of body, or plucking out hair or feathers. It is observed in primates and other mammals reared in social isolation (Morris, 1964; Erwin & Deni, 1979). It is also observed in animals caged alone as adults. It appears to be especially prevalent in the category of animals classified by Morris (1964) as neophilic, i.e. those that exhibit a high degree of curiosity in nature and would therefore be expected to require higher levels of sensory input in captivity. In social animals, the absence of group mates may trigger the behaviour, which in its most extreme form may involve gnawing of the tail and even damage to the animal's testicles (Meyer-Holzapfel, 1968). Parrots caged alone in a very small cage frequently exhibit feather plucking and continue to do this even when subsequently put in a social group. This behaviour may also be a form of redirected aggression, where the animal is showing aggressive behaviour to one in an adjacent cage, and being unable to reach the target animal redirects the behaviour towards itself.

Coprophagia and eating of vomitus are types of behaviour most frequently observed in captive primates, particularly the great apes, but they have never been observed in the field. Both are difficult to eliminate once an individual has become fixated in the behaviour: the answer appears to be to stop the behaviour developing. Various theories have been put forward as to their cause: Meyer-Holzapfel cites an example of repeated vomiting in a sloth bear, which was due to the aggressive behaviour of the male, and both this behaviour and a stereotypic weaving ceased when she was removed to a cage on her own. However, in the great apes it is probably a result of boredom, and is certainly more prevalent in chimpanzees caged alone than in grouped animals. As Maple (1980) summarized in his review, apes kept with companions in a complex environment where novel stimuli are introduced do not develop such behaviour. In the wild, apes spend considerable time foraging and feeding, whereas in the captive environment the time spent feeding is much reduced, and other stimuli have to be introduced instead. This aspect will be further discussed in the section on environmental enrichment schemes.

Non-pathological responses.   *Failure to breed:* some species (e.g. gorilla, cheetah, giant panda) do not breed well in captivity owing to the male's lack of copulatory behaviour (Hediger, 1950; Morris, 1964). The stimulus required for the male to copulate with the female is absent or at too low an intensity. This could be due to the absence of other strange males or to the fact that the female is too familiar, and one or both animals require the stimulus of a strange (novel) animal.

Inventing new types of behaviour: Morris (1964) gives several examples of animals inventing activities adapted to the captive environment; these often involve interactions with the public. Examples are object throwing by great apes and

188

elephants, or urine spraying by carnivores and primates. Orang-utans and chimpanzees often exhibit tool use in captivity: this is especially interesting in the case of orangs as they do not exhibit this behaviour in the natural environment. In captivity they use orang skins as cups to hold water; plait substances such as woodwool to make ropes and use sticks to obtain objects beyond arm's reach.

Food begging is a form of behaviour acquired in captivity and reinforced by the public responding with food: animals that have been well fed will still beg. The behaviour can be categorized as a substitute for foraging, which is adapted to the captive environment.

Altered feeding patterns in captivity: as I have previously outlined, species that spend a great deal of time in the wild foraging or hunting have much spare time in captivity. The only predatory behaviour that animals can exhibit in zoos is insect catching. Zoo food also tends to be monotonous for species that in the wild eat a wide variety of fruits or select certain shoots and buds. Therefore, not only is the stimulus to explore and forage lacking, but so is the reinforcement of obtaining a varied supply of foods. Grazing animals spend at least one third of the day feeding and, when in captivity and given a pelleted food, which is quick and easy to eat, they will develop aberrant behaviour such as dirt eating, wood chewing, hair chewing and fence licking (Hintz *et al.*, 1976). Therefore all species need a supply of hay or similar food that will require chewing, some grazing if possible, supplies of leaves to browse and grain scattered on the ground (Dittrich, 1976). If food is made more difficult to obtain, these types of aberrant behaviour do not develop. With terrestial primate species, burying food in gravel, hay or woodshavings, increases the time spent foraging, especially if mealworms and fine grain are also added. Chamove & Anderson (1979) found that one side-effect of this use of wood shavings was that aggressive interactions in a group of stump-tailed macaques was reduced by a factor of five.

Morris (1964) listed some exaggerated feeding behaviour that can be caused by captivity, e.g. food washing in racoons, and killing of dead prey by carnivores. Various methods have been tried to stimulate artifically prey catching in carnivores and to increase foraging time; these will be considered in the section on environmental enrichment.

Feeding *ad libitum* to species that would normally survive for several weeks without feeding can also cause behavioural changes. In the wild, the king penguin nests some distance from the sea. Parent birds take turns to incubate the single egg for two to three week periods, while the other bird goes to sea to feed (Stonehouse, 1960). In pairs of king penguins at Edinburgh zoo, each bird incubates the egg, on average, for three to four days, as food is provided each day.

7.5 Environmental Factors

It is beyond the scope of this chapter to discuss all the environmental variables that may cause behavioural changes in captivity. In this section I shall briefly discuss some of these, and the results of some environmental enrichment projects.

7.5.1 Stress and Captivity

Archer (1979) reviewed the behavioural and physiological consequences of stressful stimuli in captive animals. He pointed out that these responses are only beginning to be understood, but must be a major factor when interpreting the behaviour of a wild animal in a captive environment. In this section, I examine environmental stresses that may affect the captive animals' responses to novel and changing stimuli.

Crowding. This tends to be a vague and poorly defined term, with little agreement on how it should be measured (Erwin, 1979). However, most species show behavioural changes when kept in conditions of extreme crowding. Mongooses, for example, showed a change in frequency of social interactions, infanticide and loss of locomotor activity (Rasa, 1979), while subordinate tree shrews showed pilo-erection of the tail and spent 90% of time motionless (von Holst, 1976). Elton (1979) found that juvenile baboons exhibited autobiting, and pulled out the hair of conspecifics, while subordinates became socially withdrawn and showed a higher frequency of self-directed behaviour. Thus the crowding may inhibit an animal's normal response to stimuli.

Novelty can provide a stimulus for exploration or can be overarousing and stress-inducing, and produce other responses. Moving familiar animals to a completely novel environment can elicit exploration but also aggression (Archer, 1976) and fearful and avoidance responses (Russell, 1979). Novel objects placed in the home cage before eliciting exploration may initially produce fear and avoidance. This degree of neophobia may be greater in animals reared in deprived and sterile conditions (Baldwin & Baldwin, 1977; Russell, 1979). Rowell & Hinde (1963) found that the fear and alarm responses were greater in solitary animals than in those in a social group. Glickman & Sroges (1966) illustrated that there are both species-specific and individual differences in responses to novelty.

The response threshold is probably altered in domestic species (Ratner & Boice, 1975) and this could also be true for species maintained for several generations in laboratories and zoos. Poole (1972) showed that the polecat, when moved to an unfamiliar environment showed extreme caution in exploration and frequently returned to a familiar cage, whereas the domestic ferret showed no fear response and commenced exploration, showing much less neophobia. However the ferrets did not habituate to novel stimuli as quickly as the polecats.

7.5.2 Comparisons with Field Observations

As Mitchell (1970) remarked, we are unable to deduce the effects of captivity

190

without direct comparisons between the same species in the wild using similar group compositions and comparable methods of data collection and analysis. To date, there have been insufficient studies of this nature to come to any definite conclusions, but some of the general findings are of interest to interpretations of behaviour in captivity.

Kummer & Kurt (1965) showed that hamadryas baboons exhibited behaviour in the wild that was not observed in captivity, and *vice versa*. They also showed that the repertoire exhibited by animals born in captivity was not the same as that of wild-caught animals, i.e., behavioural activities could be 'lost' in the captive situation. Similar results were found by Klein & Klein (1971) with spider monkeys. Rowell (1967), in comparing captive with wild baboons, found that captive animals showed four times more social interactions than in the wild population, and of these, a higher percentage were agonistic in nature. She also demonstrated that wild animals were frequently inactive: it can be a misconception to think of captive animals as inactive and wild ones as active.

There is some evidence that the development of independence in infant chimpanzees may be more rapid in captivity owing to lack of inhibition from the mother (Nicolson, 1977). Observations in Edinburgh on a chimpanzee infant whose mother lived in a complex environment with other chimpanzees agree with this conclusion, as mother–infant contact was broken four weeks earlier than the earliest observation from the field, and carrying by siblings commenced three weeks earlier. Similar effects were noted in captive compared with wild common marmosets (Stevenson & Rylands, 1983).

Behaviour may be performed in a different context in captivity owing to the absence of appropriate stimuli. In the wild, common marmosets eat gum that they obtain by gnawing at the bark of certain tree species; they then anally scent mark these gouges. During intergroup displays at territorial boundaries, group members move with pilo-erected coats and display to the other group, but do not anally scent mark. Sutcliffe & Poole (1978) found that the animals although unable to obtain gum in captivity, gnawed holes in branches and anally scent marked certain areas of the cage, which became high-density marking areas. However, during intergroup displays in captivity, animals were observed to pilo-erect and anally scent mark, and the two types of behaviour were closely linked. This is probably due to the absence of the correct stimulus for gum production, and the presence of the marked gouges throughout the small captive environment.

7.5.3 *Environmental enrichment projects*

There are three main methods of increasing the amount of sensory stimulation in the captive environment: the first is by increasing complexity and providing novel objects, while at the same time trying to provide as natural an environment as possible for the species, the second is by the use of mechanical devices to provide supplies of food at intervals; and the third is by operant conditioning of the animals to perform certain types of behaviour for rewards.

Considering the first method, an interesting study was carried out in Edinburgh Zoo by Watson (1973), in which chimpanzees were caged in bare sparse cages, in the unnatural grouping of pairs of animals. Watson tried to enrich the sparse environment by providing novel objects, but was unable to change the social groupings. For enrichment he used clothing, water, receptacles, sand, ropes and bedding material. Before the addition of the objects, the animals had shown overgrooming (both auto and allo-), inactivity, and manipulation of faeces. The addition of objects increased their activity and reduced acts such as faeces handling, but also produced a more natural daily cycle. In the wild, chimps may spend 6–8 h/day foraging, and they rest during the midday period, when most social interaction takes place. In the enriched environment, the animals started performing more of their social interactions during the midday period. Now the zoo has a mixed group of adult and infant chimps, and these have recently been provided with a complex outdoor enclosure with moving objects and climbing frames. An artificial termite mound is also provided where the animals 'fish' with sticks for such substances as honey and yoghurt. This has resulted in a high level of activity, loss of abnormal behaviour and much social interaction, this occurred even though five of the animals were the deprived animals studied by Watson (1973). Maple (1979, 1980) and van Hooff (1973) both stress the need for a complex environment with changing objects and complex climbing equipment for the arboreal apes. Maple (1980) cites an example from San Francisco Zoo where the pair of orang-utans had only one dead tree as climbing equipment, and they spent 30% of the day under sacks. After the provision of a complex climbing frame with moving parts, the animals spent less time under the sacks, pacing movements ceased, and they were much more active.

Hancocks (1980) details several methods of making zoo enclosures suitable for the species caged in them and the advantages of hiding food supplies, burying food under hay or shavings, and providing constant changes in the cage furnishing: these simple improvements cause the species to perform more of their natural behavioural repertoire.

Considering now the use of mechanical devices to provide food at intervals, Markowitz et al. (1978) suggested that predatory behaviour could be stimulated in carnivores by providing artificial prey in the form of 'flying meatballs'. They found that before the introduction of the meatballs, three servals performed stereotyped pacing and showed a high level of inactivity. After installing the apparatus which provided flying meatballs several times per day, activity increased and pacing decreased. Similar reduction of stereotypic movement was noted in polar bears when a machine that delivered fish into the pool was installed. A pair of orang-utans in San Francisco zoo spent much time on the floor, showing stereotypic pacing and low activity levels. After the installation of a device that produced monkey chow when a lever was pressed, the animals were more active, used the climbing frame more and reduced their stereotypic movements (Murphy, 1976).

Markowitz & Woodworth (1978) also used operant methods to increase the activity levels of a group of gibbons. In response to a light, the animals learned to pull a lever and then travel across the cage to obtain a food reward. A similar machine and technique was designed for a group of diana monkeys. Myres (1978) describes experiments in which animals (e.g., baboons) competed with the public for speed in switching off a lighted button on a panel. Jaguar were trained to work a 'paddle' to obtain food. These more extreme operant methods have been criticized (Hutchins *et al.*, 1978) in that they cause the animal to perform unnatural acts of behaviour, which may develop into stereotypic movements. Providing food at frequent intervals for species such as jaguar, which would normally eat only once every few days, is also unnatural. However, these methods are useful, in that they do increase the animals' activity, and more research on these techniques would be beneficial. However, care should be taken to try and adapt operant methods to suit the natural behaviour and activity of the species.

7.6 Conclusions

Zoos and laboratories have only recently begun to consider the effect of the captive environment on the behaviour of caged wild animals. This environment is relatively sterile and lacking in stimulus change, but it is not possible to interpret the effects on an individual without some knowledge of the behaviour of the species in the wild. Neophilic species (Morris, 1964) may be more likely to develop aberrant behaviour than neophobic ones. The degree of deprivation during early rearing will also affect the animal's responses to stimuli as will the degree of sensory stimulation it received as an infant. Thus the environment is a complex combination of cage size and complexity, group size and composition, diet, climate and proximity to humans and other animals (Fig. 7.1). The resultant behaviour is a combination of the animal's responses to environmental stimuli and its previous experience. (Fig. 7.2).

There is no species of which we have sufficient knowledge of the natural behavioural repertoire, to be able to state what is abnormal and what is normal. There are now several examples from the field of intraspecific variation in behaviour and social organization, depending on the environment and abundance of food. Some aberrant forms of behaviour have been observed under certain conditions in the wild, and therefore their occurrence in captivity cannot be considered an artifact. Some species (e.g. lions) are inactive in the wild and therefore their inactivity in captivity is simply a reflection of this.

Parent-reared young animals experience many novel stimuli to which they show differing responses, depending on the ontogenetic stage. To the adolescent and adult animal, the captive environment must lack stimuli, and the opportunity to explore for food and other resources. The wild animal in captivity must also go through some degree of domestication; this, together with the nature of the environment, will make its responses to certain stimuli different from its wild counterpart.

One of the commonest types of aberrant behaviour is stereotypic movement: this can result from several factors, including early experience. Other forms of behaviour, directly attributable to boredom or low sensory input, are self-mutilation, coprophagy, eating of vomitus, failure to breed, behaviour involving interaction with the public, begging, and aberrant feeding patterns.

Many aspects of captivity, such as crowding and moving to a new enclosure, are stress-inducing, and these will produce behavioural changes. However, it is only by making direct comparisons between the repertoire of a species in the wild and in captivity that one can come to definite conclusions on the degree of change. There have been few studies of this type, and few that compare the same species in different captive environments.

Several methods of enriching the environment have been applied, and the most profitable approach would appear to be to make the complex features of the cage as near to those utilized by the species in the wild, while producing stimulus change, and novelty, where possible.

References

ARCHER, J. (1976) The organization of aggression and fear in vertebrates. In *Perspectives in Ethology, Vol. 2* (Eds. P. P. G BATESON and P. H. KLOPFER). New York: Plenum Press.

ARCHER, J. (1979) *Animals under Stress.* (Studies in Biology No. 108). London: Edward Arnold.

BALDWIN, J. D and BALDWIN J. I. (1974) Exploration and social play in squirrel monkeys (*Saimiri*). *American Zoologist* **14**, 303–315.

BALDWIN, J. D. and BALDWIN, J. I. (1976) Effects of food ecology on social play: a laboratory simulation. *Zietschrift fur Tierpsychologie* **40**, 1–14.

BALDWIN, J. D. and BALDWIN J. I. (1977) The role of learning phenomena in the ontogeny of exploration and play. In *Primate Bio-social Development: Biological Social, and Ecological Determinants* (Eds. S. CHEVALIER-SKOLNIKOFF and F. E. POIRIER). London: Garland Publishing Inc.

BALDWIN, J. D. and BALDWIN, J. I. (1978) Reinforcement theories of exploration, play creativity and psychosocial growth. In *Social Play in Primates* (Ed. E. O. SMITH). London: Academic Press.

BERLYNE, D. E. (1960) *Conflict, Arousal and Curiosity.* New York: McGraw-Hill.

BERMAN, C. (1981) Paper given at the XVII International Ethological Conference, Oxford.

BERTRAM, B. C. R. (1975) Social factors influencing reproduction in wild lions. *Journal of Zoology (Lond.)* **177**, 463–482.

BERTRAM, B. C. R. (1978) *Pride of Lions.* London: Dent.

BIGALKE, R. C. (1972) Observations on the behaviour and feeding habits of the springbok, *Antidorcas marsupialis. Zoologica Africana* **7**, 333–359.

BROADHURST, P. L. (1963) *The Science of Animal Behaviour.* London: Pelican Books.

CHAMOVE, A. S. and ANDERSON, J. R. (1979) Woodchip litter in macaque groups. *Journal of the Institute of Animal Technicians* **30**, 69–74.

CLUTTON-BROCK, T. H, ALBON, S. D., GIBSON, R. M. and GUINNESS F. E. (1979) The logical stag: adaptive aspects of fighting in red deer (*Cervus elaphus* L.). *Animal Behaviour* **27**, 211–225.

CROOK, J. H. (1965) The adaptive significance of avian social organizations. *Symposia of the Zoological Society of London* **14**, 181–218.

CROOK, J. H. (1970) The socio-ecology of primates. In *Social Behaviour of Birds and Mammals* (Ed. J. H. CROOK). London: Academic Press.

CURTIN, R. and DOLHONOW, P. (1978) Primate social behavior in a changing world. *American Scientist* **66**, 468–475.

DAVIES, N. B. (1978) Ecological questions about territorial behaviour. In *Behavioural Ecology: an Evolutionary Approach* (Eds. J. R. KREBS and N. B. DAVIES). Oxford: Blackwell.

DITTRICH, L. (1976) Food presentation in relation to behaviour in ungulates. *Inter national Zoo Yearbook* **16**, 48–54.

DITTUS, W. P. J. (1977) The social regulation of population density and age sex distribution in the torque monkey. *Behaviour* **63**, 281–322.

DRAPER, W and BERNSTEIN, I. (1963) Stereotyped behavior and cage size. *Perceptual and Motor Skills* **16**, 231–234.

ELTON, R. H. (1979) Baboon behavior under crowded conditions. In *Captivity and Behaviour* (Eds. J. ERWIN, T. L. MAPLE and G. MITCHELL). New York: Van Nostrand Reinhold.

ERWIN, J. (1979) Aggression in captive macaques: interactions of social and spatial factors. In *Captivity and Behaviour* (Eds. J. ERWIN, T. L. MAPLE and G. MITCHELL). New York: Van Nostrand Reinhold.

ERWIN, J. and DENI, R. (1979) Strangers in a strange land: abnormal behaviors or abnormal environment? In *Captivity and Behavior* (Eds. J. ERWIN, T. L. MAPLE and G. MITCHELL). New York: Van Nostrand Reinhold.

GLICKMAN, S. E. and SROGES, R. W. (1966) Curiosity in zoo animals. *Behaviour* **26**, 151-187.

GOODALL, J. (1971) *In the Shadow of Man.* Glasgow: Collins.

GOODALL, J. (1979) Life and death at Gombe. *National Geographical Magazine* **155**(5), 592–621.

HANCOCKS, D. (1980) Bringing nature into the zoo: inexpensive solutions for zoo environments. *International Journal for the Study of Animal Problems* **1**, 170–177.

HARCOURT, A. H. (1981) Intermale competition and the reproductive behaviour of the great apes. In *Reproductive Biology of the Great Apes* (Ed. C. E. GRAHAM). London: Academic Press.

HARCOURT, A. H., FOSSEY, D. and SABATER-PI, J. (1981). Demography of *Gorilla gorilla. Journal of Zoology (Lond.)* **195**, 215–233.

HEBB, D. O. (1955) Drives and the CNS (conceptual nervous system). *Psychological Review* **62**, 243–254.

HEDIGER, H. (1950) *Wild Animals in Captivity.* London: Butterworth.

HEDIGER, H. (1955) *Studies of the Psychology and Behaviour of Captive Animals in Zoos and Circuses.* London: Butterworth.

HINDE, R. A. (1972) Social behavior and its development in subhuman primates. Eugene, Oregon: Condon Lectures.

HINTZ, H. F., SEDGEWICK, C. J. and SCHRYVER, H. F. (1976) Some observations on digestion of a pelleted diet by ruminants and non-ruminants. *International Zoo Yearbook* **16**, 54–62.

HOLST, D. VON (1976) Social stress in the tree-shrew: its causes and physiological and ethological consequences. In *Prosimian Behaviour* (Eds. R. D. MARTIN, G. A. DOYLE and A. C. WALKER). London: Duckworth.

HOOFF, J. A. R. A. M. VAN (1973) The Arnhem zoo chimpanzee consortium: an attempt to create an ecologically and socially acceptable habitat. *International Zoo Yearbook* **13**, 195–203.

HRDY, S. B. (1974) Male-male competition and infanticide among langurs (*Presbytis entellus*) of Abu, Rajasthan. *Folia Primatologica* **22**, 19-58.

HRDY, S. B. (1979) Infanticide among animals: a review, classification and examination of the implications for the reproductive strategies of females. *Ethology and Sociobiology* **1**, 13-40

HUMPHREY, N. K. (1976) The social function of intellect. In *Growing Points in Ethology* (Eds. P. P. G. BATESON and R. A. HINDE). London: Cambridge University Press.

HUTCHINGS, M. HANCOCKS, D. and CALIP, T. (1978) Behavioural engineering in the zoo: a critique. *International Zoo News* **25**, **26**, 155-157.

INHELDER, E. (1955) Zur Psychologie einiger Verhaltensweisen-besonders des Spiels-von Zootieren. *Zeitschrift für Tierpsychologie* **12**, 88-144.

JARMAN, P. J. (1974) The social organisation of antelope in relation to their ecology. *Behaviour* **48**, 215-267.

KILEY-WORTHINGTON, M. (1977) *Behavioural Problems of Farm Animals*. Stocksfield: Oriel Press.

KLEIN, L. and KLEIN, D. (1971) Aspects of social behaviour in a colony of spider monkeys, *Ateles geoffroyi*. *International Zoo Yearbook* **11**, 175-181.

KRUUK, H. (1972) *The Spotted Hyena*. Chicago: University of Chicago Press.

KUMMER, H. and KURT, F. (1965) A comparison of social behaviour in captive and wild hamadryas baboons. In *The Baboon in Medical Research* (Ed. H. VAGTBORG). Austin : University of Texas Press.

LOY, J. (1970) Behavioural responses of free-ranging rhesus monkeys to food shortage. *American Journal of Physical Anthropology* **33**, 263-272.

MAPLE, T. (1975) Fundamentals of animal social behaviour. In *The Behaviour of Domestic Animals* (Ed. E. S. E. HAFEZ). London: Bailliere Tindall.

MAPLE, T. (1979) Great apes in captivity: the good, the bad, and the ugly. In *Captivity and Behavior* (Eds. J. ERWIN, T. L. MAPLE and G. MITCHELL). New York: Van Nostrand Reinhold.

MAPLE, T. (1980) *Orang-utan Behaviour*. New York: Van Nostrand Reinhold.

MARKOWITZ, H. and WOODWORTH, G. (1978) Experimental analysis and control of group behavior. In *Behavior of Captive Wild Animals* (Eds. H. MARKOWITZ and V. J. STEVENS). Chicago: Nelson-Hall.

MARKOWITZ, H. SCHMIDT, M.J. and MOODY, A. (1978) Behavioural engineering and animal health in zoos. *International Zoo Yearbook* **18**, 190-194.

MASON, W. A. (1968) Early social deprivation in the nonhuman primates: implications for human behavior. In *Environmental Influences* (Ed. D. C. GLASS). New York: Rockefeller University Press.

MEYER-HOLZAPFEL, M. (1968) Abnormal behaviour in zoo animals. In *Abnormal Behaviour in Animals* (Ed. M. W. FOX). London: Saunders.

MITCHELL, G. (1970) Abnormal behaviour in primates. *Primate Behaviour* **1**, 195-249.

MORRIS, D. (1964) The response of animals to a restricted environment. *Symposia of the Zoological Society of London* **13**, 99-118.

MUCKENBECK FRAGASZY, D. (1979) Titi and squirrel monkeys in a novel environment. In *Captivity and Behaviour* (Eds. J. ERWIN, T. L. MAPLE and G. MITCHELL). New York: Van Nostrand Reinhold.

MURPHY, D. E. (1976). Enrichment and occupational devices for orang utans and chimpanzees. *International Zoo News* **137**, 24-26.

MYRES, W. A. (1978) Applying behavioral knowledge to the display of captive animals. In *Behavior of Captive Wild Animals* (Eds. H. MARKOWITZ and V. J. STEVENS). Chicago: Nelson-Hall.

NICOLSON. N. A. (1977) A comparison of early behavioral development in wild and captive chimpanzees. In *Primate Biosocial Development : Biological, Social, and Ecological*

196

Determinants (Eds. S. CHEVALIER-SKOLNIKOF and F. E. POIRIER). London: Garland Publishing Inc.

ODBERG, F. O. (1978) Abnormal behaviours: stereotypies. Proceedings of the First World Congress of Ethology Applied to Zootechnics, Madrid.

ODBERG, F. O. (1981) Ethologische bijdrage tot de studie van stereotypieën. Dierpsychologische experimenten over de invloed van omgevingsfactoren en van psychofarmaca. Ph. D. Thesis, State University of Ghent, Belgium.

POOLE, T. B. (1972) Some behavioural differences between the European polecat, *Mustela putorius*, the ferret, *M. furo*, and their hybrids. *Journal of Zoology (Lond.)* **166**, 25-35.

RANDRUP, A., SCHEEL-KRUGER, J., FOG, R. and MUNKVAD, I. (1978) A short survey of animal psychopharmacology. *Proceedings of the first World Congress on Ethology Applied to Zootechnics*, Madrid.

RASA, O. A. E. (1979) The effects of crowding on the social relationships and behaviour of the dwarf mongoose *(Helogale undulata rufula)*. *Zeitschrift für Tierpsychologie* **49**, 17-25.

RATNER, S. C. and BOICE, R. (1975) Effects of domestication on behaviour. In *The Behaviour of Domestic Animals* (Ed. E. S. E. HAFEZ). London: Bailliere Tindall.

RHINE, R. J., NORTON, G. W., ROERTGEN, W. J. and KLEIN, H.O. (1980) The brief survival of free-ranging baboon infants *(Papio cynocephalus)* after separation from their mothers. *International Journal of Primatology* **1**, 401-409.

ROWELL, T. E. (1967) A quantitative comparison of the behaviour of a wild and a caged baboon group. *Animal Behaviour* **15**, 499-509.

ROWELL, T. E. and HINDE, R. A. (1963) Responses of rhesus monkeys to mildly stressful situations. *Animal Behaviour* **11**, 235-243.

RUSSELL, P. A. (1979) Fear-evoking stimuli. In *Fear in Animals and Man* (Ed. W. SLUCKIN). London; Van Nostrand Reinhold.

SACKETT, G. P. (1968) Abnormal behaviour in laboratory-reared rhesus monkeys. In *Abnormal Behaviour in Animals* (Ed. M. W. FOX). London: Saunders.

STEVENSON, M. F. (1978) Ontogeny of playful behaviour in family groups of the common marmoset. In *Recent Advances in Primatology, Vol. 1* (Eds. D. J. CHIVERS and J. HERBERT). London: Academic Press.

STEVENSON, M. F. & RYLANDS, A. (1983) The marmoset monkeys: genus *Callithrix*. In *Ecology and Behaviour of Neotropical Primates, Vol. 2*. Rio de Janeiro; Academia Brasileira de Ciências.

STONEHOUSE (1960) The King penguin *(Aptenodytes patagonica)* of South Georgia: I Breeding and development. *Falkland Islands Dependencies Survey*, Scientific Reports No. 23, 1-81.

SUTCLIFFE, A. G. and POOLE, T. B. (1978) Scent marking and associated behaviour in captive common marmosets *(Callithrix jacchus jacchus)* with a description of the histology of scent glands. *Journal of Zoology (Lond.)* **185**, 41-56.

UEXKÜLL, J. VON (1934) Streifzuge durch die Umwelten von Tieren und Menschen. Translated in *Instinctive Behaviour* (1957) (Ed. C. H. SCHILLER). London: Methuen.

WATSON, C. J. M. (1973) *Chimpanzees at Edinburgh zoo: a study in environmental enrichment*. B. Sc. Thesis, University of Edinburgh.

WRANGHAM, R. W. (1981) Drinking competition in vervet monkeys. *Animal Behaviour* **29**, 904-910.

197

CHAPTER 8

Exploration in Farm Animals and Animal Husbandry

David Wood-Gush, Alex Stolba and Candace Miller

8.1 Introduction

Berlyne (1960) suggested that one function of exploratory behaviour would be to alter sensory input in animals. In wild animals, patrolling will be partly appetitive and partly exploratory in function. Observations on baboons, for example, show that they often make detours from their usual routes after feeding, and that, although these are unconnected with feeding, they enable the animals to check their environment and its resources. This sort of activity is the primary expression of exploratory behaviour in the wild animal, but, since the farm animal is kept in unvarying and cramped conditions, their main expression of exploratory behaviour becomes the investigation of objects. This may take the form of either investigating a new item in the familiar environment or checking a familiar object in that environment, probably to see if it has changed in any way. In either case the result will be to increase sensory input and arousal. Concomitant with this hypothetical function is the hypothesis that the causation is a homeostatic mechanism that is activated by any disparity between incoming information and the animal's internal model of its environment (see Chapter 3). Such a homeostatic mechanism could serve to bring the animal into a balanced state of arousal (Berlyne, 1960) or into a balance of arousal and security (Bischof, 1975). Although arousal theory has drawbacks (see Chapter 2), it nevertheless seems a useful concept in the case of animals confined in very restricted conditions. In intensive husbandry conditions, farm animals will try to escape if the environment causes a surfeit of arousing stimuli (if, for example, things are unpredictable) or if there is too little stimulation from the unchanging environment. The desired level of stimulation will vary from species to species, and within a species it will probably vary from time to time and from individual to individual depending on physiological state and experience. In practice, while one might expect an animal in an unsuitable environment to select one that would compensate with regard to arousing stimuli, one might also expect that it would overshoot at first and would choose one that was too high or too low in terms of arousal, before finding the optimum.

For many wild species, exploratory behaviour is of vital importance and there will have been strong selection pressure to ensure its continuation (see Chapters 1 and 6). Domestication is unlikely to have abolished such important motivation, although, as is the case in many other behaviour patterns, domestication may have changed the threshold at which it will become operative. We may conclude that, in the absence of strong human selection against it, there will still be a strong intrinsic tendency to explore in our farm stock. Indeed, there has been no conscious selection against it. This stance makes us disagree with views that would lump exploratory behaviour and appetitive behaviour into a single category (e.g. Barnett, 1975). Although distinction on a practical level may be difficult, it seems possible that detailed studies using sequence analysis will show that exploratory motivation, like play, combines many behaviour patterns originating from different motivational systems (Meyer-Holzapfel, 1956). Among other things, exploratory behaviour can be distinguished from play in some species on the grounds that sequences of exploratory behaviour may often end in marking and elements indicating ownership, whereas sequences of play rarely do (Lorenz, 1978).

8.2 Experiments on Exploratory Behaviour in Farm Livestock

8.2.1 Domestic Fowl

Several studies have been carried out on the chick's response to novel stimuli and environments, mostly with a view to studying 'emotionality' rather than exploration. In one such study Murphy & Wood-Gush (1978) investigated the effect of age, strain and different rearing systems on the birds' responses to new environments. Two stocks of birds were used; one was a Flighty White Leghorn strain, and the other a docile strain derived from a Rhode Island Red — Light Sussex cross. In the initial experiment, 14 females of each strain were tested at 9 months of age, 10 females of each strain at 14 weeks of age (sexual maturity is at about 22 weeks of age), 12 females of each strain at 10 weeks of age, 15 of each at 6 weeks old, and finally 84 chicks reared either in visual isolation from other chicks or in groups of 4 were tested at one of three ages — 4, 7 or 14 days. The strange environment was a cage in a soundproof room, a large one for the older birds and a small one for the chicks. The room was brightly lit and warmth was provided for the chicks.

Exploration in the young chick, uninhibited by fear, takes the form of readily moving from one object to another, picking at them and scratching, if the substrate is suitable. Locomotion might sometimes give way to running towards an object and this may be accompanied by trills. In the case of the juvenile and adult birds, much of the time in the novel environment was spent in standing or lying and looking around. Most intermittently preened, 'yawned', defaecated, scratched the floor and called. Such locomotion as there was, was extremely wary in manner. There were very few strain differences at these ages. However, strain, age and early rearing all had significant effects in the chicks. In general, chicks from the docile stock spent more time standing, took more steps and spent more time peeping than the Flighty strain chicks. Four day old chicks performed these behaviour patterns more than older chicks, and chicks reared in isolation more than chicks reared in groups. Because of the silence of the testing room, it was felt that most birds had been too frightened and that this had masked any differences in exploratory behaviour between strains. In a second experiment, adult females of both strains that had been kept in cages from hatching were tested in a strange pen with litter on the floor and with familiar noises in the background. Each bird was placed in a starting box and its behaviour in the box after the door had been opened was observed. Striking differences were then apparent. The Flighty strain hens spent 449 $\pm$ 109 s in the box before emerging whereas the docile hens spent 2245 $\pm$ 598 s before doing so. The latter, once out, took significantly fewer steps in the pen. However the quantitive data did not give a true representation of the strain differences. Once out of the starting box, the docile birds walked about in a relaxed manner whereas the Flighty strain hens showed obvious signs of attempted escape. These results indicate that the traditional view that the number of squares entered is an index of exploratory behaviour cannot be applied to fowls, as it can for many other species (see Chapter 1), as birds can readily carry out stationary exploration in an area the size of a pen. An example of patrolling in a limited area by hens is given in an experiment by Duncan & Hughes (1972). These hens were individually housed in a Skinner box where they had a choice between earning food by pecking at a disc or obtaining identical food from a trough. After several days on this regimen only food in the trough was available, but the hens continued to peck at the disc a few times a day.

In general, the study by Murphy & Wood-Gush (1978) shows that in fowls, strain, early experience and age can affect exploration and that different criteria for exploration from those used with rodents have to be employed. Sex can also affect the response to strange environments in young chicks (Jones, 1977). Further, with fowls, some exploratory behaviour is difficult to distinguish from other forms, since pecking and scratching in the litter may easily typify either the appetitive component of feeding behaviour or exploration. Possibly, detailed sequence analysis would reveal differences, but this has not been attempted so far, and little attention has been paid to the exploration of novel objects in familiar environments.

8.2.2   Pigs

Most studies on pigs have largely neglected their exploratory behaviour, which is surprising, as in choice experiments they obviously show considerable ability to deal with new and complex situations (Baldwin & Meese, 1977). Observations in natural environments on wild boar (Meynhardt, 1978) and on domestic Large White pigs in semi-natural enclosures (Stolba & Wood-Gush, in prep.)

200

demonstrate that pigs spend considerable time actively searching and investigating. The latter study found that, although being fed a generous daily maintenance ration, adult and sub-adult pigs still spent 53% of the active daylight time foraging, i.e. browsing, rooting, sniffing at food items and chewing them. During an average day, they investigated and manipulated objects in various other contexts in 5% of the scanning samples and moved and explored from a distance in 18%. In the remaining time they mainly interacted with social partners or rested for short periods. Thus exploratory information was gained by patrolling and by close investigation of food and non-food items during approximately 29% of the time spent active.

The generation of exploratory motivation includes internal causes ('need for certain specific stimuli' — Tembrock, 1969), as well as external ones (Berlyne, 1960), as is generally postulated for most motivational systems (see also Chapter 3). Since the pigs spend such a large proportion of their time exploring, it is reasonable to suppose that, in addition to obvious dependence on external stimuli, the motivation is also likely to have a large internal component. Under modern husbandry conditions, fattening pigs are usually kept in mono-caste groups in very bare pens. Thus their physical as well as social environment is distinctly deficient in structural and temporal complexity and variation. This means that there will be a lack of many key stimuli that in the semi-natural environment are important in releasing, enhancing and orienting many behavioural patterns. Various consummatory acts — e.g. in the case of exploration, close investigation of novel features — may therefore be impeded, and the animal's appetitive behaviour — searching — will remain unfulfilled. This stifling of exploratory sequences might thus have serious effects on the pigs' motivational balance, affecting their level of reactivity.

A series of tests measuring the reaction towards unfamiliar stimuli has been conducted to detect such an effect of behavioural restraint (Stolba & Wood-Gush, 1980). In each of 4 different environments, five groups of 10 to 14 juveniles aged 4–6 months were presented with a hanging tyre close to their nest. The trials, in which the pigs were tested as a group, lasted up to 80 min and were repeated on different days. The environments were: (a) an indoor Danish pen with a concrete, partially slatted floor; (b) a straw-bedded, open-front pen; (c) an enriched pen with straw bed, rooting area and various furnishings; or (d) a large semi-natural wooded enclosure where the juveniles were in families with adults and sub-adults.

The barer the environment, the more strongly the group reacted towards the stimulus: in the semi-natural enclosure, no attention was paid to the tyre in any trial after 10 min and in the enriched pen in any trial after 30 min. On the other hand, strong reactions to the tyre were seen in the first two environments even after 80 min. In the Danish pen 72 min, and in the straw-bedded pen 28 min, elapsed before the tyre was left untouched for 30 s. The mean proportion of animals of a group reacting towards the stimulus during the group reaction time was also significantly greater the barer the environment. In addition, significantly more aggressive interactions per animal per unit time were observed at the tyre in the barer environments.

An essential quality of the exploratory reaction is the inclusion of behavioural elements from many different functional systems that normally do not occur in juxtaposition (Lorenz, 1978) and such sequences of behaviour were seen in the pigs' responses. Interest in the tyre started with investigative sniffing followed mostly by aggressive elements or by nosing or chewing. While courtship elements were rarely shown, the more frequent transitions in the behavioural sequence were those leading to material gathering and nest-building and then to comfort or to marking behaviour. In the strawless pen, while their reaction consisted of a mixture of elements, the pigs tended to perform a high proportion of manipulative behaviour patterns and elements related to the preparation of food, e.g. tugging and tossing the tyre. Marking, displacement and nosing were significantly more frequent at the end of the reactive sequence than other behaviour patterns. The pigs therefore seem at first to test what the tyre can be used for, and then sometimes apparently take possession of it, before they put it aside.

In bare environments, the reactions to novel objects are generally intensified. If a moderately frightening stimulus, such as the sudden opening of an umbrella, is presented to the pigs, they again overreact in the extremely bare Danish pen. There, the initial flight reaction of a few pigs standing close by quickly spreads to many neighbouring animals, sometimes even developing into hysterical reactions and inhibiting the subsequent exploratory approach. Stimuli can easily elicit fright reactions instead of exploratory ones, as noted by van Putten (1978). However since this obviously is more likely to happen in severely impoverished environments, it suggests that arousal is generally more easily increased there.

8.2.3 Cattle

In domestic cattle, one major expression of exploratory behaviour is likely to be patrolling. This is so because of the ecological niche occupied by the species, and because of the species' group structure. Cattle form stable herds, occupying a home range within which the location of shelter sites, water sources, and particular vegetation types is likely to be well known to the older animals. Further, although their food source may be time-consuming to ingest and digest, it is not particularly difficult to locate, and in common with other environmental features important to cattle is fairly predictable in time and space. Hence the species has not been required to develop the same complexity of exploratory behaviour as one whose resources are more patchy in distribution and which may require some ingenuity in acquisition. Juvenile animals must learn the topography of their herd's home range, but this is information likely to be assimilated in the course of the daily movements and requiring little further exploration. A further form of exploratory behaviour likely to be shown by cattle is the sampling of unknown species of plants encountered. This is not really likely to be shown by stock on managed grassland, but is probably quite important for the virtually free-ranging herds in, for example, the Argentine.

Domestication of cattle has removed them from the free-ranging lifestyle they would naturally adopt. However, most cattle are maintained out of doors for a considerable proportion of each year, and in fairly stable and long-lived herds to whom the grazing pastures will be at least familiar, if not well known to the oldest members. Thus the only times one is likely to observe environmental exploration in adult cattle are at spring turn-out, or when a group is transferred to a new field.

Mackay & Wood-Gush (1982) observed the behaviour of a group of 9-month-old beef calves for the first 7 h after release from winter-housing, and found that calf distribution and activity were controlled primarily by the levels of excitement and apprehension induced by sudden release from confinement into a strange environment. Initially high levels resulted in exploratory behaviour and excited running, with tight groupings and the animals showing a preference for boundary areas. This was followed by increasing spread of animals across the field and an increase in grazing, as excitement and fear subsided with increasing exposure to the novel environment, and food-choice factors apparently came to assume control over activity and distribution.

When housed, adult cattle are not usually subjected to the same type of cramped intensive conditions as other forms of farm livestock. For dairy cows and suckler cows in beef production, the housing systems still allow expression of some exploratory behaviour through patrolling of the environment in which they are housed, albeit a much smaller area than when at pasture. The calf, however, is more commonly kept in fairly intensive conditions, e.g. the cramped, individual pens used to house many veal calves, and some dairy and beef calves. This is done particularly during the pre-weaning period, at which stage it could be argued that the calf's motivation to explore would be high in order that it would learn sufficient about the topography of its surroundings to be self-supporting after weaning.

Mackay & Wood-Gush (1980) examined the behaviour of calves from two different rearing environments in a novel area, and although interested primarily in responsiveness, their findings are relevant to this discussion. The behaviour of single-suckled beef calves when placed in a novel environment, and when presented with a novel stimulus in that environment, was observed. The calves were drawn from two housing systems: in one, calves were able to move freely and to interact with their peers and dams ('loose' housing), whereas in the other they were restricted in their movements and social interactions by being individually penned ('restricted' housing). A qualitative comparison of the behaviour shown revealed differences between calves from the two systems. Calves from the 'restricted' housing investigated more different areas of the novel environment and showed a greater tendency towards approach to the novel stimulus than did calves from the 'loose' housing. Calves from the loose-housing system were as likely to approach the stimulus as they were to withdraw from it or to continue with the behaviour in which they were engaged at the time of stimulus presentation, i.e. they took less notice of it.

When approaching the stimulus object, the calves from the 'restricted' system adopted a 'non-confident' posture, suggesting a conflict between the tendencies to approach and withdraw from the stimulus object. Overall, results indicated that the motivations for display of fear responses and exploratory responses were higher in calves from the 'restricted' system than those from the 'loose' system. Although social deprivation undoubtedly had an influence on the behaviour of calves from the 'restricted' conditions, denial of opportunities for exploration was also likely to be of importance. Calves in the 'loose' system were free to perform at least some of the exploration and learning they would normally exhibit during this period. However, this was totally denied to the single-penned calves under the 'restricted' conditions. This is similar to the experiment by Stolba & Wood-Gush (1980), reported above, in which pigs from various environments were presented with an unfamiliar stimulus. It would appear that the general responsiveness of calves from the 'restricted' conditions has been increased, and their threshold for display of exploratory behaviour lowered, over that of calves reared in the 'loose' housing system.

Cattle generally exhibit fairly low levels of exploratory behaviour, except when confronted with unfamiliar objects or situations. For adult animals, husbandry systems usually provide some opportunity for exploratory behaviour, even if it is only the checking of food troughs in order to ascertain which contains the most or the best food. For younger animals, however, housing practices are often such as to deny even this. In such cases, the responsiveness of the calf to novel situations and objects may be affected, something which could be important to the management of that animal.

8.3 Abnormal Behaviour Patterns that may be Connected with Frustrated Exploratory Behaviour

As we mentioned earlier, when chickens are placed in an isolated unchanging environment such as a Skinner box, they will perform an operant response for food, even when identical food is freely available from a trough within the Skinner box (Duncan & Hughes, 1972). In that experiment, 10 well-trained female Brown Leghorns were used, and it was reported that when these birds were placed singly into the Skinner box for 2 h/day and given the choice between earned and free food, only a small percentage of their food was earned. In a later phase of the experiment when they were again in the Skinner box for only 2 h/day, the earned food amounted to 44% of the total, indicating that learning had occurred. In the final part of the experiment, each bird was housed singly in the apparatus for 24 h/day and given the choice, but this time only their responses were reported. Under these conditions they made between 150 and 400 responses/day for the earned food, one response allowing the bird 5 s access to the food. This was then followed by 11 days when only free food was available, but a peck at the disc operated the mechanism as before causing a light to come on and the empty food hopper to bang into position. On the first day that earned food was withheld, the birds increased their response rate very dramatically and then it fell to a very low rate until day 17, when earned food became available again. Thereafter the responses rose to about 500/day and remained between 150 and 500 over the next 7 days, when the experiment ended. The authors dismiss boredom as a motivating factor, on the grounds that when the food reward was withheld, responses dropped after the initial increase, suggesting an experiential factor. However, it seems very difficult to dismiss boredom as a contributing factor, as the birds' responses increased with increasing knowledge of the Skinner box. The authors felt that if the birds had been bored, the flashing of the food light and banging of the hopper would have been sufficiently rewarding for the birds to respond at a high rate. Nevertheless, it is possible that the small number of responses shown, which we earlier classified as patrolling behaviour, was enough to satisfy the exploratory motivation of the birds, for we do not know how much variability in sensory input is required by the fowl. Further, it must be emphasized that the response rate probably was depressed as those stimuli were associated with frustration.

Many environments used in the pig industry are very bare, but none so barren as that of the tethered sow, for in most others the animals are in groups that allow social interactions of various sorts, although there, too, the physical environment is very bare. One such environment is the flat-deck cage for piglets weaned prematurely. Wood-Gush & Beilharz (1982) observed 12 groups of early weaned piglets in flat-deck cages, 6 of which had a trough of sterilized earth attached to the side of the cage. This was avidly used by all the piglets in those groups, particularly immediately before feeding and drinking and sometimes before lying down, defaecating and playing. The most striking difference between the two treatments, however, was in lying inactive, which was much more frequent in the cages without earth ($p < 0.02$). Further, in the experimental cages, lying inactive was correlated with ambient temperature; the hotter it became the more inactive were the piglets, while at moderate temperatures they were more active. In the control cages, on the contrary, there was no such relationship; the frequency of lying inactive was not correlated with high or moderate temperatures. This suggests that, in the absence of suitable physical features in the environment, the piglets adopt a strategy of torpidity or 'cut-off'.

A similar behavioural strategy is seen in gilts when housed for the first time in dry stalls (Stolba et al., in prep.). Gilts 'drowsily' lie, stand, sit or kneel during significantly more intervals than sows and are thus likely to reduce adverse sensory inputs from this barren and initially frightening environment. If active they are mainly occupied with the straw ration, which they use for much longer than do the older sows; only rarely are they seen to perform stereotyped activities. During the next two pregnancies, the sows go through a phase of increased investigative behaviour, but inactive stances are also frequent. However they do not show the symptoms of the 'drowsiness' of the gilts. In the higher parities the sows are mostly active during the same periods following feeding, but the patterning of behaviour becomes more and more stereotyped. Thus it seems that the sows go through several phases in which they try to overcome the behavioural problems of the stalls, such as the long-term thwarting of many motivational systems, by various methods. One of these, the occupation with straw, might be particularly interesting, since this multipurpose substrate might act as a substitute for several specific key stimuli that are normally required by the pig for the elicitation and direction of its different behavioural actions, such as exploration. The effects of this occupation with straw on the behaviour of stalled sows has been investigated by Fraser (1975) in the same dry sow house. He found that the daily administration of as little as 1 kg of unchopped straw had similar effects on behaviour as 3 kg given daily for full straw bedding. The sows were clearly less restless and less aroused than those without straw or with chopped straw. Therefore it seems that straw sheaves have a recreational effect, lowering the performance of head weaving, vacuum chewing, nosing, licking and biting of stall structures that is seen in those sows without a supply of loose straw.

However, in spite of the enriching effect of a portion of loose straw, conventional sow stalls obviously remain a boring environment, as with repeated visits stereotypies still emerge and increase in frequency (Stolba *et al.*, in prep.). The acquisition of stereotypies may therefore be an attempt by the animal to increase sensory input, because its level of arousal is likely to be too low in this unvarying environment. Thus the responses of these animals to novel objects is of interest, for although one might expect them to react strongly to such stimuli, they fail to do so. However this source of environmental variation is interesting for sows not having acquired fixed stereotypies. Thirty sows showing different degrees of stereotyped behaviour were tested for their responsiveness to a tightly rolled sack that was dangled into the stall for 10 min. The number of reactions with the sack was inversely related to the general level of stereotypy. Interactions with the sack ranged from 110 to 0; the sows with no stereotypies manipulated it 44.2 ± 37.3 times, sows with occasional stereotypies 33.3 ± 20.6 times and sows with frequent stereotypies 14.5 ± 13.9 times. The response of sows with fixated stereotypies always was of low intensity, whether they were performing stereotyped or variable behaviour immediately before the presentation of the stimulus. In this respect, they resemble the chickens with fixated stereotypies, reported by Duncan & Wood-Gush (1972), that could not respond normally once the source of frustration had been removed. One cause for not paying great attention to the test stimuli might be that the animal has learned that the environment is unlikely to provide suitable and varying stimulation, so that it then seemingly prefers the self-generated stimulation freely obtainable from the established stereotypies. Similar behaviour problems have been reported in individually stalled calves, but they have not been linked specifically to exploratory behaviour.

8.4   Conclusions

An important question in farm livestock that has yet to be tackled is: how much exploratory behaviour do they require for their mental well-being? Would adequate exploratory behaviour cut down the high levels of aggression and abnormal behaviour often seen in intensively housed animals? A consideration of the evolutionary forces affecting exploratory behaviour may be of use in this respect. In a species relying on essential resources (food, nesting sites, water, etc.) that are patchily distributed and not easily found, one might expect exploratory behaviour to be relatively prominent compared with a species whose resources were easily obtainable. Of course the cognitive abilities of the species will also affect its exploratory behaviour. If, for example, two species both exploit a similar source of food, the one with the greater cognitive capacities may show more exploratory behaviour. Manipulative play behaviour as opposed to social play might be expected to be related to the complexity and degree of exploratory behaviour of the adult, so that in species in which the young show a high level of manipulative play one might expect a relatively high level of exploratory behaviour in the adult. This relationship indeed appears to hold for most farm livestock. The ancestral pig or wild boar has its food patchily distributed and the piglet shows a high level of manipulative play and, as shown above, there are indications of frustrated exploratory behaviour when they are kept in barren environments. Cattle, on the other hand, show less manipulative play than piglets as calves, and do not show such a high level of exploratory behaviour as do pigs. In chickens there is no evidence of manipulative play, and other play is minimal, so this relationship between play and exploration is absent.

Exploration in the developing animal may vary with different developmental stages, and, as with other motivational systems, a period of very frequent performance can be expected during the emergence of the system in ontogeny. Thus, in general, the young of a species may be expected to be more strongly motivated to explore and to seek appropriate stimulation than the adult of that species. Young mammals before weaning will seek stimuli that are related to their future food resources. Piglets in semi-feral conditions often come close to the sow or older companions when the latter have found food items and actually remove the item from the mouth of the older animal (Stolba & Wood-Gush, in prep.). Similarly, young foals at about the time of onset of grazing behaviour explore and chew a number of items and apparently only commence to graze grass if another equid is grazing nearby (Glendinning, 1977). We might postulate, therefore, that at these ages and in these species high levels of exploratory behaviour would be expected in relation to potential food items, regardless of the environment. Furthermore, such exploratory behaviour is not the normal appetitive behaviour related to hunger, for it may be seen in satiated animals. Chicks also follow this pattern; when with the hen, for example, they are highly responsive to her pecking movements at food items. In industrial conditions it is likely that this exploratory behaviour is still present, but probably directed towards pecking at other chicks in the brooders. Later, in the older juveniles and sub-adult stage, sheep (Geist, 1971) and pigs, in particular, seem to acquire important knowledge about trials and the location of resources. At this developmental stage, one might expect exploratory behaviour to be at a relatively high level, and that it will then involve much walking.

Translating these concepts into practical terms for animal welfare, one might see that different types of stimuli will be necessary for animals of different ages within the same species to avoid frustration. However, in order to be able to meet the specific requirements of the different age and sex classes within husbandry practices, further research is required. Possibly, in species such as the pig, whose evolutionary history has brought about exploration to exploit patchily distributed food, an operant response mechanism yielding food items on a variable schedule of reinforcement might fulfil this role. In the fowl, which is a visual animal, visual stimulation might suffice.

References

BALDWIN, B. A. and MEESE, G. B. (1977) Sensory reinforcement and illumination preference in the domesticated pig. *Animal Behaviour* **25**, 497–507.

BARNETT, S. A. (1975) *The Rat: A Study in Behaviour*. London: University of Chicago Press.

BERLYNE, D. E. (1960) *Conflict, Arousal and Curiosity*. New York: McGraw-Hill.

BISCHOF, N. (1975) A systems approach towards the functional connections of attachment and fear. *Child Development* **46**, 801–817.

DUNCAN, I. J. H. and HUGHES, B. O. (1972) Free and operant feeding in domestic fowls. *Animal Behaviour* **20**, 775–777.

DUNCAN, I. J. H. and WOOD-GUSH, D. G. M. (1972) Thwarting of feeding behaviour in the domestic fowl. *Animal Behaviour* **20**, 444–451.

FRASER, D. (1975) The effect of straw on the behaviour of sows in tether stalls. *Animal Production* **21**, 59–68.

GEIST, V. (1971) *Mountain Sheep. A Study in Behaviour and Evolution*. London: University of Chicago Press.

GLENDINNING, S. A. (1977) The behaviour of sucking foals. *British Veterinary Journal* **133**, 192.

JONES, R. B. (1977) Sex and strain differences in the open field responses of the domestic chick. *Applied Animal Ethology* **3**, 255–261.

LORENZ, K. (1978) *Vergleichende Verhaltensforschung Grundlagen der Ethologie*. Bonn: Springer Verlag.

MACKAY, P. C. and WOOD-GUSH, D. G. M. (1980) The responsiveness of beef calves to novel stimulation: An interaction between exploration and fear. *Applied Animal Ethology* **6**, 383–384.

MACKAY, P. C. and WOOD-GUSH, D. G. M. (1982) Behaviour of 9-month-old beef calves at Spring turn-out. *Applied Animal Ethology*, in press.

MEYER-HOLZAPFEL, M. (1956) Das Spiel bei Saugetieren. *Handbuch der Zoologie* **8**, 1–36.

MEYNHARDT, H. (1978) *Schwarzwild-Report*. Melsungen: Verlag J. Neumann-Neudamm.

MURPHY, L. B. and WOOD-GUSH, D. G. M. (1978) The interpretation of the behaviour of domestic fowl in strange environments. *Biology of Behaviour* **3**, 39–61.

PUTTEN, F. VAN (1978) Spezielle Ethologie des Schweines. In *Nutztierethologie* (Ed. H. H. SAMBRAUS). Berlin. Verlag Paul Parey.

STOLBA, A. and WOOD-GUSH, D. G. M. (1980) Arousal and exploration in growing pigs in different environments *Applied Animal Ethology* **6**, 382–383.

STOLBA, A and WOOD-GUSH, D. G. M. (in prep.) Behaviour patterns of domestic large white pigs in a semi-natural environment.

STOLBA, A., BAKER, N. and WOOD-GUSH, D. G. M. (in prep.) The characterisation of stereotyped behaviour in stalled sows: the measurement of informational redundancy.

TEMBROCK, G. (1969) Allgemeine Grundlagen des Verhaltens bei Haustieren. In *Das Verhalten landwirtschaftlicher Nutztiere* (Ed. E. PORZIA). Berlin: VEB Deutscher Landwirtschaftsverlag.

WOOD-GUSH, D. G. M. and BEILHARZ, R. (1982) The enrichment of a bare environment. *Applied Animal Ethology*, in press.

CHAPTER 9

Play and Exploration

Dorothy F. Einon

9.1 The Problems of Definition

Classification is the very basis of biology. Before we study a living organism we tend to describe it both in terms of its physical attributes and in terms of its relationships with other living organisms. We classify it, and in doing so we tend to emphasize those aspects of the organism that are easily described or that fit neatly into our categories (e.g. if it has fur and suckles its young, it fits into our categories of mammal) while placing less emphasis or even ignoring aspects of the organism that cannot so easily be categorized. This lulls us into a false security: we tend to think in terms of simple straightforward categories and to forget, as Hinde (1974) points out, that most categories have fairly solid centres, but rather fuzzy edges. This is particularly true of behaviour. Who, for example, would believe from reading most of the psychological literature on feeding in rats that food-seeking could be anything but a simple and well understood behavioural category?

There are however, exceptions, things we hate to classify, behaviour we see as all fuzz and no hard centre: play is one such behaviour, exploration is another. Welker (1961) wrote in his review of play and exploration:

I find it virtually impossible to continue to think of play and exploration as unique behavioural categories with characteristics distinct from other phenomena within the behavioural repertoire of mammals.

Why should this be? It is not, I think, because play and exploration are inherently difficult to define. They may be, but so is sexual behaviour if we look beyond copulation. How, for instance, do we differentiate in females between masturbation and washing the genitals? We do so by talking about the intensity of the ·response, its repetition, and by appealing to assumed underlying motivation (or its lack), by discussing bodily posture or facial expression, in fact by using exactly the same sort of arguments that are used in distinguishing play from exploration (Hutt 1970; see Chapter 10). Yet we do not, as Fagen (1981)

210

so rightly points out, agonize over the definition of sexual behaviour at the beginning of each new paper.

Why then do we feel the need to define play and exploration? I believe there are two basic reasons. The first is that we are unsure of what motivates play and exploration whereas we tend to feel that all feeding behaviour is motivated by hunger and all sexual behaviour by a sexual drive. Perhaps more importantly, there is no obvious consummatory behaviour in the case of play and exploration, whereas the consummatory behaviour is clear for sex and feeding. Thus we readily classify together behaviour that usually terminates in feeding, even when the consummatory behaviour is implied rather than observed.

In practice, laboratory researchers mean by 'feeding' little more than the response of actually eating. If 'play' were similarly restricted (say, classified in terms of a play face) it would be easily defined, as exploration would be if we included only the manipulation of a novel object. But if we include food gathering and preparation, in the category of feeding, it would become as difficult to define as either exploration or play.

It is of little concern to those studying, say, courtship behaviour that it might be difficult to produce an unambiguous yet inclusive definition. Similarly, it is of little concern to those studying play or exploration that these lack a clear definition. The problem of definition assumes more importance when we look for function (and then only if we look for a unitary function), or when we wish to compare exploration or play across species or after some treatment. For example, if we wished to say that the hippocampus was concerned with the exploration and mapping of the environment (O'Keefe & Nadel, 1978; see also Chapter 5) or that the administration of small doses of amphetamine increased exploration (Robbins & Iversen, 1973), we would need to distinguish between object manipulation, scent marking, non-specific locomotor activity and patrolling. But if we wished only to say *how* an animal reacted to a novel object, we could not improve on an accurate description of the behaviour itself.

Have the energies expended on trying to define play and exploration been wasted? On the whole I think they have, since the definitions tend to be broad enough to be virtually meaningless, but the agonizing has one big advantage. We go into the study of play and exploration knowing they are fuzzy concepts, and thus aware of potential problems. Probably the best known 'fact' about play is that it is a difficult concept to define.

9.2   Three Different Types of Play

One of the reasons that play and exploration are such fuzzy concepts is that both tend to be overinclusive. They tend to be a ragbag for a number of behaviour patterns that often only have in common that they cannot be, or have not been, clearly defined. When we place a hungry rat in a large, novel enclosure with some food, it will investigate its environment before eating. We say it is exploring, and, since it explores before it eats, that exploration is primary to hunger in this situation. We do not usually say that the animal is trying to escape, or checking that there are no predators hiding, or that it is searching for a place of safety; nor do we say that the rat is investigating whether another food is on offer before eating, or looking for water (rats tend to drink after eating). We say it is exploring, whatever the underlying motive might be (and it could be fear reduction, or water seeking) because the rat is performing a set of behavioural activities that have no obvious consummatory response, except implied knowledge of its environment. Had we placed a small ping-pong ball in the rat's home cage, we would also call its behaviour towards the ball exploration, but the act of exploring and possibly the motive for exploration would differ. (This point is discussed in more detail in Chapter 1.)

In the same way, many types of behaviour are classed as play because they are in a certain sense related. They may, for example, share some of the following characteristics: they are pleasurable, but lack obvious motivation or consummatory activities; behaviour patterns are exaggerated, there is a degree of flexibility in the behavioural sequences, and compared with adult behaviour, sequences are truncated; they are characteristic of the young and have no obvious functional significance; they are organism-dominated rather than stimulus-dominated, and are apparently conducted for their own sake with relative relaxation.

To the biologist, the term play denotes three distinct but related sets of behaviour patterns (Fagen, 1981):
1. Social rough-and-tumble play.
2. Locomotor exercise — including post-mastery behaviours.
3. Object play.

9.2.1 Social Rough and Tumble

The most clearly defined and obvious category of play is social rough and tumble. We may take as our basis Aldis' (1975) description:

> Almost everyone would agree that chasing and playfighting in young animals is play. The serious counterparts of these behaviors may be broadly classified as agonistic behaviors — predation, aggression, and flight. In play, these behaviors are usually accompanied by play signals and are modified in certain ways (lower intensity, relaxed muscle tone) from their serious conterparts. In addition, some serious behaviors may be omitted, new behaviors may be added, and the order may be changed. The causation of play may also differ from that of serious behavior.

One may add to this that play fighting is characterized by rapid role reversals. Thus when two rats or puppies wrestle, one participant, then the other will hold the upper position, and most chases are reciprocated, with chaser and chased frequently changing roles (Bekoff, 1974; Meaney & Stewart, 1981). Just before maturity the reciprocal nature of this juvenile play begins to break down: one animal may begin to dominate another, it will tend to chase, rather than be chased and will tend to be on top during wrestling bouts. Eventually such play fighting merges into real adult fights (Bekoff, 1974; Meaney & Stewart, 1981; Poole, 1967; 1978; Steiner, 1971).

Bouts of play are frequently preceded by some form of 'invitation': a play bow in dogs, a bouncy gait in mink, peeping through the legs in primates, pouncing in rats, and are accompanied by play signals, the most obvious being the open mouth playface. Even without such signals play-fighting can be fairly easily categorized as 'play' by naive observers (Humphreys, 1982; Loizos, 1967; Mason, 1965; Miller, 1973).

Play fighting is distinguished from real fighting by the absence of biting and by the context in which the behaviour occurs. Fighting occurs when there is 'something to fight about': violation of personal space or territory, lack of food, or sexual competition. Play fighting occurs when young animals are well fed and watered, well rested and on familiar ground. Play fighting is seen in young primates, and carnivores; it also occurs in many social rodents, such as the Olympic and Alpine marmots (Barash, 1973; 1976), the prairie dog (King, 1955), the Californian (Steiner, 1971) and Columbian (McDonald, 1977) ground squirrels, and in the Norwegian (Poole & Fish, 1975) and Black rat (Ewer, 1971). But it is absent in such solitary rodents as grey squirrels (Horwich, 1972), hoary marmots (Barash, 1973), mice (Poole & Fish, 1975), and voles (Wilson, 1973).

There are other activities that are sometimes classified as social play. They are not related to rough and tumble. Some, such as sniffing and riding conspecifics (Wilson & Kleiman, 1974) are probably amicable behaviours. Others, such as sexual play (Horwich, 1972) are seen by some observers (Smith, 1982) as direct practice rather than play. We have mentioned the 'fighting' that occurs in adolescent rats (Meaney & Stewart, 1981), dogs (Bekoff, 1974), and ground squirrels (Steiner, 1971). This is distinct both from the 'play' that preceeds it and the serious fighting that follows it (Humphreys, 1982). In rodents that do not engage in rough-and-tumble play, similar 'gentle' fights may occur, and these have often been called play. (It is not known whether such fighting influences dominance in these animals.) They differ from rough and tumble in several ways: chases are unreciprocated; fights tend to occur in specific places, such as the nest, the food cup, or the water bottle (Rowell, 1961), and there is frequently a 'victor' (Einon, unpublished observations).

In *Octodontomys* the mutual upright posture (Wilson & Kleiman, 1974) may be such a behaviour. It is described thus:

> The dyad simultaneously adopts the bipedal position with the nasal/mouth area in contact . . . The body of one or both of the dyad may become tense, with the forepaws of the animal pushing against the other's shoulders . . . and a dyad may sway from side to side . . . If separation does not occur one of the pair may emit high pitched 'protest' squeaks until they do . . . the squeaking young would sometimes run to the mother.

Sometimes such a sequence ends with more amicable behaviours as in the chipmunk (Elliott, 1978), but as the animals became older, the behaviour merges into 'real fights'.

Neither rough-and-tumble play fighting nor other social-play behaviour show any obvious relationship to exploration. In a book concerned primarily with exploration, they obviously do not warrant extensive discussion. It is important to note, however, that probably most studies of animal play are concerned with rough-and-tumble play, perhaps because they form such a clear-cut category. Human-play studies, although they do encompass such behaviour (Aldis, 1975; Blurton-Jones, 1967) are more concerned with locomotor, object and fantasy play. These, as we shall see, are more difficult to distinguish from exploration.

9.2.2   Locomotor Exercise

Perhaps the most familiar locomotor play is the gambolling of lambs or the leaps and backward leg kicks of young horses. Children show similar inclinaions (Rhys, 1930 — *After leaving Mr McKenzie*):

> When you were happy about nothing you had to jump up and down, 'Can't you keep still, child, for one moment?' No, of course you couldn't keep still. You were too happy, bursting with happiness. You ran as if you were flying, without feeling your feet. And all the time you ran, you were thinking, with a tight feeling in your throat: 'I'm happy-happy-happy . . .'

There is other behaviour that is categorized frequently under 'locomotor play'. Head shaking, body twisting and turning have, together with running and jumping, been called Locomotor Rotatory Movements (LRM) (Wilson, 1973; Wilson & Kleiman, 1974). But are they always play? The behaviour that leads to such movements can include: urinating, urine sniffing, sand bathing and perineal dragging, unreciprocated body sniffing and circling. In voles, LRM are known to be related to the release of a certain chemical (Wilson, 1973). Although LRM movements may be exaggerated, and repetitive, this is also true of the animal's behaviour following a low dose of amphetamine (Randrup & Munkvad, 1970) or very high levels of light or noise (Einon & Morgan, 1978). Yet we would not wish to call the exaggerated sniffing and head shaking of rats who have received CNS stimulants 'play'.

Most descriptions of locomotor play include 'post-mastery' behaviour. Some examples might make this term clear. At about 9 or 10 months babies may learn to pull themselves up onto their feet and to sit back down again. They will then spend a great deal of each day pulling themselves up on various pieces of furniture, sitting down, crawling across the room and pulling themselves up again. At 2 years of age they may spend a great deal of time performing ever-increasing 'big jumps' from higher and higher pieces of furniture, or more alarmingly from further and further up the stairs. Some Ibex kids (Meyer-Holzapfel, 1958) also 'practise' their skills on more and more difficult terrain.

But a child's new motor skills are not just *locomotor* skills, and 'post-mastery skills' merge into object play and object investigation as the following example illustrates (Bruner, 1973, p. 302: quoted by Fagen, 1981, as an example of post-mastery behaviour):

> The six-month-old infant, having learned to hold on to an object and get it easily to his mouth, now begins a program of variation; when he takes the object now, he holds it

214

to look at, he shakes it, he bangs it on his high chair, he drops it over the edge, and he manages shortly to fit the object into every activity into which it can be put.

A child who has learned to open a door may spend a great deal of time opening and closing doors, or having learned to put something inside a box will spend hours putting all manner of objects into the box. Such behaviour is often considered 'play', but would not fit many of the definitions of play. It is when considering such behaviour that our lack of clear definitions may produce problems. I have, for example, watched my daughter spend the best part of a morning transferring the berries of a holly bush between the bush, two toy buckets, and a small wheelbarrow. She did so with a relaxed posture, but with a solemn and intent expression. The behaviour was in no sense truncated or unordered; all berries were placed in one bucket before being transferred to the wheelbarrow, and all were placed in the wheelbarrow before being transferred to the bucket. Sometimes she would break off to push the wheelbarrow or even to ride her bike, at other times stones, sticks or even leaves, would be included with the berries. Is it exploration? Probably not, for the behaviour was repeated on nearly every occasion she went into the garden over the next few weeks. We might call it post-mastery practice, or 'serious play' (Kohler, 1925), but as such it obviously merges into object play, just as jumping on the stairs or swinging on the bars of a cage may merge into the gambolling, jumping, and twisting of locomotor play.

There is one further point to be made about post-mastery play behaviour. If we are to define play as having no 'obvious function' (Smith, 1982), then such behaviour is not play. It seems highly unlikely that jumping from the stairs or manipulating spoons will not improve jumping or manipulatory skills.

9.2.3   Object Play

Beyond saying that object play is play that incorporates objects, it is impossible to define object play: at least it is impossible to produce a definition to cover all instances of behaviour that have been described as object play. In general usage, object play becomes a term that refers to a child's/young animal's interaction with an object that is in a sense inappropriate for that object. Thus when a baby bangs a spoon on a chair, or drops it on the floor this is 'playing with the spoon'. Such play is clearly distinct from the example given by Gilmore (1966):

> A young child takes a piece of cloth and, as if the cloth were human, makes it go to sleep.

or from Uttley (1943):

> We picked the rye grass, which we called 'Tinker tailor grass' and we counted the little ears to find out whom we should marry. Tinker, tailor, soldier, sailor, rich man, poor man, beggar man, thief. We asked it this year, next year, sometime, never.

Or an example of object playing in Japanese Macaque (Candland & French, 1978):

After the bar had remained on the ground for a period of several weeks, we noted that it had been bent into the shape of an S, inserted into the metal framework within the enclosure and was being used as a swing by the juvenile.

Or indeed from perhaps the most common example of object play in animals: the kitten playing with a ball or a piece of string.

Clearly all these might be considered play, but there is a sense — and this is the basis of most discussions of the relationship between exploration and play — in which many of the activities that are called 'play with an object' might be called 'investigation of an object'.

Let us consider each type of object play in turn and decide in what sense it is 'play'.

Playing with a spoon. We discussed Bruner's example of playing with a spoon in the context of post-mastery behaviour. Many of the very young child's interactions with objects could be so classified. They learn to pick up an object and to put it down. Play is a repetition and extension of this newly learned behaviour. It has a great deal in common with jumping for the sake of jumping, or climbing more and more 'difficult' trees. But how long can we call something 'post mastery'? When a 2-year-old jumps over a stick or down two steps we can call it 'post-mastery play' since it is likely that the skill was recently acquired. But what do we call the behaviour of older children when playing at jumping off the wall or leaping over the stream?

We might consider the child's building with bricks in a similar way. We could say that the child learns to place one play brick with another then gradually 'elaborates' by combining bricks in post-mastery play. But children carry out such 'post-mastery play' over a number of years, and it obviously merges with a form of object play that one could only rather arbitrarily call post mastery.

We can view the child's playing with a spoon in another context. The child is given the spoon, it holds it, turns it over, sucks it, bangs it, drops it. It is given the spoon a second time. It bangs it and drops it again. Hutt (1970) would argue that the initial investigation of the spoon was exploratory, the subsequent behaviour play. At first the child asks 'What does this object do'? and subsequently 'What can I do with this object'?. Hutt (1979) suggests the following distinctions between play and exploration: When a child explores, its behaviour is directional, it is elicited by, or oriented towards certain environmental changes. Its behaviour is systematic, stereotyped and accompanied by intent facial expression and tense body posture. Play, however, occurs in a familiar environment, when the properties of the object are known, and is accompanied by a more relaxed body posture and facial expression (see Chapter 10). The point I wish to make here is that there is a clear analogy between exploring an object, and subsequently playing with it, and mastering a skill or action and subsequently 'playing with that skill'. Rather than saying 'What does this object do: what can I do with this object'? The child says 'How do I do that'? and 'What can I do with this new skill?'. We can in effect talk about a relationship between skill and play that is similar to that between exploration and play.

216

Play by this criterion is what the child does after it has mastered a skill, or discovered an object.

Weisler & McCall (1976) have suggested that there is a continuum between exploration and play: that in practice we cannot draw a dividing line between the two. But to place skill/play along a continuum is to imply that play is a further development of skill, just as placing exploration and play along a continuum is to imply that object play is an extension, a further stage, of exploration. The term 'play' then becomes merely a convenient label for one end of the continuum rather than a behaviour in its own right. It is this denial that play is a behaviour in its own right that has caused people such as Bekoff (1974), Fagen (1981); and Hutt (1979) to object to a position such as Weisler & McCall's (1976). One of the major problems in defending 'play' as a separate behaviour is that learning and play, like exploration and play (Weisler & McCall, 1976) become admixed in natural behaviour sequences. In theory this is not important. Admixing of behavioural acts is a common occurrence and it does not imply that the acts are related; consider for example (Fagen, 1981) a food-gathering animal scanning for predators every few seconds. There is however, a practical problem. Play does not have a unique set of behaviour patterns. It shares them for example with exploration and learning. We distinguish play from other behaviours by observing body posture and facial expression, or by considering whether the child's response is systematic or stereotyped. These are not simple, clear-cut distinctions. When two behaviour patterns are difficult to distinguish, the fact that they tend to occur in the same sequence of behaviour makes distinctions between them exceedingly arbitrary. They may be distinct in theory, but it is hard to demonstrate this in practice. Such problems are not unique to the exploration/play 'continuum'. They are inherent in exploration. How would one draw the line *in practical terms* between exploration and food gathering, or between exploration and predatory avoidance? (See also Chapter 4 for further discussion of this question).

The kitten chasing the ball.   The most frequently cited example of play in animals is that of the kitten chasing a ball. When defining play by a series of examples this one is almost invariably used. It is surprising, therefore, that the evidence that such behaviour is 'play', in the sense that it is distinct from immature predation, is so very weak.

There is an increase in the kittens' play as the need for predation arises: When the kitten is weaned, object play (and to some extent social play) increases, and this increase is found even when weaning occurs at an earlier date than is normal (Bateson & Young, 1981). Further, predatory play and prey catching use the same motor patterns; stimuli that elicit a particular motor pattern in prey catching will also elicit that response in play. The closer the object is to prey (e.g. small size, fur, animal smell, movement) the more like predation is play. Egan (1976) describes the kitten's predatory play thus:

> Typically an object is first sniffed and/or patted; the stimulation received determines whether or not it is bitten (fur is the stimulus most effective in eliciting biting). If it is bitten it might then be picked up in the mouth, then shaken or thrown (with live prey

217

this would serve to stun it) or carried (with prey to a corner perhaps, where it might eventually be eaten). Alternatively, the initial patting might cause the object to roll, in which case it might elicit crouching and pouncing (movement being the stimulus for these patterns) which, as with prey, would serve to immobilize it. A fur-less object is seldom bitten, carried, shaken or thrown; playing with it therefore entails the repetition of other than mouth patterns. Similarly, since with objects there can be no progression to the consummatory acts of killing and eating, it is logical to expect that if the cat sustains any interest in them, sequences will be repeated.

Probably the best substitute for 'prey' that a kitten or puppy has available is its siblings. It does not, however, throw them in the air or kill them — although it stalks and pounces upon them. In predatory play with its siblings the predatory sequence is truncated, threats and hard bites are absent, bouts are longer, and there is more variation in, and repetition of, behaviour units (Bekoff, 1974). It is of course these aspects of the kitten's behaviour which leads us to call it play. But the truncated nature of this behaviour may be an artifact; one can hardly expect the full predatory sequence from a kitten when its 'prey' is engaged in predation upon it. The 'eliciting stimuli' will obviously not occur in the correct order. It is not surprising therefore that the predatory sequence is not completed.

There are other grounds for considering object play in kittens as an immature form of predation. First, food deprivation does not affect the type or amount of play with objects (Egan, 1976). Nor, according to Leyhausen (1956), is adult catching and killing of prey influenced by hunger, whereas food deprivation reduces social rough-and-tumble play (Baldwin & Baldwin, 1974). Second, the presence of other kittens stimulates object play in a way analogous to its effects on predatory behaviour (Egan, 1976). Third, although the experience of prey as a kitten may improve adult predatory ability (Baerends-van Roon & Baerends, 1979; Caro, 1980a, b; Kuo, 1930; Leyhausen, 1956), the advantages gained by experience with a *particular* prey may be specific to that prey (Caro, 1980a, b). Experience with mice improves mouse killing, experience with birds does not. Caro (1979) also found that there was a significant correlation between adult prey-catching ability and the frequency with which a particular kitten engaged in some, but not all forms of social play. If we define play as having no obvious immediate benefit, we cannot call the kitten's behaviour with objects, play.

There is other immature behaviour that we might similarly dismiss as play since it shows obvious improvements in efficiency, and functionally these benefits are clear. Birds 'learning' to fly is an obvious example. Smith (1982) suggests that nest building (van Lawick-Goodall, 1968) and allomothering (Lancaster, 1971) might be examples, as might sexual play (Horwich, 1972). Indeed the behaviour patterns that we have referred to as post-mastery are also in a sense *pre*-mastery. Learning how to put one item inside another may be the learning of a specific response, but post-mastery play generalizes this skill, and one might expect improvements in efficiency. We shall return to this point at the end of this chapter.

One possible reason for the high incidence of object play in domestic cats and dogs is that most kittens, and many puppies, are isolated from conspecifics

218

during the major play period. Guyot *et al*. (1980) found that kittens raised without siblings (but with their mother) played with objects more than kittens reared with siblings. Most pet kittens leave their mother (and litter mates) at about 6 weeks of age, which according to West (1974) is the time that social play begins. Puppies are typically purchased at about 8 or 9 weeks of age, which is about the middle of the play period (Bekoff, 1974). A large proportion of 'predatory play', especially stalking and pouncing, is normally directed towards siblings. In the absence of siblings, pet cats and dogs may substitute objects.

Most examples of object play in mammals other than primates fall within the category of predatory play. Although rats investigate objects, I do not think they play with them. By this I mean they do not look to me to be playing, since I do not know how I would show that rats played with objects. They are not primarily predators, and so predatory play is absent. Most of the criteria for making the dissociation between exploration of objects and manipulatory play (Hutt, 1970) simply do not apply to rats. Rats do, however, use objects to run around during chasing and wrestling bouts. They may also climb onto an object in order to leap onto a play partner, and like many other small mammals (kittens, ferrets, mink) may enter a small object, such as a box or a tube, in order to wrestle with another animal.

It is only among the primates that one finds complex forms of object manipulations, the use of an object as an exploratory tool, and nonstereotypical, novel uses of objects as vehicles of play (Candland & French, 1978). The more complex forms of interaction with objects only occur in the more highly evolved forms of primate life. There is little evidence of object orientated play in wild prosimians (Doyle, 1974), or wild New World monkeys, although there is some evidence for object manipulation in captive members of both orders. There are many reports of object play in Old World monkeys, but it is in the lesser and greater apes that we see the widespread incorporation of objects into play sequence (Fagen 1981). As Candland & French (1978) suggest, one factor that influences the distribution of object play is the ability to manipulate. This is dependent upon the structural complexity and efficient functioning of the primate hand (Bishop, 1962).

Putting a cloth to sleep.   From the age of about 18 months the play, of the child gradually becomes more imaginative and symbolic. Indeed according to Susannah Miller's 5-year-old daughter (Miller, 1968) play is 'only when you pretend'. When we think of children playing we think of imaginative or fantasy play. Although as Fagen (1981) suggests we can imagine chimpanzees pretending to be leopards or baboons, such games have never been observed. (There is an anecdotal report of imaginary play in a hand-reared chimpanzee (Hayes, 1952).)

In the child, fantasy play initially involves objects, drinking from a toy cup, rocking dolls or teddys to sleep. But although the objects initially need to be realistic, they are in a sense incidental to play. They anchor make-believe (Fein, 1975), offering it realistic support. As the child gets older (and has learned to make believe) the objects are no longer necessary, one does not need the toy cup in order to drink, and imaginary babies can be rocked to sleep (whether bits of cloth as in Gilmore's example or just cupped arms). Games get more elaborate. Chairs make trains or aeroplanes, whole sequences of daily life can be enacted. But the objects as objects are less important. As this example of Catherine Garvey's (1977) shows:

> A child is able to arrange utensils on a table, serve another child, tell him not to eat with his knife, and warn him that the food is very hot — all quite realistically — she may also appropriate the iron to serve as a teapot, if a proper one is missing. She will be quite happy to serve apple sauce from an empty pan. She may be oblivious to the fact that the dining table was, moments ago, the family car, or she may tell her partner to use a stuffed animal for a chair . . . It appears that the complex action plan, here the notion of serving and dining, has become more important than the objects themselves.

Overtly fantasy play declines after about 7 years of age. But it would be difficult to say whether this is because fantasy play decreases, or whether, as Singer (1973), suggests such play simply becomes the day dreaming of the adult.

9.3 Is Play a Unitary Category?

As we have seen, play may be divided into several subcategories, such as locomotor play, object play, social play and fantasy play. I want here to consider whether play is a unitary behaviour or whether each 'type' of play may be considered as a separate entity. The question is one that has been raised several times in the literature on animal play. The position is not one on which violent disagreements are held, rather one on which people favour a different emphasis. The two positions can be characterized by the following quotations:

> What has to be done, therefore, is to investigate each of these different aspects of play separately and to find out what controls them and what function they perform in the infant's development.   (Chalmers, 1979)

> Grand syntheses are easier to proclaim than to achieve. However, I remain reluctant to dismiss the perceived unity of play . . . As long as this question remains open, the analysis of play will need to continue accepting evidence of all kinds.   (Fagen, 1981)

Let us consider the grounds for separating the behaviour into separate classes. One obvious reason for doing this is that not all animals that 'play' engage in all types of play. Locomotor play of some sort is found in most mammals, social rough-and-tumble play is found in social rodents, carnivores and primates. Apart from primates, social rough and tumble appears to be mainly confined to animals living in fairly complex social groups or in animals that hunt. Play differs in these two groups: in predators predatory sequences are commonly incorporated into social rough and tumble, which is not true of non-predators; compare for example Poole's work on rats (Poole & Fish, 1975) and ferret/polecats (Poole 1967, 1978). It is interesting to note that according to Fagen (1981), the skunk (which is the only *solitary omnivorous* mustelid) may not show any social rough-and-tumble play. Predatory object play is found in some captive and domesticated carnivores (particularly cats and dogs), but is surprisingly, though not completely, absent from most other carnivores (see Fagen, 1981, for details). Object manipulatory play is similarly common in captive primates, but is uncommon in most wild primates except apes (Candland & French, 1978). With the possible exception of home-reared apes (Hayes, 1952), fantasy play has only been observed in humans.

There is nothing odd about this distribution. It would be suprising to find animals 'playing' with a skill that they do not possess when adult. How could one see fantasy play in an animal that was not capable of abstract thought or symbolic processing? Probably the only surprising element in the distribution of play is that not all animals engage in social rough and tumble. The corresponding adult behaviour pattern (adult fighting) is present in mice, in squirrels, and in many other small mammals that do not play in this way. Since mice are sexually mature at 30 days, they have little time to play, but squirrels, gerbils and marmots have rather more youth than the rat: but they do not spend it in rough and tumble.

9.4   Is Play Distinct from Exploration?

Much of what constitutes animal play — rough-and-tumble fighting and chasing play, predatory and sexual play, play mothering as well as locomotor twists gambols and kicks — bears little relationship to exploration. The behaviour that constitutes similar play in children, the wrestling, running, jumping, chasing, fleeing and beating of rough and tumble play (Blurton-Jones, 1967), locomotor play, games and sports as well as fantasy and imitative play are not obviously related to exploration (not at least in the sense that the term is used in the present book). Nor, except by rather tortuous argument, does much of what constitutes post-mastery play (such as jumping from the stairs or swinging from rails) relate to exploration.

In fact, much of the behaviour that constitutes 'play' in children and all of the behaviour that constitutes 'play' in sub-primate mammals are quite distinct from exploration. The explicit (Welker 1961) or implicit (Hayes, 1958; Thorpe, 1963) assumption that play and exploration are equivalent behaviours is clearly misguided. The literature (Hutt, 1970; Weisler & McCall 1976; Welker, 1961) is not always clear on this point. When these authors discuss whether or not we can distinguish 'play' from 'exploration', they are in fact asking if we can distinguish *'exploratory' manipulation* of objects from *'playful' manipulation* of objects. It is a rather different question.

In Chapter 10, Hughes discusses some of the evidence for making this distinction. Her work, and that of Hutt (1970, 1979) has been mainly concerned with the temporal properties of manipulative play and exploration, and with the physiological correlates of exploratory and playful behaviour.

One other means of approaching the same question is exemplified by Weisler & McCall's (1976) review paper, in which they examine the variables (age, stimulus complexity, rearing environment) that influence play and exploration. It would be helpful to have some more systematic studies in this area. Those studies that are available (Lowe, 1975) suggest that exploration precedes play (ontogenetically as well as phylogenetically). It is almost certainly the case that compared with play it occurs relatively more frequently in adults than it does in children.

9.5 Is Play Motivated?

Although in the past, play was considered as 'goalless' (Patrick, 1916), or 'useless in the eyes of the beholder' (Schlosberg, 1947), there is an increasing tendency to see it both as a functional behaviour (Fagen, 1981; Smith, 1982) and as a motivated behaviour (Fagen, 1981). The evidence that locomotor and rough- and-tumble play is motivated is quite stong: first both children and animals invite play from one another. If children or animals are well fed and in a familiar place they will almost invariably play. If deprived of locomotor or rough-and-tumble play, in the classroom (Smith & Hagen, 1980) or when dogs or rats are deprived of playmates (Bekoff, 1964; Einon et al., 1978; Panksepp & Beatty, 1980) they will show 'rebound' effects; play will occur at the first oppor- tunity and will continue for longer than normal. Rats will even learn a maze in order to engage in rough and tumble with a playmate (and will learn as quickly as they would for food). Moreover, they will learn to choose the more playful of two companions (Humphreys & Einon, 1981).

But is more 'serious' or post-mastery play motivated? Perhaps the most characteristic aspect of play in children is the frequency with which it occurs. A well nourished 10-month-old child will manipulate objects for most of its waking day. Similarly a 3-year-old will spend a large proportion of each day in post mastery and fantasy play. There is, to my knowledge, no evidence of 'rebound effects' in manipulative play, but there is considerable evidence that manipula- tion may serve as a reinforcer in monkeys (Harlow et al., 1956; Mason et al., 1959). And surely, at some time most parents will have used play as a rein- forcer; they will have bribed their children to perform a nonpreferred task in order to engage in a favourite game. Indeed one method by which parents get 'difficult' children to eat or to get dressed is to turn the whole thing into a game.

9.6 Is Human Play Distinct from Animal Play?

My brief in writing this chapter was to link the human and animal literature on play and exploration. It is frequently implied that play and exploration are diffi- cult both to define and to differentiate and I have tried to show how limited this problem is: most play is, as we have seen, clearly distinct from exploration. I want in this section to consider whether or not we can see human play as a continuation of animal play.

Locomotor play, jumping, running and leaping is seen in similar forms in most mammals from lambs to humans. Social rough and tumble also shows very similar forms in rats, kittens, monkeys and humans. This continuity

222

implies (though in no way proves) that such behaviours may have a common function.

Fagen (1976, 1981) has made a very strong case for considering locomotor play as physical training. He argues that animals incur the cost of energy expenditure in active physical play in order to get the future benefits of well exercised muscles and superior general physical capacity. The evidence for this hypothesis is discussed at length by Fagen (1981), and more briefly by Smith (1982). Social rough and tumble is often considered in terms of practice for adult fighting skills (Smith, 1982) or the development of dominance (Symonds, 1978). However, there is no evidence in animals or in humans that social rough and tumble is related to agonistic dominance (Strayer, 1977; Symonds, 1978), or to individual differences in aggression (Blurton-Jones, 1972; Di Pietro, 1981). I have argued elsewhere (Einon, 1980; Einon et al., 1981) that the distribution of rough and tumble play in mammals is in any case inconsistent with such a view, and have suggested that rough and tumble social play induces social flexibility with secondary benefits in behavioural flexibility.

Locomotor play and social rough and tumble show a continuity across mammalian species. Although there are several reports of object play in zoo animals, such as the giant panda (Wilson & Kleiman, 1974) and the rhinoceros (Inhelder, 1955), there are no reports of object play in feral members of these species. Many animals can be taught to perform 'playful' tricks (I have taught rats to push balls through tubes, and pigs can be taught to vacuum the floor — Breland & Breland, 1966), and for this reason we should perhaps be cautious of reports of object 'play' in zoo animals. It is possible that object play would occur in the well fed feral members of a number of species if they lacked social companions, but probably, the combination of ample food, and no companions would not occur in the wild.

The 'predatory' object play of the kitten is found in several carnivores (again more frequently in captivity), but the playful manipulation of objects occurs only in the great apes and humans.

Bruner (1972) has suggested that one of the major factors in the emergence of object play in the great apes is the very large increase in a type of observational learning that Kohler (1925) refers to as serious play. Bruner (1972, pp. 156–157) quotes the following example:

> I would call the following behaviour of a chimpanzee imitation of the 'serious play' type. On the playground a man has painted a wooden pole in white colour. After the work is done he goes away leaving behind a pot of white paint and a beautiful brush. I observe the only chimpanzee who is present, hiding my face behind my hands, as if I were not paying attention to him. The ape for a while gives much attention to me before approaching the brush and the paint because he has learned that misuse of our things may have serious consequences. But very soon, encouraged by my attitude, he takes the brush, puts it into the pot of colour and paints a big stone which happens to be in the place, beautifully white. The whole time the ape behaved completely seriously. So did others when imitating the washing of laundry or the use of a borer.

I think it is possible to see in this example a continuity between the great apes and the human child, between for example Jane Van Lawick-Goodall's (1968) Chimpanzee Flint who:

> When he was 2.8 years old, was twice observed using grass tools out of context. Both instances occurred during the termite-fishing season: once he pushed a grass carefully though the hair on his own leg, touched the end of the tool to his lips, repeated the movement and then cast the grass aside. On the other occasion he pushed a dry stem carefully into his elder sibling's groin three times in succession.

and May Edel's report (Leacock, 1971) of the Chiga of Uganda:

> Playing with a small gourd, a child learns to balance it on his head, and is applauded when he goes to the watering-place with the other children and brings it back with a little water in it.

Such 'serous play' can be seen as direct practice of adult skills. It requires, as Bruner suggests, the ability to model one's behaviour, to engage in what we have called elsewhere 'post-mastery play': the trying out of new skills in a different context. It requires also the ability to observe one's own behaviour as it were 'from outside' (Bruner, 1972) and to adjust behaviour to fit that of the model. In the great apes we see this ability in 'play' at termite fishing or nest building. In children, such modelling pervades the child's whole behaviour. It 'plays' with each skill as it develops: thus manipulatory play with objects is observed from about 5–6 months when manipulatory skills develop, and make believe play is at its height between the ages of 18 months and 7 or 8 years, when children learn to refer to objects in their absence, and to communicate by language and gesture. In each case the child might be said in some sense to be engaging in post-mastery play. But the functions of such play may well be 'pre-mastery': the development of more complex skills.

When Kohler used the term 'serious play' he meant rather more than play with a serious intent. Post-mastery play and fantasy play *is* more serious: it lacks the 'joie de vivre' that is so characteristic of locomotor or rough-and-tumble play. It is locomotor play or rough and tumble that appears to the observer to be enjoyed for purely its own sake (Tinkelpaugh, 1942) or expresses a joy of living (Pycraft, 1912). When we say we recognise play when we see it, or that naive observers can agree that a behaviour is 'play', it is this 'Joie-de-vivre' which we sense (Beach, 1945):

> Even the most militant and objective 'behaviourist' cannot seriously object to the statement that the dog, which romps through the snow barking, leaping, dashing wildly hither and yon, or plays fetch with his master, is enjoying and experience.

The group glee of nursery school children described by Sherman (1975) may be related to this playful exuberance.

Are functions of 'serious' and 'exuberant' play different? Locomotor gambolling and social rough and tumble are not direct practice for adult behaviour, although indirectly they do influence adult abilities (Einon *et al.*, 1978). But it is hard to imagine that serious or post-mastery play does not serve as indirect practice, or as a means of developing skills. The changing forms of children's play tend to reflect newly acquired abilities. The changes in play are

224

also associated with normal growth and maturation; indeed, the failure of play to evolve often signals developmental problems (Garvey, 1977).

The study of development has traditionally placed great emphasis on the long-term effects of early experience. Bowlby's (1951) work on maternal deprivation in children and Harlow's (1961) work on maternal deprivation in monkeys are in this tradition (both stem from a Freudian psychoanalytical approach to development). Hebb's (1949) rather different approach also emphasized the dependence of later learning upon earlier experience (see Denenberg, 1972, or Scott, 1968). Play, however, has always been outside this tradition.

In 1974 Lazar & Beckhorn criticized studies of play because, they claimed, the study of play distracted from the study of development. They suggested that by calling behaviour 'play' we direct our investigations towards the behaviour of young animals as young animals, ignoring the ways in which immature behaviour develops. In 1974, the criticism was perhaps more valid than it is today. There have been several recent longitudinal studies of play and development (Bateson & Young, 1980; Caro, 1979; Meaney & Stewart, 1981), although these have perhaps been more influenced by Kagen's (1978) and Bateson's (1981) claim that there is little evidence that the young animals' experience necessarily predicts the adults' behaviour. (Clarke & Clarke, 1978, reach a similar conclusion following an analysis of the human literature.) But both the viewpoints that are typified on the one hand by Bowlby's (1951) and Hebb's (1949) writing and on the other by Kagan's (1978), Bateson's (1981) and the Clarkes' (1978) are supported by these longitudinal studies. Object play and immature predation in cats may point to a continuity between some 'play behaviour' and adult predation. (But this does not explain why so much of the kittens' behaviour is playful.) But although, in cats, object play resembles mature predatory behaviour, not all immature behaviours are less complex versions of adult behaviour (Kagen, 1978). Indeed the young sometimes have specially adapted capacities for a particular stage in their life cycle, filial imprinting in birds (Bateson, 1979) or suckling in mammals being obvious examples. Exuberant play is almost certainly another example: it is not direct practice for adult behaviour.

The gentle fighting that follows rough and tumble in many mammals, and the immature predation of objects and siblings, may gradually merge into adult fighting or predation; but it would be wrong to assume that all 'post mastery' and 'serious play' is such literal practice for adult skills. Bateson (1981), and Kagan (1978) both suggest that progress from one stage of development to another is not always smooth; that is, that there is discontinuity in development. This has long been the view of those who study human development where the study of developmental stages, and the progress between them, has long been an acceptable research strategy.

Is play distinct from exploration? Most of the behaviour that constitutes 'play' in children and all of the behaviour that constitutes 'play' in sub-primate mammals is quite distinct from exploration. Is human play distinct from animal play? Human play certainly departs from that of animals; much of it is 'serious' play, and much of it involves fantasy or formal rules, but then humans depart from other mammals in so many abilities. If the play of the young reflects the abilities of the adult, we should not be surprised by this difference whether or not we call post mastery and 'serious play' play, or indeed whether we call the kittens predation of ping-pong balls play, is clearly a matter of definition.

References

ALDIS, O. (1975) *Play Fighting*. New York: Academic Press.

BAERENDS-VAN ROON, J. M. and BAERENDS, G. P. (1979) *The Morphogenesis of tne Domestic Cat, with Special Emphasis on Prey Catching Behaviour*. Amsterdam: North Holland.

BALDWIN, J. D. and BALDWIN, J. I. (1974) Exploration and play in squirrel monkeys (*Saimiri*). *American Zoologist* **14**, 303-315.

BARASH, D. P. (1973) The social biology of the Olympic marmot. *Animal Behaviour Monographs* **6**, 171-245.

BARASH, D. P. (1976) The social behaviour and individual differences in free living alpine marmots (*Marmota marmota*). *Animal Behaviour* **24**, 27-35.

BATESON, P. P. G. (1979) How do sensitive periods arise and what are they for? *Animal Behaviour* **27**, 270-486.

BATESON, P. P. G. (1981) Discontinuities in development, and changes in the organisation of play in cats. In *Behavioral Development* (Eds. K. IMMELMANN, G. BARLOW, M. MAIN and L. PETRINOVICH). Cambridge: Cambridge University Press.

BATESON, P. P. G. and YOUNG, M. (1981) Separation from the mother and the development of play in cats. *Animal Behaviour* **29**, 173-180.

BEACH, F. (1945) Current concepts of play. *American Naturalist* **79**, 217-238.

BEKOFF, M. (1974) Social play and play-soliciting by infant canids. *American Zoologist* **14**, 323-340.

BISHOP, N. (1962) Control of the hand in lower primates. *Annals of the New York Academy of Sciences* **102**, 316-337.

BLURTON-JONES, N. G. (1967) An ethological study of some aspects of social behaviour of children in nursery school. In *Primate Ethology* (Ed. D. MORRIS), pp. 347-368. Chicago: Aldine.

BLURTON-JONES, N. G. (1972) Categories of child-child interaction. In *Ethological Studies of Child Behaviour* (Ed. N. G. BLURTON-JONES), pp. 97-127. London: Cambridge University Press.

BOWLBY, J. (1951) *Maternal Care and Mental Health*. Geneva: World Health Organization.

BRELAND, K. and BRELAND, M. (1966) *Animal Behaviour*. New York: Macmillan.

BRUNER, J. (1972) The nature and uses of immaturity. *American Psychologist* **27**, 687-708.

BRUNER, J. (1973) Competence in infants. In *Beyond the Information Given* (Ed. J. M. ANGLIN). New York: Norton.

CARO, T. M. (1979) Relations between kitten behaviour and adult. *Zeitschrift für Tierpsychologie* **51**, 158-68.

CARO, T. M. (1980a) Effects of the mother, object play, and adult experience on predation in cats. *Behavioral and Neural Biology* **29**, 29-51.

CARO, T. M. (1980b) The effects of experience on the predatory pattern of cats.

Behavioral and Neural Biology **29**, 1–28.

CANDLAND, D. K. and FRENCH, J. A. (1978) Object play: test of a categorized model by the genesis of object-play in *Macaca fuscata*. In *Social Play in Primates* (Ed. E. O. SMITH). New York: Academic Press.

CHALMERS, N. (1979) *Social Behaviour in Primates*. London: Edward Arnold.

CLARKE, A. M. and CLARKE, A. D. B. (1978) *Early Experience: Myth and Evidence*. London: Open Books.

DENENBERG, V. H. (1972) *Readings in the Development of Behavior*. Stanford: Sinauer Associates.

DI PIETRO, J. A. (1981) Rough and tumble play: a function of gender. *Developmental Psychology* **17**, 50–58.

DOYLE, G. A. (1974) Behavior of posimians. In *Behavior of Nonhuman Primates*, Vol. 5 (Ed. A.M. SCHRIER and F. STOLLNITZ), pp. 155–353. New Yorke: Academic Press.

EGAN, J. (1976) Object play in cats. Reprinted in *Play: its Role in Development and Evolution* (Eds. J. BRUNER, A. JOLLY and W. SYLVA). New York: Basic Books.

EINON, D. F. (1980) The purpose of play. In *Not Work Alone*. (Eds. J. CHERFAS and R. LEWIN). London: Temple Smith.

EINON, D. F., HUMPHREYS, A. P., CHIVERS, S. M., FIELD, S. and NAYLOR, V. (1981) Isolation has permanent effects upon the behaviour of the rat, but not the mouse, gerbil, or guinea pig. *Developmental Psychobiology* **14**, 343–355.

EINON, D. F. and MORGAN, M. J. (1978) Habituation under different levels of stimulation in socially reared and isolated rats: a test of the arousal hypothesis. *Behavioral Biology* **22**, 553–558.

EINON, D. F., MORGAN, M. J. and KIBBLER, C. C. (1978) Brief periods of socialisation and later behaviour in the rat. *Developmental Psychobiology* **11**, 213–225.

ELLIOTT, L. (1978) Social behavior and foraging ecology of the eastern chipmunk (*Tanias striatus*) in the Achirondack mountains. *Smithsonian Contributions to Zoology*, Number 265.

EWER, R. F. (1971) The biology and behaviour of a free-living population of black rats (*Rattus rattus*) *Animal Behaviour Monographs* **4**, part 3.

FAGEN, R. M. (1976) Exercise, play, and physical training in animals. In *Perspectives in ethology, Vol. 2* (Eds. P. P. G. BATESON and P. H. KLOPFER). New York: Plenum Press.

FAGEN, R. (1981) *Animal Play Behavior*. New York: Oxford University Press.

FEIN, G. (1975) A transformational analysis of pretending. *Developmental Psychology* **11**, 291–296.

GARVEY, C. (1977) *Play*. London: Fontana/Open Books.

GILMORE, J. B. (1966) Play, a special behaviour: In *Current Research in Motivation* (Ed. R. N. HABER). New York: Holt Rinehart and Winston Inc.

GUYOT, G. W., BENNETT, T. L. and CROSS, H. A. (1980) The effects of social isolation on the behaviour of juvenile domestic cats. *Developmental Psychobiology* **13**, 317–329.

HARLOW, H. F. (1961) The development of affectional patterns in infant monkeys. In *Determinants of Infant Behavior* (Ed. B. M. FOSS). London : Methuen.

HARLOW, H. F., BLAZEK, N. C. and McCLEARN, G. E. (1956) Manipulatory motivation in infant rhesus monkeys. *Journal of Comparative and Physiological Psychology* **49**, 444–448.

HAYES, C. (1952) *The Ape in Our House*. London: Gollancz.

HAYES, J. R. (1958) The maintenance of play in young children. *Journal of Comparative and Physiological Psychology* **51**, 788–790.

HEBB, D. O. (1949) *The Organization of Behavior*. New York: John Wiley.

HINDE, R. A. (1974) *The Biological Bases of Human Social Behaviour*. New York: McGraw-Hill.

HORWICH, R. H. (1972) The ontogency of social behavior in the grey squirrel (*Sciurus carolinensis*). *Zietschrift für Tierpsychologie* Suppl. 8.

HUMPHREYS, A. P. (1982). The behavioural significance of animal play. Unpublished Ph. D. thesis, University of Durham.

HUMPHREYS, A. P. and EINON, D. F. (1981) Play as a reinforcer for maze-learning in juvenile rats. *Animal Behaviour* **29**, 259–70.

HUTT, C. (1970) Specific and diversive exploration. *Advances in Child Development and Behaviour* **5**, 119–180.

HUTT, C. (1979) Exploration and play. In *Play and Learning* (Ed. B. SUTTON-SMITH). New York: Gardner Press.

INHELDER, E. (1955) Zur Psychologie einiger Verhaltensweisen-besonders des spiels. *Zeitschrift für Tierpsychologie* **12**, 88–144.

KAGAN, J. (1978) Continuity and stages in human development. In *Perspectives in Ethology, Vol. 3.* (Eds. P. P. G. BATESON and P. H. KLOPFER). New York: Plenum Press.

KING, J. A. (1955) Social behavior, social organization, and population dynamics in a black-tailed prairie dog town in the Black Hills of South Dakota. *University of Michigan Contributions to the Laboratory of Vertebrate Biology*, No. 67.

KOHLER, W. (1925) *The Mentality of Apes*. New York: Routledge and Kegan Paul.

KUO, Z. Y. (1930) The genesis of the cats responses to the rat. *Journal of Comparative Psychology* **11**, 1–35.

LANCASTER, J. B. (1971) Playmothering: the relation between juvenile females and young infants among free-ranging vervet monkeys (*Cercopithecus aethiops*) *Folia Primatologica* **15**, 161–182.

LAWICK-GOODALL, J. VAN (1968) The behaviour of free-living chimpanzees in the Gombe Stream Reserve. *Animal Behaviour Monographs* **1**, 161–311.

LAZAR, J. W. and BECKHORN, G. D. (1974) Social play or the development of social behavior in ferrets (*Mustela putorius*) *American Zoologist* **14**, 405–414.

LEACOCK, E. (1971) At play in African villages. *Natural History Magazine*: Special Supplement on 'Play'.

LEYHAUSEN, P. (1956) Verhaltensstudien bei Katzen. *Zeitschrift für tierpsychologie. Beiheft 2*.

LOIZOS, C. (1967) Play behavior in higher primates: a review. In *Primate Ethology* (Ed. D. MORRIS). Chicago: Aidine.

LOWE, M. (1975) Trends in the development of representational play in infants from one to three years: an observational study. *Journal of Child Psychology* **16**, 33–48.

MASON, W. A. (1965) Determinants of social behavior in young chimpanzees. In *Behavior of Nonhuman Primates, Vol. 2* (Eds. A. M. SCHRIER, H. F. HARLOW and F. STOLLNITZ). New York: Academic Press.

MASON, W. A., HARLOW, H. F. and RUEPING, R. R. (1959) The development of manipulatory responses in the infant rhesus monkey. *Journal of Comparative and Physiological Psychology* **52**, 555–558.

McDONALD, D. L. (1977) Play and exercise in the California Ground Squirrel (*Spermophilus beecheyi*), *Animal Behaviour* **25**, 782–784.

MEANEY, M. J. and STEWART, J. (1981) A descriptive study of social development in the rat. *Animal Behaviour* **29**, 34–45.

MEYER-HOLZAPFEL, M. (1958) Boquetins en captivite. *Mammalia* **22**, 90–103.

MILLER, S. (1973) Ends means and galumphing: some leitmotifs of play. *American Anthropologist* **75**, 87–98.

MILLER, S. (1968) *The Psychology of play* Harmondsworth: Penguin Books.

228

O'KEEFE, J. and NADEL, L. (1978) *The Hippocampus as a Cognitive Map.* Oxford: Clarendon Press.

PANKSEPP, J. and BEATTY, W. W. (1980) Social deprivation and play in rats. *Behavioral and Neural Biology* **30**, 197–206.

PATRICK, G. T. W. (1916) *The Psychology of Relaxation.* New York: Hougton Mifllin.

POOLE, T. B. (1967) Aspects of aggressive play in polecats. *Zeitschrift für Tierpsychologie* **24**, 351–348.

POOLE, T. B. (1978) Social play in polecats. *Animal Behaviour* **26**, 36–49.

POOLE, T. B. and FISH, J. (1975) An investigation of playful behaviour in *Rattus norvegicus* and *Mus musculus* (Mammalia). *Journal of Zoology (Lond.)* **175**, 61–71.

PYCRAFT, W. P. (1912) *The Infancy of Animals.* London: Hutchinson and Co.

RANDRUP, A. and MUNKVAD, I. (1970) Biochemical, anotomical, and psychological investigations of stereotyped behaviour induced by amphetamines. In *Amphetamine and related compounds* (Ed. E. COSTA and S. GARRATINI). New York: Raven Press.

RHYS, J. (1930) *After Leaving Mr Mackenzie.* London: Jonathan Cape.

ROBBINS, T. W. and IVERSEN, S. D. (1973) A dissociation of the effects of *d*-amphetamine on locomotor activity and exploration in rats. *Psychopharmacologie (Berlin)* **28**, 155–164.

ROWELL, T. E. (1961) The family group in golden hamsters: its formation and break up. *Behaviour* **17**, 81–94.

SCHLOSBERG, M. (1947) The concept of play. *Psychological Review* **54**, 229–251.

SCOTT, J. P. (1968) *Early Experience and the Organization of Behaviour.* Belmont, California: Wadsworth.

SHERMAN, L. (1975) An ecological study of glee in small groups of preschool children. *Child Development* **46**, 53–61.

SINGER, J. (1973) *The Child's World of Make Believe.* New York: Academic Press.

SMITH, P. K. (1982) Does play matter?: Functional and evolutionary aspects of animal and human play. *The Brain and Behavioral Sciences* **5(1)**, in press.

SMITH, P. K. and HAGEN, T. (1980) Effects of deprivation on exercise play in nursery school children. *Animal Behaviour* **28**, 922–928.

STEINER, A. L. (1971) Play activity of Columbian ground squirrels. *Zeitschrift für Tierpsychologie* **28**, 247–261.

STRAYER, J. (1977) Social conflict and peer-group status. In *Ethological Perspectives on Preschool Social Organization* (Ed. F. F. STRAYER). Memo de Recherche, Department of Psychology, University of Quebec.

SYMONDS, D. (1978) The question of function: dominance and play. In *Social Play in Primates* (Ed. E.D. SMITH). New York: Academic Press.

THORPE, W. H. (1963) *Learning and Instinct in Animals.* Harvard: University Press.

TINKLEPAUGH, O. L. (1942) Social behavior in animals. In *Comparative Psychology* (Ed. F.A. MOSS). New York: Prentice Hall.

UTTLEY, A. (1943) *Country Hoard.* London: Faber and Faber.

WEISLER, A. and McCALL, R. B. (1976) Exploration and play: Resumé and redirection. *American Psychologist* **31**, 492–508.

WELKER, W. I. (1961) Ontogeny of play and exploratory behaviors: a definition of problems and a search for new conceptual solutions. In *The Ontogeny of Vertebrate Behaviour* (Ed. H. MOLTZ). New York: Academic Press.

WEST, M. (1974) Social play in the domestic cat. *American Zoologist* **14**, 427–436.

WILSON, S. (1973) The development of social behaviour in the vole (*Microtus agrestis*). *Zoological Journal of Linnean Society* **52**, 45–62.

WILSON, S. C. and KLEIMAN, D. G. (1974) Eliciting play: a comparative study. *American Zoologist* **14**, 341–370.

CHAPTER 10

Exploration and Play in Young Children

Miranda Hughes

10.1 Introduction

Imagine a child, sitting alone in a room, surrounded by familiar toys, smiling and talking to itself, and engrossed in an idiosyncratic game. Then imagine the same child, led by an adult into the same room which still contains some of those familiar toys together with a strange new object it has never seen before. The former situation is universally recognized as 'playful', but in the latter situation most children are irresistibly drawn to the strange new object; they are inquisitive about its origins and its possible purpose; their faces take on a serious expression and they do not immediately incorporate the new toy in the kinds of game they play with familiar toys; they 'explore' it first. In an experiment that mimicked these conditions, Hutt (1966) described in detail exploratory and play behaviour. In a subsequent review (Hutt, 1970), she encapsulated the nature of these two types of behaviour by articulating the questions that are implicit in them: during exploration a child asks 'what does this object do?', during play it asks 'what can I do with this object?'.

Of course, exploration is not confined to the investigation of specific objects. Berlyne (1960) distinguished the kind of 'specific exploration' described above from 'diversive exploration' in which a child might be searching round a room looking for something to do. Typically, such a child might have a slightly bored facial expression and would engage in desultory investigation of previously ignored objects (such as light switches). Thus, to return to the imaginary situation of the child in a room, it is possible to identify three behavioural states: '*playful activity*' during which a child is relaxed and happily engaged in a game involving familiar toys; '*specific exploration*' in which attention is focused on a particular new toy and the child is actively investigating its properties; and '*diversive exploration*' in which enjoyment of familiar toys is apparently temporarily satiated and the child is looking for something else (undefined) to do.

The intuitive temporal relationship between these three behavioural states is examined in more detail in a review by Nunnally & Lemond (1973). They propose that there is a continuous cycle for any organism in which the encounter of a new stimulus is followed first by attention and exploration, then by play activity, and finally by further searching. This cycle is depicted in Fig. 10.1, in which the inside of the parabola describes the presumed covert cognitive processes that underlie the observable behaviour.

There are three important aspects of exploration and play to which particular attention will be paid in this chapter: firstly, the motivational antecedents of the different behavioural states; second, their specific morphological features; and finally, their consequences in development.

10.2 Motivational Antecedents of Exploration and Play

When a child encounters any object, the behavioural response will depend largely on the 'information' (or perceived novelty and complexity) inherent in the object itself, but also depends on the endogenous state of the child. The first of these factors is amenable to experimental manipulation, the second is both more difficult to define and less amenable to measurement and manipulation; however, the importance of state is evident when one considers that some children (autists) find any novelty so aversive that they engage in little exploratory behaviour and show 'an intensive preoccupation with maintaining sameness' (Stroh & Buick, 1970, p. 161).

The extent to which object novelty affects exploratory activity has been consi-

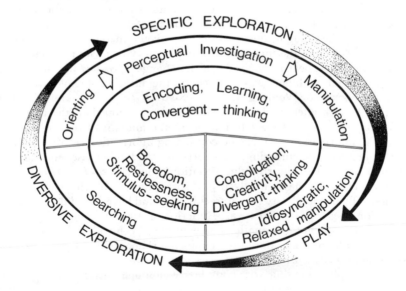

Fig. 10.1   The exploration-play cycle.

dered by Hutt (1966) using the following experimental paradigm. Children who had become accustomed to spending 10-min periods playing alone in a room (with an adult observer present), were confronted with a novel toy; the toy consisted of a red box (12 in × 6 in × 6 in) mounted on four brass legs, with a lever that could activate a bell, a buzzer, and four digital counters. Four experimental conditions were observed, under each of which the toy differed in complexity:

1. no sound or visual feedback (bell and buzzer switched off and counters covered);
2. vision only (noises off, but counters visible);
3. sound only (bell and buzzer on, counters covered);
4. sound and visual feedback (noises on, counters visible).

In general, when the children entered the room they looked immediately at the novel toy; they would then examine the object manually or inspect it visually while holding the lever, and finally engage in active manipulation of the lever. The children's behaviour was observed for 10 min; they then left the playroom but returned for five subsequent 10-min sessions at daily intervals. Hutt reported that exploratory responses to the toy ('those responses that involved visual inspection, and feeling, touching or other manipulations accompanied by visual inspection', p. 69) decreased over sessions and that there was a slower rate of decay in exploration with the more complex forms of the toy.

Schneider (1981) has used a similar experimental design, but manipulated the novelty and complexity (or information value) of the toy in a slightly different manner. In his study, the contingent effects of the lever changed at varying time intervals: thus, a forward movement of the lever might operate a buzzer for one minute, and then the light for the second minute. It was predicted that the changing effects of the lever would increase the toy's novelty and thereby lengthen the time spent in exploratory behaviour. In fact, some children did not appear to be aware of the changes; *perceived* novelty was not therefore altered, and there was no effect on the duration of exploration.

Studies reported by Wohlwill (1975), by Switzky et al. (1974), and by Switzky et al. (1979) have attempted to evaluate the proposition that 'the amount of exploratory behaviour is directly related to the amount of time required to resolve the information conflict (the competing information relative to identifying, labelling, remembering, categorizing, and otherwise encoding the stimulus) inherent in the stimulus situation' (Switzky et al., 1974, p. 321). These experiments have involved the presentation of shapes that vary systematically in complexity to young children, and have found that voluntary exploration does tend to increase as a function of stimulus complexity but that the relationship is not systematic. For example, Wohlwill (1975) found that 8-year-old children spent more time exploring shapes with 20 turns (corners) than those with 40 turns; kindergarten children, however, showed a monotonic increase in exploration time with complexity although the absolute differences between complexity conditions were very small (a mean of 22 s spent exploring triangular shapes compared to a mean of 28 s spent with 40-turn shapes).

232

It is well established, then, that stimulus novelty affects the time that children spend in exploration, although measures of stimulus novelty are often based on measures of complexity that are intuitive rather than absolute. The other important variable affecting the motivation of exploratory behaviour is a child's psychological 'state': an infant in a mildly stressful situation (for example, temporarily separated from a caretaker) is less likely to engage in active exploration of new toys (Rheingold & Eckerman, 1969, 1970), than an infant whose caretaker is present.

Considerable experimental effort has been expended in trying to develop an acceptable measure of psychological state in terms of physiological arousal. Hutt (1979), for instance, argued that the protracted latency to, and cursory mode of exploration in, autistic children could be explained by their chronically high neurophysiological arousal. However, the correlations between different measures of physiological arousal (electroencephalogram (EEG), heart-rate (HR), galvanic skin response (GSR), respiration, pupillary dilation, etc.) are not consistent across experimental conditions and cannot be shown to be systematically related to behavioural states (Lacey, 1967; Lacey & Lacey, 1970). Thus, the idea that there may be a physiological arousal system that acts as a motivational substrate for exploratory behaviour has not been substantiated. Nonetheless, there is tentative evidence that a psychophysiological model of exploration and play might have some validity: exploratory behaviour has been shown to correlate with suppression of heart-rate-variability (HRV), whereas play is associated with high HRV (Hughes & Hutt, 1979). These findings cannot, however, be regarded as evidence of a *motivational* system that can be described in physiological terms; it seems more likely that motivation to explore will be better understood in terms of individual differences in perceived novelty, and the reinforcement of contingent responses: see Stratton (1982) for further discussion of this.

The transition from exploratory to playful behaviour does not occur with either the inevitability or the smoothness that Fig. 10.1 might suggest. Play only occurs when environmental conditions provide absolute security; for example, Sutton-Smith (1971) has found that play occurs relatively rarely in subsistence cultures where demands are made on children to contribute to the pressing needs of survival (e.g. food and water collection and care of infants), and Fein (1981) has documented several sources of evidence that indicate that high levels of anxiety (clinically defined) disrupt play behaviour.

Early writers (e.g. Spencer, 1855) believed that surplus energy provided the primary motivation for play, and that when the demands of the environment did not require the use of a child's total energy potential a surplus accumulated which was used during play. However, this view was subsequently refuted by Groos (1898) who pointed out that play often occurs when an organism is tired; he thought (*loc cit.*, p. 368) that two main principles were implicated in motivating play '. . . the discharge of surplus energy and recreation for exhausted powers. They may operate simultaneously'.

It is suggested by Hughes & Hutt (1979) that play behaviour may be largely motivated by a child's desire to maintain information processing at optimal

233

levels. That is, when a child engages in play behaviour he or she maintains stimulus input, and thereby physiological state, at an optimal level to respond to novel environmental stimuli. In this way, the motivation for play may be regarded as *intrinsic*, in contrast to the motivation for specific exploration which is *extrinsic* (i.e. exploration is a behavioural response to some novel external stimulus). Similarly the motivation for diversive exploration is also intrinsic: a child actively seeks out novelty when interaction with the stimuli available no longer maintains information processing within optimal limits.

Thus, the motivational antecedents of exploration and play are quite distinctive: external factors have greater salience in motivating specific exploration, whereas play and diversive exploration appear to be largely intrinsically motivated.

10.3 Morphological Features of Exploration and Play

Groos's book *The Play of Man* (1898), was an attempt to provide a scholarly analysis of human play. He was perhaps the first author to acknowledge that it is the inventive nature of play that makes it impossible to encapsulate the full meaning of the term in a brief definition; Beach (1945, p. 539) subsequently alluded to this problem and concluded that 'any serviceable definition of play must be based on a number of predominating characteristics'. In effect, this requires that any definition of play should be a description of behavioural characteristics. Beach (1945) himself, for example, listed the outstanding characteristics of play behaviour as follows:

1. It carries an emotional element of pleasure.
2. It is usually characteristic of the immature animal rather than the adult.
3. It has no immediate biological result affecting the existence of the individual or species.
4. Its forms are relatively species specific.
5. Its amount, duration and diversity within a species are related to the phylogenetic position of that species.

Loizos (1966) refers to the re-ordering, exaggeration, repetition and fragmentation of behavioural elements that occur during play; and Einon (Chapter 9) has given some descriptions of playful behaviour of this type in both animals and children. Einon further alludes to the paradox inherent in using the term 'play' to subsume post-mastery behaviour that does not have any very evident expression of emotional pleasure. Hutt (1979) attempted to deal with this problem by proposing a 'playfulness' spectrum of play behaviour that ranged from exploratory to ludic states: the post-mastery behaviour described by Einon could presumably be allocated in the centre of this spectrum and might be amenable to the descriptive definitions of the type that Loizos (*loc. cit.*), Beach (*loc. cit.*), Welker (1961) and others have used for play.

Although clear behavioural description enables an observer to distinguish exploration from play, the scientific aspirations of behavioural research have

234

provoked some attempts to quantify these differences. For example, it has been demonstrated that when first confronted with a novel toy most children do the same things, in the same order; this loose statement can be quantified in terms of the probability of a child initially selecting one behavioural element (e.g. visual inspection) and the contingent probabilities of a transition from this to another specified behavioural element (e.g. touching the toy with one finger). A sequential probability analysis of this type is reported by Hughes (1978, 1979); it uses the same behavioural element definitions for both exploration and play, and defines an 'uncertainty' (U) measure such that $U = -\sum_{i=1}^{i} p_i \log_2 p_i$ where p_i is the probability of occurrence of behavioural element i. This measure (which is basically a measure of constraint) is then amenable to statistical analysis, and reveals a statistically significant difference in the relative sequential constraints of behaviour during exploration and play: exploration being more constrained than play.

Table 10.1 contains a summary of the distinctive features of specific exploration, play and diversive exploration. This summary owes much to the formulation posited by Hutt (1970), but extends that analysis by drawing a distinction between diversive exploration and play. Nonetheless, these three behavioural categories are still inadequate to subsume the range of behaviours in what Nunnally & Lemond (1973) regard as a continuous cycle: it has already been suggested that there is a set of 'post-mastery' behaviour that occurs temporally between exploration and play (and this set would be analogous to the Phase II exploratory behaviour described by Nunnally & Lemond), but there is further need to extend our analysis of the category 'diversive exploration'. In Section 10.1, it was indicated that once a child had finished playing its facial expression might become bored, and it would engage in desultory manipulation of surrounding objects. However, this type of behaviour is distinct both from a conscious 'seeking-out' of novel stimuli and from the behaviour that Wohlwill (1981, p. 6) has termed 'vigilant exploration':

> a continuous perceptual scanning and frequently locomotor traversal of a given environment to minimize threats from unknown stimuli and facilitate appropriate action under potentially unstable environmental conditions.

Yet all three of these behaviours are preliminary to the encounter of a novel stimulus that would provoke specific exploration.

10.4 Exploration and Play: Consequences for Later Development

The distinctions that can be made between exploration and play in terms of their motivational antecedents and behavioural characteristics indicate that there may be some validity in investigating possible differences in outcomes. In the previous section, it was suggested that exploration and play are part of a continuous cycle of behaviour that also incorporates the non-playful practice of certain skills. This description subsumes only those types of behaviour that are

235

Table 10.1 Characteristics of Specific Exploration, Play and Diverse Exploration

	Specific exploration	Play	Diversive exploration
1.	Implicit query 'what does this object do?'	Implicit query 'what can I do with this object?'	Implicit query 'where can I find something to do?'
2.	Intent, concentrated, facial expression	Relaxed facial expression	*not documented*
3.	Stereotyped sequence of behavioural elements	Elements essentially brief	*not documented*
4.	Extrinsically motivated (elicited by novel stimuli)	Intrinsically motivated (never shown in presence of novel stimuli)	Intrinsically motivated
5.	Consummatory response *to* stimulus change	Maintenance of stimulus input information processing	Instrumental response *for* stimulus change
6.	Decreases as linear function of time after stimulus encounter	Is a quadratic function of time after stimulus	Probability of occurrence increases with length of time since stimulus encounter
7.	Physiological parameters reflect information processing (suppressed HRV)	Physiological parameters reflect readiness to respond to new stimuli (high HRV)	*Physiological state not documented*

essentially object-oriented, and whose developmental consequences are therefore likely to be related to the subsequent use of those objects. It is these outcomes that are to be discussed in this section. In children, this may seem an excessively narrow perspective to take, since many developmental theorists have adopted the view that play is related to such factors as social adjustment (Singer, 1972), language development (Garvey, 1976), general intellectual development (Piaget, 1951) and creativity (Lieberman, 1977). However, these wider claims (which depend on a very loose definition of 'play') have depended on correlational measures, or the influence of intervention strategies to assess their validity, and the resulting arguments are not wholly convincing.

In the experimental studies reported by Hutt (1966), Hughes (1978, 1979) and Schneider (1981), it was shown that children's exploratory interactions with a novel toy were characterized by intent facial expression, tentative handling, and visuo-motor coordination; in contrast, during their play the toy was incorporated into games in which the child might manipulate the toy, but would not necessarily be concentrating on this action, and facial expressions became far more relaxed. The organization of exploratory behaviour was consistent among all children observed, and Hutt (1970) speculated that if a child failed to discover one of the properties of the novel toy during exploration, he or she was unlikely to discover it during subsequent play.

Reports by Sylva et al. (1974) and Smith & Dutton (1979) both indicate that children who have some pre-exposure time to materials later to be used in a problem-solving task, are at an advantage to children who have simply been shown the properties of the materials. In the Sylva et al. experiment, children sat in a chair with 3 sticks and a G-clamp at their side, and were asked to reach a piece of chalk in a box that was out of reach. To solve the task, children had to clamp the 2 longer sticks together and use the joined stick to reach the chalk. Hints were given if the children had difficulty. There were two experimental groups (E1 and E2) and a control group C. The children in E1 were shown how to use the clamp and then allowed some 'free play' time with the materials; the children in E2 were given a demonstration of the appropriate construction to solve the problem; and the children in C were shown only how to use the clamp. There was no difference in the number of hints children needed in the two experimental groups; however, children in the control group did require more hints. In a second experiment, using the same problem-task, Sylva et al. yoked the children in the play condition (E1) of the first experiment to two new groups: a demonstration group (D) and a training group (T). Each child in the D and T groups either saw an adult *demonstrate* the configurations of sticks and clamps that had been made by a child in E1, or they were *trained* to build those configurations. Thus, for each child in the E1 group, there was a matched child in the D group who had had a play demonstration, and a matched child in the T group who had been trained to make the same configurations that the E1 child had spontaneously made during play. Both the T and D groups required more hints than the E1 group to solve the task and the authors argue that the play experience was superior to the demonstration and training experience as a means of learning about the materials. They draw an analogy between their experiment, and those of Jackson (1942) and Birch (1945) who each found that chimps who were given play experience with a stick were later able to use the stick in a skilled way to solve a task requiring the acquisition of a distant lure; and Schiller (1957) in a similar experiment, also found that play with several interlocking sticks had a significant impact on chimps' later use of the sticks to acquire a lure.

There are however, some problems with Sylva et al.'s experiments. In the first experiment, the children were not exposed to the materials for an equal amount of time. The play group (E1) was allowed to handle the materials for 10 min, whereas the demonstration group (E2) and the control group received exposure times of 2 min and 1 min, respectively. In view of the ultimately similar performance of groups E1 and E2 it might be concluded that demonstrating to a child how to do a task is the most efficient way of teaching him or her the properties of the materials involved! A second difficulty, applicable to both experiments, is that task performance was evaluated as a function of the number of hints given, with no adjustment for the level of the hint. Since the hints were scaled to reveal increasing amounts of information, two hints at the beginning of the task were not really comparable to two hints at the end of the task; the experimenters did not attempt to make any discrimination on this basis. A third difficulty is really a semantic quibble: were the children in E1 playing in the ludic sense, or were they exploring? In the absence of any behavioural observations there can be no definitive answer, but a replication of this experiment with some simple behavioural observations would examine the question of whether children do indeed 'learn through play' or whether they 'learn through exploration'.

Smith & Dutton (1979) tackled some of the design problems of the experiment: first, the training experience was of the same duration as the play opportunity, and second, the experimental and control groups were all given an initial familiarization time with the materials 'to allow some brief exploration' (p. 831). They also introduced a further problem for the children, which required them to join three sticks (and was therefore considered harder; Smith & Dutton suggest that it requires innovative problem-solving). Their results showed that children in both the play and training conditions performed significantly better than children in the control condition who had merely had the 3-min pre-task familiarization period. In the second (more difficult) task children who had been in the play condition were more likely to solve the problem spontaneously than children in the training condition.

Smith & Dutton (1979, p. 835) argued that the relatively greater efficacy of play opportunity over direct training for more innovative problem-solving is a consequence of 'flexible', combinational activity:

. . . learning an innovative behaviour sequence which combines behaviour elements, or sub-routines, in ways which are new is unlikely to be learned directly by non-playful practice.

However, they do not document whether any children in the play condition did actually 'discover' the appropriate elements or sub-routines to solve the problem. A study reported by Hughes (1981) attempted to examine the way in which children use materials during a period of pre-exposure to a problem, and to relate this to subsequent performance on a problem-solving task.

The two sets of materials used in Hughes' (1981) experiment are shown in Fig. 10.2. Set A comprised three brightly coloured sticks (each 18 in length), and three strip (keys) of copper tubing (2 mm diameter, 2½ in long with rounded end); each stick had a small slot at one end and a rounded section of copper tubing (insert) at the other. Two sticks could therefore be joined by placing the insert from one stick into the slot of another, and sliding a key through the insert to secure the join. Set B comprised a similar set of materials,

238

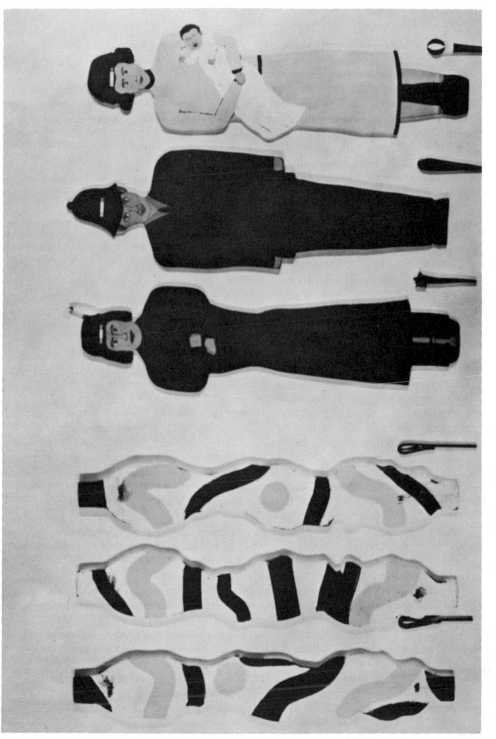

Fig. 10.2   Apparatus used in problem-solving task.

except that the 'sticks' were designed to look like dolls: there was a policeman, a red indian, and a woman holding a baby; and the 'keys' were designed to look like a small truncheon, a tomahawk, and a baby's rattle. It was hypothesized that Set B would elicit more play from the children than Set A because Set B could be more readily incorporated into representational play. Set A was expected to elicit more exploratory behaviour because of the more ostensibly unusual features of the materials.

After 5 min spent with one set of these toys, each child was confronted with a 'problem'. A strip of white tape had been placed down the centre of the playroom before the experiment began, and the child was told that he or she could not now cross this white line. A jelly baby was placed in a paper cup on the opposite side of the line to the child, and the child's problem was to obtain the jelly baby. A series of hints was used to help the children, none of whom were immediately able to solve the problem.

As predicted, the children who spent the pre-task period with Set A were more likely to spend time exploring the materials than children with Set B; no child made a full construction appropriate to the problem (i.e. joined all the sticks), but children using Set B were less likely to discover the way in which the sticks fitted together. During the problem, the children whose pre-exposure period had been spent with the doll-type sticks needed more hints than the other children.

One surprising aspect of this study was the degree of application that children showed in trying to solve the problem; it is in marked contrast to Smith & Dutton's study where more than one-third of their subjects in a 'training' and three-quarters of their subjects in the control condition (which was 3 min familiarization time with the materials) were unwilling to concentrate on the task presented to them. In effect, the present study distinguished the effects of 'epistemic' and 'ludic' play behaviour, and they were equally potent in maintaining the children's interest in the problem; but it is not clear exactly why the children in this study did not lose interest in the same way as the children in Smith & Dutton's experiment. One possible reason is the different nature of the subject sample, another possibility is the lack of constraint on the children's behaviour in the present study: Smith & Dutton required their subjects to sit formally at a table; the subjects in the present study were permitted a good deal more freedom of activity during the pre-task period, and they may therefore have felt less constrained by the adult presence. As Loizos (1967) and Bruner (1972) have both pointed out, a child will not play in surroundings that create a feeling of insecurity; the children in the Smith & Dutton study may well have found the experimental conditions so aversive that they engaged in displacement activities which distracted them from the task ahead.

The present study does exemplify that when children respond to objects as having a familiar use (the dolls in Set B), they do not examine the less familiar features that may be present. Their behaviour is 'ludic', in that it is relaxed and incorporates the objects into various activities; children who are confronted with materials that are relatively unfamiliar, and have no obvious use, 'explore' the properties of those materials. It is exploration that gives children an ultimate advantage in using the materials in a problem-solving situation.

The finding that exploration facilitates the type of 'convergent thinking' necessary for the problem-solving task described above cannot necessarily be generalized to the proposition that exploration facilitates *all* problem-solving activities. For example, since it is during ludic behaviour that children typically use materials in different ways ('what can *I* do with this object?' — Hutt, 1970), it may be that ludic behaviour facilitates divergent thinking, whereas exploratory behaviour facilitates convergent thinking.

Experiments reported by Dansky (1978) and Dansky & Silverman (1973, 1975) found that children who spent a period of free play with a set of everyday objects (paper clips, corks, etc.) were able to suggest more possible uses of these objects than children who had spent the same length of time watching or imitating the actions of an experimenter with the objects. Since we can probably assume that the familiar nature of these items would not elicit exploratory behaviour, the children in the free-play condition may have been able to use the pre-problem period to engage in idiosyncratic behavioural sequences (typical of play, rather than exploration), which in some way facilitated the divergent style of thinking required by the problem.

In terms of consequences, then, it is possible to distinguish exploration and play on two grounds: firstly, that exploration is associated with learning, whereas in play, information obtained during exploration is used (and thus possibly consolidated); and second, exploration is more closely allied to convergent-thinking processes, whereas play reflects divergent cognitive style. These conclusions draw attention to the value of distinguishing different behavioural categories in the exploration–play cycle in order to illuminate the role of these types of behaviour in development.

10.5 Play and Biological Fitness

The question of whether (or how) play might promote biological fitness has provoked fairly wide speculation (Fagen, 1977, 1981; Vandenberg, 1978). Sutton-Smith's (1973) suggestion that the relatively low levels of play observed in subsistence cultures indicates the low priority that play behaviour has in the motivational hierarchy is unable to account for widely observed individual differences *within* a culture. Indeed, not all forms of play are absent from subsistence cultures; in particular post-mastery play is frequently observed (see, for example, Einon, Chapter 9).

The most elegant model of the manner in which play could be related to biological fitness is propounded by Fagen (1976, 1977). He broadly accepts the function of play described in the previous section, arguing that it provides a source of behavioural variability that generates innovative and sometimes useful acts that can then be absorbed into existing cultural patterns (the behaviour of the Japanese macaques described by Bruner, 1975, is a fine example of this). He further points out, however, that the biological value of innovative potential in a population of animals that are also capable of observational learning, must be

241

weighed up against any disadvantage inherent in the expression of that potential. Fagen proposes a model that attaches mathematically defined values to innovation through play and the associated deficits that might be incurred by playing but failing to innovate. In subsistence cultures, the biological cost of play may be very high: it could, for example, result in the failure to collect adequate provision or provide adequate shelter. In more highly technologically developed cultures, however, a child is unlikely to incur any biological cost through play. Fagen (1976) described a model in which genes for 'playfulness' are initially randomly distributed throughout a population; some members of that population will incur the biological benefits of others' play through observational learning. According to the principles of population biology, a population will eventually reach a steady state in which a balance of 'players' and 'observers' will maximize the fitness of each individual within that population. The steady state for any population will then depend on both environmental and species factors.

Such a simple model offers an elegant explanation of the evolution of individual differences in play, and of the relative paucity of play in some cultures.

10.6 Summary and Conclusions

Berlyne (1969) wrote:

> . . . there is some justice in the view that our ignorance is the main factor that holds together the category of play . . . psychology would do well to give up the category of play in favour of both wider and narrower categories of behaviour.

Weisler & McCall (1976) continued the lament that, despite a plethora of studies, experimental studies of exploration and play were dogged by the imprecision of definitions and the lack of a widely acceptable theoretical perspective. Recent studies of children's play have, however, reflected consistent attempts to define the particular categories of play to which reference is being made, and to distinguish play from exploratory behaviour. In particular, attempts have been made to investigate the special significance that symbolic play may have in the development of human symbolic thought (see Fein, 1981, for a review).

This chapter has focused attention on exploration and play with objects. Specific and diversive exploration have been shown to be quite distinct from play in terms of motivational antecedents, behavioural features and physiological correlates, and developmental consequences. It has been further suggested that post-mastery behaviour might be usefully regarded as a component of the exploration-play cycle depicted in Fig. 10.2. Our ignorance is slowly, but firmly, being eroded (*pace* Berlyne), and the exhortations of Weisler & McCall (1976) have made at least some impact.

References

BEACH, F. (1945) Current concepts of play in animals. *American Naturalist* **79**, 523–541.

BERLYNE, D. (1960) *Conflict, Arousal and Curiosity.* New York: McGraw-Hill.

BERLYNE, D. E. (1969) Laughter, humor and play. In *Handbook of Social Psychology.* (Eds. G. LINDSEY and A. ARONSON). New York: Addison-Wesley.

BIRCH, H. G. (1945) The relation of previous experience to insightful problem-solving. *Journal of Comparative Psychology* **38**, 267–283.

BRUNER, J. (1972) Nature and uses of immaturity. *American Psychologist* **27**, 1–28.

BRUNER, J. (1975) The importance of play. In *Child Alive* (Ed. R. LEWIN). New York: Anchor Books, Doubleday.

DANSKY, J. (1978) Why does 'free play' enhance associative fluency? *TAASP Newsletter* **4**.

DANSKY, J. and SILVERMAN, I. (1973) Effects of play associative fluency in pre-school children. *Developmental Psychology* **9**, 38–43

DANSKY, J. and SILVERMAN I. (1975) Play: a general facilitator of associative fluency. *Developmental Psychology* **11**, 104.

FAGEN, R. (1976) Modelling how and why play works. In *Play* (Eds. J. BRUNER, A. JOLLY and K.SYLVA). Harmondsworth: Penguin.

FAGEN, R. (1977) Selection for optimal age-dependent schedules of play behaviour. *American Naturalist,* III (1979), 395–415.

FAGEN, R. (1981) *Animal Play Behavior.* New York: Oxford University Press.

FEIN, G. (1981) Pretend play in childhood: an integrative review. *Child Development* **52**, 1095–1118.

GARVEY, C. (1976) *Play.* London: Fontana

GROOS (1898) *The Play of Man* (trans. by E. BALDWIN from the 1898 original). London: Heinemann (1901).

HUGHES, M. (1978) Sequential analysis of exploration and play. *International Journal of Behavioural Development* **1**, 83–97.

HUGHES, M. (1979) Exploration and play re-visited: a hierarchical analysis. *International Journal of Behavioural Development* **2**, 215–224

HUGHES, M. (1981) The relationship between symbolic and manipulative (object) play. Paper presented at the conference 'Curiosity, Imagination and Play', Berlin.

HUGHES, M. and HUTT, C. (1979). Heart-rate correlates of childhood activities: play, exploration, problem-solving and day-dreaming. *Biological Psychology* **8**, 253–263.

HUTT, C. (1966) Exploration and play in children. *Symposia of the Zoological Society of London* **18**, 61–81.

HUTT, C. (1970) Specific and diversive exploration. In *Advances in Child Development and Behavior*, Vol. 5, (Eds. H. REESE and L. LIPSITT). New York: Academic Press.

HUTT C. (1979) Exploration and play. In *Play and Learning* (Ed. B. SUTTON-SMITH). New York: Gardner Press.

JACKSON, T. A. (1942) Use of the stick as a tool by young chimpanzees. *Journal of Comparative Psychology* **34**, 223–235.

LACEY, J. (1967) Somatic response patterning and stress: some revisions of activation theory. In *Psychological Stress: Issues in Research* (Eds. M. APPLEY and R. TRUMBELL). New York: Appleton-Century-Crofts.

LACEY, J. and LACEY, B. (1970) Some autonomic–central nervous system relationships In *Physiological Correlates of Emotion* (Ed. P. BLACK). New York: Academic Press.

LIEBERMAN, J. (1977) *Playfulness: its relation to imagination and Creativity.* New York: Academic Press.

LOIZOS, C. (1966) Play in mammals. *Symposia of the Zoological Society of London* **18**, 1–9.

LOIZOS, C. (1967) Play behavior in higher primates: a review. In *Primate Ethology* (Ed. D. MORRIS). London: Weidenfeld and Nicholson.

NUNNALLY, J. and LEMOND, L. (1973) Exploratory behavior and human development. In *Advances in Child Development and Behavior, Vol. 8*, (Ed. H. REESE and L. LIPSITT). New York: Academic Press.

PIAGET, J. (1951) *Play, Dreams and Imitation in Childhood* (trans. by GATTEGNO and F. HODGSON). London: Heineman.

RHEINGOLD, H. and ECKERMAN, C. (1969) The infant's free entry into a new environment. *Journal of Experimental Child Psychology* **8**, 271–283.

RHEINGOLD, H. and ECKERMAN, C. (1970) The infant separates himself from his mother. *Science* **168**, 78–83.

SCHILLER, P. H. (1975) Innate motor action as a basis of learning: manipulative patterns in the chimpanzee. In *Instinctive Behaviour* (Ed. S. H. SCHILLER). London: Methuen.

SCHNEIDER, K. (1981) Subjective uncertainty and exploratory behavior in pre-school Children. Paper presented at the conference 'Curiosity, Imagination and Play', Berlin.

SINGER, J. (Ed.) (1972) *The Child's World of Make-Believe*. New York: Academic Press.

SMITH, P. K. and DUTTON, S. (1979) Play and training in direct and innovative problem solving. *Child Development* **50**, 830–836.

SPENCER, H. (1855) *Principles of Psychology*. London: Longmans-Green.

STRATTON, P. (1982) Contingency, control and competence. *Developmental Medicine and Child Neurology*, in press.

STROH, G. and BUICK, D. (1970) The effect of relative sensory isolation on the behaviour of two autistic children. In *Behaviour Studies in Psychiatry* (Eds. S. J. HUTT, and C. HUTT). Oxford: Pergamon Press.

SUTTON-SMITH, B. (1971) Child's play: a very serious business. *Psychology Today* **5**, 66–69.

SUTTON-SMITH, B. (1973) Spiel als Mittler des Neuen. In *Das Kinderspiel* (Ed. A. FLITNER). Munich: Piper and Co.

SWITZKY, H., HAYWOOD, C. and ISETT, R. (1974) Exploration, curiosity and play in young children: effects of stimulus complexity. *Developmental Psychology* **10**, 321–329.

SWITZKY, H. LUDWIG,, L. and HAYWOOD, C. (1979) Exploration and play in retarded and non-retarded preschool children: effects of object complexity and age. *American Journal of Mental Deficiency* **83**, 637–644.

SYLVA, K., BRUNER, J. and GENOVA, P. (1974) The role of play in the problem-solving of children 3–5 years old. In *Play* (Eds. J. BRUNER, A. JOLLY and K. SYLVA). London: Penguin (1976).

VANDENBERG, B. (1978) Play and development from an ethological perspective. *American Psychologist* 724–738.

WEISLER, A. and McCALL, R. (1976) Exploration and play: resume and redirection, *American Psychology* **31**, 492–508.

WELKER, (1961) An analysis of exploratory and play behaviour in animals. In *Functions of Varied Experience* (Eds. D. FISKE and S. MADDI). Illinois: Dorsey Press.

WOHLWILL, J. (1975) Children's voluntary exploration and preference for factually presented nonsense shapes differing in complexity. *Journal of Experimental Child Psychology* **20**, 159–167.

WOHLWILL, J. (1981) A conceptual analysis of exploratory behavior: the 'specific-diversive' distinction revisited. In *Advances in Intrinsic Motivation and Aesthetics* (Ed. H. DAY). New York: Plenum Publishing Corp.

CHAPTER 11

Novelty and Human Aesthetic Preferences

W. Sluckin, D. J. Hargreaves and A. M. Colman

It is a view widely held and well supported by evidence that novelty evokes curiosity and fear in animals, both at the same time (Russell, 1973). Repeated exposure to a novel stimulus object can overcome the subject's fear of it, and may result in exposure learning (Sluckin, 1972), that is, in a development of an attachment to, or a preference for, the object. There is no reason to believe that in this regard human beings are exceptional. In animals, fear of a given figure is incompatible with attachment behaviour directed to it. In human beings, too, what is feared cannot at the same time be preferred. As novelty wears off, however, and fear wanes, the initial unfavourable view of a given stimulus object will diminish, and may well gradually turn into liking; but the unfavourable attitude can later return as a function of satiation and boredom (Sluckin *et al.*, 1980). Thus, one of the factors influencing favourability, or aesthetic preferences, is the position of the stimulus object on the novelty/familiarity continuum.

As Berlyne (1971) points out, novelty can refer to several distinct states of affairs. When a stimulus is unlike anything encountered before, we are dealing with absolute novelty — strictly speaking, a very rare occurrence. Novelty in most cases is really relative novelty, that is, unprecedented combinations of previously experienced elements. Further, novelty may be short-term, in the sense that the stimulus is different from stimuli experienced only recently, say, during the last few minutes or hours. However, novelty may also be long-term — an experience of a kind not encountered for a very much longer period. In all cases novelty is said to be arousing to some extent. Whether it is specifically fear-arousing, and therefore 'off-putting', will depend on the kind and intensity of the novelty in question. Although some novel stimuli will be disliked, others — at a given time relatively novel to the subject, but previously highly familiar — will be well liked (having now lost their boringness associated with excessive familiarity). For this reason, works of art viewed, or heard, at infrequent intervals may be aesthetically highly satisfying.

Familiarity, too, can vary in character. Generally, although some elements of a configuration may be very familiar, others may be less familiar or unfamiliar.

This can occur in any sensory modality: a photograph can contain both familiar and unfamiliar elements; a well-known melody may be heard with new rhythms or harmonies. It has been traditionally said that such variation, or unity-in variety, is at the root of aesthetic appreciation. Indeed, variations on a familiar theme may be just what is needed to prevent favourability, which initially rises as novelty wears off, from ever setting on a path of decline.

It is, of course, difficult to consider aesthetic preferences in real-life situations with reference only to novelty/familiarity ignoring the influence of such factors as complexity and interestingness of what is being judged or appreciated (Berlyne, 1974b). However, it was clear from early on to some investigators that if experimental studies were to make progress towards a better understanding of everyday human likes and dislikes, experiments had to be so designed as to relate favourability to novelty/familiarity and to keep initially other factors constant as far as possible. This is what investigators such as Cantor (1968) and Zajonc (1968) set out to do in the early days of the 'new experimental aesthetics'.

We therefore begin by providing a brief historical review of studies concerned with relationships between novelty/familiarity and aesthetic preferences; both experimental findings and explanatory theories will be considered. We then turn to our own work. To start with, some comments will be offered on experimental procedures in this field of research. Next, we review our studies of preferences for such things as letters of the alphabet and words. We continue by dealing with preferences for surnames and Christian names; in relation to the latter we shall introduce our preference-feedback hypothesis. We subsequently consider at some length the question of aesthetic appreciation of music — a topic not often tackled by experimental psychologists. Finally, an attempt is made to arrive at some broad conclusions; in the process we refer to different stimulus categories that evoke likes and dislikes, and also refer to changing fashions in aesthetic preferences.

11.1   Novelty, Familiarity and Liking: an Introductory Review

In an influential monograph, Zajonc (1968, p. 1) examined evidence related to the hypothesis that 'mere repeated exposure of the individual to a stimulus is a sufficient condition for the enhancement of his attitude toward it'. This hypothesis can be traced to William James (1890, p. 672) and Gustav Theodor Fechner (1876, pp. 240–243), although Zajonc was the first to subject it to careful empirical investigation. His review of existing evidence and his own experimental work suggested that the relationship between exposure and liking is best described by a rising but decelerating curve in which liking is a logarithmic function of exposure frequency. The *mere exposure* hypothesis asserts that the effect of exposure on liking — other things being equal — is always positive, although the effect may be more pronounced for novel than for relatively familiar stimuli.

This hypothesis contradicts certain widely held beliefs, such as those implied by the proverbs 'familiarity breeds contempt' and 'absence makes the heart grow fonder', but an impressive body of empirical evidence has accumulated in support of it (see Harrison, 1977; and Stang, 1974, for reviews). As we shall see, however, the existing evidence is not all consistent with the mere exposure hypothesis, and recent theoretical and empirical work, including our own, suggests that the underlying functional relationship between novelty/familiarity and liking may be non-monotonic, rising only at relatively low levels of exposure and declining at higher levels.

In his original monograph, Zajonc (1968) devoted a great deal of attention to correlational evidence in support of the exposure hypothesis. The most important correlational evidence was based on the relative frequencies of usage of antonym pairs, i.e. words of approximate opposite meaning, in the Thorndike–Lorge (1944) word count. Several previous researchers had noticed that words with positive affective connotations have higher frequency counts, in general, than negatively toned words. *Happiness*, for example, occurs more than 15 times as frequently in written English as *unhappiness*; *beauty* is 41 times as frequent as *ugliness*; *love* is almost 7 times as frequent as *hate*; *find* is 4.5 times as frequent as *lose*; and so on. A similar relationship between frequency and favourability has more recently been found in French, German, Spanish, Russian, Urdu, and other languages (Harrison, 1977; Zajonc, 1968).

In order to investigate this phenomenon more closely, Zajonc asked 100 subjects to indicate which member of each of 154 antonym pairs expressed 'the more favorable meaning'. The subjects nominated in 82 % of cases the one with the higher Thorndike–Lorge frequency count. It seems odd, however, to deploy this type of evidence in support of the mere exposure hypothesis. The implication is that the positive connotations of words like *happiness* and *beauty* are a consequence of their frequent usage, and this in turn implies that the connotations of such words were relatively unfavourable before they became frequent in the language; another improbable implication is that words like *ugliness* and *hate* would lose their unfavourable connotations if they were used more frequently. But the correlation of frequency and favourability among words can be explained without recourse to the mere-exposure hypothesis. Instead of assuming that exposure causes increased favourability, it seems more reasonable to postulate that favourability causes increased exposure. There is, in fact, evidence (Boucher & Osgood, 1969; Osgood, 1964) showing that people tend to pay greater attention in their thought and speech to positive than to negative aspects of their conceptual universe. This predilection for positive concepts, which Osgood called the *Pollyanna effect* (alluding to the optimistic heroine of a series of children's novels), provides a more natural explanation than the mere exposure hypothesis for the correlation of word frequency and favourability.

Some of the other evidence presented by Zajonc can be reinterpreted in a similar way. High school students were asked to rate on a seven-point scale how much they liked various trees, fruits, vegetables and flowers, and their preferences were found to be nearly proportional to the logarithms of the frequencies of these items in the Thorndike–Lorge word count: correlations ranged

247

from 0.80 to 0.89. The three best liked fruits, for example, were (in descending order) *apple*, *cherry* and *strawberry*, and their average preference ratings were 5.13, 5.00 and 4.83, respectively. Rather than demonstrating that exposure leads to increased liking, however, these data may simply provide further evidence for the Pollyanna effect: there may be a tendency for popular trees, fruits, vegetables and flowers to be spoken and written about more frequently than those that are less popular.

In order to establish a causal link between exposure and liking, Zajonc reported some controlled experiments, and his experimental design and methodology have served as a model for numerous subsequent investigations. Nonsense words like *iktitaf* and *civadra*, diagrams resembling Chinese ideographs and photographs of human faces were used as stimuli in these early experiments. The subjects rated each of the stimuli belonging to one of the above classes for assumed favourability of meaning (in the case of the nonsense words and ideographs) or liking (in the case of the faces) after 0, 1, 2, 5, 10, or 25 exposures. Stimuli and exposure frequencies were counterbalanced in Latin square designs to avoid confounding effects. In each case a strong, positive and nearly linear relationship was found between log-transformed exposure and rated favourability of meaning or liking. These findings have been replicated in numerous subsequent experiments (Brickman *et al.*, 1972; Hamid, 1973; Harrison, 1969; Harrison & Crandall, 1972; Harrison & Zajonc, 1970; Harrison *et al.*, 1974; Janisse, 1970; Matlin, 1974; Moreland & Zajonc, 1976, 1977; Zajonc *et al.*, 1971). The external validity of the mere-exposure effect has been extended through field experiments in which subjects were asked to rate the favourability of nonsense words previously placed in their mailboxes a pre-determined number of times (Rajecki & Wolfson, 1973) or inserted in newspaper advertisements (Zajonc & Rajecki, 1969). The effect has been found even when the stimuli were live human beings and exposure was manipulated by varying the number of interpersonal encounters (Saegert *et al.*, 1973). Most experiments have involved a maximum of only a few dozen exposures, although Zajonc *et al.* (1974) reported a steady increase in liking of Chinese ideographs up to 243 exposures.

Some investigations have, however, yielded results at variance with the mere-exposure hypothesis. Berlyne (1970) reported that simple representational and abstract works of art were rated as progressively *less* pleasing as frequency of exposure increased. Cantor (1968) and Cantor & Kubose (1969) found that children gave more positive ratings of liking to unfamiliar than to familiar geometric patterns taken from the Welsh Figure Preference Test. Using line drawings of familiar objects and simple meaningless patterns, Faw & Pien (1971) found that both adults and children liked both types of stimuli better when they were novel than when they were relatively familiar. Siebold (1972) familiarized children with both simple and comparatively complex geometric patterns, and found that both kinds of stimuli were better liked when they were novel to the subjects than after familiarization. All of these findings are in direct opposition to the predictions of the mere exposure hypothesis. To complicate the picture further, several studies (reviewed by Crandall *et al.*, 1973) have

248

reported an initial increase in liking with moderate degrees of familiarization, followed by a decline with increased familiarization. Our own studies, discussed later in this chapter, have confirmed this finding with several classes of stimuli.

Several theories, all but the most recent of which are discussed and critically evaluated in Harrison (1977), have been proposed to explain the empirical evidence on familiarity and liking. Some of these theories have fared badly in experimental tests, and others seem either inadequate to account for the full range of empirical evidence or are deficient on other grounds. The most persuasive theories share the common assumption that the universal relationship between familiarity and liking takes the form of an inverted U, with liking rising at low levels of familiarity and then declining. Various factors have been proposed to account for the parameters of this hypothesized function. The peak of the curve may occur at very high levels of familiarity under certain conditions, leading to a monotonic increase in liking — a mere-exposure effect — across the limited range of exposure that it is possible to investigate in experiments based on the methods pioneered by Zajonc. Under different conditions, the peak may occur at very low levels of familiarity, yielding a monotonic decrease in liking across most of the exposure range as found in some of the studies mentioned in the previous paragraph.

The inverted-U curve, in the form originally suggested by Wundt and later adapted by Berlyne (1971) and others, is depicted in Fig. 11.1(a). According to Berlyne, the *hedonic value* of a stimulus is a function, which rises to a peak and then falls, of a person's *arousal*; and arousal is hypothesized to be directly related to the novelty of the stimulus. We have indicated elsewhere (Sluckin *et al.*, 1980) that the notion of zero novelty implies total familiarity. However, such complete familiarity can never, strictly speaking, be achieved; rather, familiarity may be regarded as increasing, with continued exposure to the stimulus, *ad infinitum*. Complete unfamiliarity, on the other hand, is more easily conceived of; it occurs with nil exposure to the stimulus. Fig. 11.1(b) shows favourability as a function of familiarity, the latter increasing from zero to infinity. In this formulation, a strange stimulus is assumed to be initially somewhat unattractive rather than of neutral affective value; this is consistent with a great deal of empirical evidence, in spite of the widespread belief that there is something inherently attractive about novelty (Harrison, 1977).

The most influential theories concerning the relationship between familiarity and liking are the response-competition and two-factor theories. These theories will be discussed briefly in the following paragraphs. We shall also say a few words about the recently proposed scheme theory.

According to response-competition theory (Harrison, 1968; Matlin, 1970), an unfamiliar stimulus usually contains elements reminiscent of a diversity of previously encountered stimuli, and these elements generally elicit mutually incompatible or antagonistic cognitive and behavioural tendencies. The coexistence of mutually incompatible response tendencies in a person confronted with an unfamiliar stimulus is held to result in an aversive drive state leading to negative affect and to a dislike of the stimulus. Subsequent exposure leads to cognitive restructuring: one class of response tendencies typically gains

249

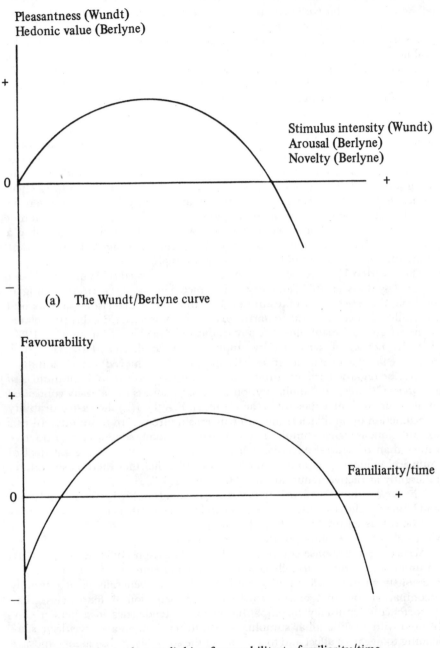

(a) The Wundt/Berlyne curve

(b) The hypothesized curve linking favourability to familiarity/time

Fig. 11.1 Inverted U-curves. (Reproduced from W. Sluckin, A. M. Colman and D. J. Hargreaves (1980) *British Journal of Psychology*, 71, 163–169, by permission.)

dominance over the others as the stimulus is fitted into a meaningful conceptual framework, and incompatible tendencies are weakened or suppressed. The reduction of response competition alleviates tension and negative affect, and leads to increased liking — or, strictly speaking, decreased disliking — for the stimulus.

In its original form, response-competition theory provides an explanation for the mere-exposure effect but fails to account for the negative and inverted-U effects found in some experiments. The theory has therefore been modified to take account of these findings. Saegert & Jellison (1970) proposed that an *intermediate* level of response competition is maximally pleasurable, so that beyond a certain point increased exposure, by reducing response competition below the optimal level, leads to a decline in liking. The number of exposures required to reach the critical point should be relatively small if the stimulus is simple, since in that case few associative response tendencies will be elicited. If, on the other hand, the stimulus is complex, the optimal level of response competition should be reached only after a relatively large number of exposures, since many potentially antagonistic response tendencies will initially be elicited by it.

Two-factor theories are based on the assumption that exposure produces a pair of opposing tendencies that in combination may result in positive, negative, or inverted-U effects. Berlyne (1970, 1971) suggested that exposure generates both a *habituation* or *reduction of uncertainty* effect leading to increased liking, and a *satiation* or *boredom* effect whose influence on liking is negative. When a stimulus is unfamiliar, habituation predominates and exposure therefore leads to increased liking. Once a stimulus has become familiar, however, satiation gains ascendancy and further exposure leads to decreased liking. If the stimulus is simple, the habituation phase will be completed after relatively few exposures and the predominant trend will be a decline in liking; but if it is complex, the peak of the favourability curve may never be reached through laboratory exposures. A slightly different two-factor theory has been proposed by Stang (1974, 1975): according to this version the opposing tendencies are *progress of learning* and *satiation*.

According to Stang's theory, repeated exposure is accompanied by learning about the stimulus, and as learning progresses the stimulus becomes more pleasing. Once the stimulus has been learned, an unpleasant state of satiation, or boredom, is hypothesized to develop, causing the pleasingness of the stimulus to decline. If this theory is correct, conditions of repeated exposure that favour learning and minimize satiation (e.g., spaced exposure of complex, novel stimuli) should produce familiarity–favourability functions resembling learning curves; but conditions favouring both learning and satiation should produce inverted-U functions (Stang, 1975).

The most recent theoretical contribution is Eckblad's (1981, pp. 83–89) scheme theory. According to this theory, the process of learning new perceptual schemes for recognizing, classifying and discriminating among unfamiliar stimuli is inherently pleasurable, but repeated exposure to stimuli that are already recognizable in terms of existing perceptual schemes generates neutral

251

or negative affect, manifested by inattention or boredom. The location of the peak of the curve, according to scheme theory, depends on the degree of recognizability of the stimuli. The larger the number of exposures required to build up the schemes necessary for recognizing the stimuli, the later the peak of the curve. When the requisite schemes are more-or-less complete, liking passes its maximum and begins to decline.

Response-competition, two-factor, and scheme theories all postulate a universal inverted-U function linking familiarity and liking. The parameters of the curve are assumed to depend, among other things, on the complexity or recognizability of the stimuli. Monotonic mere exposure effects, such as those discussed earlier in this section, are assumed to represent only the rising part of the underlying inverted U. Using the traditional experimental procedures pioneered by Zajonc (1968), initially unfamiliar stimuli can be exposed only a few hundred times at most, and the peak of the curve may often lie beyond the reach of such investigations. Our own research methodology discussed in the following sections, on the other hand, allows a vastly wider range of familiarity, from complete novelty to literally millions of exposures, to be investigated.

11.2   Experimental Procedures

Experimental findings and conclusions in studies of aesthetic preferences are to a degree determined by the methods used in the experiments. We have already seen that if the type of stimulus material chosen is generally unfamiliar to the particular group of subjects, then the less strange the stimuli the better they will be liked; and the risk is that a generalization will be formed that liking is simply an ever-increasing function of stimulus familiarity. What may be more important is that experimental procedures for assessing aesthetic preferences — e.g. whether pair comparisons or rankings are used — could influence results. Likewise, experimental findings can be affected by the choice of familiarity measures — whether a subjective scale of familiarity is used, or an objective measure of time or frequency of exposure of subject to the stimulus is employed. Our own experimental studies have tended to differ procedurally, sometimes slightly and sometimes radically, from previous relevant investigations. Therefore, it seemed worthwhile to focus attention in the first place on the methodological aspects of our work, and only afterwards report our findings stage by stage.

We have refrained from adopting the well-known 'before-and-after' procedure of testing attitudes. In some of our work we have used stimuli with which our experimental subjects would be familiar to varying degrees as a result of everyday experience outside the laboratory. In the case of each stimulus we obtained an assessment of our subjects' familiarity with it, and we proceeded to assess their liking for it. Thus, we tested each subject for favourability not twice, before and after an experimental exposure to the stimulus, but only on a single occasion. There are two advantages in this method. One may be called procedural: a once-only testing session is simple to organize and enables the experimenter to 'round up' relatively large numbers of subjects without worrying about getting them back for a second testing session or exposing them to tedious repetition. The other advantage may be described as methodological: prior real-life experience of stimuli can provide for a very wide range of stimulus familiarity; this is important if our main aim is to study liking as a function of familiarity.

In some of our more recent studies we have assigned our subjects in a random manner either to a group in which each subject rates stimuli for familiarity or to a group in which each subject rates stimuli on a scale of liking. Technically this is a between-subjects experimental design. It has been used occasionally in earlier studies (Harrison, 1969; Moreland & Zajonc, 1977). The advantage of this design over the within-subjects one is that judgments of familiarity and favourability cannot mutually influence each other. Such influence could 'contaminate' findings when the subjects have some ideas, as many might have, as to how familiarity and liking are related.

In some of our experiments stimulus familiarity was inferred from the stimulus type. For example, nonsense syllables were considered to be unfamiliar stimuli, uncommon words were classed as somewhat familiar, and very common words as very familiar stimuli. In other experiments we used the subjects' own subjective assessments of stimulus familiarity. Other workers preferred in the past to rely on objective measures of familiarity, such as those based on the duration of exposure of the subject to the stimulus. However, subjective measures indicate the subject's familiarity with the stimulus in the most direct manner. Further, it has been shown (Harrison, 1977) that at least in some situations subjective assessments are better than objective measures of familiarity at predicting aesthetic preferences.

11.3   Preferences for Letters and Words

It is somewhat surprising that people should have preferences among ordinary letters of the alphabet — that they should like some and not others. However, whenever presented with a card displaying two letters children in our own investigations have always readily said which of the two they liked the better; and their replies have turned out to show a consistent pattern. An early study involved the use of capital Roman-alphabet and Cyrillic-alphabet letters as stimuli (Sluckin et al., 1973). The subjects were 147 children recruited from schools in Louisville, Kentucky, USA, at a time when one of us (W.S.) was on a research assignment at the University of Louisville. One group of subjects ranged in age from 4.3 years to 6.6 years, with a mean age of 5 years 1month. The other group ranged from 9.4 years to 11.11 years, the mean age being 10 years 7 months. Very briefly, each subject was tested individually by the pair comparison method; he/she had to say which of the two things shown on a card he/she liked the better. 72 cards were presented to each subject in a random order. The Roman and Cyrillic letters, and examples of cards used, are shown in Fig. 11.2.

D Б   Б D

Fig. 11.2 Roman and Cyrillic letters and examples of cards used. (Reproduced from W. Sluckin, L. B. Miller and H. Franklin (1973) *British Journal of Psychology*, 64, 563–567, by permission.

The younger children were at the stage of just learning to read whereas the older children were already well able to read. Thus, the younger group were fairly familiar with ordinary Roman letters, and the older children were very familiar indeed with such letters. The Cyrillic letters were, from the point of view of all the children, simply letter-like shapes. All in all, we found that the younger children very strongly preferred the Roman-alphabet letters. Since the two sets of letters had been fairly alike with regard to straight and curved line components, the most probable reason for our finding was that the letters that were preferred had been quite familiar, whereas the non-preferred Cyrillic letters had been unfamiliar to the younger children. The older children also liked better the familiar shapes than the strange ones, but this preference was much less marked than in the case of the younger children. The conclusion from our study was that the liking of children for letters was *initially* a direct function of familiarity, resulting from exposure of the children to the letters. However, much more exposure to letters did not lead to an increased preference for them over the letter-like shapes and, on the contrary, extra exposure resulted in a reduction of preference for the familiar shapes. There could also, of course, be less fear of novelty with increasing age in children; or both effects, less neophobia and a decline in the liking for highly familiar stimuli, could occur all at once as children advance in age.

Some years later some of us set out to investigate the preferences of children and young adults for common words, uncommon words and nonsense words (Colman *et al.*, 1975). Two separate experiments were conducted. In the first of them, the subjects were (a) 15 6- to 7-year-old children, (b) 15 10- to 11-year-old children, both from a primary school in Northamptonshire, and (c) 17 18- to 20-year-old Combined Studies students from the University of Leicester. All the stimuli were consonant-vowel-consonant trigrams. Eight words were used, *viz*. BAG, TAP, LEG, PEN, LID, DOT, JUG and CUP; and eight non-words, *viz.* YAD, VAB, FEP, KEB, MIB, JOM, VUD and CUG. Every possible combination of word and nonsense syllable was printed in lower-case letters on a separate card, once with the word on the left and once with the word on the right, adding up to 128 cards altogether. The children were tested individually for preference as between the two stimuli on each card. In this experiment all the groups of subjects showed a preference for words over non-words. Most probably this simply reflected a preference for the familiar stimuli over the unfamiliar ones.

In the second experiment in the study mentioned above, the subjects were (a) 20 7-year-old children, (b) 20 9- to 10-year old children and (c) 20 18- to 21-year-old students. The stimuli this time were six very common words, *viz.* APPLE, WINDOW, TRUMPET, BOTTLE, RABBIT and TEACHER, and six relatively uncommon words (roughly matching the common ones), *viz.* GUAVA, CORNICE, CORNET, CARAFE, WOMBAT and MENTOR. The pair-comparison method, as between common and uncommon words, was used again. The results were this time markedly different from those of Experiment I (but not altogether unexpected). Children in both groups preferred common to uncommon words, but young adults showed a significant preference for the uncommon words. It looked as if the uncommon, less familiar words were perhaps more interesting to the young adults; at any rate, they were certainly more pleasing.

The results of both experiments may be brought together to make sense in the manner shown in Fig. 11.3. Within the Cartesian coordinates one graph represents the way familiarity and favourability are related in the case of children. Broadly, the more familiar the stimuli — progressively non-words, uncommon words and common words — the more they are liked. The other graph represents the relationship between familiarity and favourability for young adults. Here the very unfamiliar stimuli (non-words) and the very familiar ones

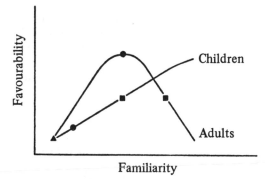

Fig. 11.3   ▲, Non-words; ●, uncommon words; ■, common words. (See explanation in text.) (Reproduced from A. M. Colman, M. Walley and W. Sluckin (1975) *British Journal of Psychology*, **66**, 481–486, by permission.)

(common words) are liked less than the stimuli of intermediate familiarity (uncommon words); thus the relationship for adults is, at least partly, of the inverted-U kind. It may be surmised that in the case of children even the common words are not yet familiar enough to have reached the peak of the inverted-U curve; a great deal more exposure to words may be needed before some of them can become so ordinary and boring as to diminish in their aesthetic appeal.

Several years later we set out once again to investigate people's likes and dislikes of words as a function of the experienced frequency of their occurrence (Sluckin *et al.*, 1980). The method of investigation this time was quite different. Our subjects, 33 adults, ranging in age from 19 to 43 years, had to rate either the familiarity of each one of 100 words on a five-point scale or the liking for each of the words, also on a five-point scale. Thus, the between-subject design, mentioned in a previous section, was used. Seventeen subjects were randomly assigned to the familiarity condition and sixteen to the favourability condition. The words were selected randomly from a dictionary, but those regarded as emotionally charged were discarded. Naturally, some objectively very uncommon words were judged by our subjects as entirely unfamiliar; and at the other end of the scale, some words were judged by our subjects as very familiar indeed. On the scale of liking, the distribution of ratings was pretty even, ranging from words disliked to words liked.

In Fig. 11.4 each dot represents the position of each word in relation to the familiarity and favourability co-ordinates. An inspection of the scatter diagram shows that on the whole unfamiliar words were rated low or lowish on favourability; very familiar words were on the average marginally less well liked than the moderately familiar words. A full statistical analysis confirmed this impression. The straight rising line in the figure shows the fairly steep average increase of liking for words up to the familiarity rating of 2.5 chosen by inspection. Then, at the high levels of familiarity there is some decline, albeit less steep, in favourability as a function of familiarity. Our published paper gives a full mathematical analysis of the data that shows clearly that our results fit a theoretical inverted-U function. Our data so far do not allow any clear-cut inference as to the parameters of the inverted-U curve — how its shape in any given circumstances may depend for instance on such factors as the complexity or discriminability of stimuli. We shall offer, however, some comments on this matter in the concluding section of this chapter.

11.4 Preferences for Names and the Preference-Feedback Hypothesis

Once a new word or phrase has gained a foothold in the language, it tends to win rapid popularity, so much so that sometimes the 'newcomer' turns into a cliché and begins to be shunned. We wondered to what extent something similar occurs in the case of names. Before looking more closely at this, it seemed desirable to start by investigating simply the relationship, at any given time,

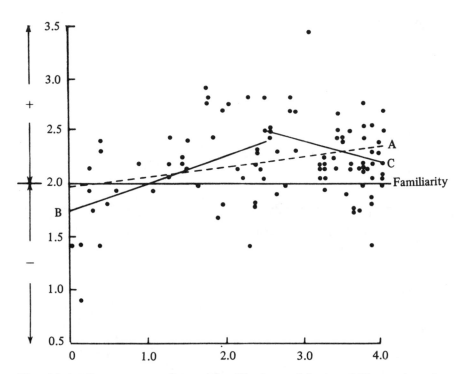

Fig. 11.4   Scattergram of mean familiarity and favourability ratings for 100 words, with regression lines (A) for the whole sample, (B) for those words with familiarity < 2.5 and (C) for those words with familiarity > 2.5 (Reproduced from W. Sluckin, A. M. Colman and D. J. Hargreaves (1980) *British Journal of Psychology*, 71, 163–169, by permission.)

between experienced familiarity with, and liking for, Christian names among various populations.

As it happens, the first opportunity for such research arose when one of us (W. S.) was on Study Leave in 1978 in Melbourne, Australia. We were able before long to collect similar data in Leicester. In the two experiments we used in all 160 subjects. In each case there were 40 men and 40 women. Their ages ranged in Melbourne from 18 to 50 (median, 22 years) and in Leicester from 15 to 68 (median, 34 years). Briefly, 40 subjects in Melbourne and 40 correspond-ing subjects in Leicester rated their own familiarity *either* with 100 randomly chosen male Christian names *or* with 100 similarly chosen female Christian names. Likewise, 40 other subjects in Melbourne and 40 in Leicester rated their liking for the same male and female names (Colman *et al.*, 1981a).

The results of the two studies are summarized in Fig. 11.5. Significant and strong positive linear relationships between familiarity and favourability were found for male and for female names, whether judged by males or females, both

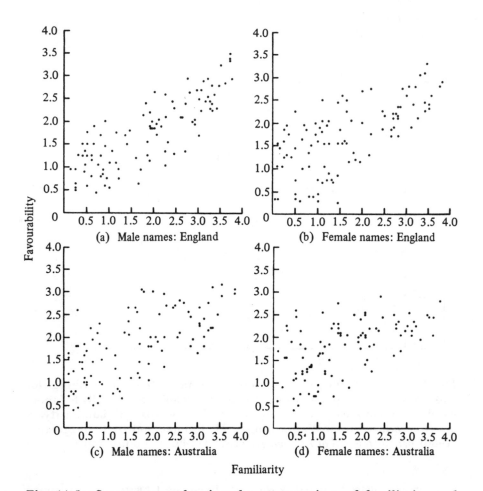

Fig. 11.5 Scattergrams showing the mean ratings of familiarity and favourability (liking) for male and female Christian names given by English subjects and Australian subjects. (Reproduced from A. M. Colman, D. J. Hargreaves and W. Sluckin (1981) *British Journal of Social Psychology*, 20, 3–5, by permission.

in Melbourne and in Leicester. To illustrate, among the four best liked male names in Australia were David and Peter; and these two were also among the four most familiar names. In England the best liked names were David, Peter and Richard in that order; and these three were among the four most familiar names. Names such as Cedric and Fulbert were both unfamiliar and disliked in Australia. Further similar examples could be quoted; full details will be found in Hargreaves *et al*. (1979) and in Sluckin *et al*. (1979).

It may at first sight be thought that the essentially straight-line positive correlations between familiarity and favourability could be explained in terms of the mere-exposure hypothesis. A closer analysis of the situation leads to a different explanation. First we may note that in the case of words, favourability is a function of familiarity and that, up to a point, favourability rises with familiarity. In the case of Christian names the causal relationship is partly reversed and, therefore, more complex. The best-liked names tend to be given most often to newborn infants; and so these names gradually become the most frequently-occurring and familiar of all the names. Thus we have a self-regulating mechanism in name-giving. It ensures that no names are given so frequently as to bring about an antipathy for them; and no single name can become so prevalent as to become markedly disliked. The preference or lack of preference for names eventually influences the frequency of their occurrence and, hence, their familiarity. This feedback of preference accounts for the non-existence of the inverted-U relationship in the case of Christian names. Thus, the positive linear correlation, such as we have found, can be satisfactorily explained in terms of our preference-feedback hypothesis.

The case of surnames is different. They are not commonly chosen at will. Therefore, like ordinary words, they may be expected to obey the inverted-U law. It seemed to us worthwhile to put this prediction to an empirical test. We carried out an investigation, using 80 subjects who rated either their familiarity with, or their liking for, 60 surnames randomly selected from a telephone directory (Colman et al., 1981b). We were unlucky that comparable data gathered by one of us (D.J.H.) while on Study Leave in Chicago, USA, were later lost (strictly speaking, stolen!) in New York, with other belongings.

The results, showing the relationship between familiarity and favourability, are displayed in Fig. 11.6. Very unfamiliar names — examples being Bamkin, Bodle, Nall, Codling — were disliked. At the other end of the familiarity range were Smith and Brown; they, too, were disliked. The best liked names were of intermediate familiarity, for example, Shelley, Cassell, Burton. A regression analysis shows that a large and highly significant proportion of the variance is accounted for by an incremental quadratic component. Further, the overall non-linear relationship for surnames is well exhibited by a piecewise linear-regression analysis. Thus, the linear component of the trend in the lower third of the familiarity scale is strongly positive with a slope of 0.82; in the upper third the linear trend is quite strongly negative, with a slope of -0.43; the middle third of the familiarity scale shows not much departure from the horizontal, the slope being somewhat negative (-0.18).

11.5 Aesthetic Appreciation of Music

Though musical theorists (e.g. Meyer, 1956) have long debated various important issues concerning the aesthetic and affective response to music, the experimental psychologist is better equipped to carry out objective, empirical tests of the hypotheses proposed. Berlyne's (1974a) distinction between 'synthetic' and 'analytic' approaches in experimental aesthetics, perhaps more

259

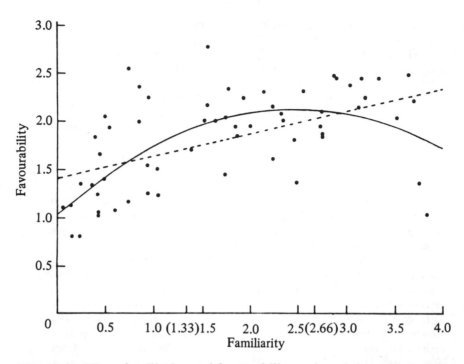

Fig. 11.6   Mean familiarity and favourability ratings (ranges 0–4) of 60 randomly selected surnames, showing least square linear regression line (FAV on FAM) and least square parabola. ——, least square parabola; -----, least square line. (Reproduced from A. M. Colman, W. Sluckin and D. J. Hargreaves (1981) *British Journal of Psychology*, 72, 363–369, by permission.)

appropriately called experimental and naturalistic respectively, has clear parallels in research on the psychology of music. The experimental approach is that which characterizes most of the work that has been described in this chapter so far, as well as most of the 'new experimental aesthetics'. It consists of presenting subjects with simple, often artificially contrived stimuli in which specific independent variables are manipulated, and investigating the effects on specific dependant variables. Research in which this approach has been applied to music has been extremely scarce and limited in scope, and as Radocy & Boyle (1979) point out, this approach holds much promise for the systematic evaluation of the aesthetic response to music.

The naturalistic approach, on the other hand, uses stimuli drawn from real-life works of art and represents an attempt to study them under relatively lifelike conditions. The two approaches may be thought of as being at opposite ends of a continuum; many studies, including our own research on music (Hargreaves & Colman, 1981; Hargreaves *et al.*, 1980), fall somewhere in between, drawing on techniques characteristic of both approaches. In this section we shall review some research on the role of novelty in the aesthetic response to music. We shall look first at those studies that are closest to a purely experimental approach in their manipulation of the novelty of musical stimuli; then at empirical studies of the effects of repetition of music, which use a mixture of experimental and naturalistic techniques.

A straightforward application to music of the inverted-U theory, as we have developed it so far, raises a new set of theoretical problems, since musical events are ordered in the dimension of time; this applies both *within* the duration of a single musical piece and *between* different playings of the same piece. Focusing on the latter, familiarity with a given piece might be thought of as an inverse function of its novelty, in terms of the number of times the piece has been heard. Thus we may dislike a piece when we hear it for the first time; with further playings liking rises to a peak, and then declines. The existence of inverted-U curves of this type could easily be demonstrated by observing the changes in position of popular songs in the 'charts' over a period of several weeks. This phenomenon is a good example of the cyclical vogues that will be discussed in the last section of this chapter.

Another inverted-U theory of musical preference, which concentrates on likes and dislikes for different pieces at a given point in time rather than changes in liking for individual pieces over time, has been developed by Davies (1978). Davies' account derives from Berlyne's work, which we mentioned earlier, and has much in common with our own views; we shall attempt a brief summary here. The initial premise is that people tend to like music that provides them with information, i.e. that reduces their uncertainty about subsequent events. They tend to dislike music that is very familiar to them, as it contains no new information; similarly, they tend to dislike very unfamiliar music, since extreme novelty gives rise to uncertainty about future events. People therefore tend to prefer pieces of music that, for them, contain an intermediate amount of information, i.e., music that is moderately familiar to them. Davies draws next on Berlyne *et al.*'s (1968) suggestion that the information conveyed by a stimulus is related to its *subjective complexity*, and this concept is central in making predictions about people's liking for different pieces. The amount of information conveyed by a piece is a function both of its objective complexity, and of the familiarity of the listener with music of that type; the subjective complexity of a piece thus summarizes the levels of both of these interacting variables. The inverted-U curve that emerges from this conceptualization is one with subjective complexity as the abscissa; people's liking is greatest for music with intermediate levels of subjective complexity.

It is possible to carry out precise experimental manipulations of the objective complexity, or information content, of musical elements, and empirical researchers in this area have done so in various ways. Davies (1969) constructed tone sequences that vary in objective uncertainty levels in an analogous way to Miller & Selfridge's (1953) 'statistical approximations to language'. He presented a group of musicians from different musical disciplines with either a single written note or several written notes in a sequence, and asked them to write one more note that might reasonably follow. By passing the sequence on to the next musician, then the next, and so on, Davies was able to generate musical material varying in predictability; sequences in which each note was based on the preceding one, or on three, or five, or seven notes were constructed. Crozier (1974) and Vitz (1966) also manipulated the informational content of tonal sequences, and investigated the effects on subjects' ratings of pleasantness and other variables. Vitz found an inverted-U relationship between the two; pleasantness ratings increased with 'stimulus variation' up to a moderate amount, and then declined. He also found that his more musically sophisticated subjects preferred sequences with larger amounts of stimulus variation than did subjects with little training and interest in music.

Heyduk (1975) obtained preference ratings for four piano compositions that were specially constructed to represent different degrees of complexity, and presented one of them to his subjects 16 times. His findings support an inverted-U-type 'optimal complexity' model of musical preference. Further, he found (Heyduk, 1975, p. 84) that:

> . . . the affective consequences of repeated exposure varied depending upon whether the repeatedly exposed composition was more or less complex than the subject's preferred complexity level.

Now this finding is an important corollary of the subjective complexity model that was outlined earlier, and it corroborates Vitz's (1966) results. Generally speaking, repeated exposure to a piece of music tends to reduce its subjective complexity. When the initial subjective complexity of the piece is too high, further listening will tend to increase liking for it, as this will reduce its complexity, which will move nearer to the subject's optimum level. When the initial level is too low, however, repeated exposure will tend to decrease liking for the piece, since its subjective complexity moves still further away from the subject's optimum level. This model should enable us to predict, to some degree, how a person's musical preferences might change and evolve: the characteristics of any individual inverted-U function relating liking to novelty will depend on the objective complexity of the piece, and the musical experience of the listener.

The 'repeated exposure' paradigm employed by Heyduk has been used extensively in research in the new experimental aesthetics, and Heyduk adopts a typically experimental approach to the stimulus material. We shall now briefly review some research that uses the same experimental paradigm, but which is essentially naturalistic in its use of 'real-life' musical pieces as stimuli.

Verveer et al. (1933), like Heyduk, found an inverted-U curve for liking with repetition over time. They repeatedly played the same two 'jazz selections' to groups of undergraduate psychology students in two testing sessions one week apart. The subjects' pleasantness ratings (on a 20-point scale) tended to increase to an affective peak at an optimal degree of familiarity; further repetition produced a decline in pleasantness. After an intervening time interval, however (one week in this case) the ratings rose again. The authors suggest that some apparently discrepant results in this field may be resolved by distinguishing between the contrary effects of *continuous repetition* and *repetition at intervals*.

262

Neither Krugman (1943) nor Mull (1957), however, found any evidence for an inverted-U curve. Krugman played recordings of classical and swing music once a week for 8 weeks to 7 undergraduate subjects, and found that their pleasantness ratings tended to increase over this period for both types of music. Mull played modern serious music (selections from Hindemith and Schoenberg) to 16 music students during two sessions of 1 h each, in two successive weeks; she also found a general increase in liking for the music over this period, though she concluded (Mull, 1957, p. 161) that 'neither of the compositions studied was generally much liked, even at the end of the familiarizing process'.

No clear effects of type of music have emerged so far; according to the theoretical model outlined in the last section, more complex pieces of music should be more likely to show an increase in liking with repetition than should less complex pieces. Schuckert & McDonald (1968) may have found such an effect in their study of 20 pre-school children. They obtained initial preference judgements from the children on jazz as well as classical pieces, and then systematically exposed each subject to the less preferred musical type in four different play situations. A re-test for shifts in preference showed that although the magnitude of the preference shift was not statistically significant, twice as many children shifted their preference from jazz to classical music as in the opposite direction as a result of the exposure. Whether or not this demonstrates that the classical piece used (*Liebestraum*, as recorded by the Boston Pops Orchestra) had greater subjective complexity for the children than the jazz piece (*Blue Rondo*, by Dave Brubeck) is unclear; the authors suggest that the greater rhythmicity of the latter may partly explain their results.

This kind of research has clear practical implications for so-called 'plugging' effects in music broadcasting. Although a certain amount of research on this topic was carried out under the auspices of the Office of Radio Research at Columbia University (Lazarsfeld & Stanton, 1944), it is rather surprising that there has been virtually no further interest in it since the Second World War. Wiebe's (1940) study of the effect of radio plugging on students' opinions of popular songs is one of the very few in this area to incorporate some degree of experimental control. In summary, he found that plugging did not affect the liking ratings of initially well liked songs, but that it did slightly increase the ratings of those songs that were initially less well liked. The explanation of these results by the subjective complexity model would be that the initially well liked songs were of lower subjective complexity to the students, though of course this would be virtually impossible to test retrospectively.

We may conclude this section by characterizing the aesthetic appreciation of music as an area in which empirical evidence lags well behind theoretical speculation. Music is a complex area of study, and musical stimuli tend to be less convenient to handle in the laboratory than stimuli such as shapes, letters, words or names. It is probably for this reason that no consistent findings emerged from the repetition studies reviewed above. These studies used various different samples of subjects, types of music, experimental procedures, and methods of analysis. Nevertheless, it may well be that some form of inverted-U theory provides the most useful, general framework for integrating what appear at first sight to be diverse and even contradictory findings. There can be little doubt that this applies to the research reviewed earlier, though a good deal of empirical flesh remains to be put on the theoretical skeleton.

11.6   Conclusions

As we mentioned early on in this chapter, there has been no dearth of interesting theories concerning the inverted-U relationship between novelty/familiarity and aesthetic preferences. Both the modified response-competition theory and the two-factor theory, as well as the more recent scheme theory, have their appeal. However, they do not readily generate conflicting predictions, and hence empirical findings have not the power of differentiating between then. Therefore, for the present, theorising about the underlying causes of the inverted-U relationship remains tentative.

We have seen earlier how Christian names and surnames differ with regard to the relationship between familiarity and favourability. Much more generally, this difference between, respectively, a positive rectilinear and an inverted-U relationship is characteristic of two broad categories of naturally occurring stimuli (Colman *et al.*, 1981b). Category A, which includes Christian names, is one in which exposure to the stimuli depends largely on voluntary choice. This is very well exemplified by musical pieces that we choose, or do not choose, to listen to. Examples somewhat comparable to Christian names include garments and shoes of different styles. Category B comprises stimuli such as surnames, but also, typically, letters of the alphabet, words, geometrical shapes and so on, that is, cases where frequency of exposure is essentially outside the subject's voluntary control. The two categories are in reality two ends of a continuum of stimuli, because the *degree* of voluntary control of exposure that is achievable will vary with the nature of the stimulus.

Individuals will differ, of course, with regard to the extent of their familiarity with the various stimuli within Category B. Some of these stimuli can be so ubiquitous in any given culture that they are on the descending section of the inverted-U curve. For instance, we have found that some words, and even surnames, are in that position. Stimuli in Category A, however, are prevented from reaching the requisite high levels of familiarity, because voluntary choice on the part of the individuals reduces the extent of their exposure to excessively frequently occurring stimuli, such as particular pieces of music, or clothes that are frequently worn, or even Christian names that are regarded as common. This cutting down of exposure by choice reduces sufficiently the popularity of any given stimulus to prevent it from becoming overly unattractive. This self-regulation, or preference feedback, accounts for the absence of the inverted-U relationship between familiarity and favourability for stimuli in Category A.

Over a period of time the self-regulating mechanism just referred to appears to be responsible for the fluctuations in popularity of, for example, hair styles, shoe styles and the like. A given style ceases to be aesthetically pleasing when it is very common, but begins to return to favour when it is relatively uncommon. Thus we witness the rise and fall of fashions; what is in vogue today will not be so in a few years' time, but may return in a decade or two. Of course, this is only a very partial account of fluctuations of popularity. Some fashions disappear never to reappear again, perhaps because they have been found to be incompatible with more modern living conditions, or because they have been condemned by some authority, and so on. Rather than old stimuli re-emerging, some entirely new stimuli may emerge as aesthetically pleasing, perhaps for prestige reasons to begin with, then rapidly becoming favourites of many. But, this is not to say that the preference-feedback mechanism does not go some considerable way towards explaining the fluctuations of fashion.

In the case of changing positions of popular songs in the 'charts', such cycles have a fairly short periodicity. The greater complexity of most serious music would lead us to predict that if similar curves exist, their periodicities should be much longer. Farnsworth's (1969) studies of the changes in eminence rankings of the great composers made by members of the American Musicological Society in 1938, 1944 and 1951 are of interest in this connection. Although the question of cyclical vogues was not directly under investigation, Farnsworth found some interesting and marked average shifts in preference over the thirteen year period. The 1951 rankings correlated 0.95 with those obtained in 1944, and 0.85 with those obtained in 1938.

We may return now to Category B stimuli where, provided the range of familiarity is wide enough, the inverted-U relationship between familiarity and favourability obtains. The interest here centres on the parameters of the U-curve, e.g., the factors influencing the height of the peak of the curve, the position of the peak on the familiarity scale, and the symmetry or asymmetry of the curve. There is evidence to suggest that, as far as the position of the peak is concerned, maximal favourability tends to occur early with stimuli that are subjectively simple, highly discriminable and predictable. On the other hand, the peak of favourability tends to be reached late on the scale of familiarity with stimuli that are subjectively complex, poorly discriminable and, perhaps, relatively unpredictable (Colman & Sluckin, 1976). This would indicate which things are likely to have a quick appeal but soon become boring, and which are slow in becoming attractive but are longer-lasting in their aesthetic appeal.

As we mentioned at the beginning of this chapter, neither novelty nor familiarity is a unitary entity. On the contrary, each can refer to several distinct situations. Therefore, when we talk about a quantitative novelty-familiarity continuum we oversimplify matters; we do not do justice to the qualitative complexity of the continuum. Empirical studies do sometimes take this complexity into account; research work has, for instance, been carried out on the effects of massed and distributed exposure (see Stang, 1974). In this chapter, however, we have focused on the fundamentals of the relationships between novelty/familiarity and liking, whereby a tacit assumption is made that novelty/familiarity is unidimensional.

It is sometimes believed that novelty, as such, is aesthetically attractive. Empirical studies do not bear this out. On the contrary, perhaps because novelty tends to evoke wariness, novel stimuli are not generally liked as much initially as they are liked later, when their novelty has worn off. Of course, the understanding of human aesthetic preferences is only very partially illuminated by the study of the novelty-favourability relationships. Nevertheless, as this chapter has attempted to show, a close experimental and theoretical analysis of these relationships can be quite revealing.

11.7 Synopsis

Much of the so-called new experimental aesthetics is concerned with liking as a function of novelty/familiarity. The mere-exposure hypothesis, suggesting that liking is the result of 'mere repeated exposure' of the individual to the stimulus, is critically discussed. The view is then considered that, more generally, the relationship between novelty/familiarity and liking takes the form of an inverted U. Theories purporting to explain this relationship are then briefly described. Next, our own experiments on letters, words and surnames, which show results consistent with the inverted-U function are reported. However, for a certain category of stimuli, where the preference-feedback effect is in evidence, the relationship between novelty/familiarity and liking is more like a positive rectilinear one. This is well illustrated by our findings concerning preferences for Christian names. This brings us to the topic of vogues. A survey of studies of aesthetic appreciation of music highlights, among other features, the presence of cycles of fashion of varying periodicities. The chapter ends up with some tentative general conclusions about aesthetic preferences in relation to novelty.

References

BERLYNE, D. E. (1970) Novelty, complexity, and hedonic value. *Perception and Psychophysics* **8**, 279–286.

BERLYNE, D. E. (1971) *Aesthetics and Psychobiology.* New York: Appleton-Century-Crofts.

BERLYNE, D. E. (Ed.) (1974a) *Studies in the New Experimental Aesthetics.* New York: Wiley.

BERLYNE, D. E. (1974b) Novelty, complexity and interestingness. In *Studies in the New Experimental Aesthetics* (Ed. D. E. BERLYNE). New York: Wiley.

BERLYNE, D. E. OGILVIE, J. C. and PARHAM, L. C. C. (1968) The dimensionality of visual complexity, interestingness and pleasingness. *Canadian Journal of Psychology* **22**, 376–387.

BOUCHER, J. and OSGOOD, C. E. (1969) The Pollyanna hypothesis. *Journal of Verbal Learning and Verbal Behavior* **8**, 1–8.

BRICKMAN, P., REDFIELD, J., HARRISON, A. A. and CRANDALL, R. (1972) Drive and predisposition as factors in the attitudinal effects of mere-exposures. *Journal of Experimental Social Psychology* **8**, 31–44.

CANTOR, G. N. (1968) Children's 'like–dislike' ratings of familiarized and nonfamiliarized visual stimuli. *Journal of Experimental Child Psychology* **6**, 651–657.

CANTOR, G. N. and KUBOSE, S. K. (1969). Preschool children's ratings of familiarized and nonfamiliarized visual stimuli. *Journal of Experimental Child Psychology* **8**, 74–81.

COLMAN, A. M. and SLUCKIN, W. (1976) Everyday likes and dislikes; the psychology of human fancy. *New Society* **38** (No. 733), 123–125.

COLMAN, A. M. WALLEY, M. and SLUCKIN, W. (1975) Preferences for common words, uncommon words and non-words by children and young adults. *British Journal or Psychology* **66**, 481–486.

COLMAN, A. M., HARGREAVES, D. J. and SLUCKIN, W. (1981a) Preferences for Christian names as a function of their experienced familiarity. *British Journal of Social Psychology* **20**, 3–5.

COLMAN, A. M., SLUCKIN, W. and HARGREAVES, D. J. (1981b) The effect of familiarity on preferences for surnames. *British Journal of Psychology* **72**, 363–369.

CRANDALL, J. E., MONTGOMERY, V. E. and REES, W. W. (1973) 'Mere' exposure *versus* familiarity, with implications for response competition and expectancy arousal hypotheses. *Journal of General Psychology* **88**, 105–120.

CROZIER, J. B. (1974) Verbal and exploratory responses to sound sequences varying in uncertainty level. In *Studies in the New Experimental Aesthetics* (Ed. D. E. BERLYNE). New York:Wiley.

DAVIES, J. B. (1969) *An Analysis of Factors Involved in Musical Ability, and the Derivation of Tests of Musical Aptitude.* Ph. D. thesis, University of Durham Library.

DAVIES, J. B. (1978) *The Psychology of Music.* London: Hutchinson.

ECKBLAD, G. (1981) *Scheme Theory: A Conceptual Framework for Cognitive-Motivational Processes.* London: Academic Press.

FARNSWORTH, P. R. (1969) *The Social Psychology of Music (2nd edn.).* Ames: Iowa State University Press.

FAW, T. T. and PIEN, D. (1971) The influence of stimulus exposure on rated preference: effects of age, pattern of exposure, and stimulus meaningfulness. *Journal of Experimental Child Psychology* **11**, 339–346.

FECHNER, G. T. (1876) *Vorschule der Aesthetik.* Leipzig: Breitkopf & Härtel.

HAMID, P. N. (1973) Exposure frequency and stimulus preference. *British Journal of Psychology* **64**, 569–577.

HARGREAVES, D. J. and COLMAN, A. M. (1981) The dimensions of aesthetic reactions to music. *Psychology of Music* **9**, 15–20.

HARGREAVES, D. J., COLMAN, A. M. and SLUCKIN, W. (1979) Aesthetic preferences for names in relation to their experienced familiarity. II. England. *Melbourne Psychology Reports* **No. 59**, 1–20.

HARGREAVES, D. J., MESSERSCHMIDT, P. and RUBERT, C. (1980) Musical preference and evaluation. *Psychology of Music* **8**, 13–18.

HARRISON, A. A. (1968) Response competition, frequency, exploratory behaviour, and liking. *Journal of Personality and Social Psychology* **9**, 363–368.

HARRISON, A. A. (1969) Exposure and popularity. *Journal of Personality* **37**, 359–377.

HARRISON, A. A. (1977) Mere exposure. *Advances in Experimental Social Psychology* **10**, 39–83.

HARRISON, A. A. and CRANDALL, R. (1972) Heterogeneity-homogeneity of exposure sequence and the attitudinal effects of exposure. *Journal of Personality and Social Psychology* **21**, 234–238.

HARRISON, A. A. and ZAJONC, R. B. (1970) The effects of frequency and duration of exposure on response competition and affective ratings. *Journal of Psychology* **75**, 163–169.

HARRISON, A. A., TUFTS, J. W. and STRAYER, J. B. (1974) Task difficulty and the

267

reinforcement effects of high and low frequency stimuli. *Journal of Personality and Social Psychology* **29**, 628–636.

HEYDUK, R. G. (1975) Rated preference for musical composition as it relates to complexity and exposure frequency. *Perception and Psychophysics*, **17**, 84–91.

JAMES, W. (1890) *The Principles of Psychology, Vol. 2*. New York: Holt.

JANISSE, M. P. (1970) Attitudinal effects of mere exposure: a replication and extension. *Psychonomic Science* **19**, 77–78.

KRUGMAN, H. E. (1943) Affective response to music as a function of familiarity. *Journal of Abnormal and Social Psychology* **38**, 388–392.

LAZARSFELD, P. F. and STANTON, F. (1944) *Radio Research 1942–43*. New York: Duell, Sloan & Pearce.

MATLIN, M. W. (1970) Response competition as a mediating factor in the frequency-affect relationship. *Journal of Personality and Social Psychology* **16**, 536–552.

MATLIN, M. W. (1974) Frequency-affect relationship in a simultaneous spatial presentation. *Psychological Reports* **35**, 379–383.

MEYER, L. B. (1956) *Emotion and Meaning in Music*. Chicago: University of Chicago Press.

MILLER, G. A. and SELFRIDGE, J. A. (1953) Verbal context and the recall of meaningful material. *American Journal of Psychology* **63**, 176–185.

MORELAND, R. L. and ZAJONC, R. B. (1976) A strong test of exposure effects. *Journal of Experimental Social Psychology* **12**, 170–179.

MORELAND, R. L. and ZAJONC, R. B. (1977) Is stimulus recognition a necessary condition for the occurrence of exposure effects? *Journal of Personality and Social Psychology* **35**, 191–199.

MULL, H. K. (1957) The effect of repetition upon the enjoyment of modern music. *Journal of Psychology* **43**, 155–162.

OSGOOD, C. E. (1964) Semantic differential technique in the comparative study of cultures. *American Anthropologist* **66**, 171–200.

RADOCY, R. E. and BOYLE, J. D. (1979) *Psychological Foundations of Musical Behavior*. Springfield, Ill.: C. C. Thomas.

RAJECKI, D. W. and WOLFSON, C. (1973) The rating of materials found in the mailbox: effects of frequency of receipt. *Public Opinion Quarterly* **37**, 110–114.

RUSSELL, P. A. (1973) Relationships between exploratory behaviour and fear: a review. *British Journal of Psychology* **64**, 417–433.

SAEGERT, S. C. and JELLISON, J. M. (1970) Effects of initial level of response competition and frequency of exposure on liking and exploratory behavior. *Journal of Personality and Social Psychology* **16**, 553–558.

SAEGERT, S., SWAP, W. and ZAJONC, R. B. (1973) Exposure, context, and interpersonal attraction. *Journal of Personality and Social Psychology* **25**, 234–242.

SCHUCKERT, R. F. and MCDONALD, R. L. (1968) An attempt to modify the musical preferences of preschool children. *Journal of Research in Music Education* **16**, 39–45.

SIEBOLD, J. R. (1972) Children's rating responses as related to amount and recency of stimulus familiarization and stimulus complexity. *Journal of Experimental Child Psychology* **14**, 257–264.

SLUCKIN, W. (1972) *Imprinting and Early Learning*. London: Methuen.

SLUCKIN, W., MILLER, L. B. and FRANKLIN, H. (1973) The influence of stimulus familiarity/novelty on children's expressed preferences. *British Journal of Psychology* **64**, 563–567.

SLUCKIN, W., HARGREAVES, D. J. and COLMAN, A. M. (1979) Aesthetic preferences for names in relation to their experienced familiarity. I. Australia. *Melbourne Psychology Reports* **No. 55**, 1–18.

SLUCKIN, W., COLMAN, A. M. and HARGREAVES, D. J. (1980) Liking words as a function of the experienced frequency of their occurrence. *British Journal of Psychology* **71**, 163–169.

STANG, D. J. (1974) Methodological factors in mere exposure research. *Psychological Bulletin* **81**, 1014–1025.

STANG, D. J. (1975) Effects of 'mere exposure' on learning and affect. *Journal of Personality and Social Psychology* **31**, 7–12.

THORNDIKE, E. L. and LORGE, I. (1944) *The Teacher's Word Book of 30 000 Words.* New York: Teachers College Press, Columbia University.

VERVEER, E. M., BARRY, H. and BOUSFIELD, W. A. (1933) Changes in affectivity with repetition. *American Journal of Psychology* **45**, 130–134.

VITZ, P. C. (1966) Affect as a function of stimulus variation. *Journal of Experimental Psychology* **71**, 74–79.

WIEBE, G. (1940) The effect of radio plugging on students' opinions of popular songs. *Journal of Applied Psychology* **24**, 721–727.

ZAJONC, R. B. (1968) Attitudinal effects of mere exposure. *Journal of Personality and Social Psychology, Monograph Supplement* **9**(2), Part 2.

ZAJONC, R. B. and RAJECKI, D. W. (1969) Exposure and affect: a field experiment. *Psychonomic Science* **17**, 216–217.

ZAJONC, R. B., SWAP, W., HARRISON, A. A. and ROBERTS, P. (1971) Limiting conditions of the exposure effect: satiation and relativity. *Journal of Personality and Social Psychology* **18**, 384–391.

ZAJONC, R. B., CRANDALL, R., KAIL, R. V. and SWAP, W. (1974) Effect of extreme exposure frequencies on different affective ratings of stimuli. *Perceptual and Motor Skills* **38**, 667–678.

269

Author Index

271

273

275

Salzen, E.A., 12, 31, 38, 39, 40, 45
Samuelson, R.J., 135, 155
Satinder, K.P., 32
Sawyer, C.H., 163
Schallert, T., 122
Schiller, P.H., 237
Schlosberg, M., 222
Schneider, G.E., 36
Schneider, K., 232, 237
Schneider, W., 89, 90
Schneirla, T.C., 45
Schuckert, R.F., 263
Schultz, D.P., 79
Schutte, W., 94
Schwaltz, S., 87
Scott, J.P., 225
Scourse, N.J.S., 7
Seggie, J., 134
Selfridge, J.A., 261
Seligman, M.E.P., 7
Segall, J.N., 36, 74
Shafer, J.N., 33, 128
Sheldon, M.H., 10, 46, 78, 165
Shepard, R.N., 95
Sherman, L., 224
Sherrick, M.F., 35
Shiffrin, R.M., 89, 90
Shillito, E.E., 148
Shorten, M., 147, 159, 168
Siddle, D.A.T., 8
Siebold, J.R., 248
Silverman, I., 241
Simmel, E.C., 4, 10
Sims, R.A., 157
Sinclair, J.D., 35
Singer, J., 220, 236
Sinnamon, H.M., 135
Slovic, P., 87
Sluckin, W., 245, 249, 253, 254, 255, 256, 257, 258, 260, 265
Small, W.S., 22, 147
Smedslund, J., 86, 87
Smith, J.N.M., 158
Smith, P.K., 213, 215, 218, 222, 223, 237, 238
Smith, S., 75
Sokolov, E,.K., 7, 38, 92, 103
Soskin, R.A., 77
Southern, H.N., 147
Spence, K.W., 13, 77
Spencer, H., 233

Spencer, M.M., 34
Spiker, C.C., 55
Spinner, N., 5
Srebro, B., 5
Sroges, R.W., 11, 33, 184, 190
Stahl, J.M., 36
Stang, D.J., 247, 251, 265
Stanton, F., 263
Steiner, A.L., 212–213
Stellar, E., 118
Stevens, D.W., 88
Stevens, R., 135
Stevenson, M.F., 178, 181, 191
Stewart, J., 212, 225
Stickle, L.K., 157
Stoddart, R.C., 160
Stolba, A., 200–201, 204, 205, 207
Stonehouse, 189
Stratton, P., 233
Strayer, J., 223
Strickney, K.J., 127
Stroh, G., 231
Studelska, D.R., 73, 76
Suarez, S.D., 30, 31
Sutcliffe, A.G., 191
Sutherland, N.S., 35, 68
Sutherland, R.J., 123, 128, 139
Sutton-Smith, B., 233, 241
Sweatman, H.P.A., 158
Switzky, H., 232
Sylva, K., 237
Symmes, D., 97
Symonds, D., 223
Szechtman, H., 123

Tanji, J., 125
Tapp, J.T., 74
Taylor, G.T., 37, 149, 164
Teitelbaum, P., 117, 118, 119, 121, 122, 123, 124, 125
Tembrock, G., 201
Terry, W.S., 73, 90
Thistlethwaite, D.L., 73, 84
Thomas, H., 94, 95
Thompson, R.F., 7
Thompson, W.R., 43, 74, 75, 78
Thor, D.H., 97
Thorndike, E.L., 247
Thorpe, W.H., 221
Tiira, E., 75
Tinbergen, L., 8

276

Subject Index

278